THE SOVIET CENTURY

THE SOVIET CENTURY

MOSHE LEWIN

Edited by Gregory Elliott

VERSO

London · New York

First published by Verso 2005
© Michael Levine 2005
All rights reserved

The moral rights of the author have been asserted

1 3 5 7 9 10 8 6 4 2

Verso
UK: 6 Meard Street, London W1F 0EG
USA: 180 Varick Street, New York, NY 10014–4606
www.versobooks.com

Verso is the imprint of New Left Books

ISBN 1–84467–016–3

British Library Cataloguing in Publication Data
A catalogue record for this book is available from the British Library

Library of Congress Cataloging-in-Publication Data
Lewin, Moshe, 1921–
    The Soviet century / Moshe Lewin.
        p.   cm.
    Includes bibliographical references and index.
    ISBN 1–84467–016–3 (cloth : alk. paper)
    1.   Soviet Union—History.   I. Title.
    DK266.L474 2005
    947.084–dc22
                                                                2004015478

Typeset in Bembo by YHT Ltd, London
Printed and bound in the UK by The Bath Press

CONTENTS

PREFACE

The Soviet Union is no more. As some like to put it, 'It's history' –
meaning 'Forget all that.' Politicians, academics and the media elaborate
on this formula in accordance with their specific interests and perspectives. But the term 'history' is rich in meanings and the Soviet era is
still recent history. Even if their numbers are declining, the majority of
the populations of Russia and the other republics of the ex-Soviet
Union were formed in the USSR and many are even nostalgic for it. It
is still part of the biographies of millions of people, and in this sense the
'past' is still relevant to their lives.

This 'biographical' dimension is only one index of the persistence of
the past. The question of the country's national identity preoccupies
Russian citizens, and this debate involves different attitudes to, and
conceptions of, the USSR. Yet when such an important collective
analysis is conducted without serious knowledge of the past – which is
still frequently the case – national debate turns to farce.

For historians and for all those who are aware of the myriad ways in
which history, however distant, makes its presence felt, 'Forget all that'
is an utterly absurd attitude. Especially in the last fifteen years of its
existence, the USSR did not cope with its present. Yet in so far as it
now belongs to the past, it represents an immutable reality that cannot
be altered by successive interpretations of it: it is – and will remain – a
crucial part of the dramatic twentieth century. And who seriously
believes that we no longer require a knowledge of the twentieth century?

Soviet Russia remains a weighty component of Russia's cultural and
political tradition, which continues to influence the country to this day

– not unlike the Tsarist past, which continued to shape the USSR. Can this be ignored by anyone who is interested in their country's destiny and reflects on it?

Thus, the USSR as 'past' is needed in the present for the simple reason that it is impossible to dispose of history. One of the contentions of this book is that the USSR remains an ill-understood system. The veil of secrecy that was the hallmark of the Soviet system has been lifted for earlier periods (including the Stalin period), which can now be, and are being, studied systematically. Previously, the lack of access to archives and other indispensable sources of information made studying Soviet history a very frustrating and arduous enterprise. Coming across data that contained useful pointers, or hitting upon a well-documented Soviet publication, was a signal event.

So when Soviet archives became accessible, historians had to take advantage of them. For me personally, obtaining such material, whether found by myself or published in documentary collections by others, became my main activity for a number of years. The more I read, the richer the reality began to look to me. But at the same time I experi-enced renewed frustration because of the lack of access to material dealing with the later stages of the Soviet era.

In this work, I endeavour to bring out what I consider to be unknown or neglected aspects, even though they afford greater insight into the guts of the system. I have made little use of Western sources here – something I intend to do in the more systematic future work I have in mind. Here reliance on new materials – archives, memoirs, autobiographies or documentary publications – is an objective in itself. But it is also a kind of self-examination: after consulting a mass of new evidence, what remains of my former understanding of the Soviet phenomenon? How has it changed? Where did it err? Most of what I say in the forthcoming pages answers these questions, as the new materials revealed things I knew little about and allowed me to for-mulate problems I could not raise before.

The other privileged source in these pages is current work by Russian scholars, who either have access to first-hand information, or have worked in governmental institutions, or who were already writing knowledgeably and critically in Soviet times.

I also thought that readers would benefit from the opportunity to get a feel for what these sources consist in, what they 'say', and what the regime knew or could know on the basis of the information commu-nicated by its various agencies. In order to lay bare the building-blocks of my interpretation, and offer readers a sample of what Soviet leaders were themselves reading, I have therefore both summarized and quoted extensively from these documents and authors.

Thus it turns out that although society was poorly informed – and often seriously misinformed – the regime, especially in the post-Stalinist period, often had at its disposal a mass of good material and, in addition, rigorous analyses of the country and of the outside world. But good information never helps mediocre leaders. The problem lay in what these leaders were able to understand, what they wanted to know, what they did know – even if they were incapable of doing anything with it – but also in what they had absolutely no desire to know.

These questions take us to the heart of our inquiry into the Soviet system's mechanisms and underpinnings.

INTRODUCTION

Power games and personal ambitions are part of history. They also exert strong pressure for history to be written in such a way as to serve interests or causes. From its inception, the Soviet regime presented a radical challenge, which was reinforced during the Cold War with the polarization of the world and the arms race, and the ensuing unprecedented propaganda war. All this created the conditions in which propaganda was readily mistaken for analysis. Both sides paid a heavy price for this fallacy, impairing their own ability to understand themselves and the world around them. The Soviet Union, which prohibited free social, political and historical research, was more damaged. It was also much poorer. Ideological frenzy, with its natural bent for propaganda, cost the USSR dearly in terms of its ability to grasp its own – and global – reality and to respond with appropriate strategies.

During the 1960s and '70s, the Soviet leadership did in fact allow some scope for published, and particularly unpublished, research and debate. It created high-quality research institutes, which enabled it to learn about the other side. Given its democratic character, in the US statistics and all sorts of information about the country were available; and this was helpful to the Soviets, notably from the 1960s onwards, when they were ready to use such data. In fact, specialists provided leaders with a sufficiently accurate picture of both the external world and Russia itself. What was done with this knowledge is another story; it depended on the leaders' conservative mentality. Even so, at various stages the USSR was ready to play the card of 'peaceful coexistence' and reduce tension. Aware of its inferiority (especially in the final stages of its history), it sought to implement policies that reflected a realistic appreciation of things.

In the US, the fact that independent research could be pursued, and alternative ideas and positions debated, did not necessarily mean that they counted. After all, freedom to publish critical analyses is not everything. It then has to be asked: Who pays any attention to them? Some analyses served as a cover for dubious policies and misconceptions, which were supposedly true simply by virtue of originating in the Free World.

A single illustration will suffice at this point. A group of specialists who have analysed the work of the US intelligence services[1] maintain that an organization like the CIA (and, in their turn, the leadership circles dependent on it) incorrectly assessed the strengths and weaknesses of the Soviet Union; in any event, it did not have a clue about where the USSR was headed. Yet it was capable of listening in on Brezhnev's phone conversations and, in all likelihood, of counting the exact number of Soviet missiles. Evidently, the blinding force of ideology and the logic of power (personal or imperial), as well as an obsession with secrecy, were not the monopoly of the Soviet 'propaganda state', even though they were highly potent there and served the interests of conservative elements to the country's detriment. But cognitive capacities are not the exclusive property of any one system. The Cold War, which encouraged innovation in some spheres of technology, was also a great simplifier when it came to grasping global realities; and in this regard the West was by no means faultless.

In addition to these problems, the West, including the US, suffered from the 'security complex', with the enormous role accorded to the secret services and their mindset of 'anything goes' in the line of duty – launching covert operations, hobnobbing with criminal or semi-criminal military formations, detecting communism and subversion anywhere and everywhere, buying off media outlets, infiltrating different social organizations. The obsession with security had a damaging effect on democratic institutions and created a powerful cover for the growth of internal anti-democratic forces, which were hard at work undermining American democracy. And the fact that Stalinism was worse, with its terror and witch-hunts, is little comfort. The faintest resemblance between the two systems – the very possibility of such a

---

1   See Craig Eisendrath, ed., *National Insecurity: US Intelligence after the Cold War*, Philadelphia 2000, pp. 8–9.

thing – was a danger to the liberties that furnished the battle-cry and the alleged stakes of the great contest.

Despite the contribution of genuine scholars committed to rigorous research, representations of the Soviet system were significantly influenced by the ideological and political realities of a bipolar world. Public opinion was guided in a particular direction by the large-scale diffusion of rooted ideological judgements, shaped by government agencies, the media and publicists with little interest in supporting their declarations with facts or arguments. While many other problems, countries and histories were open to debate, when it came to Soviet Russia a 'public discourse' emerged, based on deeply ingrained but unverified assumptions.

Setting aside the unilateral focus on misdeeds and crimes characteristic of propaganda, we shall instead point to limitations of a methodological kind. In fact, objective, methodologically sound research came up against rigid thought patterns that were widespread among publics and opinion-formers alike. These consisted in:

(1) Concentrating on leaders and government agencies as prime movers, instead of making them an object of study in order to grasp what they were engaged in and what determined their actions

(2) Studying the USSR essentially in terms of its 'undemocratic' status, which meant endlessly listing all the features of a 'non-democracy' and dealing with what it was not, rather than attempting to deal with what it was. Let us recall that even today democracy is not the only system on the planet and that the other systems must be understood in their own right.

(3) Disregarding the historical context in which leaders operated and to which they reacted. Ahistoricism is a very common error and the gravest fault of all, because human action does not occur in a void; it is not a *deus ex machina*. To take an example, in 1916–17 Lenin was not someone who sought to destroy a healthy, thriving system. Quite the reverse, he (like millions of others) faced a world that was literally in a state of collapse and a disintegrating Russia, and he sprang into action without any guarantee that he would not perish before he had even begun to confront the ongoing and impending catastrophes. Or to take a subsequent example, which further clarifies the importance of attending to context, the world economic crisis of the 1930s is crucial for understanding the prestige Soviet Russia had in many people's eyes, and helped to legitimize

Stalinism. The Second World War likewise threw a veil over Stalin's mass atrocities, at a time when the regime and his own power were already decaying because of their own internal maladies.

These considerations mean that readers can expect historical background and context, both internal and external, to play a key role in the arguments presented below.

But we have not yet done with surveying the obstacles to a real knowledge of the USSR. We must also draw attention to even more convoluted thought patterns that use and abuse the notion of Stalinism.

What I have in mind is the tendency to 'demonize' Stalin, by piling up on him and his system a ludicrously inflated, impossible, and quite unverifiable number of victims, involving the victims both of the terror and of his political and economic policies. When it transpires, for example, that the human losses attributed to his crimes also include major demographic losses expressed in estimates of unborn children, one can only scratch one's head in disbelief. Why is such a calculation necessary? And for whom? Deflating these figures and other arithmetical sleights of hand was a laborious business for specialists (especially when the archives were closed to them). But it has now been done successfully, allowing us to deal with Stalin and Stalinism as they actually were. We are left with quite enough horrors to condemn what needs to be condemned, but also to disentangle the threads of a drama which, having occupied centre-stage, made for a different episode following the dictator's death. In fact, the terror itself underwent changes; and in history it is indispensable to distinguish between different periods. The tendency to perpetuate 'Stalinism', by backdating it to 1917 and extending it to the end of the Soviet Union, pertains to those 'uses and abuses' of history of which there are many examples.

In this respect, mention should be made of the *Historikerstreit* (the 'historians' controversy') set off by conservative German historians. In their attempt to justify representatives of the non-Nazi German Right who had helped Hitler to power, and by the same token to rehabilitate Hitler and his infernal designs on the world, they resorted to a rather predictable stratagem, counting on Western connivance encouraged by the Cold War. They wished us to believe that Hitler's madness could somehow be attributed to Stalin, who supposedly created the atrocious precedent that inspired him. In particular, so it was claimed, the Holocaust was modelled on the treatment meted out to the kulaks. And Hitler's aggression, although it began with attacks on countries other than Russia, was nothing but a defensive war against the war Stalin some day planned to launch against Germany.[2] The anti-communist indoctrination characteristic of the Cold War permitted this kind of ideological manoeuvre in the West. Fortunately, enough voices were raised to condemn the operation and persevere with the project of understanding the dynamic of the Soviet system.

This book does not aim to offer a history of the USSR. It is restricted to a presentation of general aspects of the system. It has three parts. Part One is devoted to the Stalinist period, with an emphasis on its specific characteristics, but also its fluctuations. Part Two deals with the post-Stalinist period (from Khrushchev to Andropov), identified as a different model that reinvigorated the system for a time, but which then sank into stagnation (*zastoi*). Part Three broaches the 'Soviet era' as a whole, attempting a bird's-eye view of the system's historical trajectory. It underscores the general features and specificities of this trajectory, as well as the historical underpinnings of its success and subsequent failure. Both these moments had worldwide resonance and both, we might add, were equally unpredictable and surprising. What we stress is the complexity and richness of this historical process (however gruesome many of its chapters), but also the importance of an awareness of the specifically historical dimension, including when reflecting on the course of post-Gorbachev Russia.

The political philosopher V. P. Mezhuev, of the Russian Academy's Institute of Philosophy, addressed precisely these problems during a conference in Moscow in 1999:

> Ask yourself what in the past is dear to you, what must be continued, preserved, and that will help you to face the future ... If the past contains nothing positive, then there is no future and it only remains to 'forget it all and sink into slumber' [*zabytsia i zasnut'*]. A future without a past is not the historical destiny of Russia. Those who want to erase the twentieth century, a century of major catastrophes, must also bid a permanent farewell to a great Russia.[3]

This is well put, and we shall return to these considerations in our conclusion. But we wish to insist on one point: we are perfectly aware

---

2 See Peter Baldwin, ed., *Reworking the Past: Hitler, the Holocaust and the Historians' Debate*, Boston 1990.

3 V. P. Mezhuev, 'Otnoshenie k proshlomu-kliuch k budushchemu', in *Kuda Idet Rossiia? Krizis Institutsional'nykh Sistem: Vek, Desatiletie, God*, Moscow 1999, p. 47.

that historical research is a difficult undertaking and it seems to us crucial that it be conducted in a dispassionate and unbiased fashion. When an author professes to offer a work of scholarship, a short disclaimer is in order: intentions, however sincere, are no guarantee of success. The pitfalls en route are many and varied: sources and evidence, degree of professional mastery, personal biases, but also the infinite complexity of historical realities, which are fluid, ambiguous and manifold – and resist being reordered in any explanatory schema. And yet, if they do not attempt precisely that, historians would not even produce a convincing story. There would simply be false stories, or rather the same one endlessly trotted out.

PART ONE

A REGIME AND ITS PSYCHE

INTRODUCTION

The 1930s occupy a very special place in the relatively short history of the Soviet system. First, because they took the form of a high-intensity drama in a country that had not yet fully recovered from the aftermath of the First World War and the Civil War of 1918–21. Second, because the short-lived New Economic Policy (NEP) of the 1920s, although quite successful in restoring the country to minimal levels of physical (biological) and political viability, still left it short of what was required to confront the internal, and especially external, challenges that were looming on the horizon. The sudden launch of the five-year plans (*piatiletki*) triggered a chain of utterly unexpected, startling events. The first surprise was the Stalinist 'big drive', which occurred against the backdrop of the deep economic recession that engulfed the US and Europe but stopped short at the borders of the USSR. The second was a series of internal upheavals consequent upon this new policy. The unprecedented national effort dictated and executed by a determined elite and a ruthless supreme leader, heavily reliant on the state's coercive machinery, generated a spate of radical changes in all directions, which had a significant rebound effect on the regime itself. They shaped it in a way that amounted to the formation of a new, *sui generis*, state system, which, at least in its early stages, seemed to some actors, but also to outside observers, to embody the aspiration to a higher form of social justice. Others – especially some years later – regarded it as a new form of state slavery.

It might legitimately be asked how one and the same system could elicit such incompatible judgements in these years. But one fact is undeniable: the country was undergoing extremely rapid changes. A (hypothetical) party or government official, who for some purpose or other had been on a foreign mission during the first years of the plan, would certainly have been struck on his return by the astonishing changes that had occurred in the interim. Much more so, at any rate, than a White Russian returning to the country in the 1920s (there were such cases) and comparing Russia under the NEP with Tsarist Russia. However irritated by the novelties introduced by the regime, the latter would still have seen all around him the 'Mother Russia' he knew. He might even have felt quite reassured. By contrast, the Soviet official returning to Moscow in the 1930s would have found virtually none of the institutions he was familiar with in the 1920s. The press, the *nepmen*, the stores, the supply system, the political debates, most cultural life – all this had gone. The workplace, the pace of life, the slogans, and also (on closer inspection) the party itself – all were transformed. Political life and the policies adopted were different and impetuous. Stalin's image and slogans extolling him now covered the walls of towns and village squares alike. Initially portrayed alongside Lenin, he soon invariably came to be represented alone. The meaning of these iconographic switches would not as yet have been readily apparent.

This state system early on received the name of 'Stalinism', and the man at the helm was manifestly and unambiguously in control. This does not mean that the system's characteristics are to be ascribed exclusively to its head. In many ways, they transcended the leader's way of running things. The considerable changes that occurred in the way the regime was managed after Stalin's death indicate this. But the converse is also true: many basic characteristics remained in place. Determining what actually did change, and what endured, is a key problem in understanding the country's history. But it also presents the historian with a recurrent obstacle, which pertains to the philosophy of history: how much can be attributed to an individual leader? Is he an independent agent, i.e. an autonomous factor? If so, all we need is a biography. Or is he a product of historical circumstances and conditions, of the country's traditions, of its potential and limitations? In that case, we need a work of history.

The 1930s do not present historians with an easy task, regardless of whether they are dealing with personal or objective factors. As has been suggested, these years contain enough contradictory elements for some people to depict them in glowing colours, while for others they were nothing but a Calvary. And many autobiographies reveal their authors oscillating between these extremes. The fact that so many people, at the time or subsequently, refused to believe in the image of Stalin as the criminal organizer of a regime of terror may have had much to do with those aspects of his policies that unquestionably served the country's interests. As many Russian and non-Russian observers agree, the USSR's victory in the Second World War was an epic that saved the country and had great international impact. But it could not have been achieved by Tsarism or a similar regime. On the other hand, ignorance – fruit of the secretive character of the Stalinist state – also certainly contributed to the successful propagation of the image of the 'great Stalin' as imposed by its subject.

A scholarly approach cannot ignore these 'extremes'. But its purpose does not consist in wavering between such determinist notions as 'There was no alternative' and 'Stalin was inevitable', or contrary views stressing the fortuitous, usurpatory and arbitrary dimensions of the Stalinist phenomenon. It is preferable to concentrate on the actual course of history, analysing the context – i.e. the full interplay of relevant factors – that contributed to the making of a regime which abandoned the requisite rules of the political game – rules it still unquestionably possessed in the early years of the NEP. Stalinism was precisely the flip side of a party system that had lost control over its political existence. That many vital state functions continued to be taken in charge does not alter this fact. However, it is also an incentive to carry on exploring the way in which the various factors remained active. Stalin's arbitrary power was never immune from the rebound of developments – from what was advancing or slowly decaying in the country, around him and, ultimately, inside him.

The period 1928–39 unquestionably stands out because, although brief, it condenses all the past and future problems of the Soviet system. Understanding the Stalinist period is indispensable. But this does not mean that we subscribe to the widespread cliché according to which that is all there is to know. It cannot be repeated too often that many features distinguished the Stalinist system both from the NEP and from the post-Stalinist system, and yet at the same time all three periods have much in common. Study of the 1930s should help to clarify not only this point, but also a series of other problems that constitute so many knots in the historical tangle of Russia.

We are now in a position to disclose one of our findings: it transpires that while history had rendered Stalin's regime profoundly dysfunctional, it also prepared the factors and actors that would make it possible to proceed to the subsequent chapter in Soviet history.

I

STALIN KNOWS WHERE HE WANTS TO GET TO – AND IS GETTING THERE

Stalin died some fifty years ago. New sources have become available and fine books are in the process of being written. Notwithstanding this wealth of material, however, it remains difficult to get the full measure of his character inasmuch as assessments and first-hand testimony offer contrasting portraits and snapshots. Some present a matter-of-fact, well-informed, often polite, and even benevolent leader – in other words, a rational statesman. Others offer a cold, manipulative tactician. Yet others depict a control freak, distrusting everyone and everything, an irate, vindictive monster who could barely contain his fits of rage; or worse, a capricious madman who believed the massacres he committed were his greatest political invention. Ham actor on a grand scale or skilful organizer? For many, he was nothing but a pathetic figure who made a mess of everything. Was he talented, even a genius (however evil)? Or just a vulgar and perverse mediocrity?

This kaleidoscopic picture is further complicated by the fact that observers who had pronounced on the subject in one setting subsequently revised their judgement when they saw the same man in different situations.

Such diametrically opposed assessments (some of which do reflect the reality and nature of Stalin) are bewildering. Given, however, that we are dealing with a figure known for meticulously staging his appearances, a case can be made for the idea that all the various Stalins glimpsed by observers were authentic. At all events, we must state the obvious: the whole phenomenon had a beginning and an end, dictated not merely by the banal fact of mortality, but also because the phase of systemic aberration the USSR endured under Stalin had its natural limits. This obliges us to reinsert Stalin into the historical flux from which he emerged, to which he contributed, and from which he departed in dying a natural death. This tortuous, bloody, intensely dramatic and deeply personal path was also one component of a historical 'motherboard' – in other words, it was also an impersonal product. Some of these aspects will be clarified here; others will be broached in Part Three.

We shall begin by querying what is usually regarded as incontestable. Stalin was a member of the Bolshevik Party, a Leninist like everyone else in the leadership. Or so it appeared. He did indeed belong to the leading circles, was a member of the Central Committee, and later of the Politburo. Especially during the Civil War, he served as Lenin's man on special assignments. And yet, intellectually and politically Stalin was different from most of the historical figures in the Bolshevik movement. The other Bolshevik leaders were often political analysts, who knew the West well because they had lived there. More 'European', easier to 'read', they were interested in theoretical questions and intellectually superior to Stalin. He was less well-educated, with little experience of the outside world. Capable of leading discussions and conducting arguments, he was no orator. He was secretive, intensely self-centred, cautious and scheming. His highly sensitive ego could be soothed, if by anything, only by a sense of his own greatness, which had to be unreservedly acknowledged by others.

Acquiring personal power seemed to Stalin the surest way to compel others to bow to him. Despite his high position (he entered the Politburo on its creation in 1919), he was overshadowed not only by Lenin and Trotsky – the two top-ranking leaders – but also by a pleiad of others who did not know – and could not have conceived – that they would one day have to yield to him completely. Stalin must have compensated for this relative inferiority by mobilizing his own fantasies of greatness and assigning himself a much larger part than he actually played. He did it by gathering around him an expanding group of insignificant acolytes and sycophants like Voroshilov or Budenny; the abler but still uncouth Ordzhonikidze; the skilful but very young Mikoyan; and, somewhat later, Molotov, who became, perhaps unwittingly at the outset, the future dictator's main support and a high priest of his cult.

These features of a profoundly authoritarian personality were given free rein during the Civil War – an experience that contributed considerably to Stalin's vision of the form that the new state emerging from its ravages should take and of how it should be governed. At the same time, such ideas represented an ingredient of the psychological urge for self-aggrandizement. In short, one cannot but be struck by the difference between his personality and what we know about the other members of the 'old guard', Lenin included. Stalin's world was initially quite naturally shaped by the traditions of his native Caucasus, and subsequently by his experience of the depths of popular Russia. By contrast, the impact on him of the Second and Third Internationals was minimal, if not non-existent. Accordingly, it was no wonder that he and his intimates emerged from the Civil War with a quite different approach to what should be done in Russia from that of Lenin, Trotsky, Kamenev and their ilk, whether the issue was their conception of socialism or the kind of state that should run the country. Thus, two very different political and cultural universes coexisted within what was presented as 'Bolshevism', and this coexistence endured as long as everyone shared the same key objective. Once the regime defeated the 'Whites', the two divergent orientations surfaced and clashed: one concentrated on equipping Russia with a state that defended the interests of the majority of the population; the other focused its strategy on the state itself – an approach shared by many in Russia, not least in the ranks of Civil War veterans.

At this stage, dictatorship was the only available option. The Civil War had temporarily concealed the fact that the term did not denote a single unequivocal reality. This is far from being the case: dictatorial regimes come in different shapes and colours, just like other political regimes – including democracies, which all too often fluctuate, and sometimes dangerously, between authoritarian, liberal and social-democratic variants. Once peace had returned, and the issue was to construct a peacetime state, two antagonistic models came to the fore. The differences revolved around representations of Russia, the type of state power required to handle the nationalities problem, cooperation, the peasantry, party structure, development strategies, and the kind of social transformation to aim at. Two politically opposed camps found themselves within what was supposedly the same party. Predictably, the one that ended up winning preserved the old name for a time. But we know what it became – and how rapidly.

Because for the most part Stalin kept his goals concealed, other party leaders were outmanoeuvred. By the time they realized the trap they had set for themselves, it was too late. Lenin himself was fooled for quite a while. When he finally understood what he was dealing with, again it was too late for effective remedial action. Stalin's rise was greatly facilitated by the fact that Lenin was seriously ill from late 1920 onwards. On and off medication, subject to extensive treatment, for long periods he had to abandon political activity – especially for much of 1922 and part of 1923. As we have stressed, however, the problem went deeper than 'deciphering' Stalin's personality, for with the latter went a whole vision of the political line to be pursued in future years. Implicit in his political behaviour, this had not yet been explicitly formulated. Even so, the two different programmes emerged very clearly during 'Lenin's last struggle', as attested mainly (but not exclusively) in his so-called 'testament'. Stalin's position became evident in his plans for the constitutional form of the USSR, which were debated and adopted in 1922–3 under his rule (he had become party general-secretary in 1922). The documents relating to the construction of the USSR contain the most revealing material about the clash between Lenin and Stalin, even though the polemic went much further and deeper than the nationalities problem in the Soviet state. It ran virtually the whole gamut of system-building: ideology, the respective roles of party and state, economic policy, and especially the strategically crucial issue of policies towards the peasantry [1]

Materials that became available after perestroika enable us to appreciate not only how far-reaching the differences were, but also the profound personal hostility that had developed between Lenin and the figure he had himself selected as general-secretary – a post that at the time was not meant to have the importance it subsequently acquired. Stalin's hostility towards Lenin and Lenin's growing irritation with Stalin – a deepening personal and ideological divide that was concealed from all but a few insiders – can be sampled, or rather guessed at, from a previously unknown letter by Stalin to Lenin, written some time in 1921.[2] This letter, which deals with the party apparatus, Lenin's wife Krupskaya, and the Politburo, offers a rare insight into how Stalin's political mind worked. As it transpires from the text, the story began with a complaint from Krupskaya to Lenin (she kept her ailing husband informed on many subjects): Stalin had created a large party agitprop department that 'looks like a full-blown new commissariat', with virtually the same tasks and objectives as the political education department she headed in the education commissariat, thus undermining it. After carefully reading her memo, Lenin forwarded it to Stalin with his

---

1   I could not have known all this when writing *Lenin's Last Struggle* in 1967.
2   See *Istoricheskii Arkhiv*, no. 2, 1994, pp. 220–3.

remarks, requesting him not to concern himself with agitprop. Stalin's reply was that of a *kinto* – Georgian for 'street-urchin' (the nickname he had been given in his youth). He behaved like a petty, insolent intriguer, exploiting the fact that his correspondent was not in the best of health. He denied the figures Krupskaya had given for the number of officials recruited to the department. He claimed that he had been forced to take on this department, but now refused to give it up, 'explaining' to Lenin that it was in his interests for him to stay on since, if not, 'Trotsky will conclude that Lenin is only doing this because of Krupskaya'. In short, Stalin refused to knuckle under.

The ruse is obvious. It was not, of course, a question of what Trotsky would say. It was Stalin's way of telling Lenin that he knew the story came from Krupskaya; and of giving him to understand that faced with the formidable Trotsky, who at the time was in conflict with Lenin on a series of issues, the latter, weakened by illness, could not be certain of commanding a majority in the Politburo without Stalin's help.

Nineteen twenty-one witnessed more of these skirmishes, which are just as revealing. The Trotsky card that Stalin played to contain Lenin emerged during this period, which was dominated by a rather sterile dispute about the role of trade unions between a Trotsky-led minority and Lenin's majority in the Politburo. Trotsky, who had been rebuffed that year when he proposed a change of course to an NEP-type system, could see no other way of handling the economic devastation than by temporarily persisting with quasi-military methods for mobilizing manpower. For his part, Lenin could not as yet envisage a new economic policy, but wanted to allow the unions, rooted in the working class, greater autonomy. The two factions manoeuvred to win over a majority of delegates to the upcoming Eleventh Party Congress. As Mikoyan testified in his autobiography *Tak Bylo* ('It happened like this'), if Lenin participated in some of the meetings held to refine tactics to counter Trotsky, it was Stalin who conducted the whole operation.

Making common cause with Lenin against his *bête noire* – Trotsky – seemed to Stalin a good way of manipulating the former. And this is what he was also up to in the 'Krupskaya affair'. But it is possible that these machinations – and Stalin's grudge against Lenin himself – developed even earlier, during the Civil War, but had passed unnoticed because of urgent military tasks and the fact that the chief target of Stalin's intrigues at the time was Trotsky. Stalin's total lack of respect and, soon, hatred, for Lenin – this is my point here – were indirectly fed by his obsessive hatred of Trotsky, who stood in the way of Stalin's self-image as a great military strategist and statesman. The object of numerous derogatory (and often unpublishable) epithets directed at him by Stalin and his supporters, Trotsky was the creator of the Red Army, the People's Commissar for War, and co-leader of the 1917 revolution – nothing to do with Stalin's depiction of him. Trotsky's name was associated with Lenin's – something Lenin never openly disavowed – and this more than anything else irked Stalin. The incessant intrigues and the pressures he and his acolytes brought to bear on Lenin with the aim of eliminating Trotsky from his military post, but also from the leadership *tout court* (a story long familiar to biographers of Lenin and Stalin), make this interpretation of Stalin's attitude plausible.

Apart from a few moments of hesitation, this 'siege' of Lenin was unsuccessful. Lenin relied on Trotsky and his prestige. He worked closely with him – and not just on military matters. Moreover, he maintained daily, confident contact with Trotsky's right-hand man on the Military Revolutionary Council and in the Defence Commissariat – Yefraim Skliansky – who doubtless played the role of trusted intermediary between the two men. Documents dating from the Civil War reveal his absolutely critical importance in the everyday activity of the centre. Yet very little is known about him, or the circumstances of his drowning when boating on a river in 1925.

This close network of relationships was bound to fuel Stalin's profound hostility towards Lenin. But it only emerged when Lenin was dying and Stalin was already in almost total command. Openly attacking a healthy Lenin would not have suited Stalin's calculating, cautious character, but with Lenin's illness – of whose details Stalin was fully informed – things changed. As general-secretary, Stalin was charged by the Central Committee with supervising Lenin's medical treatment, which allowed him unabashedly to spy on the sick man. Lenin's secretary, Fotieva, may have reported to Stalin about every piece Lenin dictated to her, even though he had stipulated that they were to remain confidential for the time being. One can imagine Stalin's state of mind when he realized that Lenin wanted to demote him from his current position and perhaps destroy his political career altogether. If Fotieva did not inform him of this earlier, he learnt it at the same time as the Politburo from the text Lenin delivered to them on the eve of the Twelfth Party Congress for which it was intended. Here Lenin demanded the removal of Stalin from his post and explained why. But at precisely this moment Lenin became totally incapacitated and could no longer be consulted on anything. At the time, Lenin's demand was known only to the Politburo. Not until Khrushchev thirty-three years later was his text revealed to the Soviet public.

The debate on the place of nationalities in the nascent USSR, which was conducted in the seats and corridors of power, reveals the depth of the disagreements about the future state and the shape it should take. These differences of opinion elicited some extremely sharp reactions from Lenin who, although seriously ill, managed, astonishingly enough, to formulate his own ideas with the utmost clarity.

Stalin's conception of the future Soviet state was largely shaped by his experience immediately following the revolution, when he was in charge of nationalities. His first government position after 1917 was Commissar for Nationalities, and the first book he published, written before the revolution at Lenin's request and with Bukharin's editorial aid, dealt with the 'national question'. Dabbling in such endlessly complicated and conflict-ridden problems may have convinced him that all those highly diverse, unruly and combative nationalities might at any moment throw a spanner in the works of central government.

Lenin's last stand on this subject was a manifesto containing the most powerful and clearest analysis he had produced in the entire post-Civil War period. According to him, Stalin wished to give the non-Russian nationalities 'autonomy' – meaning that they would become part of Russia (at the time named the RSFSR or Russian Federation) or, in other words, administrative units subordinate to Russia. The debate over this approach, but also about other proposals for the shape of the future state, was fierce; and the clash between Lenin and Stalin on precisely these points was at its epicentre, with far-reaching consequences for the system's future. This is why it is a story well worth telling.

2

'AUTONOMIZATION VERSUS FEDERATION' (1922–3)

The Russian editors of the collection that constitutes our main source on this subject[1] write in their introduction that Lenin's ideas on the place and role of nationalities in the state underwent a major transformation. He moved from a firm belief in the virtues of centralism to a 'recognition of the inevitability of federalism'. At the outset, he believed that national specificities should be accommodated inside a unitary state, but then he proceeded to defend the creation of states on an ethnic basis which would enter into contractual relations with one another. He switched from outright rejection of cultural autonomy to acknowledging the territorial and extraterritorial aspects of such autonomy. The opinions of Trotsky, Rakovsky, Mdivani, Skrypnik, Makharadze, Sultan-Galiev and other people close to Lenin developed in a similar direction, usually independently of each other (with the exception of Lenin, none of them would die of natural causes).

Stalin was a consistent supporter of what his opponents called 'unitarism'. His report on problems of federalism, delivered as early as January 1918 to the All-Russian Soviet Congress, was an ardent plea for this doctrine. Later, in a note to Lenin dated 12 June 1920 which does not feature in his *Collected Works*, he wrote: 'Our soviet form of federation suits the nations of Tsarist Russia as their road to internationalism ... These nationalities either never possessed states of

---

1 See A. P. Nenarokov, V. A. Gornyi, V. N. Dobrokhotov, A. I. Kozhokina, A. D. Kotykhov and A. I. Ushakov, *Nesostoiavshiisia Iubilei: Pochemu SSSR ne Otprazdnoval svoego Semidesiatiletiia*, Moscow 1992: a very rich collection of documents, with articles by the editors.

their own in the past or, if they did, long ago lost them. That is why the soviet (centralized) form of federation is accepted by them without any particular friction.' On numerous occasions during 1918–20 Stalin stressed the centralized character of the Soviet Federation, which was manifestly the direct heir of the Tsarist federation 'one and indivisible'. It included such 'autonomies' as Poland, Finland, the Ukraine, Crimea, Turkestan, Kirgizia, Siberia and the Transcaucasus, which might one day tend to become separate entities. But Stalin firmly underlined that 'autonomy does not mean independence and does not involve separation'. The central power should retain all key functions firmly in its own hands. According to the editors of the collection we are using, for Stalin granting autonomy was mainly an administrative device en route to a 'socialist unitarism'. Stalin's argument was nothing but an expression of the Russian notion of a 'super-state' (*derzhava*, a term we shall often have to employ) – the product of an expansion based on Russia's messianic role. In this conception, incorporating other nations served the cause of progress. The Russian editors, we might interject, may not have realized that other imperialisms suffered from comparable messianism. What was new was Stalin's emphasis on the 'supra-Russian' (*sverkhrusskost'*) dimension of his own imperial policy when contesting Lenin's conceptions, which were now presented by Stalin as a *nationalist deviation* harmful to the interests of the Soviet state.

On 10 August 1922, the Politburo decided to create a commission to examine the relations between the Russian Federation and the other republics, which for now enjoyed the status of independent states. Stalin, the nationalities expert since before the revolution, who became party general-secretary in the same year, declared himself ready to present his plan the very next day. The five independent Soviet states, linked by a form of contractual agreement, were the Ukraine, Belorussia and the three Transcaucasian states: Georgia, Armenia and Azerbaidzhan. What Stalin proposed for them was 'autonomization', which simply meant that the republics would formally become part of the Russian Federation. The status of the remaining areas – Bukhara, Khorezm, the Far Eastern Republic – was to be left open for the time being. Treaties should be signed with them on customs, foreign trade, foreign and military affairs, and so on. The governing bodies of the Russian Federation – the Central Executive Committee, the Council of Commissars, the Council of Labour and Defence – should formally encompass the central soviet institutions of the republics being incorporated. Their own commissariats of foreign affairs, foreign trade, defence, railways, finance and communications should merge with those of Russia. The remainder – justice, education, internal affairs, agriculture, state inspection – would remain under their jurisdiction. And, not surprisingly, the local political police were to be merged with Russia's own GPU.

Stalin explained that these proposals should not be published yet; they should be debated by the party's national central committees and later translated into formal legislation by the soviets of the republics – their executive committees or congresses of soviets. In the most straightforward manner imaginable, the principle of 'independence', which was in any case nothing more than 'verbiage' as far as Stalin was concerned, would be eliminated, with these republics becoming mere administrative units of a centralized Russian state.

Waves of protest soon mounted against this policy. On 15 September 1922 the Georgian Central Committee rejected 'autonomization' as 'premature'. Ordzhonikidze, Kirov, Kakhiani and Gogoberidze voted against this decision. They were all of them Stalin's men from the 'Transcaucasian Party Committee' – a body imposed by Moscow to oversee the three republics that was a source of endless friction with national party leaderships. On 1 September 1922, Makharadze, a leading Georgian communist, complained to Lenin: 'We are living in confusion and chaos.' In the name of party discipline, the Transcaucasian Committee was imposing all sorts of decisions on the Georgian party that undermined the country's independence. 'Georgia', he stressed, is 'neither an Azerbaidzhan nor a Turkestan.'

In a letter addressed to Lenin on 22 September 1922, Stalin likewise complained about the 'total chaos' in relations between the centre and the periphery, with its train of conflicts and grievances. But all fault now lay with the other side. Stalin railed against the small republics 'playing the game of independence'. According to him, 'the unified federal national economy is becoming a fiction'. The alternatives were as follows. Either full independence, in which case the centre would withdraw and not meddle in the affairs of the republics, leaving them to run their own railways, trade, and foreign affairs. Common problems would require constant negotiations between equals and the decisions of the Russian Federation's supreme bodies would not be binding on other republics. Or they should opt for genuine unification in a single economic unit, with the other republics submitting to the decisions of the Russian Federation's higher instances. In other words, an imaginary independence would be replaced by an authentic internal autonomy for the republics in the spheres of language, culture, justice, internal affairs and agriculture. And Stalin lectured his colleagues:

> In four years of Civil War, we were obliged to display liberalism towards the republics. As a result, we helped to form hard-line 'social-independentists' among them, who regard the Central Committee's decisions as simply being Moscow's. If we do not transform them into 'autonomies' immediately, the unity of the soviet republics is a lost cause. We are now busy bothering about how not to offend these nationalities. But if we carry on like this, in a year's time we'll be verging on the break-up of the party.

In his text, Stalin reiterated the main lines of his 'autonomization' project. He did not anticipate Lenin's reaction.

The least that can be said is that Lenin was not content with Stalin's memorandum; he sensed trouble. In a note to Kamenev dated 26 September 1922, he asked the latter to examine the proposals for the integration of the republics into the Russian Federation. He had already discussed the issue with Sokolnikov, would be seeking a meeting with Stalin, and was tomorrow seeing Mdivani, the Georgian leader accused of the deviation of 'independentism' (*nezavisimstvo*) by Stalin's supporters. He added that in his view, 'Stalin tends to rush things too much', and that amendments would be required. Lenin had already sent some to Stalin and the latter had accepted the first and most important of them, replacing his formula – 'joining the Russian Federation' – by Lenin's – 'a formal unification with the Russian Federation in a Union of Soviet Socialist Republics of Europe and Asia'. And Lenin explained: we must not destroy their independence; we must construct a higher tier, consisting in a federation of independent republics enjoying equal rights. There were further amendments Lenin wanted to discuss with Stalin and he also wished to meet with other leaders. The amendments he had proposed thus far were just preliminary; more would be sent out to all members of the Politburo. This note was simply a first draft: after discussing matters with Mdivani and other leaders, he would suggest new changes. But he requested that the text in its current form be communicated to the whole Politburo.

Stalin's reaction to Lenin's proposals was acerbic. In a note he sent to members of the Politburo on 27 September 1922, he professed himself in agreement with the changes to paragraph one suggested by Lenin. He had no choice. But he rejected all the others with snide remarks like 'premature', 'absurd', 'pointless', and so on. He sought to turn the accusation of undue haste back against Lenin: 'His haste risks encouraging the independentists' and demonstrated the error of Lenin's 'national liberalism'. The argument is not very coherent. Stalin was furious because he had to retreat from his project of 'autonomization'. Unable to contain himself, he sought to retrieve the initiative by pointing to a 'deviation' ('national liberalism') that could rally his own supporters against Lenin. Defeat was not something that Stalin could easily live with. But it was just around the corner.

In an exchange of notes between Kamenev and Stalin during a Politburo meeting on 28 September 1922, Kamenev scribbled that Lenin had 'decided to go to war on the issue of independence' and had asked him to 'go to Tbilisi to meet the leaders offended by Stalin's supporters'. In response Stalin wrote: 'We should get tough with Ilitch [Lenin]. If a few Georgian Mensheviks can influence some Georgian Communists, who in turn influence Lenin, one can ask: what does all this have to do with "independence"?' But Kamenev warned him: 'I think that if V. I. [Lenin] persists, *opposing him* [Kamenev's emphasis] would only make things worse.'

What was Kamenev up to? Was he not being duplicitous in doing Lenin's bidding, while informing Stalin? Or did he think that Lenin would not be around much longer?

Stalin responded to the last note as follows: 'I don't know. Let him do as he sees fit.' This was a practice in which Stalin excelled: manoeuvring to present his retreat in the best possible light. He wrote to all members of the Politburo to inform them that 'a slightly abridged, more precise version' was in the process of being prepared, and that he and his committee on relations between the republics would be submitting it to the Politburo. But the revised text was Lenin's: all the republics (including Russia) were joining to form a common Union of Soviet Socialist Republics, but retained the right to leave it. This state's highest body was to be the 'Union Executive Committee', on which all republics would be represented in proportion to their populations. This Committee would nominate a Union Council of Commissars.

Since Stalin's game is what interests us here, we shall not linger over the details of the government constitution. Compelled to give way on his project of autonomy, Stalin did not give up on attaining his main objective by roundabout means, manipulating the language that defined the prerogatives of the Moscow-based future commissariats (i.e. ministries) so as to nip any desire for independence in the bud, whatever the constitutional niceties. For their part, the republics were all too aware of what was at stake: without proper, clearly stated constitutional guarantees, the ministries based in Moscow would in fact be in the hands of the Russian Federation or, in plain language, in Russian hands.

This point was broached in a lengthy memorandum to Stalin from Christian Rakovsky, the head of the Ukrainian government, on 28 September 1922. In essence, this is what he said: Your draft refers to independent republics deferring to the centre. But it says nothing about their own republican rights, executive committees, or councils of commissars. The new nationalities policy would deal a blow to efforts to revive local economies, since it would significantly hamper their room for initiative. They had no material means and were being deprived of the rights required to develop their wealth and acquire what they currently lacked.

While Rakovsky appreciated the need for a federal government that was in a position to act, he thought that this could be achieved provided republican interests were secured by clearly formulated rights. He saw in Stalin's proposals not so much the project of a federation as the liquidation of the republics. This, he thought, could only harm the USSR internally and internationally. Lenin had the same concerns and was now ready for a fight. It was the so-called 'Georgian incident' that sounded the final alarm in his mind.

During the Georgian Central Committee's struggle against forcible incorporation into the Transcaucasian Federation, Stalin's irascible representative Ordzhonikidze had slapped one of the Georgian leaders.[2] Following this incident, the Georgian Central Committee collectively resigned, while vigorously criticizing the new project for the USSR in its entirety. There was a danger of the affair turning into a prolonged scandal. Lenin initially misunderstood what had occurred, but he rapidly made inquiries and learned that Stalin had sent Dzerzhinsky, accompanied by two other non-Russians, to investigate the conflict. Stalin's envoys sided unambiguously with Ordzhonikidze. Deeply disturbed by this incident, Lenin arrived at the conclusion that on the national question Stalin and his associates were behaving as 'representatives of a domineering great power' (*velikoderzhavniki*) – the term used by Lenin, but possibly inspired by the Georgians who were in constant touch with him. On 6 October 1922 he wrote a letter to Kamenev that began half-jokingly and ended in deadly earnest: 'I am declaring war on great-Russian chauvinism: it is necessary to insist *absolutely* that the Union's

---

2   The episode is described more fully in Lenin's *Sochineniia*, fifth edition, vol. 45; and, in more detail, in the sources published in Nenarokov *et al.*, eds, *op. cit.*

Central Executive Committee be chaired in turn by a Russian, Ukrainian, Georgian, etc. *Absolutely.*'

Lenin's programmatic text on the national question, dictated on 30–31 December 1922, reflects this new perception of the state of the system.[3] It was a unique – critical and self-critical – document, in which Lenin expressed his sense of guilt before the country's workers for not having intervened sufficiently firmly and energetically on the 'notorious problem of autonomy', officially called the problem of the USSR. Illness had hitherto prevented him from doing so. The gist of what he said is as follows: The unity of the apparatus is a prerequisite, but what apparatus are we referring to? An apparatus borrowed from the Tsarist past, a mixture of Tsarist and petty bourgeois chauvinists, traditionally used to oppress the people. We should at least wait until this apparatus improves, since otherwise the much-bruited principle of the right to secede from the Union will be nothing but a piece of paper, offering the other nationalities no protection against the *istinno russkii chelovek, biurokrat, nasil'nik, velikorusskaia shval'* – a set of derogatory epithets that is difficult to translate, but which basically refer to the brutish Russian nationalist oppressor. And Lenin pursued his indictment: Defenders of the project claim that administration deemed important for the preservation of local cultures and mentalities is being turned over to the republics. But is this really the case? And another question: What measures are being taken to defend the ethnic minorities (*inorodtsy*) from the authentically Russian bully (*ot istinno russkogo derzhimordy*)? The answer is: none.

It is important to understand the vehemence of Lenin's condemnation of the oppressive characteristics of the Russian bureaucracy and Russian ultra-nationalists. Such oppression dated back centuries – hence the need to dispel the distrust of the ethnic minorities who had suffered so much injustice, and who were (Lenin insisted) particularly sensitive to any form of discrimination. And he proceeds: 'In his haste and his infatuation with administrative methods, not to mention his animosity towards social nationalism, Stalin has played a fatal role. Animosity [*ozloblenie*] is the worst thing in politics.' With these words, Lenin put his finger on something that should have disqualified Stalin from a position of power in the first place.

---

3 Lenin, 'K voprosu o natsianalnostiakh ili ob "avtonomizatsii"', in *Sochineniia*, vol. 45, pp. 356–62.

What was to be done? Lenin responded by stating that the creation of the USSR was necessary; the diplomatic apparatus (the best thing we have) should remain in the centre. The use of national languages should be firmly guaranteed. Ordzhonikidze should be punished. Stalin and Dzerzhinsky were responsible for this whole Russian nationalist campaign. More generally, the USSR project should be rethought in its entirety and, if necessary, redrawn. This could be done at the next Congress of the Soviets. Let the centre retain military and diplomatic functions; all other functions should revert to the republics. Lenin reassured his audience that there was no reason to fear a fragmentation of power. If deployed judiciously and impartially, the party's authority would be sufficient to achieve the requisite unity. 'It would', Lenin wrote,

> be unacceptable, just as the East is awakening, for us to undermine our prestige by bullying and committing injustices against our own national minorities. We must criticize foreign imperialism. But it is even more important to understand that when we ourselves adopt an imperialist attitude towards oppressed nationalities, if only on points of detail, we are reneging on our own principled commitments.

It should by now be obvious that Lenin's attack on Stalin was part of an attack on what he regarded as a replica of the old great-Russian imperial ideology (*velikoderzhavnichestvo*). And there can be no doubt about it: Lenin was identifying and attacking political enemies. He sensed what was going to happen (we might speak of foresight, even inspiration). For this was indeed the direction in which Stalin was going and which, in due course, would become official policy.

It is no wonder, then, that in his 'testament' Lenin made it clear that Stalin should be removed from his party post. Aware of his physical debility, Lenin asked Trotsky in a note of 5 March 1923 to 'please take upon yourself defence of the Georgian case in the Central Committee'. The same day, in a letter addressed to the Georgians Mdivani and Makharadze, he wrote: 'I am following your case with all my heart.' But his political activity ceased abruptly four days later, on 9 March. On that fatal day, a further extremely powerful stroke incapacitated him for good. Henceforth, until his death on 21 January 1924, he was incapable of doing anything except listening to Krupskaya read him press articles. He could understand what he was hearing, but bereft of speech he was able to react only by inarticulate sounds and by moving his eyes.

In the meantime, as requested, Trotsky had on 6 March 1923 written a strongly worded memorandum for the Politburo, in which he declared that ultra-statist tendencies must be resolutely and ruthlessly rejected and criticized Stalin's theses on the national question. He stressed that a significant section of the Soviet central bureaucracy regarded the creation of the USSR as a way of beginning to eliminate all national and autonomous political entities (states, organizations, regions). This should be fought as an expression of imperialist and anti-proletarian attitudes. The party should be warned that, under the cover of so-called 'unified commissariats', the economic and cultural interests of the national republics were in fact being discounted.

Yet the following day, in a letter to Kamenev, Trotsky adopted a rather puzzling position. He wrote: 'Stalin's resolution on the national question is worthless and a sharp turn is needed' – which accorded perfectly with Lenin's personal appeal to him. But thereafter, one has the sense that Trotsky, aware of Lenin's second stroke, was unsure of the next step. He suddenly displayed great magnanimity and a conciliatory attitude towards Stalin. He declared himself opposed to *perestroika* and did not wish to punish anyone:

> I am against liquidating Stalin and expelling Ordzhonikidze. But I agree with Lenin in principle: nationalities policy should be radically changed, persecution of the Georgians must cease; administrative methods of pressurizing the party must come to an end; industrialization should be pursued more resolutely; and we must establish a collaborative spirit at the top. The intrigues must stop. We need honest collaboration.

Was Trotsky daydreaming out loud?

On 7 March 1923, Kamenev informed Zinoviev that Lenin had disavowed Ordzhonikidze, Stalin and Dzerzhinsky; had expressed his solidarity with Mdivani; and had sent Stalin a personal letter breaking off personal relations on account of the latter's mistreatment of Krupskaya. Kamenev adds that Stalin responded with a brief, sour-tempered apology that will hardly satisfy the *starik* (old man). Lenin 'will not be satisfied by a peaceful settlement in Georgia, but obviously *wants certain organizational measures to be taken at the top*' (Kamenev's emphasis). 'You should be in Moscow at this time', Kamenev concludes.

In the interim, Stalin had conducted a retreat, since the situation had become critical for him. He ordered Ordzhonikidze to go easier on the Georgians and seek a compromise (7 March 1923). The same day, he wrote to Trotsky accepting his amendments as 'incontrovertible'. Fotieva, Lenin's secretary, had meanwhile sent him the latter's memorandum on the nationalities, adding that Lenin (by now stricken) intended to have it published, but had not given her any formal instructions to this effect. Fotieva also wrote to Kamenev, with a copy to Trotsky, to tell him how important this text and the nationalities issue were to Lenin. Kamenev declared himself in favour of publication. Trotsky wrote to other Central Committee members, explaining how Lenin had sent him this text and inviting them to read it.

On 6 April 1923, Fotieva wrote to Stalin again, offering him an escape clause: Lenin did not consider the text finished and ready for publication and Maria Ulianova (Lenin's sister) had advised her that Lenin had not given instructions for it to be published. All that could be done was to communicate it to participants in the forthcoming Twelfth Party Congress.

It is likely that Stalin 'suggested' this to one or other of the women, but it is ultimately irrelevant. He got what he wanted: there were to be no direct attacks on him at the congress. On 16 April he declared to Central Committee members: 'as it turns out, Lenin's article cannot be published'; and attacked Trotsky for having kept such an important document from the delegates who were gathering – an act he described as 'disloyal'. In short, he lied, but had no hesitation about lying further: 'I think it should be published, but unfortunately, as Fotieva's letter indicates, the text cannot be published because it hasn't yet been revised by comrade Lenin.'

The Presidium of the Twelfth Party Congress made all Lenin's notes on the national question available to members of the very restricted 'council of elders' (*sen'orenkonvent*). It also informed them of the decisions of the Central Committee plenum on the Georgian question. But participants in the session dealing with these questions, although deeply involved with them, were not to see these materials.

The Presidium also declared that the Central Committee had only learned of the content of Lenin's notes on the eve of the congress, not as a result of the action of any its members but solely on account of Lenin's instructions and his deteriorating health. The rumour that someone on the Central Committee had blocked their publication was sheer slander. Trotsky was thus exonerated from Stalin's charge of keeping the text from congress delegates.

This bickering about what to do with the texts, and about whom to show them to, were so many petty intrigues. But the stakes were high: who would stay in power and what was the shape of that power to be. Was the dictatorship to pursue (or resume) the populist and social orientation of Bolshevism? Or was it going to adopt, in theory and practice, a deeply conservative great-power orientation (*velikoderzhavnost'*) directed against Bolshevism, whose cadres were still socialists and opposed to the perpetuation of a form of state harking back to past models?

Astonishingly, in his note to Kamenev Trotsky lost his sense of reality. If Stalin's orientation represented such a threat, was it really sufficient, in order to fight it, to offer the partisans of great-power chauvinism (*velikoderzhavniki*) a feeble compromise, asking them to demonstrate more loyalty and call a halt to their intrigues and posturing? Asking Stalin for loyalty? The episodes reveals how little Lenin's closest collaborators understood Stalin's ability to manipulate and outmanoeuvre them at will. The 'old man' was not just very irate, as Kamenev seemed to think. For him, removing Stalin and co. meant exorcizing the spectre of an ideology and political orientation that was alien to Bolshevism and represented a mortal danger for Russia's future. As subsequent developments were to demonstrate, Lenin proved truly prophetic.

The decision to leave Stalin and his supporters in power indicates that at this fateful moment Trotsky understood neither Lenin nor Stalin. Known for his many brilliant analyses, historical and conjunctural, Trotsky was at the nadir of his political vigilance in 1923. Stalin had never been so vulnerable. A Leninist coalition, or a majority supporting Lenin's positions, was still possible. Revealing the whole of Lenin's testament to the Twelfth Congress and provoking a debate, rather than playing the game of 're-educating Stalin', was the last serious chance for a new course. But Trotsky let it slip, even though we know that he soon moved into outright opposition to Stalin. The other two supposed Leninists in the Politburo, Zinoviev and Kamenev, were also deeply confused; deprived of Lenin's leadership, they lost their bearings. Subsequently, they would form a 'triumvirate' with Stalin against Trotsky.

Was illness or extreme fatigue a factor in this massive failure of political acumen on Trotsky's part, of which there were to be further examples? No doubt this is a possible explanation.[4] But broader con-

---

4 RGASPI, f. 17, op. 84, d. 304, no page number, dated 26 June 1922. Five doctors, members of a concilium convened to examine and probably treat Trotsky – Ramonov, Voitsik, Semashko, Professor Klemperer and Professor Ferster (the latter two German doctors invited to treat Lenin) – signed the following diagnosis: Trotsky suffers from 'a chronic functional colitis, a slight hypertrophy of the heart and a tendency to fainting fits, due to anaemia'. In their judgement, Trotsky required a special diet (feeding up) and should avoid physical and intellectual exertion. (The copy of the report was difficult to read; I have carefully transcribed it.)

figurations of social and political forces, and the available alternatives at a given moment, are the framework in which leaders can win or lose, with the outcome sometimes seeming fortuitous. Yet 'accidents' happen when the factors in play are developing, are fluid, or are in a temporary stalemate.

It was utterly symptomatic that the 'national question' – i.e. the way in which the USSR and its government were to be constructed – should lead to a huge battle over the form and future of the Soviet state. Its outcome indicates that what was called 'Bolshevism' (or 'Leninism') was at this point vulnerable and in disarray, as it confronted both the enormous postwar task of putting the country on its feet again and, at the same time, the regime's hitherto invisible negative features. The situation called for a good deal of rethinking, regrouping and adaptation. In other words it was a classic situation where the personalities of leaders can make an enormous difference in the choice of direction.

Lenin's performance here was unique. Impressive at a political and human level amid this extraordinary imbroglio, it was the action of a dying, semi-paralysed man who remained lucid until the last fatal stroke.

For Stalin, of course, the issue was not so much the nationalities as the choice of strategic orientation: his project of 'autonomization' indicated one alternative for the regime and the character of state power. A careful reading of Lenin's texts demonstrates that his priorities were different. Power considerations were not foreign to Lenin, but in this instance the way that the nationalities were treated was an issue in its own right – one that the state must supply an adequate response to. Thus, in both versions what was at stake was the soul of the dictatorship. In Lenin's eyes, Stalin's project basically harked back to an old-style imperial autocracy. And he intended to take advantage of the next session of the Supreme Soviet to rewrite the legislation on the USSR that had just been adopted and to restore to the republics the ministerial prerogatives befitting their independent status, retaining only foreign affairs and defence for the centre.

In fact, the numerous Union-level ministries proposed by Stalin were a bone of contention and source of resentment. The republics were in no doubt that they would merely be confiscated by Russia. And this was precisely Stalin's goal. His clear and simple vision was inspired by the Civil War. Military power had settled the issue then. Now that peace had been restored to the country, a yet more powerful instrument must be forged: an untrammelled, unfettered, ultra-centralized and self-serving power – a war machine in peacetime. The role Stalin intended to play at the summit and the way in which he intended to set about reaching it – including the type of party he envisaged (if any) – were at the heart of his jigsaw puzzle.

3

'CADRES INTO HERETICS'

The documents presented thus far have provided us with a good deal of insight into Stalin's political designs and personality. The next two topics will illuminate them still further.

Some years after the events we have recounted, when he held all the levers of power in his own hands, Stalin continued to imagine himself a great man and leader – but he knew how to simulate a modest and unassuming personality, a simple follower of the great founder of the party. Taciturn and forever cautious, he seemed to be cool-headed – and was generally described as such. He affected a role of unassuming simplicity, casting himself as the modest follower of a great man. Yet his political activity – in fact, much of the puzzle – is readily decipherable: behind this image there lay hidden a quite different persona. We already know something about the kind of state he envisaged. Moreover, his utterances on the tasks and role of state and party cadres disclose the way in which he conceived the exercise of power, including his own part in it. These statements are revealing, even if their meaning eluded his contemporaries or observers. Perfectly clear in his own mind, his positions were publicly expressed during the Thirteenth Party Congress in 1924:

> A cadre must know how to carry out instructions, must understand them, adopt them as his own, attach the greatest importance to them, and make them part of his very existence. Otherwise, politics loses its meaning and consists merely of gesticulating. Hence the decisive importance of the cadres department in the apparatus of the Central Committee. Every functionary must be closely studied, from every angle and in the most minute detail.[1]

---

1 Stalin, *Sochineniia*, vol. 5, pp. 210–11.

Mention of the cadres department (*uchraspred*) should not be taken to mean that Stalin attributed any importance to the party itself. This becomes clearer if we refer to one of his later declarations to 'future cadres', students at the Sverdlov Party University. Here he basically explained that 'for us, objective difficulties do not exist. The only problem is cadres. If things are not progressing, or if they go wrong, the cause is not to be sought in any objective conditions: it is the fault of the cadres'.

Thus, for this 'Marxist', objective conditions do not exist: the leader is free to set tasks, but cannot be held responsible for poor decisions or results. These short texts contain the substance of Stalinist philosophy and practice in its entirety, as formulated by Stalin himself. With good cadres, nothing is impossible. The policies decided at the top are always correct; failures are attributable to the leader's entourage or underlings. As expressed here, the essence of Stalin's conception of his personal power consists in the idea that such power should be 'naked'. Stalin never wrote anything resembling a *Mein Kampf* – a book that anyone who wished to understand Hitler and his aspirations had only to read. But his conception of an unaccountable personal power, at the head of a state responsible only to him – in other words, his conception of an 'irresponsible dictatorship' – was succinctly articulated early on, in a couple of sentences that could easily escape the attention of even quite seasoned party members. This conception had already been put into practice in emergency situations – when the party was underground, during the revolution or Civil War – when militants had simply to obey. But the same logic was now to be transposed to a quite different situation – in which routine, not emergency, was the everyday reality – and applied to the state administration and the various party apparatuses and bureaucracy. The leader was demanding a type of behaviour that had its place in wartime, when an army is besieged on all sides. This exigency – an 'untrammelled dictatorship' – could only lead to deformations at the most elementary level.

A highly illuminating example can be found in the memoirs of Stalin's interpreter, Valentin Berezhkov.[2] Unaware of Stalin's 1925 text and its implications, he recounts an episode that occurred during the war, when he worked under Molotov in the Foreign Affairs Ministry. Stalin's 'illogical logic' was explained to him by Molotov, who was one

2 See Valentin Berezhkov, *Riadom so Stalinym*, Moscow 1999, pp. 244–5.

of its connoisseurs. When something went wrong, Stalin demanded that 'the culprit be found and severely punished'. The only thing to do was to identify someone, and Molotov would do just this. One day it was noticed that a telegram from Stalin to Roosevelt had not been answered. Molotov ordered Berezhkov to investigate and identify the guilty party. Berezhkov discovered that no one on the Soviet side was responsible; he concluded that the fault lay with the American State Department. On hearing his report, Molotov mocked him, explaining that every failing was attributable to someone. In the case to hand, someone had decided a procedure for transmitting and monitoring telegrams. This involved the Soviet side alone. Stalin had given orders for the culprit to be found, and so it could only be the person who had established the procedure. Finding him was assigned to Molotov's deputy, Vyshinsky who did so without difficulty. The ill-fated head of the cipher department was immediately relieved of his duties, expelled from the party, and disappeared without a trace. Stalin's order had been executed to the letter. The source of this insane logic was clear: if there was no culprit for failures that occurred at lower levels, they might be attributed to those at the top. And that was out of the question.

The methods employed by Stalin to 'construct' the image of his power involved some other dimensions. Thus, he composed the various scenarios in his mind and everything else followed – usually without the least imagination. One of the simplest consisted in appropriating the lingering images of the power and influence associated with Lenin and Trotsky. Trotsky was a recurrent figure in this phantasmagoria: he was systematically vilified and had every possible calumny heaped on his head. There can be no doubt that he played a special role in Stalin's psyche and that is why mere political victory would not suffice. Stalin would not rest until he had issued the order for Trotsky's assassination. He also wished to erase him from Soviet history – via censorship, obviously, but also (astonishingly) by ascribing Trotsky's achievements to himself. The country would thus be offered films in which the military exploits of his sworn foe – for example, Trotsky's role in the defence of Petrograd against General Yudenich's army in December 1919 – were attributed to Stalin. This is only one example of his incredible pettiness and envy.

The appropriation of Lenin took the more convoluted and curious form of the 'oath to Lenin', sworn before the Supreme Soviet on 26 January 1924, the day before Lenin's funeral. The decision to embalm Lenin's body, despite his family's vigorous protests, formed part of the scenario. As for the oath itself, it was a long incantation in which Stalin listed the commandments supposedly bequeathed by Lenin to the party and then solemnly pledged, in the party's name, faithfully to obey them. Now that we have a better understanding of Stalin's real attitude to Lenin, it is obvious that this 'apotheosis' was not a sincere gesture of respect, but a way of preparing the launch of his own cult. As some of Stalin's opponents noticed at the time, the oath made no reference to any of the ideas that were at the heart of Lenin's real testament. In short, the whole script was self-serving.

STALINISM AND THE HERESY SYNDROME

Stalin's recourse to the symbols of the Orthodox religion is also revealing. His foreign biographers have discerned this when commenting on the liturgical form of the 'oath', which probably dates back to his years in the Orthodox seminary where he received his only systematic education. Such influences were evident again later, in the rituals of confession and repentance imposed on his political enemies, which never sufficed: by definition, even when forgiven, a sinner remains a sinner. In this context, it is worth reflecting for a moment on the concept of heresy and its use in politics. For Stalinism, the equivalent of 'sin' was 'deviation', to be extirpated in the manner of a heresy. 'Heresy syndrome' is the appropriate term for the rituals and propaganda and the persecution of those who had – or, more often, might have had – opinions that differed from what was supposed to be a common creed. In one of his speeches, Stalin 'explained' in characteristic fashion that a 'deviation' begins as soon as one of the party faithful starts to 'entertain doubts'.

In connection with this theme, let us cite Georges Duby, who has studied heresy in the Middle Ages – a period when highly elaborate methods were perfected for rooting out dissidence and ensuring conformity:

> We have seen that orthodoxy incited heresy by condemning and naming it. But we must now add that orthodoxy, because it punished, because it hunted people, put in place a whole arsenal that then took on a life of its own, and which often survived the heresy it was supposed to be fighting. The historian must attend very carefully to these screening bodies and their specialist personnel, who were often former heretics making amends.
>
> Because it hunted and punished people, orthodoxy also instilled particular

mental attitudes: a dread of heresy, the conviction among the orthodox that heresy is hypocritical because it is concealed and, as a result, that it must be detected at all costs and by any means. On the other hand, repression created various systems of representation as an instrument of resistance and counter-propaganda; and these continued to operate for a very long time ... Let us also reflect, much more straightforwardly, on the political use of heresy, of the heretical group treated as a scapegoat, with all the desirable amalgamations at any particular moment.[3]

This analysis of the Middle Ages sounds as if it were really about Stalinism and its purges. Heresy-hunting was part of Stalin's strategy and the construction of the cult of his personality. What actually justifies the use of the term 'cult', as practised, say, by Catholicism or Orthodoxy, is not simply the attribution of superhuman qualities to the supreme ruler, but also the fact that the practice of this cult is underpinned by a whole technology of heresy-hunting (with the heresy invariably being invented by it) – as if the system could not survive without such underpinnings. In fact, the furies unleashed against heretics represented the optimal psycho-political strategy for justifying mass terror. In other words, the terror did not result from the existence of heretics; heretics were invented to justify the terror Stalin required.

The parallel with ecclesiastical strategies is even more obvious when we consider that Trotsky was available as the perfect embodiment of the 'apostate' for many people, whether religious or anti-religious, nationalist, anti-Semitic, and so on. Rejection of him outlasted the adulation of Stalin. Even after the collapse of the Soviet Union, a persistent hatred of Trotsky was extremely widespread, whether among contemporary Stalinists, nationalists or anti-Semites. The question is worth asking: Should it be seen as some kind of concentrate of hatred of socialism? Of internationalism? Of atheism? A careful reading of the arguments offered by Stalin's apologists would doubtless reveal the ingredients that render Trotsky odious to so many positions on the Russian ideological spectrum, where he is rarely studied with a minimum of detachment.

Besides the Orthodox religion, other things from the past appealed to Stalin. Comparisons between his position and that of a Tsar did not develop immediately. On the other hand, the decision to construct 'socialism in one country' (to put it plainly, 'we can do it on our own') indicates that ideology was manipulated as required, in the direction of

---

3   Georges Duby, 'Hérésies et sociétés', in *L'Europe pré-industrielle, XIe–XIIe siècles,* Paris–La Haye 1968, p. 404.

the 'great-power chauvinism' his opponents accused him of. Even before turning into sheer ideological and political intoxication, the slogan was capable of seducing an audience largely composed of the victors in a civil war. The domination over the Church exercised by the Tsars was closely bound up with the symbols of the Church, with the Tsars appropriating this supra-terrestrial legitimacy for themselves. In contrast, the case of Stalin and his cult was not a religious phenomenon. It was a purely political construction, which borrowed and utilized symbols of the Orthodox faith, regardless of the question of how far Stalin himself shared elements of this faith and its psychological underpinnings. To my knowledge, no information exists that could help us answer this question. But there is every reason to suppose that personally he was an atheist.

It is essential that we understand that Stalin was executing a systematic policy designed to transform the party into an instrument for controlling the state, even into a tool *tout court*. Once again, this emerges from his 'cadres philosophy'. Visible early on, the project was practically completed by the end of the NEP in 1929. It followed logically from the cavalier statement that 'objective difficulties do not exist for us'. Such a conception of the role of cadres required more than mere transformation of the party. It was already changing rapidly in any event, owing to massive recruitment of new members and the expulsion of successive oppositions, not to mention the considerable numbers of resignations, which went officially unacknowledged. All this feverish 'traffic' dictated the expansion of the party apparatus, which had hitherto been rather small and not perceived as a danger by Bolshevik cadres, most of whom sooner or later turned to open or silent opposition. The modest but indispensable Central Committee apparatus, which had been established in 1919, did not at the time know how many members the party had. In the hands of Stalin, however, especially after he was appointed to the post of general-secretary in 1922, it began to play a quite different role.

Stalin possessed an unerring sense of the levers of power. 'Old Bolsheviks' preferred to work in state administration (commissariats and other governmental agencies). He tightened his control over the 'Secretariat' – an instrument that was indispensable not only for assimilating the raw mass of newcomers, but for dominating the party, including veteran cadres. It took the 'old Bolsheviks' time to understand this process. Not until 1923 did some begin to criticize, and then deplore, the growing power of the 'Secretariat machinery'. By then, it was evidently past master in the art of fixing the composition of delegations to party conferences and congresses in accordance with the Politburo's wishes. Historians seem agreed that the Thirteenth Congress in 1924, when Stalin was re-elected general-secretary, was 'packed'. The party as known to its first members, and to those who had joined its ranks during the Civil War, was fast disappearing. Henceforth everyone other than rank-and-file members was a 'cadre' – in other words, worked in an apparatus where each person held a precise post in a hierarchy of disciplined functionaries. Some appearances were still preserved, as in the case of the Central Committee, which for a few more years continued to be elected, to deliberate, and to vote on resolutions. But the selection of its members was completely outside the control of party members.

In this way, Stalin accomplished his 'master plan' to become sole ruler. The party was stripped of the very thing Stalin wanted to strip it of: the ability to change its leadership through elections. Bolshevism – and this point must be underscored – still possessed this ability. Destroying such a mechanism was consequently a precondition for Stalin's success; contrary to the widespread idea that the Soviet Union was 'ruled by the Communist Party', it tolled the bell for any political party. Under Lenin, something like this did obtain; under Stalin, the government and party executed policies in precisely the fashion 'cadres' were supposed to, so long as they gave satisfaction.

All this must be studied in detail, for dictatorships come in different guises. Some 'one-party systems' retain a capacity to master their fate, or at least the composition of their leadership. When this is not the case, a 'one-party system' is merely the scenery, not the play itself. The principal roles are played by the apparatus that administers the country, in accordance with the dictates of the summit, whatever it might be. The history of the Soviet system reveals a radical change in the rules of power, and not mere inflections over time. It is to this issue that we must now turn in more detail.

4

THE PARTY AND ITS APPARATY

As yet, neither the state nor the party bureaucracy has a 'history', and we can only deal with a few of their key features here. For clarity's sake, we must employ distinct terms for the personnel of the two ruling bodies. The state bureaucracy can be classified as the 'administration', while its upper echelons are often referred to as *upravlentsy* (the equivalent of 'managers') in Soviet sources. For its part, the party administration is best designated an 'apparatus' or *apparat*, and the apparatchik is precisely someone who holds a post in the party's own administration. It is not always possible to distinguish clearly between these two categories, but even so the terminology is serviceable.

We have already alluded to the fact that from the time of its emergence the 'apparatus' created problems for party members. As early as 1920, voices were raised denouncing the increasing disparity between the *verkhi* (those at the top) and the *nizy* (those at the bottom), and they were taken seriously by both the rank and file and the leadership. Something that was to become obvious a few years later to the Soviets and outside observers alike – namely, the inequality between upper and lower echelons – was still a shock for members of a party that remained Bolshevik. In the miserable year of 1920, which I shall return to in Part Three, the leadership was embarrassed by the problem and allowed it to be aired in the party press. During the 1920s, the lack of equality and democracy inside party ranks was one of the key issues raised by the opposition while it could still express itself. But it was met with demagogic denials. Until the end of the 1920s (and even later), the battle against bureaucratic tendencies – 'bureaucratization' – in the state administration was officially authorized, and seemingly supported by the party leadership. It lent itself to scapegoating officials. Attacking bureaucratization in the party itself, especially when such criticism emanated from the successive oppositions, was an altogether different matter. Still, the party, which at the end of the 1920s had more than a million members and thousands of apparatchiks, could not afford to bury reactions to internal bureaucratization within its ranks, even though opposition had been practically eliminated.

Thus, it turned out that if an administration is a tool, it also takes its toll. The problem came under the jurisdiction of the party's Central Control Commission (CCC). In June 1929, the chairman of its Presidium, Ia. A. Iakovlev, presented it with an outline of the intervention he intended to make on the theme of bureaucratization at the Sixteenth Party Conference. Not everything he said was included in the published record, but what does feature there is highly informative.[1]

Iakovlev, one of the 'old guard' still in post, did not hide his concerns: a struggle of the utmost vigour must be conducted against bureaucratization inside the party itself. According to him, the phenomenon could be explained by the fact that so many party members worked in the state administration and acquired there pernicious habits with which they were 'contaminating' the party. To counteract this trend, the party needed to fight for a democratic spirit within Soviet institutions and other governmental bodies, where those in charge were concentrating all power in their own hands and substituting themselves for the formal leading bodies of state and cooperative organizations. Democratization, he suggested, was the only way to treat the disease at source.

Such an approach by an old Bolshevik, who was known as an intelligent, competent administrator, testifies to a time when the party no longer tolerated being perceived as responsible for anything negative. He understood that if, as so often before, he engaged in a real analysis of the problem without quotation marks, he risked being accused of belonging to some opposition or other. Yet calls for more democracy and less bureaucracy, including within the party itself, featured in a mass of material addressed by local party organizations to the Control Commission and other leading bodies complaining about party bosses. These complaints were still being summarized in the 1920s by the party's Information Service and circulated in a bulletin for the use of its top cadres. The bulletin also contained other documents deemed important,

---

1   RGASPI, f. 613, op. 1, d. 79: materials of the Collegium of the Central Control Commission.

issuing from the trade unions and the GPU. At least twice a month it provided briefings on the mood and opinions of specific social groups, especially workers. It referred to strikes, but also to the reactions of party members who had participated in them. Certainly, in 1929 *Pravda* was not somewhere one would find the bitter accusations of workers who were party members and on strike against their bosses, who were themselves members. But the leadership was kept informed of such matters and regularly discussed what to do in response, for the most part without much publicity. Readers should also be aware that, regardless of what conclusions they might care to draw from the fact, during the 1920s GPU reports on labour disputes were mainly critical of both administrative and party bosses, who were accused of indifference and incompetence when it came to dealing with workers' legitimate grievances. The reports often vindicated strikers and criticized the behaviour of union leaders. GPU and party information bulletins from the 1920s contain a mass of material of this type.

It was not inaccurate to say that the state apparatus was contaminating the party. But this was due to the existence of an apparatus peculiar to the party, which did all it could to prevent public animus against bureaucrats rebounding on it. The Central Committee had launched a major campaign, particularly during the struggle against the various oppositions in the 1920s, to defend and celebrate the party apparatus – those referred to as *politrabotniki* (party cadres) or even the party's 'faithful guard'. Nevertheless, non-party people and members who had remained loyal to Bolshevik ideals continued to amalgamate both types of cadre into the single category of 'bureaucrat'. There were good reasons for this.

Once an apparatus has been set up, especially if it is intended to control other, larger apparatuses, it operates in an environment that secretes shared habits, behaviour and a mindset. The use of the term 'comrade' loses its magic if the 'comrade' is a superior who issues orders and determines your salary and promotion prospects. The new reality, which is now part of daily life, is very simple: 'We are not on an equal footing but on a ladder, comrade Ivanov, and I am not your comrade, comrade Ivanov.'

The secretariat machinery was a pyramid. At its apex were the Politburo, Secretariat and the Orgburo; at its base, the party secretaries with their own secretariats at district level (the *raiony*, or lowest administrative levels). It was a system designed to serve the top party leadership in keeping tabs on two much larger pyramids: the scaffolding of the soviets and the much more powerful governmental administration, from the Council of People's Commissars to its local agencies. The soviets, from the Supreme Soviet down to the local soviets, which further complicated an already intricate organizational structure, may be left to one side here. Their only reality consisted in accomplishing local administrative tasks. As a pyramid capped by the supreme soviets of each republic and by the Supreme Soviet of the USSR at the summit, they were scarcely more than a fiction preserved in order to claim residual allegiance to the revolutionary past and the popular sovereignty it had supposedly established. The local soviets were in fact subordinate to the Council of Commissars (renamed 'ministries' in 1946) and their departments. The whole bureaucratic set-up, composed of 'pyramids' and 'scales', was subject to control by a parallel party apparatus. The division between the two major administrative spheres was somewhat attenuated at the top inasmuch as the Prime Minister, and sometimes one of his deputies, was also a Politburo member. Similarly, interconnection between party and state bodies at the bottom of the ladder was ensured by the presence in every workplace of a party cell, which was itself integrated into a party organization covering the whole firm or ministry. If we add to this the fact that the great majority of important posts in the administration were held by party members, thanks to the so-called *nomenklatura* procedure (which we shall return to), we might wonder how much more supervision and control were required to render the system 'crash-proof'. Were a planetary insurance company to exist offering insurance policies to states, it would probably take its cue from the Soviet method of handling such things.

Nevertheless, at every stage of our journey through the 1930s we shall encounter a sort of 'permanent insecurity' system, whose shadow hung over an apparatus that was intended both to run the party and to control the strategic layers of the *upravlentsy*. This mission came up against numerous fault-lines throughout the system. We shall have more than one occasion to ask whether one small apparatus can effectively master a much larger one, with the ultimate aim of controlling the whole society.

It is now time to offer some data about the party apparatus and the apparatchiki. 'Bureaucratization', frequently bemoaned since its onset, had rapidly assumed such proportions that it was a feature of all ruling and other bodies. Regularly criticized by ad hoc institutions formally designed to correct such faults, the phenomenon was reduced in public to an enumeration of bureaucratic malfunctions, with reassuring words to the effect that remedies existed whose results would be seen ... one day. On the other hand, it should be noted that unpublished documents, especially in the post-Stalin era, were often quite frank and sometimes of good analytical quality. The effects of bureaucratization on Soviet citizens and party members alike, whether persons of integrity or careerists, were multiple.

THE TEDIUM OF PARTY APPARATUS WORK (1924–34)

Many party members, particularly idealistic ones who were ready to serve their country by taking on responsible positions at a local level or in 'vanguard' institutions, were often deeply disturbed by what bureaucratization was doing to the party and to them personally. Some did not dare use it as an explicit term of criticism: they just told their superiors that they felt they could do a better job elsewhere. But others would draw more far-reaching conclusions. A few examples from among a myriad of others will illustrate the difficulty of being a party apparatchik, even before the term had become established. Those who had previously waged the revolutionary struggle in clandestine activities, in prison or on the battlefield, and who were now engaged in the prestigious task of helping to build socialism, suddenly perceived – or gradually discovered – that working in a hierarchical apparatus was far from edifying. Quite the reverse: amid the tedious routines boredom predominated. Two examples, drawn from different years, reveal this malaise.

A well-known militant, Ksenofontov, wrote to Kaganovich on 4 November 1924.[2] He had served in the Cheka, taken part in suppressing the Kronstadt uprising, and participated in restoring calm to the country thereafter. He had then asked to be released from such duties and transferred to a position where he could help to build the party-dominated system. Attached to the Central Committee, he was appointed head of its Business Administration department. He had been there for more than three years. Everything was highly organized, and his work was utterly routine. So he now wanted to move on and was hoping for another job from the Central Committee, provided it was not in the economy, trade or the cooperative sector, which did not attract him. At this time, such requests could be submitted without fear

---

2 RGASPI, f. 17, op. 84, d. 488, L. 68.

of reprisals – though telling Kaganovich that working for him had been uninteresting was perhaps not very prudent. Ksenofontov was authorized to switch to a job in education.

The second example, which dates from ten years later (November 1934), concerns another erstwhile revolutionary who complains about the profound tedium of work at the top of the apparatus. The story here is somewhat more convoluted. A certain Khavinson, deputy head of the 'Department of Culture and Propaganda of Marxism-Leninism', reported to his superiors about one comrade Slepchenko. A disciplined and steady worker, who chaired a party committee responsible since 1933 for checking membership lists, Slepchenko had been experiencing difficulties and asked to be transferred to work in production. 'Working in the apparatus depresses me', he is reported to have said. Such a statement, made when he had been asked to become aide to the Central Committee's Industry Department, could have caused him problems. He too had written to Kaganovich, stating that after three years working in the apparatus he had not been able to adapt to it: 'With every passing day, I am losing my identity.' Khavinson was of the opinion that he should be accommodated and it is likely that he was allowed to quit, 1934 being (as we shall see) a good year.[3]

Such personal statements, which were acceptable despite their implicit criticism of the apparatus, can be usefully supplemented by a third example, containing a direct critique of the system. This denunciation was based on a solidly argued analysis and its author was a fine political sociologist, Christian Rakovsky. We have already spoken of him when he was head of the Ukrainian government in 1923 and opposed Stalin's plans for the USSR. Accused of Trotskyism, he was exiled in 1928 to Astrakhan, a city whose climate was very bad for his heart condition. He nevertheless managed to hold out until 1934, while all the time producing critical studies of the state of the Soviet system. He 'capitulated' in 1934 when in urgent need of medical treatment. But it was not his heart that finally killed him.

The substance of his diagnosis went as follows: The party is now an aggregate of hundreds of thousands of individuals. What unites them is not a shared ideology, but the trepidation each has about his own fate. The question arises as to how a communist party can be recreated out of such an amorphous mass. There is no other way but to restore inner-

---

3   RGASPI, 17, 114, d. 685, L. 235, 29.

party democracy.[4] But restoring the party of Rakovsky's past was an illusion – and he knew it. In another part of the same text, probably written somewhat later, he comments on the ongoing debate in the party over versions of the second five-year plan (1933–7) which, according to official declarations, was to be a 'sober five-year plan'. In Rakovsky's view, the years corresponding to this 'sober' plan would consummate the 'total separation of the bureaucracy from the working class' and witness the former transform itself into a 'ruling stratum supported by the state apparatus'. Some thirty years later, in a widely acclaimed book,[5] the Yugoslav Milovan Djilas supposedly made a theoretical innovation when he suggested that the USSR was now run by a 'new class'.

These cases of disillusionment among highly placed cadres close to the corridors of power must be supplemented by information on the way in which ordinary party members lost their enthusiasm. It was long assumed that under Stalin it was not possible to leave the party without inviting reprisals. But the opening of the archives led to the discovery that such cases were real enough – sometimes even numerous – but rarely ostentatious, which explains why the phenomenon remained invisible for so long. The available data indicate that between 1922 and 1935 approximately one and a half million members left the party, mostly by failing to pay dues and thereby letting their membership lapse. Others changed workplace and address without re-registering with the local party branch. In other words, they drifted away and many of them were subsequently expelled. There were many workplaces where the number of those who had left the party exceeded current membership levels.[6]

These former members, and those excluded during the wave of so-called 'pre-purges' in 1935–6 when membership cards were being checked, afforded an automatic target for the onslaught of 1937–8. The one and a half million people who had left the party represented a huge pool of self-declared 'enemies of the people' for the NKVD to cast their nets in.

---

4 'VKP(b) i oppozitsiia' – a file from RGASPI, f. 17, op. 120, d. 68, L. 6, which reproduces for internal party information various Left Opposition documents, copied from Trotsky's *Biulleten' Oppozitsii*, published abroad. Trotsky somehow continued to receive this and other texts by Rakovsky, which he then published.

5 See Milovan Djilas, *The New Class: An Analysis of the Communist System*, New York 1957.

6 RGASPI, f. 17, op. 120, d. 278, containing material on the various pre-1937 purges and the party ranks and apparatus.

ADDITIONAL REMARKS ON THE PARTY AND STATE
ADMINISTRATION

During the 1930s, the party apparatus grew ever larger and more complex. Stalin had the first and last word on everything, on every meeting and every institution. In one sense, this should have simplified decision-making and policy execution alike. But this simplification – it certainly seemed such to Stalin – was nothing but an illusion: the party apparatus continued to swell, which could only complicate things.

The number of People's Commissariats also kept increasing – from ten in 1924 to eighteen in 1936 and then forty-one in 1940 – as did 'state committees' with Commissariat status like Gosplan, Grain Procurement, Higher Education and Artistic Affairs. Their staffs expanded at the same rate. The logic of party control as practised at the time dictated a corresponding adaptation. At every level, and especially at the centre, each party organization was instructed to create in its own apparatus branch departments, equipped with the appropriate personnel: heads, deputies, instructors, technical staff.[7] By 1939 the Central Committee apparatus contained large structural directorates for each branch of state administration, as well as a massive 'directorate for cadres' (*upravlenie kadrov*). When Malenkov was its secretary, the Central Committee was composed of forty-five departments – one for practically each branch of government activity. At republican district levels, the party apparatuses were also constantly expanding, with ever more rigid hierarchies.

The conduct of internal party affairs was strictly centralized. Virtually everything of any importance ended up on the agenda of the Politburo, which took the final decision. This amounted to hundreds of items which, in a less centralized system, would never have been dealt with at this level. Predictably, with such a vast number of items to get through, the Politburo did not have time to go into the genuinely important ones. It operated on the basis that they would have been thrashed out en route from the Secretariat to the Orgburo. The overload at the top, and the exponential expansion of the party apparatus and state administration, created a vicious circle; and the system's efficiency was almost inevitably relegated to the lowest priority. As long as increased staffing was primarily a means of meeting the obvious need to control a sprawling, unruly reality, amid a constant shortage of supplies and very

---

7 V. G. Kolychev, in D. A. Volkogonov, otvet. red., *Tridtsatye Gody: Vzgliad iz Segodniia*, Moscow 1990, pp. 24–5.

low living standards, this vicious circle could not be broken. The truth of this claim can be attested by glancing at how things looked to those at the bottom of the ladder.

In a very gloomy letter, written following a tour of inspection of the party organization in the Far Eastern Province (*Dal'kraikom*) accompanied by a Central Committee instructor, Shcherbakov, head of the Central Committee's Cadres Department, reported that what he had discovered resembled a 'railway station in total chaos'. In one year (1 January 1933 to 1 January 1934), party membership in the region had shrunk from 44,990 to 23,340: 7,651 members had been expelled, 1,892 downgraded to the status of 'sympathizers', 1,557 had left the area with authorization and 6,328 without (they had simply deserted). Among the last group were people with a solid party record, but also irreplaceable specialists who were urgently required. According to the two inspectors, the reasons for the exodus were as follows: 'an excessively bureaucratic attitude' towards members displayed by the provincial party committee; neglect of their recreational and cultural needs; and scandalous housing conditions for workers and specialists alike. Some of them were still living in dug-outs; one family was living in the toilets; other families were staying in disgusting dormitories; five people were crammed into one room of six square metres; and so on. Construction materials and builders were being sent to the province every year, but the housing situation remained lamentable and public services were completely neglected (public baths, crèches, hospitals, theatres). The food situation was very bad and the provincial party committee was doing nothing. It simply expelled those who had deserted and constantly shuffled cadres around from place to place. In fact, no one knew for sure how many party members there were.

The apparatchik who wrote this gloomy report requested that the situation be investigated by the Orgburo (the level below the Politburo), or even be put on the agenda of the party's Control Commission, in order to remedy things.

This sorry state of affairs involved a remote, low-priority region that would anyway have been assigned second- or third-rate leaders. But malfunctioning in local party organizations and administrative agencies was endemic in many more central regions. The constant expansion in the number of tasks and difficult living conditions easily outstripped the ability of party cadres to handle such problems. These regions lived in something like a permanent state of emergency, which they coped with reasonably, badly, or not at all – as in the just-cited case of the

Dal'kraikom. Itself expanding rapidly, the party's control apparatus could make reports, but was probably overwhelmed by what it found.

We have already seen that any mess, often caused by the centre's own policies, was arbitrarily imputed to lower-level cadres. This was inherent in the Stalinist method of government. Any mishap, catastrophe, tragedy or chaotic situation could readily be interpreted as an act of sabotage. In this respect, party cadres enjoyed no privileges; as cadres, they were potentially guilty – and the higher the rank, the more likely this was. At a higher level of responsibility, they were capable of inflicting more damage than lower ranks could and for this reason were 'naturally' under suspicion.

This paranoiac system of government had an additional twist. There was no reason to wait for the danger actually to materialize. That would have been imprudent. Great leadership involved 'preventive medicine'. Our initial analysis of the 'cadre philosophy', but also the disruption and human suffering we observe towards 1933 – consequent on the failures of the 'collectivization' of the peasantry and breakneck industrialization, not to mention the famine that struck the Ukraine and parts of Russia – mean that we are not in the least surprised to find massive recourse to such 'preventive medicine', in the form of large-scale bloody purges. A storm of protest was brewing against the government's policy, especially in the countryside, and Stalin risked becoming the focus of it. This was quite unacceptable to him, and a spectacular campaign was launched to shift the blame elsewhere. Repressive measures were adopted and there were signs that something more was in the offing. In his speech to the Central Committee meeting of January 1933 on the state of the country, Stalin referred to a host of enemies undermining the regime's foundations like termites. And yet, despite these ominous signals, the policy actually adopted in May 1933 took the opposite course, making the unanticipated 'interlude' of 1933–4 all the more remarkable. A country in the throes of famine may not buy the idea that the supreme leader has nothing to do with it. So the economic situation had to improve, and Stalin's prestige be restored, before the mass terror was unleashed and took on the appearance of a manifestation of strength. Stalin was in the process of planning his killing frenzy, but he was doing it very methodically.

THE 'INTERLUDE'

The Seventeenth Party Congress was held in April 1934. Dubbed the 'Congress of the Victors', it sang the praises of the main victor among them: Stalin. But it also epitomized the line of internal appeasement initiated a year earlier. It offered oppositionists the chance to appear before it, mainly to repent their errors in public. Just as remarkable were the decision substantially to reduce the growth rates fixed for the second five-year plan (1933–7) and an appeal for greater respect for legality in the country. The new line was proclaimed with much fanfare, and signals were sent to the effect that the regime finally had its feet firmly on the ground. A Writers' Congress took place the same year, which seriously discussed literary issues and celebrated the passing of the sectarian Writers' Union. Less noticed at the time was a short speech by one Andrei Zhdanov – a party secretary, not a writer – laying down, almost *sotto voce*, the line of 'socialist realism' in all the arts. If it went largely unremarked, it was because it was overshadowed by spectacular interventions from Bukharin, Radek and Ehrenburg, and many others, which were much more open and intellectually stimulating.

These moves were important ingredients of the 'new line'. In a letter to Stalin of 13 September 1934,[8] Ehrenburg took it seriously. His hopes were raised by the USSR's new foreign policy, with entry into the League of Nations and 'common fronts' between communists and social-democrats in response to the rise of fascism. But he complained about the Soviet organization responsible for relations with foreign writers, denouncing its sectarianism and taste for petty quarrels which repelled internationally renowned writers. Only a few writers of such stature, like André Malraux and Jean-Richard Bloch, had been invited to the congress. As for the others, it would have been better not to invite them. Amid the mounting power and aggressiveness of fascism, Ehrenburg believed that it was possible to create an anti-fascist writers' association in the West, which would rally leading literary figures and help defend the Soviet Union. Such an initiative was now more realistic: foreign participants had been impressed by the serious open exchanges between communists and non-communists and persuaded of the flourishing state of culture and literature in the USSR. But the new organization must not, he insisted, be run by sectarians.

---

8 RGASPI, f. 3, op. 3, d. 439.

In a handwritten note to Kaganovich, Stalin registered his agreement with Ehrenburg. Such an organization should be established and organized around the two themes he had suggested: anti-fascism and defence of the USSR. He was proposing some names and awaited a response. Here we see a businesslike Stalin, quite different from the one sniffing out 'termites' everywhere. The 1934 interlude was still under way. Kaganovich, number two in the Politburo at the time, was vigorously promoting the 'new line' aimed at strengthening respect for the law: 'We can now punish people via the legal system without resorting to extra-judicial means as in the past. Many cases that went exclusively through the GPU will now be handled by the courts.'

Kaganovich made this statement on 1 August 1934 during a special conference convened by the Prosecutor General's Office, whose sphere – when it received authorization at least – was precisely 'legality'. Kaganovich also reminded his audience that the GPU itself would be undergoing changes and merged into a new ministerial department, the NKVD (Commissariat of Internal Affairs). He explained that the Prosecutor General's Office was the central institution in the legal system, and that with the creation of the NKVD it would have many more cases to process. Henceforth the main task was to educate the population and legal personnel to respect the law. Such, he said, was the line decided by Stalin. A major obstacle to surmount was the lack of education within the legal system itself. Judges were supposed to operate on the basis of codes, but all too often their pronouncements were unclear. Everyone now had to learn the text of the law: 'Citizens have to know that there are laws and that they also apply to the apparatus.'

We might mention in passing that on the basis of this new enhanced role, the legal apparatus requested a significant salary increase. Kaganovich stalled, suggesting that the new line should not be ushered in with such a selfish move . . .

These outpourings of moderation, level-headedness and good sense contained not the slightest hint as to what was brewing, and which would explode after Kirov's assassination at the end of 1934. Sometimes attributed to other leaders, the 'liberal interlude' was in fact Stalin's own – just like what was to follow.

As the evidence available to us today indicates, Stalin never forgot or forgave past critics. Take the case of Bukharin. On the face of it he was forgiven, became editor-in-chief of *Izvestiia*, and kept up a friendly correspondence with Stalin. He felt entitled to print all manner of opinions on industrialization, collectivization, and the NEP. He often presented analyses or assessments that differed from official pro-nouncements. For example, he laid firm stress on the fact that the high rate of investment fixed for heavy industry was having pernicious economic effects, at a time when other, more promising alternatives were available. Whereas the Bukharin of 1928 had seen Stalin for what he was, in 1934 he was playing with fire, probably in the belief that the lull of that year derived from a sincere desire to rectify a policy whose negative results he had anticipated. He regarded it as legitimating his opposition to Stalin in 1928–9. Moreover, this is precisely how Stalin read the situation. Bukharin never suspected that Stalin was setting a trap for him, encouraging other leaders to write articles against him and circulating all sorts of acerbic remarks about him in the Politburo, while concealing what he really had in mind.

Stalin enjoyed this game. He was absolutely convinced that everyone, including his current entourage, had 'offended' him at some point, had belonged to a different faction, spoken disparagingly about him, or said a good word about Trotsky. All this remained engraved in his rancorous memory. In the case of Bukharin, it cannot be excluded that his speech to the Writers' Congress and the impressive agenda he set there had rekindled Stalin's resentment.[9]

Whoever was responsible for Kirov's murder, it is clear that Stalin was by now ready to change line overnight, to write the most murderous and authentically 'Stalinist' chapter of them all. The 'other policy' – the terror – was always on his mind, ready to be activated. The interlude was nothing but a requisite pause following a spasm. Whether such increases and reductions in political tension and terror also reflected Stalin's fluctuating state of mind remains a matter for conjecture.

---

9 RGASPI, f. 56, op. 1, d. 198 (Molotov's papers). On 16 May 1934, at Stalin's behest, two memos 'for your information', written by Stetsky (a former Bukharin supporter) and Mekhlis, were circulated to Politburo members and Zhdanov. In them, the two apparatchiks attacked an article by Bukharin published in *Izvestiia* on 12 May.

5

SOCIAL FLUX AND 'SYSTEMIC PARANOIA'

THE SOCIAL FABRIC

Setting personalities to one side for a moment, let us turn our attention to an issue we touched on when evoking the situation in the Far Eastern party organization. The time has come to broaden our canvas and plunge into the social realities of the 1930s. The state and its 'psyche' continued to confront phenomena that were highly characteristic of these tumultuous years. These formed the matrix of what has been called a 'systemic paranoia' (a theme that will be explored later). The 1930s were years of unprecedented social flux, caused by tempos of development that the planners themselves did not believe in and by 'collectivization' of the peasantry. This experiment in 'social engineering' was launched with unparalleled violence whose consequences had not been considered, leaving the country short of food just as it was embarking on an equally unprecedented industrial great leap forward. The decision to collectivize formed part of an ideology that endowed industry with mythical powers: industrialize agriculture and Russia's rural past would vanish, but food supplies would still be plentiful, as if offloaded from containers. This was to overlook a 'detail': the peasantry itself. While the task had to be carried out by peasants, it was directed against them. What followed was not so much the industrialization of agriculture as its nationalization by the state – an aspect of Stalinism we have already encountered.

POPULATION AND LABOUR FORCE

To sketch the 'social panorama' of the USSR in the 1930s and its transformation, we must begin with the population statistics. But simply reciting the figures provided by two censuses – 147 million on 17 December 1926 and 170.6 million on 17 January 1939 – will not do. These significant totals were arrived at rather mechanically and gloss over the dramatic population shifts and losses that occurred in these years. The leadership ordered a census in 1937, but when it yielded a figure below expectations – 162 million – the statisticians were accused of distorting an allegedly much more radiant reality. Their ranks were decimated and a new census was ordered. Its result was virtually dictated in advance. Even so, it was quite an achievement on the part of the surviving statisticians to report a figure of 167,305,749 Soviets – neither more nor less. When this census was re-examined in 1992, experts agreed on a somewhat higher total of 168,870,700 inhabitants, arrived at by minor statistical corrections and additions. According to them, the figure published originally was not distorted, but involved a discrepancy that was perfectly acceptable in census-taking.[1] Given that the leadership had much to hide in order to escape responsibility for the population losses occasioned by 'de-kulakization' (*raskulachivanie*), the 1932–3 famine and the wave of purges, it is remarkable that the demographers of the time somehow managed to persuade the Kremlin that too flagrant a falsification would have been more compromising than the truth.

The next set of figures concerns the strategically crucial categories of the available labour force. In 1928, the approximate totals for the non-agricultural labour force amounted to 9.8 million workers and 3.9 million employees, representing some 17.6 per cent of the national total (12.4 per cent for workers, 5.2 per cent for employees). That year, industry employed 3,593,000 workers and 498,000 employees – the engineers and technicians grouped together under the category of *ITR* (where the R stands for *rabotniki*, or 'workers', as opposed to *rabochie*, which refers to manual labourers).

The picture changed dramatically towards 1939–40. By then, workers and employees constituted a mass of between 31 and 33 million people, of whom more than 21 million were workers and 11–12 million employees. Together they now represented over half the national labour

---

1   Iu. A. Poliakov and A. A. Isupov, introduction to *Vsesoiuznaia Perepis' Naseleniia 1939 goda – Osnovnye Itogi*, Moscow 1992, pp. 7–8.

force. The percentage of employees had risen from 5.2 per cent to 16 per cent of the total. In the key sector of industry, the number of workers had leapt from 3.5 to 11 million and that of employees from around 400,000 to 2 million, while a similar pattern was evident in transport, construction and communications.

Such profound structural shifts brought onto the social stage categories which yielded a labour force substantially different from that of the previous period, and whose emergence prefigured unavoidable changes in class relations and the power structure. To this must be added the massive appearance (or reappearance) of women in the world of work. This point is worth emphasizing, because their participation in production went far beyond their traditional concentration in the textile industry and services. In 1913 women represented 24.5 per cent of the labour force in large-scale industry, mostly in the textile branch. In 1928 the number of women in the 'workers-employees' category amounted to 2,795,000, but reached 13,190,000 in 1940, or 39 per cent of the average annual labour force (43 per cent in industry). They were equally present en masse in heavy industry and mining, and their role in industrialization had become decisive.

But this significant development, which seemingly represented progress, was marred by phenomena that rendered this emancipation an ambiguous affair. New positions in the industrial sector; preponderance in medicine, primary and secondary schools; equal access to education; a growing presence in scientific research laboratories – these were certainly advances. But women had little access to positions of administrative power, including in the hospitals and schools where they constituted a majority of employees; and were totally absent from positions of political responsibility (apart from some posts where they had a token presence). The disparity was obvious. Moreover, many jobs in heavy industry and other branches required physical labour often performed without any mechanical aid. Inappropriate for women, such jobs had deleterious effects on birth rates and increased the number of abortions. This situation was further aggravated by the fact that nothing was done to alleviate the burden of the daily household chores women faced with. The price they paid for entering an expanding labour market was very heavy. The patriarchal tradition still deeply ingrained in society likewise permeated the Soviet establishment, whose conservatism was actually on the increase.

The statistical data presented here for the period beginning 1928–9 are often taken from estimates that are much 'softer' than the results of the

1926 census. But since the aim is to give readers a sense of the intensity of the transformation, rather than to offer statistical precision, we have preferred (here and subsequently) to draw statistics from various sources and several authors, even if they do not always coincide.[2]

THE 'EMPLOYEES–SPECIALISTS–INTELLIGENTSIA' QUID PRO QUO

The term *sluzhashchie* (employees) was very broadly used to refer to anyone who was not a worker or peasant. The range of categories it covered rendered it rather ineffective, except when applied to office employees. The totals for 'employees' included a category of strategic importance for the country's development: namely, 'specialists', or those who had completed their studies in a higher technical institute or specialist secondary establishment. In 1928 this group numbered 521,000 (233,000 with higher education, 288,000 with specialist secondary education). By 1 January 1941 their number had reached 2.4 million (approximately 4 per cent of wage-earners) and represented 23 per cent of the total for 'employees', 909,000 had graduated from higher education and 1,492,000 from secondary. Industry employed 310,400 of these – mainly engineers and technicians. Their numbers had quintupled in twelve years. We possess a breakdown of this category of 'specialists', done at the end of 1940. It offers data for the technical, medical, economic and legal professions and, with less precision, for teachers, librarians and other cultural professions.

In the statistics we are using, the category of 'specialists' stops there: it does not include scientists, artists or writers. If we add the latter, we can very approximately quantify an additional category used by Soviet statistics (and propaganda): the 'intelligentsia'. It often overlaps with that of 'specialists', but not completely. If we add to the figure for people

---

2 See TsSU (Central Office of Statistics), *Gosapparat SSSR*, Moscow 1929, p. 47; L. I. Vas'kina, *Rabochii Klass SSSR Nakanune Sotsialisticheskoi Industrializatsii*, Moscow 1981, p. 16; and also two articles from *Statisticheskoe Obozrenie* in 1928 and 1929, as well as various documents from the TsSU archives. Many of the data used here and elsewhere derive from *Trud v SSSR: Statisticheskii Sbornik*, Moscow 1988, p. 47 and *passim*, which also contains data on 1939. As does the TsSU publication, *Itogi Vsesoiuznoi Perepisi Naseleniia v 1959*, Moscow 1962, based on the unpublished 1939 census, which is now available in *Vsesoiuznaia Perepis' Naseleniia 1939 goda*.

employed in the cultural sphere, as supplied by other tables or sources for 1 January 1941, the category of specialists, we arrive at a figure of 2,539,314.[3] Some official sources claimed almost 5 million, with the aim of making the 'cultural revolution' proclaimed by the leadership in these years more credible. To the same end, official documents used a different category, which was broader and vaguer: that of 'people primarily employed in intellectual work'. This category was quite illegitimately identified with the 'intelligentsia', making it possible to manipulate the image the government wished to present of the country's cultural development. As early as 1937, Molotov announced a huge figure for the number of such 'intellectuals'. The same fluid category probably underlay the imprudent claims subsequently made by Soviet researchers, who declared (as they were obliged to) that 'by the beginning of the 1940s, the problem of a popular intelligentsia was resolved'. But some of these researchers knew perfectly well that those who had acquired a degree from an institute of higher education accounted for only a percentage of those engaged in 'primarily intellectual work'. Most of the latter were actually *praktiki* – that is to say, people who had learnt their profession on the job or during intensive training courses, and who had no professional education, even when their jobs demanded specialist knowledge.[4] At the beginning of 1941, inadequate training was particularly widespread among those classified as 'engineers' in industry. For every 1,000 workers there were 110 engineers and technicians. But only 19.7 per cent of them had a higher education qualification and 23 per cent a secondary school qualification; 67 per cent were *praktiki* who had probably never completed the secondary school curriculum. And the picture is similar for other professional groups, all of them swept up into a process of quantitative growth that outstripped the country's ability to train them properly.

The accelerated pace of industrialization was the inevitable cause of such shortcomings, as well as of the economic and socio-cultural costs that form part of the panorama we are going to describe. If industrial workers around 1929 had on average no more than 3.5 years of primary schooling behind them, rising to 4.2 years by the end of 1939, those engaged in 'primarily intellectual work' – simply put, office employees – hardly fared better, especially when the category of 'specialists' is

---

3   See *Naradnoe Obrazovanie, Nauka i Kultura v SSSR: Statistichiskii Sbornik*, Moscow 1971, pp. 233–5, 247.

4   Ibid.

deducted from their number. Of 'employees', representing 16.6 per cent of the working population, only 3.3 per cent can be counted as 'specialists', a majority of whom had only an incomplete secondary education. This did not prevent some writers in the post–Stalin era including them under the rubric of the 'intelligentsia'.

General data on the educational levels of the active population in the towns and countryside in 1939 help to clarify the problem. For every 1,000 workers, the statistics indicate that 242 had benefited from tertiary or secondary education in the towns and 63 in the countryside. If we separate out higher education, the figure for towns is 32 and for the countryside 3. For secondary education, the figures are 210 and 60 respectively. But this is the crucial point: the statistics for 'secondary' education actually include two categories – 'complete' and 'incomplete' – and it is reasonable to suppose that the majority of individuals concerned did not in fact complete their secondary education.[5]

The emergence of new groups with a good intellectual education, and the rise in the number of those who might legitimately be included in this prestigious category,[6] are undeniable. Nevertheless, we cannot ignore the extent to which the regime inflated the figures. This manipulation (which probably also involved self-deception) sought to embellish the much less edifying reality: the generally low educational level of workers, employees, and even many of those who held responsible positions. We must keep this in mind, because the low cultural level of the whole society formed the social backdrop to Stalinism. The top leadership was sufficiently well-informed to seek to conceal and embellish this frustrating situation.

But these inflated figures – an intelligentsia numbering 5 million – also reveal a fundamental characteristic of the Soviet experience and especially the Stalinist period: its 'extensive' character, or propensity to prioritize the quantitative. The 1939 census estimated the number of people employed in 'primarily intellectual work' at 13,821,452. A breakdown by educational level in each sector of employment does lead to a figure of close on 5 million (4,970,536, to be precise). But it includes anyone with a general education, however minimal. Moreover, most of them occupied posts requiring a specialist – even higher –

---

5 *Sotsialnoe Razvitie Rabochego Klassa SSSR: Istoriko-sotsiologicheskie Ocherki*, p. 275; V. M. Selunskaya, otvet. red., *Izmeneniia Sostial'noi Struktury Sovetskogo Obshchestva, 1921 – Seredina 30-kh godov*, Moscow 1979, p. 306; and *Trud v SSSR*, p. 118.

6 *Trud v SSSR*, p. 189.

education, which they did not possess. Accordingly, they were simply *praktiki* – a huge category in these years, which remained a strong presence after the war. We even encounter it in the period following Stalin's death, though by then it was beginning to disappear.

What transpires from this is that the mass of 'blue-collar' employees who, as we have seen, mushroomed in the years between the two censuses, contained whole layers of poorly educated and trained people (including sales staff, cashiers, telegraphers), who were nevertheless better paid – sometimes substantially so – than workers. In 1940 the average monthly wage of an industrial worker stood at 30.7 roubles, while that of an office employee was 53.5. This average includes engineers and technicians (*ITR*). But even when they are excluded, an office worker fared better than a worker.[7] We therefore have the following picture: a situation where even limited skills or some basic literacy and numeracy were at a premium, against the backdrop of a much larger labour force with only basic schooling doing manual work and an even larger rural population, which was much less literate than urban workers. But even in the 'primarily intellectual' category, education rarely went beyond what could be acquired in seven years of schooling.

The benefits enjoyed by office employees (even though they were sneered at in official propaganda) and the exaggerated figures for members of the 'intelligentsia' attest to the obvious: the country's low starting point. And the generally low level of education was no social equalizer, especially in the bureaucratic agencies. Social differentiation shot up there, and people were acutely aware of it. For when living standards are low, the quantitatively small advantages obtained by some cause a keener sense of injustice among the worst-off and a feeling of solidarity among the beneficiaries, as well as hostility to those who do not enjoy them. And this stands to reason: in conditions of penury, a spare loaf of bread can be a matter of life or death.

The expanding social stratum referred to as 'employees' (neither workers nor peasants) was far from being or remaining socially homogeneous. In fact, it covered an ever more disparate social reality, including the category of 'specialists', but also an increasingly differentiated hierarchy of officials of every rank in all spheres of life. They were the recipients of most of the privileges and possessed a good deal of

---

7   *Vsesoiuznaia Perepis' Naseleniia*, Table 33, p. 112.

power. In everyday life, this growing differentiation among the ruling strata would sooner or later find its expression in official and unofficial language – notably because the powerful but spontaneous trend of 'differentiation' became in the mid-1920s, but especially from the early 1930s, a deliberate policy of motivation and social control.

As the 1930s unfolded, social and ideological divisions kept widening, strengthened by this strategy, which is best encapsulated by the term 'status revolution'. It consisted in distributing perks and privileges to the layer of 'employees', with a particular bias towards the 'intelligentsia' and the *rukovoditeli* ('office-holders') – categories that overlapped, but were concealed for ideological reasons. This policy was deemed indispensable for normalizing the social climate and imparting stability to the regime. None of those selected for preferential treatment had an easy time of it in these years. Their relations with the top leadership were, to say the least, bumpy. Whenever official policy and ideology suffered setbacks, the higher and lower strata of officialdom served as scapegoats and were sacrificed to popular indignation. This was easy to do, given the gulf between ordinary citizens and these privileged officials, especially when they were in positions of political or economic responsibility. Thus, 'privileges', much coveted by those seeking to climb the social ladder, were also a dangerous trap in the political conditions of the period.

Having dealt with the general categories of 'employees', 'specialists' and 'intelligentsia', let us now turn to a sketch of the *rukovoditeli* – the managers or office-holders.

OFFICE-HOLDERS

In Soviet statistical classifications, those holding responsible office – the *rukovoditeli* – were also called *rukovodiashchie rabotniki*, sometimes *otvet-politrabotniki*, and later simply *otvet-rabotniki*. To be included in this category, one had to be at the head of a structural unit, with at least some subordinates, in an administrative agency of the state, the party, a trade union, or some other official organization. According to the 1926 census there were about 364,816 such managers in firms, on construction sites, in administrative agencies and their departments. In the 1939 census the category numbered 445,244, to which were added 757,010 people occupying lower but still quite powerful positions in enterprises of every kind: there were 231,000 factory directors and other higher ranks in industry; 165,191 people in charge of workshops and other, less

important units; and 278,784 chairmen and deputy-chairmen of kolkhozy (sovkhoz administrators were already included under the rubric
of 'firms'). This yields a total of 2,010,275 (924,009 of them in the
countryside). Finally, at the summit of the party and state at Union,
republican and district levels, we find some 67,670 individuals heading
institutions in urban areas and 4,968 doing so in rural areas: a total of
72,638 *nachal'niki* ('top bosses') for the whole country. It was around
them, and under their orders, that the *rukovoditeli* we have just mentioned worked; and the latter were themselves supported by lower-
ranking officials, not to mention technical and service personnel
(transport, repairs, cleaning).

At this stage we must return to the broad category of the 'intelligentsia' in order to bring out various important components of it – i.e.
influential writers, scientists, architects, inventors, economists, and other
experts whom the military–industrial complex (among others) had
urgent need of. This stratum became socially and politically close to
those we have just described as high-ranking bosses, and formed an elite
with them – or, more precisely, one of the key components of the
country's elite.

The categories of *rukovoditeli* and 'intelligentsia' are important,
because they make it possible to identify layers that are now influential,
capable of articulating their own interests, exercising pressure, and often
getting what they want. The advent of social groups with the ability to
acquire powerful positions and defend their interests was something
Stalin observed with keen interest and a degree of vigilance. His concern
was precisely to prevent the emergence of such potentially 'negative
phenomena'.

RUNAWAY URBANIZATION: CITIES, HUTS, BARRACKS

The changes in the socio-professional landscape which, as we have seen,
included an expansion in the number of workers and the intellectual,
administrative and technical strata, were evident throughout the economy, including – though to a lesser degree – in agriculture. Industry,
construction and transport, as well as education and research, were
inextricably bound up with the country's urbanization. And industrialization was itself a powerful factor in urbanization, as was the
proliferation of educational, research, public health and administrative
institutions.

Urbanization was also the vehicle for a much broader process, sig-nalling a crucial phase in Russia's history: the disappearance of one kind of society (our subject here) and the emergence of another, quite dif-ferent one. The changing ratios between urban and rural populations take us to the heart of the matter. The brief period under discussion simply set the stage for a rapid, decisive turn, whose initial manifesta-tions in the 1930s were a disparate set of phenomena inherent in a transitional phase, dominated by clashes between intermingling social strata and cultures. Things would only take shape in the longer term, even if this 'long term' was not long in coming. The 1930s, meanwhile, were years of an initial, profoundly destabilizing impetus, whose repercussions were felt throughout the system.

The numbers and relative weight of the rural versus the urban population were almost constantly subjects of heated discussion among statisticians, demographers and politicians. According to results of the 1926 population census, city inhabitants reached the number of 26,314,114 (17.9 per cent), while the rural population reached 120,718,801 (82.1 per cent). The noted specialist on the peasantry V. P. Danilov claimed that the percentage of the peasants was actually higher (84 per cent according to him). He argued that census takers and demographers included in the category of 'towns' settlements that were at that time nothing more than large villages and thus artificially increased the weight of the urban population.[8] This correction affords a good introduction to one of the predominant features of the period: the ongoing urbanization occurred against the background of what were still profoundly rural realities and roots. This was something registered by many visitors, who at the end of the 1920s observed the extent to which in the cities (Moscow included) 'country and city are still playing hide-and-seek' (Walter Benjamin). The prevalence of rural origins in the present urban population was, in many ways, ubiquitous; and this socio- historical reality was far from having disappeared despite 'col-lectivization' and other 'modernizing' strategies. Exaggerated claims for the size of the 'intelligentsia', inflated pronouncements about the achievements of planning, the trumpeting of the advent of 'socialism', decreed on Stalin's whim in the *annus mirabilis* of 1937 – these conveyed a need to accelerate, at least verbally, the completion of a historical stage that was still anchored in the past. But this in no way diminished the

---

8   See V. P. Danilov, *Sovetskaia Dokolkhoznaia Derevnia*, Moscow 1977, pp. 29–30.

intensity and agonies of the transition: quite the reverse.

For the USSR in its pre-September 1939 borders, the January 1939 census recorded a total population of 170.5 million inhabitants, 114.4 million in the countryside (67 per cent) and 56.1 million in the towns (33 per cent). Accordingly, the urban population had doubled in twelve years, increasing by 30 million – an exceptionally rapid rate of urbanization by any standards. The annual growth rate for the urban population is eloquent testimony: 2.7 per cent from 1926 to 1929; 11.5 per cent from 1929 to 1933; and 6.5 per cent from 1933 to 1939. The average for the years between the two censuses of 1926 and 1939 was 9.4 per cent a year.[9]

The raw statistics are no less eloquent: between 1926 and 1929 the urban population grew by 950,000 a year; between 1929 and 1932 by 1.6 million a year; and between 1933 and 1939 by 2.34 million a year. In 1940 the urban population stood at 63.1 million inhabitants (this included 7 million in recently annexed territories). But as we have seen, this urban world was still profoundly enmeshed with the countryside and the peasantry, which remained the substantial majority of the population and served as 'reservoir' for the whole social structure. The main social changes in this short period can be encapsulated in an interaction of three powerful 'transformers': at one pole, collectivization 'de-ruralized' the countryside; at the other, urbanization did the same; and industrialization, another potent demiurge, operated at both poles.

As a result of this transformation, the growth of towns and the influx of peasants into them assumed gigantic proportions. In the years 1926–39, towns swelled by 29.6 million inhabitants – 18.5 million of them new arrivals; 5.3 million through natural growth (births, marriages, and so on); and 5.8 million through administrative decisions to attach larger rural settlements to the category of 'towns'. In 1939, 62 per cent of new town dwellers thus hailed from the countryside: endogenous population growth in towns and 'urban settlements' accounted for only 17.8 per cent; while the remaining 19.5 per cent became town dwellers by

---

9 A. S. Moskovskii and M. A. Isupov, *Formirovanie Gorodskogo Naseleniia Sibiri (1926–1939)*, Novosibirsk 1984, p. 148. The subsequent stage in urbanization (1939–59), although interrupted by the war, increased the urban population by 39.4 million inhabitants. These figures are derived from the 1939 census and A. G. Rashin, *Istoricheskie Zapiski*, no. 66, 1960, p. 269 (who gives 32 per cent, not 33, for town-dwellers in 1939, making the share of the rural population 68 per cent).

administrative fiat – meaning that 5.8 million peasants acquired such status without having to migrate.

This whole process was not restricted to the 640 towns inherited from Tsarist Russia. Approximately 450 new towns were created in the space of thirteen years. Seventy-one towns had a population of 100–500,000 – in 1926 only twenty-eight of such size existed – while eight had in excess of 500,000 (as against three in 1926). Moreover, whereas in the period 1897–1926 the fastest-growing towns were the largest ones (over 100,000 inhabitants), the years 1926–39 witnessed the development, under the impact of industrialization, of medium-sized towns (those of 50–100,000 inhabitants). Many urban areas were created in an 'empty spot' – in other words, around a new industrial building site. In 1926, 17.4 per cent of the population was urban. Thirteen years later, the percentage had leapt to 32.9 per cent.[10]

However, neither the figure for average annual growth, nor the overall total of 30 million new town dwellers, can convey the intensity of the turmoil entailed by such urban expansion. The 18.5 million peasants did not simply arrive and stay. This figure, already enormous, is the end result of population flows in opposite directions. On the one hand, millions of peasants tried out living in towns or, in the case of richer peasants, sought refuge from persecution there; on the other hand, masses of people abandoned – even fled – urban areas. This was a veritable human maelstrom.

As can readily be imagined, the country was scarcely prepared to deal with such mass migration. As a result of bad harvests and grain procurement crises, living standards had fallen considerably, as is indicated by the dramatic housing problem. Shelter was invariably to be found in barracks or in the corner of someone's room. The best scenario was where a family had a room of its own in some overcrowded communal apartment. Such difficulties were not restricted to newcomers. The housing figures underscore the gravity of the crisis: workers' barracks (often a mere roof, with no amenities) and the growing number of communal apartments (one room per family and one kitchen for four or more families) became an integral part of the Soviet urban landscape then and for years to come.

In 1928, housing was considered 'normal' in terms of hygiene and

10 Basile Kerblay, *La Société soviétique contemporaine*, Paris 1977, p. 61 (English translation, New York 1983); V. M. Selunskaya, red., *Sotsialisticheskoe Stroitel'stvo Sovetskogo Obshchetva, 1921-sered. 30kh godov*, Moscow 1979, pp. 192–3.

comfort if it possessed 6 square metres per person. But this, however modest, was just a dream – proposed as an objective in the first five-year plan and never met. In the interim, workers had to find some miserable accommodation or a corner in neighbouring villages, far from their workplace. In many industrial enterprises, the situation was actually deteriorating; apartments were falling into decay and did not meet minimal hygiene standards. On 6 January 1936, inhabitants of new urban settlements in European Russia on average had 4.4 square metres per person, compared with only 3.2 square metres in Siberia. The data for services and amenities in towns were depressing. In European Russia and Siberia, indicators for sewers, running water and central heating were extremely low. Electricity was the only exception: electric lighting was available in 92.3 per cent of houses in Russia (70 per cent in Western Siberia). In contrast, only 22.8 per cent of houses in Russia and 5 per cent in Siberia had sewers and only 43 per cent and 19 per cent, respectively, had water mains.

Such data provide a good indication of living standards in these years. They also give us an inkling of the difficulties of cohabitation in overcrowded housing, where privacy was impossible and personal and family life must have been strained to the limit. Undernourishment, poor housing, the lack of hygiene, physical and nervous exhaustion due to too little rest, not to mention the extensive participation in the labour force of women, who endured the same pressures as men (if not more) – these explain the decline in birth rates in the 1930s. In the early years of this decade, economic difficulties, famine (especially in 1932–3) and other hardships depressed population growth. Food shortages, rationing, intensive migration, 'de-kulakization', and constant flows in and out of the towns shattered traditional family life and relations within families.

From 1923 to 1928, the population had grown by an unprecedented 4 million a year, thanks to lower death rates and higher birth rates, especially in the countryside. In 1928, the birth rate was 42 per thousand, the mortality rate 18, and the rate of population growth 24 per cent. A quite different picture emerges between 1928 and 1940: rates of population growth fell, especially in 1930–1, and went on falling thereafter. In 1932, birth rates exceeded death rates by only 5.6 per cent. And for the first time, 1933 witnessed a negative demographic balance in the towns of European Russia. The years 1930–5 must have been especially alarming. In 1938, population growth improved in the same areas and returned to its 1929 level (20 per cent), before declining to 19.2 per cent in 1939 and 13.2 per cent in 1940 because of the threat of war and also because of the smaller number of people of marriageable age, resulting from the losses incurred in the First World War and Civil War.[11]

It is difficult to tell whether these statistics, drawn from Soviet sources, tell the real story. It is true that the decline in the birth rate can possibly be attributed in part to a long-term trend. But the fact that the government took drastic measures to halt and reverse the decline suggests that it possessed even more alarming figures. An improvement in living standards, although attempted, was not easy to achieve at the end of the 1930s, given the increase in arms production. Greater emphasis was placed on such draconian measures as criminalizing abortion (27 June 1936), which were largely ineffective and far from enlightened. Neither crude pro-birth policies – the image of the 'heroic mother' (an honorary title and medal bestowed on mothers for bearing ten children and a source of many jokes) – nor the butchery of women condemned to back-street abortions can account for the small improvement officially claimed for 1937 (at the height of the purges). It was followed by a new decline in 1939, back down to the 1935 level. By now, of course, an additional factor was at work: the mobilization of men into the army.

---

11 *Trud v SSSR*, p. 30.

6

THE IMPACT OF COLLECTIVIZATION

Had it consisted only in breakneck industrialization, the policy launched by the new leadership under Stalin's firm control in 1928–9 would have been unprecedented. But this huge economic effort occurred at a time when grain procurement was becoming increasingly problematic. And industrialization was perceived as being in danger unless an equally radical restructuring was undertaken in agriculture. As in the industrial sphere, this was conceived as a great leap forward, with the application of industrial methods to agriculture. Such industrialization seemed to be the quickest way of revolutionizing the agrarian economy. Once machines had replaced ploughs (the swing plough in some instances), spectacular results were bound to follow fast.

By the end of 1939, kolkhoz members (*kolkhozniki*) numbered 29 million, or 46.1 per cent of the working population. To these we must add 1,760,000 people employed in sovkhozy (state-owned agricultural factories) and similar agricultural enterprises, and the 530,000 employees of the Machine Tractor Stations (MTS).[1] But whereas in industry workers entered a pre-existing system of factories and jobs, the social and productive system in agriculture was very different. 'Reconstructing' it by coercive bureaucratic fiat, without seeking the producers' consent, amounted to expropriation of a huge mass of peasants. The unanticipated consequences of this policy were to weigh upon Soviet agriculture, as well as the Soviet state, until the very end.

A leading article in an agricultural journal indicates a key syndrome.

---

1 *Sotsialisticheskoe Zemledelie*, 10 August 1940.

In it, comrade Krivtsov, secretary of the Matveevo-Kurgansky MTS in the Rostov oblast, was criticized for not having done adequate political work among the tractor brigades. Without such work, they would never meet with success in the harvest campaign. It turns out that tractor-drivers do not read the newspapers addressed to them, are oblivious to government decrees, and are unaware that they are entitled to double pay during the first fifteen to twenty days of harvesting, on condition that they fulfil the norms.

The journal sought to publicize the warning Central Committee Secretary Andreev had issued in his speech to the Eighteenth Party Congress, where he attacked those who believed that agriculture could get along fine by its own devices. Andreev was right: 'nationalized' agriculture was incapable of functioning properly without massive political intervention, which did not just mean agitprop. For him, politics included a readiness to apply strong pressure to the producers. And agriculture now had to be managed by the local government and party agencies in exactly the same way as a ministry ran its branch, issuing orders to be executed. This meant pressure by the Agriculture Commissariat at every level, often down to the individual kolkhoz or sovkhoz, as well as state and party pressure on the commissariat and, via the party, police and local administration, directly on producers.

This involved constructing detailed plans for every stage of agricultural production for each district, which were prepared or approved by the centre. As often as was necessary, a swarm of emissaries would descend like locusts on the district and its kolkhozes to oversee the seasonal work, which was regarded as a state-run campaign. Particular attention was paid to the threshing: during this crucial stage, state officials, and specially mobilized squads, were dispatched to collect the grain quota due to the state, even before any had reached the peasants. Even more perfidious was the behaviour of a pyramid of special commissions created to assess the expected crop, which often resorted to statistical manipulation to 'decree' the size of the future harvest in advance and tax the peasants in accordance with these inflated estimates. The accumulated pressure was a disincentive to working the land honestly and helped to weaken, even eradicate, the peasant's natural attachment to the land and agricultural work. Peasants now tended to reserve most of their effort for their household plots. Without the latter, not only the peasants but the whole country would have been starving. Despite their ridiculously small size, these plots played a crucial role in feeding the countryside and also the towns. They were all that remained to the peasants for preserving themselves as a class and their villages as viable communities.

Years later, in the post-Stalinist period, and notwithstanding numerous improvements and reforms aimed at revitalizing agricultural production, the legacy of this voluntaristic agrarian policy was still exacting a humiliating price: while the 'collectives' were equipped with vast fields and fleets of tractors, and the rural population remained sizeable, the country was obliged to import grain from the USA.

The case of Soviet agriculture is an especially dramatic example of modernization running out of control. The state saddled itself with the task of managing the whole of agriculture from above. The bulk of the nation – the peasantry – now performed its productive tasks sluggishly. And even this could be obtained only under the pressure of an imposing mechanism combining control, incentives and repression. The kolkhoz system was a hybrid structure containing incompatible principles: the kolkhoz, the MTS and the private plot were forced to coexist uneasily, without ever becoming either a cooperative, a factory, or a private farm. The term 'collective' was wholly inappropriate.

'Collectivization' – about which there was nothing collective – also had a profound influence on the state system. As we have said, dictatorships come in different shapes and sizes. In the case of the USSR, the regime now had to equip itself with the vast coercive apparatus required to compel the bulk of the population to do work it had hitherto done of its own accord.

Yet whatever the fate of Soviet agriculture as a mode of production, the processes that led to the historic transformation of Russia's social landscape were accelerated by the new farming methods. Although ongoing, the transition from the millennial rural past to a new era was now in full swing. The industrial-urban component was advancing at full tilt, while the rural component, despite stagnation and upheavals, remained a massive presence. In other words, the transition was characterized by an explosive mixture of large-scale modern technical–administrative structures and a rural society which, sociologically and culturally, still lived a traditional existence with its own horizons and rhythms.

Tsarist Russia had experienced a comparable contradiction. Intense waves of capitalist development had swept over a deeply rural country dominated by an absolutist state, bringing in their wake all sorts of imbalances and crises. In the Soviet case, however, the waves of industrialization were even more intense and, in contrast to what happened in Tsarist Russia, the activity was directly steered by a rein-vigorated, determined state, prone to repression and ruled by a tight leadership group very conscious of its power. Failure to take on board the collision between a developing industrial society and the reaction – or lack of reaction – of the peasantry, as well as the impact of this complex mix on the political regime, renders the course of Russian and Soviet history in the twentieth century – 1917, Leninism, Stalinism, and the final downfall – unintelligible.

We must therefore reiterate that the country's rural component, coerced by the regime into abandoning its centuries-old ways, exacted its revenge, as it were, by compelling the regime further to strengthen its already imposing administrative–repressive machinery. For without it, it would not have extracted much from its agriculture. A string of other, equally decisive consequences followed, starting with what we might call the 'ruralization' of the towns. The influx of peasants seeking work or fleeing the countryside made urban expansion a major problem for the regime. Flight to the cities was *ipso facto* a massive rural exodus. It was a precautionary measure on the part of those who felt threatened, or the outcome of the persecution suffered by those who had been forcibly displaced to remote regions. The exodus to the towns occurred at a time when the newly established kolkhoz system was too weak to perform its seasonal tasks.

Another source of flight to the towns was the thousands of tractor and combine drivers and other agricultural specialists. Having received intensive training, or even during their professional courses, they pre-ferred to escape to an urban environment. This reflected the contradiction inherent in using material incentives to inflect behaviour: the state trained them to go and work in the fields, but they preferred to depart for the city.

Data on social flows, the chaotic population movements in and out of towns, 'ruralized' urbanization, the barracks culture typical of the urban mentality and way of life, the brutal treatment of labour on construction sites and in the kolkhozy: all these features, especially the last, must be modulated by taking into account another phenomenon. At a time when construction sites and workplaces needed large amounts of manpower, we find a rapid turnover of labour, to the despair of authorities and factory managers. Workers quit their factories, which even in peacetime was regarded as an act of desertion. Often young, they would disappear into their native villages with the support and connivance of the local administration. The same reasons that prompted the higher authorities to intensify coercion and repression against labour turnover and desertion led local authorities, especially in the country-side, to shelter young people who had fled their factory, or some other job which was too onerous, in order to join kolkhozy or sovkhozy. More puzzling, and less well studied, is the indulgence shown by courts and prosecutors in this regard. Concerned with local interests, or simply not regarding young people who refused to work somewhere against their will as criminals, prosecutors declined to pursue such cases and judges handed down lenient, non-custodial sentences.

The Stalinist state had restored the tradition of the Tsarist *ancien régime*, which (at least until the abolition of serfdom in 1861) treated the labour force as attached to its workplace (*glebae adscripti*). This was a major feature of Stalinism – with one proviso: social actors, including administrative agencies, often diluted the severity of the dictatorial state through escape-hatches and loopholes created by objective conditions and interests. These qualifications and 'relaxations' of the dictatorship's iron grip should not be overlooked. This proviso applies to Stalin's repressive policy in its entirety in the 1930s. It is true that the 'security plus terror' formula was an almost intrinsic key component of the unfolding Stalinist system, justifying the critical attention it has received. We ourselves shall have much to say about the regime's horrors, but with the same qualifications as apply to the treatment of the specific problem of manpower. The whole set of repressive and terrorist measures has too often monopolized the attention of researchers, at the expense of the broader panorama of social changes and state building. Yet the latter is indispensable if we wish to arrive at a deeper under-standing of the many and varied interactions in this complex edifice. That is why we are endeavouring here to examine at least some of the elements that allow us to delve into the social processes under way in these years.

The overall climate of the period can be encapsulated in the following features: urbanization, industrialization, collectivization, purges and show trials, the spread of education, an often demagogic depreciation of culture, the mobilization of energies and people, increasing crim-inalization of many aspects of life, hectic creation of administrative structures, and so on. All these, and more, belong to the tumultuous 1930s. These momentous events and processes, which occurred almost simultaneously, were interrelated, and impacted upon one another, generated historical changes at a rarely equalled tempo – all in an atmosphere of great confusion, even chaos. It stands to reason that the political system cannot be understood independently of the retroactive effects of its own initiatives. In other words, the political system that launched the upheaval was in turn shaped by its outcome and emerged as a very particular kind of dictatorship.

Consequently, social history cannot be ignored when dealing with the 'political system' or, more specifically, the state–party complex.

The word *tekuchka* (which can be rendered as 'spontaneous mobility of manpower') adequately encapsulates the scale of the population movements in all directions, especially during the earlier years. Millions of people circulated throughout the country: they flooded to towns and major construction sites, but then sometimes abandoned them; they fled the countryside and the threat of being expropriated and deported as a 'kulak'; they went to receive training or take a new job, which they left with equal rapidity. These different forms of *tekuchka* merged into a massive social flux, difficult to control, with a population constantly on the move, on roads or in trains, throughout the country.

Such was the backdrop that led to the situation being considered explosive. The introduction of the internal passport and the *propiska* (obligatory registration with the police in towns, in order to enjoy residence rights) was only one of the means adopted by the regime to restore order to the country. On the one hand, it resorted to the full panoply of administrative and repressive measures; on the other, it experimented with social and economic strategies.

The rudimentary planning of the urban environment was, in its initial stage, an inherent part and significant source of this social instability. Even in later years, when a degree of stability obtained, one important sociological feature persisted: in addition to partly ruralized towns, Stalin's Russia still had 67 per cent of its population in the countryside and a sizeable chunk of its working population remained pre-industrial, notwithstanding the tractors of the MTS. Their living environment continued to be composed in the main of a small or medium-sized village, sometimes clustered with other villages, but often dispersed and isolated. Larger, more populous villages certainly existed, for the most part in some areas of the steppe or the Northern Caucasus; but they were much less numerous. Moreover, they shared common features with other villages that sharply distinguished them from large towns. The neighbourhood networks that governed the system of social relations within the community; the seasonal rhythm of economic activity; a profoundly religious culture permeated by magical beliefs – these had a powerful impact on the everyday life and behaviour of rural populations.

Creating an urban culture and adapting to it is a protracted process. In the short period we are exploring here, the transition from one way of life to another would have been a very unsettling experience even in more favourable conditions. However basic they might have been, towns – particularly the larger ones – represented an enormously complex phenomenon for people who had just arrived from villages. A single point of contrast between the two worlds says it all: whereas in large towns the number of professions exercised was approximately 45,000, the corresponding figure for the countryside was 120.

Shortage of food and accommodation, to cite only the most evident and onerous aspects of urban existence, pointed to a state of crisis that could only exacerbate the difficulties encountered by rural migrants in the urban-industrial world. In a village, everyone lived in the familiar universe of their home, their livestock and their neighbours, almost all of whom they knew personally; and such familiarity translates into a veritable psychological need. By contrast, the anonymous crowd in towns is readily seen as hostile by definition. Other features we have already mentioned made adapting yet more onerous. In addition, Soviet towns were largely inhabited by young people in these years and insecurity was prevalent ('hooliganism' was the name given to a phenomenon that plagued towns). But this also made it easier for young people who had arrived straight from their village to assimilate; and they rapidly abandoned the values of their elders.

For many peasants, the only way to cope with the challenges of a difficult environment lay in preserving as many village traditions as possible. This defensive behaviour revived the rural character of many towns inherited from Tsarist Russia, recreating within them a hybrid environment and way of life that remained an enduring feature of Soviet urbanization. We must therefore insist on something that should by now be obvious: when it went to war in 1941, Stalin's Russia was not yet an important urban-industrial power, even though it was on the way to becoming one. Sociologically, but also culturally, it was in many respects an extension of its agrarian past, including in the very mould of its modernizing state.

7

BETWEEN LEGALITY AND BACCHANALIA

As yet, we have said nothing about the waves of criticism, expressions of dissent, and often harsh words issuing from the lower classes, which reached just about every government and party letterbox. The policy mix of pampering and badgering pursued with respect to administrators and the intelligentsia sought to make them a rampart for the regime and cadres in the state machinery. Any large-scale expression of popular discontent or sustained, sharp criticism was regarded as dangerous, even when not followed by disorder or demonstrations on the streets that could be dubbed 'opposition' or 'counter-revolution'. Even the reactions of members working outside the apparatus were a matter of concern for party leaders. And such discontent did not begin with the five-year plans.

PARTY MEMBERS PARTICIPATE IN STRIKES (1926)

Reports from the GPU and the party's information department noted that not all party members were strike-breakers, even if some were perceived as such and indeed were. Between January and September 1926, party members had participated in 45 of the 603 strikes recorded throughout the country.[1] Documents show some party members not only initiating, but also leading, the strikes. Reports also deplore the

---

1 RGASPI, 17, 85, 170, LL. 69–80 (a lengthy, detailed GPU document for the period January–September 1926 on the behaviour and statements of workers from many factories and regions).

negative conduct of members in various factories and stress that economic difficulties are engendering what are described as 'peasant'
attitudes: passivity in social and working life, religious and nationalistic
prejudices, hostile reactions to the decisions of the party cell.

Examples are quoted of party members making highly critical statements – for example, 'We're now more exploited than we were before.
Then we had the bourgeoisie; now we've got our managers.' Another
case is cited where the party cell demands that its members halt a strike,
prompting this response from a female communist worker: 'What do
you want? Does the party feed me? It's become impossible to survive.'
Another reaction is quoted: 'We're being squeezed to the last drop. Our
union representatives have cosied up to the factory management and pay
no attention to workers' demands.'

In a glass factory in the Krasnoyarsk province, some workers go on
strike demanding a pay rise from 42 to 52 roubles and a party member is
among the leaders. All the strikers were fired, probably because there
were so few of them. When strikes were on a larger scale, strikers'
demands were often met.

In the Nevsky shipyards in Leningrad, a strike breaks out that could
have been prevented by two party members who are highly regarded by
the workforce. But when asked to intervene by management, they
refuse.

The reports quote copiously from the criticisms made by some party
members of all aspects of party policy. To take an example, two of them
come to see their cell secretary, put their membership cards on the desk,
pay their dues for the last month, and announce that they are quitting
the party: 'Your cell works for the management; you're helping it to
oppress the workers.'

GPU reports on election campaigns in trade unions and other
organizations register considerable passivity among workers, even when
they are party members. Some workers want to leave a meeting. When
stopped at the exit, they reply: 'Why do you stop us leaving when party
members are the first to be off?'

The reports also cite anti-Semitic statements by working-class party
members. They sound familiar: 'All power is in Jewish hands'; 'The yids
are in power and oppress the workers'; 'You won't find one decent
person among the yids'; 'I've been itching to have a go at this hateful
tribe.'

We must be careful when interpreting these snippets. If such cases
were frequent, the reports, which derive from the GPU or the party's

information department, do not permit us to assess the extent of the protests. Other documents maintain that the instructions or interdictions issued by cells were rarely disobeyed by party members. This does not mean that they did not express or share opinions only openly expressed by a minority, or did not tacitly sympathize with workers' grievances. But they balanced their fear of reprisals at the hands of other workers, which were common when they evinced hostility to them or to strikes – against fear of being reprimanded by the party – which could end up with them losing their jobs. It is also clear now that rank-and-file party members, like everyone else in the workplace, were spied on by *stukachi* (unpaid informers) or secret agents.

If material from the base attests to demands for a 'democratization' of working conditions and party life alike, trends inside the regime were moving in the opposite direction and elicited a variety of reactions, including directly political ones, even among some apparatchiks. The problem was not just the emergence of criticism among these strata. Worse, dedicated old Bolsheviks or idealistic newcomers declared themselves deeply disappointed – even disgusted – with their work and no longer wanted to serve at the heart of the citadel. Some apparatchiks who had not chosen their jobs out of careerism found themselves inside a machine where their sense of vocation, political perspectives and the fate of the country were drowned in bureaucratic *vermicelli* – a term, picked up in Italy, that was often used by veteran revolutionaries. We have already cited documents to this effect. Even more negative expressions of rejection of the system and accusations of treason also circulated, invariably unsigned.

In the 1930s, however, the regime possessed more instruments than it had in the 1920s for imposing its authority on everyone, including party members – the criminal code and the secret police foremost among them. But another phenomenon proved still more potent: with the expansion of its apparatus, the party ended up becoming its mere appendix – though this was not Stalin's ultimate objective (in the 1940s he developed even more radical projects). Whether he adopted this policy in 1933 or somewhat earlier is a secondary issue. What matters is a combination of different factors. Domination of a country thrust into full-scale industrialization and 'collectivization' demanded the final emasculation of the old revolutionary party and its transformation into an obedient tool. 'Adequate' repressive agencies, as well as an ideological lexicon to justify the repression, were constructed to this end or simply updated for new purposes. Thus, the category of 'counter-

revolutionary crime' contained in the criminal code, and which sounded obvious in a revolutionary situation, was refined to meet new
requirements. A military prosecutor, V. A. Viktorov, who was very
active under Khrushchev, described the terroristic trends and practices
of the Stalinist era in highly critical terms, referring to the 'amendments
with far-reaching consequences' introduced into the criminal code in
1926, despite strenuous opposition in various circles.[2]

The article on 'counter-revolutionary crimes' originally required a
clearly proven 'intention followed by action' before prosecution was
warranted. But the newly created GPU skilfully manoeuvred so that
arrests and interrogation eluded supervision by prosecutors, who were
supposed to monitor their legality. It also succeeded in circumventing
'awkward' legal provisions in the criminal code. Amendments to the
code, and the new powers granted to the GPU by the government,
enabled the latter to prosecute and punish without real proof – i.e.,
without the 'culprit' having actually committed a crime. Investigations
no longer had to prove the existence of an 'intention followed by
action'. Viktorov's analysis indicates that the way was now open for a
type of 'legal' repression where the only requisite proof was the accusation itself. However strange it might seem, guilt was firmly established
even before the indictment was decided.

In the last analysis, the combination of this pseudo-legal manipulation
of the code and use and abuse of the 'heresy syndrome' led to a surreal
situation where guilt was genetically inscribed in all citizens, who were
liable to be prosecuted at will. Paradoxically, this juridical absurdity,
cloaked in the vaguest of terminologies, would soon be used to combat
not only what were regarded as anti-regime currents, but also – and
primarily – the ruling organization itself, in whose name the operation
was supposedly being conducted. Party members, as well as the large
pool of ex-members, became the target of a witch-hunt, at a time when
no serious opposition to Stalin remained – unless we regard as opposition the attitude of those who resigned their party duties or let them
lapse, or the numerous complaints and criticisms emanating from the
party's rank and file, and even some of its higher strata, as reported by
whoever did the reporting.

Thus, as Stalin increasingly entrenched himself at the top and the
category of 'counter-revolutionary crime' became ever more vague in

---

2   See V. A. Viktorov, *Bez Grifa 'Sekretno' – Zapiski Voennogo Prokurora*, Moscow
    1990, pp. 95–116.

the criminal code and in practice, the security agencies extricated themselves from control by the law and legal authorities and expanded the scope of their arbitrary punitive powers. A veritable machinery of terror was now available, ready to be deployed against anyone. Party membership, old or new, became irrelevant – or even dangerous. Stalin had scores to settle with many members of what was supposed to be his own party, including with some of those who had helped him acquire the tools to do just that. With the party tamed and the police completely unconstrained and directly subordinate to the 'top man', the way was free for Stalin's solo stewardship, without 'sentimentality' or checks, of a powerful centralized state. In fact, this state was a war machine ready to do battle and provided with all necessary means for that purpose. As the title of Part One puts it, this state was combined with a 'psyche'. It is remarkable how long members of the 'old guard' – with the exception of Lenin – were unaware of what Stalin was capable of. By the time they discovered it, it was too late. Were they too 'Westernized' to decipher such a dark psyche? Or just short-sighted? Or, more charitably, were they still too dominated by a socialist ideology to realize that they had embarked on a journey that was leading them back into the depths of Mother Russia, and that different means would have been required to prevent the worst?

Whatever our answer to that question, once in opposition to Stalin the different currents in the old guard – supporters of Trotsky, Zinoviev or Bukharin, each of them 'waking up' after the previous one had already been vanquished – fought as best they could for some four years. Most ended up yielding to Stalin. Trotsky, forced into exile, was the main exception. Following the defeat of the more sizeable oppositions, small groups of disillusioned top officials attempted some criticism between 1929 and 1932, but they were soon neutralized. Mention should be made of a particularly brave illegal organization headed by a former secretary of the Moscow party, Ivan Riutin. He had circulated a thousand-page document entitled 'Platform of the Marxist-Leninists', which accused Stalin of betraying the party and the revolution. According to some information, the Central Committee would not permit Stalin to eliminate him physically in 1932. We know that Riutin was sufficiently courageous and intransigent to declare to one of his interrogators: 'I will not go down on my knees.' He went to prison and subsequently disappeared. Another opposition figure whom we have already encountered – Trotsky's former associate, Christian Rakovsky – carried on writing remarkable critical analyses of Stalin's policies and regime until 1934, when he finally 'repented'. It only served to prolong his life for a few more years.

Small, sometimes tiny, currents, as well as numerous individuals, continued to express criticism. The authorities were informed of it either when the police seized material during raids on people's homes, or when such criticisms were sent by mail to the press, the party, leaders, or Stalin himself – invariably unsigned, so as to escape retribution. Researchers today are still unearthing them in large numbers in the archives.

Thus, any organized opposition, whether open or clandestine, was now impossible. But individual demonstrations, as well as politically charged collective reactions – disorder, strikes, withdrawal from the party (however discreet) – allow us to suggest that the population and many party members were not exactly mute. This is a topic that requires more research, but we already have a pioneering book, *The Year 1937*, by Oleg Khlevniuk, which offers the first evidence of the widespread existence of different forms of opposition and protest – in this case, against the purges. One of the forms of protest mentioned is a wave of suicides. Official propaganda insinuated that a suspect's suicide was proof of guilt or cowardice, but the measures adopted to reduce the number of such suicides were unavailing. Helpless in the face of state terror, some people had no other way of defending themselves. According to one source, suicides numbered in the thousands. In 1937, there were 782 in the ranks of the Red Army alone. The following year, the figure rose to 832 (not counting the navy). Such suicides were not always desperate acts by the powerless; they were also courageous gestures of protest.

The social turbulence generated by the 'great leap forward' – the massive population movements, particularly those covered by the term *tekuchka* – and the need to control those sectors where the ensuing crisis was at its most acute, impelled the regime to adopt two strategies that had contradictory dynamics:

(1) recourse to various forms of repression, referred to by the term *shturmovshchina* (storming) – i.e. the launch of huge campaigns to achieve whatever the current objectives were at any price;
(2) construction of a hypertrophied bureaucracy to control population flows by systematizing and channelling them.

Seemingly unavoidable, these strategies contradicted one another. The mobilizing campaigns alternated, or ran in parallel, with attempts to 'regularize' things: in sum, the Mr Hyde of terror versus the Dr Jekyll of bureaucracy, keen on planning, stability and 'tenure'. Both belonged to the regime's internal clock.

This alternation between stick and carrot persisted even at the height of the terror. The bloody purges of 1937–9 contained their own swings of the pendulum. The inability to pursue a steady course, the innate preference for violent acceleration, always ended up causing a trail of damage that had to be cleared away before the next mobilization.[3] This innate preference was the hallmark of a concentration of power, regarded as the only way of pursuing the chosen course to the end. Whatever the current line, whether hard or softer, the regime never relaxed its compulsive attachment to a strict centralism as the only fixed point in a chaotic situation. This approach was not altogether lacking in logic: the gigantic endeavour that had been embarked upon could never have derived from below, and could not be managed at local level either. But centralism on this scale was the source of endless imbalances. Stalinist centralism grew out of a specific situation: a powerful centre had existed since the end of the 1920s, but it had a narrow summit. The configuration of power was such that the assessment of the situation, the diagnosis, the very definition of reality and the policies to adopt depended on the opinions and views of a very small number of leaders. As the great leap unfolded, the way they had governed the country before 1929 must in retrospect have seemed like simplicity itself. The object of government was now literally in perpetual motion.

This enormous fluidity in society and institutions was, of course, the result of the speed and scale of the transformation that had been embarked on. By definition, it was inevitable, and corrigible only in the long run. However, especially in the early 1930s, the regime had to undertake its enormous economic tasks in the here and now, while confronting intense social ferment. The inexorable growth of the whole administrative apparatus – a novelty in itself on this scale – had inevitable social consequences. Even before they had learnt to do their jobs properly, administrative personnel displayed an amazing ability to express their needs, desires and interests, and hit upon means of satis-

---

3   See Oleg V. Khlevniuk, 'The Politbureau, Penal Policy and "Legal Reforms"', in Peter H. Solomon, Jr, ed., *Reforming Justice in Russia, 1964–1966: Power, Culture and the Limits of Legal Order*, Armonk (New York) and London 1997.

fying them. Thus the problem-solver generated new problems, in conformity with much else in these tumultuous years. A sketch of the bureaucratic structures of the state is now in order.

THE BUREAUCRATIC 'GENE'

A document from early 1929, and two others from 1940, cast light on some key aspects of bureaucratic state-building between these dates, or at least on the rulers' perception of it. The first derives from Kujbyshev, Politburo member and head of the State Inspectorate, composed of members of the party's Central Control Commission and the Worker–Peasant Inspectorate, which had commissariat status. The speech he made to his department heads in early 1929 was, to say the least, rather alarming: 'Nothing in our new state resembles the old Tsarist regime as much as our administration.' He listed the well-known defects of the latter and then concluded, like Lenin before him, that they were very difficult to rectify. The abuses and scandals were on such a massive scale that urgent measures were being canvassed. However, they would at best make it possible to get shot of some swindlers, who would quickly be replaced by others, sowing despair in the ranks of militants in the Worker–Peasant Inspectorate. Their commissariat was supposed to be exemplary and enjoy great authority among other government agencies. But this was dangerous: no agency could live up to it. Everyone knows, he continued, about the intra-agency disputes that are typical here and no department is prepared to accept the solutions suggested by another body, especially if they occasion the slightest inconvenience. The higher government agencies, which are supposed to coordinate the activity of lower bodies, are torn apart by the same quarrels and their decisions are often the product of nothing more than fortuitous majorities. Supra-ministerial bodies like the Council for Labour and Defence, or the economic councils at regional level, are insufficiently powerful, because the offended party appeals to the Council of Commissars and often succeeds in getting decisions overturned. 'In a word,' Kuibyshev said, 'you will not find one uncontested authority in this system.' And he added: people still hope that the Worker–Peasant Inspectorate will find a way of becoming such an authority.

Incredible as it might seem, in his diagnosis of an absence of uncontested authority, Kuibyshev did not mention the Politburo as an exception – though this might have been unintentional.

The Politburo was itself looking for ways of remedying the situation, notably by ousting old cadres from the apparatus and training new ones. We know enough about Stalin by now to guess that in his eyes such a defective organization could only be tantamount to sabotage on a grand scale.

By 1940, with the great purges already in the past, the communism 'without deformations' – particularly 'without bureaucratization' – imminently anticipated by some was still very far off. It suffices to read these lamentations from *Izvestiia*, which echo Kuibyshev's twelve years earlier: 'A great many superfluous departments and agencies have grown up in our state administration, innumerable superstructures where employees do nothing but write, "conduct inquiries", answer correspondence. And all too often, this paper trail leads to absolutely nothing.' This was a leading article. It went on to deplore the plethora of supply agencies and gave the example of Gorky, where they were pointlessly proliferating – there were sixty in this town alone. Every commissariat had several supply agencies, each agency had a large workforce, and running expenses kept on increasing. The agencies were duplicating one another, since they virtually all performed the same tasks. In Gorky, running expenses had doubled in 1940 and the editor of *Izvestiia* could not understand why. Most worrying was the fact that this was a widespread phenomenon.

Thus, the regime responsible for this situation, be it the 'social mobility' or the proliferation of bureaucracy, was in turn put to the test and forced to react to one emergency after another, each of which was perceived as a threat. This perception of things was to become the main motor of Stalinism. Not only did the threats exist, but they were necessary to the regime to mobilize the faithful and justify the terror. Yet the factors that had destabilized the social structure were not contained by the terror. The camps and the terror only compounded the instability and sense of insecurity in society, which then rebounded on the state. The leadership was haunted by the spectre of an ungovernable system and losing control of the social 'magma'. Their counter-measures consisted in strengthening state control over most, if not all, aspects of life, more centralization, and transforming the system into a fortified camp, by increasing the layers of bosses at every administrative level – precisely what *Izvestiia* denounced.

We know that bureaucracies, whether efficient or sloppy, are not that pliable a tool. Stalinism hoped to solve its problems by 'mastering the masters' – i.e. the summits of the bureaucracy. Yet this endeavour was to be complicated by an unanticipated trap, which the top leadership fell into. They had concentrated enormous power in their hands, which they justified on the basis of their tasks. Strong pressure from above was their strategy and it had its logic. The fact that so many crucial decisions depended on the capacities and psychological make-up of a small ruling group, and each of its members personally, might on the face of it have served to unify and consolidate the group. But amid the turmoil of the 1930s, the more the leadership reinforced its control and grip on power, the deeper was its sense that things were escaping its control. As they read reports or visited factories, villages and towns, they realized how many people were not carrying out their orders, were concealing the reality as best they could, or were quite simply unable to maintain the stipulated pace. They noted that thousands of their directives and decrees were not even properly filed. All this helped to spread a perception among the top ranks that their power was actually more fragile than it seemed. They shared a sense of insecurity and disorientation, leading some to doubt the validity of the whole line.

This phenomenon might be called 'systemic paranoia' – a term that encapsulates the condition of the precariousness of power. It constitutes one of the core elements of Stalinist autocracy and its 'self-beatification'.

Overwhelmed by problems and undermined by doubts, the top echelon became more vulnerable to the influence of the one of its members who seemed sufficiently strong and determined to face this historical flood tide. His toughness – even ruthlessness – seemed like the requisite qualities for the tasks of the day. It was a classically auspicious moment for a master of intrigue and backstage manipulation to gather all power in his hands, including the power to decide the fate of every other leader. It was at this point that autocratic power reached its peak. The country's destiny largely found itself at the mercy of one psyche, a personality prone to paranoia, a figure on whose shoulders the whole weight of the 1930s now came to rest. This is the conjuncture that explains the title of Part One, 'A Regime and Its Psyche'. Had a collective leadership existed, it might have attenuated the effects of such tensions. But once power was allowed to become so deeply personalized, outbursts of irrationality – including murderous outbursts – were bound to occur. 'Systemic paranoia' (at the political level) was going to crystallize in the paranoid tendencies (at the psychic level) of an individual. Spite, malice, deviousness, fury – all became components of the system's *modus operandi*.

But this is also the moment to point out that the system Stalin created was inherently recalcitrant to being 'mastered', even though the image of 'master' was the one he projected at home and abroad. Certainly, the objective of an extreme centralization of power was attained. Henceforth, however, there was nowhere else to go but to cling compulsively to the summit of power. This situation generated its own tensions and side-effects: the less power you delegate, the more it imperceptibly flows into the hands of local 'little Stalins'; the more you monopolize information, the more it is kept from you; the more you control institutions, the less you master them. As we have indicated, such a configuration was intrinsically unstable and perceived as menacing. No wonder, then, that a central dimension of Stalinism consisted in fighting hordes of enemies. It was obviously not in a position to overcome the effects of this patent over-concentration of power, for that was its very essence. And yet these 'enemies' were not individuals and the dictator's personal safety was never threatened. The real enemies were objective limitations (which Stalin had declared non-existent 'for us' in 1924): social trends and changes, institutional attrition, psychological and cultural structures. Later, we shall have the chance to see such limitations at work.

Meanwhile, if it is accepted that the essence of Stalinism consisted in accumulating all power in Stalin's own hands, we can turn to the issue of how he ruled Russia. Had he not been obsessively preoccupied by this solitary exercise of power, we might have borrowed the title of our next chapter from Merle Fainsod's *How Is Russia Ruled?* But our own research leads us to formulate the question rather differently.

8

HOW DID STALIN RULE?

Let us start with a simple, surprising discovery: the same man for whom family life meant so little (in fact, he took no interest in it), and whose personal life was a terrible mess (but did this really affect him?), chose as a ruler to personalize and privatize institutional power. No wonder: this – and not much else – *was* his life. To effect this strange project, he employed the method of fragmenting key political institutions and emptying them of their substance.

We can start with the party, which is where things are clearest. As an autonomous organization, which is what it had been under Bolshevism, the party was liquidated, transformed into a bureaucratic apparatus, and treated as such – i.e. with some considerable disdain. Symptomatically, the old party principle of 'party maximum' (whereby a member, whatever his position in the hierarchy, could not earn more than a skilled worker) was abandoned as early as 1932, along with other remnants of the initial egalitarianism, and was contemptuously referred to as *uravnilovka* (levelling down). The reason was obvious: an 'egalitarian apparatus' is as realistic as a square circle. To motivate and control the apparatchiks, they now had to climb a ladder of responsibilities and privileges. Lower-level bosses in the party and state administration (who were mostly party members) no longer played the game of 'proletarian fraternity'. The call from above was for tough, authoritarian task-masters (Stalin called them 'commanders'), forming a ruling stratum (*nachal'stvo*) whose structural hierarchy covered the whole system. They were supported and flattered, but not allowed to settle down and stabilize their position. This was something peculiar to the Stalinist dictatorship, which would be abandoned after it. As Stalin tightened his grip on power, we find him dismantling the many erstwhile party–state consultative bodies, which the Politburo used to convene systematically. He emasculated all institutions of any weight, including (surprisingly for those not already aware of it) the Politburo itself.

THE POLITBURO (1935–6)

This core institution remains little understood, and it is therefore worth taking a look at its operation in 1935–6 – years of violent tremors preceding the veritable earthquake of 1937.

On 1 February 1935, the Central Committee plenum elevated Mikoyan and Chubar to the rank of full members of the Politburo, while Zhdanov and Eikhe became candidate members. No juggling of 'moderates' and 'radicals' was involved here – just a formal procedure for filling empty posts. Mikoyan and Chubar replaced Kirov (assassinated) and Kuibyshev (deceased), because they had long been candidate members and had held high-level jobs since 1926. Eikhe, leader of an important remote region (Western Siberia), was not able to participate in meetings regularly. As for Zhdanov, it was impossible to deny him candidate membership: he had been a Central Committee secretary since 1934, worked as a de facto Politburo member, and was going to replace Kirov as Leningrad party secretary.

The redistribution of functions and responsibilities within the Politburo (27 February 1937), probably decided during a pre-meeting between some Politburo members and Stalin, was significant. Andreev left his job as Railways Commissar and became a Central Committee secretary. Kaganovich took over railways and kept his position as Central Committee secretary, but gave up his duties on the party's Central Control Commission and the Moscow party committee. Andreev joined the very powerful Orgburo (which prepared dossiers for the Politburo) and became its head. But preparation of the Orgburo's agenda was to be done in collaboration with Ezhev, who now headed the Control Commission. Andreev was also put in charge of the Central Committee's industrial department (where he replaced Ezhev) and assigned to supervise the Central Committee's transport department and its current affairs department. For his part, Ezhev was given the important post of head of the department of 'leading party organs'. All the other departments, particularly culture and propaganda, remained under Stalin's personal supervision. Kaganovich retained oversight of the Moscow regional and city party committees, but he was requested to prioritize his work at the Railways Commissariat. He was a trusted trouble-shooter and this sector required a firm hand.

This reorganization gives an idea of Central Committee activity and, in particular, of the most important departments and posts. Our source, Oleg Khlevniuk, provides us with an interpretative key, demonstrating that underlying the redistribution of duties there was a deliberate policy on the part of Stalin.[1] He was seeking to disperse and dilute the power of his close associates. Kaganovich, previously considered second in command, lost this rank. Formally, he was replaced by Andreev, who, in some spheres, shared his responsibilities with Ezhev. Andreev had important Politburo responsibilities, but a department of lesser importance (industry), whereas Ezhev, who was not a Politburo member, ran key departments and for this reason participated in its meetings. Stalin had entrusted him with major responsibilities at Internal Affairs (the NKVD). In this capacity, he organized the trial of Zinoviev. Charged with supervising the NKVD for the party, he formulated the statutes for its espionage and counter-espionage department, the GUGB (General Department of State Security), and effectively controlled the NKVD for eighteen months, before officially becoming Commissar for Internal Affairs. His first job as head of the party Control Commission was to organize the campaign for checking membership cards – a kind of 'pre-purge'. He was then responsible for the purges for one and a half years.

Zhdanov was assigned to Leningrad, but was to spend ten days a month in Moscow. Pursuing his policy of dispersal, Stalin next decided that rather than three Central Committee secretaries (himself, Kaganovich and Zhdanov), there would henceforth be five. And the post of Stalin's 'deputy' disappeared. He now saw Politburo members more rarely, according to a strict calendar, and he spent less time with Molotov and Kaganovich. It is not that they had been demoted, but in 1935–6 Kaganovich had to seek Stalin's advice (i.e. approval) on everything. His letters to Stalin now contained obsequious formulations, whereas he had previously taken quite a few final decisions himself and written to Stalin without servility. Such fawning at the highest level is a good indication of the diminishing influence of Politburo members and Stalin's growing personal power. More decisions were now taken by signing a circular containing the resolution to be approved, rather than

---

1   See Oleg V. Khlevniuk, *Politbiuro – Mekhanizm Politicheskoi Vlasti v 1930-ye gody*, Moscow 1990, pp. 96–116.

by voting at meetings. The time for criticism and reservations, which had hitherto been regarded as normal on the part of high-ranking leaders, was at an end. Requests to retire, refusals to write some report, ultimata to defend the interests of some agency – these disappeared without a trace. Frequently, the sheet containing decisions for approval did not circulate. Many resolutions carry only Molotov's stamp. Other decisions were taken by a few members who came to visit Stalin on vacation in Sochi.

Sometimes a simple telegram from Stalin would do. The famous letter announcing the nomination of Ezhev to head the NKVD and betokening the dismissal of Yagoda, who was four years late in organizing a great purge, was signed by Stalin and Zhdanov. Kaganovich received a copy on 25 September 1936. As for 'poor' Yagoda, who had not realized that he should have acted in 1932, he was of course executed. Stalin's power was now so well established and accepted by the others that he could make them swallow anything. The accusations against Yagoda are a good example: he obviously would not have been able to launch a vast purge in 1932 without being explicitly instructed to do so by Stalin.

Mastery of the Politburo was achieved by the technique of fragmenting even this small body. According to Stalin's whim, it functioned in fragments – meetings of seven, five, three or two. The only people summoned were those who had to handle some particular matter. Meetings often took the form of dinner at Stalin's dacha for those he singled out as 'friends'. This is attested by Mikoyan,[2] who explained that a quintet (Stalin, Molotov, Malenkov, Beria and himself) existed in the Politburo until 1941 dealing with foreign policy issues and 'operational matters'. After the war, Zhdanov joined this group, as did Voznesensky later. Voroshilov, who had been added at the beginning of the war, was dropped in 1944.

This is what has been called the 'narrow' Politburo, excluding Kaganovich, Kalinin and Khrushchev, all of whom were burdened with heavy administrative responsibilities outside the Politburo. The 'habit' of convening a few reliable elements had become established with the struggle of the triumvirate (Stalin, Zinoviev and Kamenev) against Trotsky, and continued with a different cast during the struggle against Rykov, when the latter was still in charge of the Sovnarkom (Council of

---

2 RGASPI, f. 39, op. 3, d. 188, L. 246. All this comes from a note to volume four of Mikoyan's memoirs, '*O Staline i Moem Otnoshenii k Nemu, 1934–53*' ('On Stalin and My Attitude Towards Him').

People's Commissars). In the 1930s, Stalin sent Molotov a letter in which he asked him to consider an important problem and talk it over with 'friends'. Not all Politburo members fell into this category and no one could count on remaining in it permanently. Before the war, members like Rudzutak, Kalinin, Kossior and Andreev were never invited to such 'intimate' caucuses, although they might have known that such meetings took place.

To summarize, the Politburo in Stalin's hands was precisely a bureau whose personnel he nominated and used as he saw fit.

THE PARTY APPARATUS

As the party lost its political identity, its apparatus – the very citadel of the system – grew ever more complex. In order to 'simplify' things and ensure greater control, a super-apparatus – variously dubbed 'special', 'political', and finally 'general' – was constructed to serve Stalin personally, without the knowledge of the rest of the apparatus. Its staff constantly expanded, as did its status vis-à-vis other Central Committee departments. Stalin's personal secretary – the ubiquitous and highly discreet Poskrebyshev – headed it and thereby acquired a promotion and salary increase. As for the Sovnarkom – a supposedly powerful institution with its departments, specialists and consultants – its authority was undermined by conspiratorial techniques at the summit. It was in fact sidestepped, since all decisions were taken elsewhere, by Stalin and Molotov. Their business was conducted via a completely secret channel of communication: Molotov submitted his proposals to Stalin and the latter corrected, approved or rejected them, sending his response, which had the force of an order, back to Molotov via the same channel. A very intimate affair! If we are aware of such details today, it is thanks to the research of Oleg Khlevniuk and his team of hardened researchers in the Soviet archives.

By way of an overview of Stalin's complex, and expanding, system of power, we might single out the following features. We are dealing with a 'security state', headed by a figure who organized his own 'cult' and resorted to a laborious method, refined down to the last detail, of running and controlling the whole enterprise. The objective was not only to guarantee its smooth operation, but also to avoid his entourage and officials at any level accumulating too much authority and power. It was achieved by fragmenting the highest institutions of state, emptying them of substance. This way of ruling – just the opposite of what might have been expected in such circumstances – created gluts and bottle-necks, to which the centre responded with emergency measures.

In a form of 'hands-on' government, Stalin personally, the Politburo, the Orgburo and the Secretariat immersed themselves in local minutiae. All this amounted to nothing less than an attempt to 'micromanage' a continent from the centre of power in Moscow.

To appreciate how the leaders and their teams engaged in such micromanaging of social groups, institutions, people and material goods, we need only glance at the minutes of the two main agencies of the Central Committee – namely the Orgburo and the Secretariat. The agendas of these two bodies charged with preparing the materials for Politburo meetings are quite simply mind-boggling, as is the number of items and documents they handled. But the best illustration of what micromanagement meant in practice is to be found in numerous tele-grams from Stalin (signed by him) to party or state agencies at the other end of the country, whether ordering someone to supply a building site with the nails it desperately needed, or build an internal railway line in a steelworks, or find some barbed wire – a product always in short supply in these years. Let us add that these countless messages always took the form of ultimata.

The Secretariat and Orgburo always proceeded in similar fashion, dealing with all manner of problems in great detail. Their work was impressive – especially their efforts to train or retrain workers, specialists and cadres in all sorts of professions, and to create courses, schools and academies, as well as compiling lists of students and teachers. It was a matter of equipping the state with the cadres it required and replacing layer after layer of specialists, who were so difficult to find.

To summarize: what we see here is the functioning of a highly centralized state, taking on a mass of tasks that are often simply not feasible. The system then suffers from a pathology of 'hyper-centralization', the cure for which is to delegate powers downwards, while retaining general policy orientation at the centre. But in the system we are concerned with, the supreme ruler mistook his own security for that of the country and perceived each failure as a fault to be punished. Such a boss had to seem omnipotent. Consequently, in a country desperately short of cadres, Stalin could declare that 'no one is irreplaceable' – a formula that harboured many demons, especially because it was false.

DOMINATING TALENTS AND UTILIZING THEM

The characteristics referred to above, including 'hands-on' management, equally apply to managing culture and, of course, the government's relations with outstanding figures in the worlds of culture and science. On this score, Stalin's dictatorship was innovative.

Once Stalin felt firmly in the saddle, a further feature of his psychology emerged: a strange fascination − a mixture of attraction and repulsion − for genius or great talent; an urge to dominate, use, humiliate and, ultimately, destroy it − rather like a child who asserts mastery over a toy by breaking it. Stalin's dealings with great writers, scientists or military figures attests to this destructive bent. He spared some of them (quite unpredictably), but the very fact that he took an interest in someone was always dangerous, if not ominous, for its object.

This subject affords insight into another important facet of Stalin's insatiable thirst for total mastery of his world. He turned to a device that would allow him to penetrate his subjects' minds and souls, their emotional systems, by using the power of fiction in novels, plays and films. He understood (and envied) the power of a writer who could single-handedly achieve a stronger grip on the thoughts and emotions of millions of people than all the agitprop in the world. He saw art as a device that could be of direct service to him, on condition that creators were coached and their work revised personally, with Stalin acting as in some sense editor and adviser or discussing with authors the behaviour of their heroes. As the reader will doubtless realize, these 'heroes' had to obey, and there was no need to be a writer to secure such obedience.

Stalin was no scientist either. Yet he personally edited, for example, Lysenko's lecture to the Academy of Science for publication. Stalin also had the last word on economic and linguistic questions and − it goes without saying − history. Since he was making history, why not personally edit a history textbook for schools? In short, Stalin's labours assumed pathological proportions: he aimed at personal mastery of a complex totality that no one had ever mastered and imposed his terms on it. Did he take himself for a genius? What we know for sure is that great talents fascinated him. Was it envy that he could assuage with the knowledge that he could destroy them at will? Or the simple pleasure of proving that he could detect errors and offer advice? It is difficult to say, but the subject is relevant to our theme of political pathology.

STALIN'S 'APOLOGY' TO TUKHACHEVSKY

His behaviour towards the brilliant Marshal Tukhachevsky, thirty-seven at the time, provides our first example of Stalin's sharply alternating attitudes towards talented figures.[3] We know that Stalin had a high opinion of himself as a military strategist. When, in 1929–30, Tukhachevsky embarked on a campaign to direct the leadership's attention to new military technology and impending changes in the character of warfare, Stalin supported Voroshilov's rejection of these ideas and wrote to him to say that Tukhachevsky was 'floundering in anti-Marxism, unrealism, even red militarism'. At the same time, he had 3,000 former Tsarist officers cashiered and arrested. The NKVD extracted 'testimony' from one of them to the effect that Tukhachevsky, himself a former Tsarist officer, belonged to some right-wing organization and was helping to plot a coup.

Stalin lapped all this up. He retained very bitter memories of the campaign against Poland in 1920, during which accusations abounded, including from Tukhachevsky, that he was a mediocre military commander. But the hour of vengeance had not yet struck. Stalin wrote to Molotov and others to say that he had personally investigated the accusations against Tukhachevsky and established that the latter was '100 per cent clean'. In 1932, he even wrote a personal apology to Tukhachevsky, with a bowdlerized copy of the letter he had sent to Voroshilov in 1930 (the allusion to 'red militarism' was omitted). He accused himself of having been unjustifiably harsh – a rare event, to say the least. In fact, Stalin had now adopted Tukhachevsky's standpoint on military technology, although in this domain, as in so many others, the targets fixed for 1932 were far from having been met. The apology did not mention the accusations fabricated by the NKVD against the marshal in 1930. It was manifestly insincere and, had Tukhachevsky understood Stalin, the duplicity would not have escaped him. Stalin's gesture actually signified: I need you for the time being, but there is a sword hanging over your head . . .

Whether naive or just plain audacious, Tukhachevsky was the only participant not to conclude his speech to the Seventeenth Party Congress in 1934 with the obligatory 'hail the leader'. The reckoning came in 1937, when Stalin destroyed his military high command. A special

---

3 One of my sources here is Lennart Samuelson, *Plans for Stalin's War Machine: Tukhachevskij and Military-Economic Planning, 1925–1941*, New York 2000.

fate was reserved for Tukhachevsky, probably the best military mind of them all. 'Information from a German source' – a total fabrication – was produced, 'proving' that the flower of the army had betrayed the country. Atrociously beaten, Tukhachevsky was dragged before Stalin for a confrontation with his accusers. Naturally, it emerged from this that he was guilty. We are dealing here with a maniac who breaks a precious object to show that it can be broken. Preferring an incompetent but obsequious Voroshilov to Tukhachevsky and the rest, and destroying the military high command, were monumental blunders. This purge alone would warrant the death penalty . . .

There is no way of knowing whether Stalin was haunted by the memory of his victims. But the strategies employed during the Second World War had been brilliantly foreshadowed by Tukhachevsky, who virtually bombarded Stalin with memos and articles about the need to prepare for a war that would require massive technological resources and in which mobile armies, geared to breakthroughs and encirclements, would play an unprecedented role. All this required a new system of command and coordination. At the beginning of the war, the Germans employed such a strategy against Soviet troops to devastating effect. Of course, no one asked Stalin why he had killed the most brilliant generals. Who was the real traitor? With the likes of Tukhachevsky, Blucher and Yegorov, the tragedy of 22 June 1941 could have been avoided.

We can cite one occasion where Stalin received a moral slap in the face, though we do not know whether he registered it at the time. After the liquidation of the high command, Stalin and Voroshilov attended a meeting of air force commanders to discuss how to rescue the air force from the lamentable state it found itself in following the purges. The officers set out the position: everything was in a woeful state – planes, weaponry, repairs, fuel, provisions, finances, administration. Training was disastrous and the number of planes and pilots lost alarming. Stalin listened carefully, requested details, and posed concrete questions to demonstrate his competence and mastery of the subject. Voroshilov took a less active part, but he was the one who closed the meeting with an explosion of anger against the officers, whom he accused of failing to mention the 'obvious fact': the situation had been caused by the sabotage and treason of the former high command, which had been justly punished. The minutes of the meeting indicate that of the dozens of officers who commented on the situation, not one uttered the word 'sabotage'. Such silence made it plain that their explanation was quite different: the dire state of the air force was due to the destruction of a group of highly capable senior officers. Voroshilov's explosion may well have been provoked by his perception that the silence implied condemnation of his leadership and his fear of Stalin's possible reaction on learning that his subordinates lacked the requisite vigilance against enemies of the USSR. We do not know what Stalin said to Voroshilov. At all events, doubtless preoccupied by the fact that the air force was far from battle-ready, he preserved his equanimity on this occasion.

Another example, which also concerns the air force, reveals Stalin's other side. It figures in the memoirs of the writer Konstantin Simonov. He recounts a high-level conference that he attended at the beginning of the war, devoted to the excessively high number of accidents involving planes and the heavy losses in terms of pilots. A young air force general came forward with a simple answer: the poorly constructed planes were veritable 'flying coffins'. Stalin was now commander-in-chief. Confronted with such a blunt accusation, his face convulsed with rage. He restrained himself from a public outburst, but murmured: 'You would have done better to keep quiet, general!' The brave young man disappeared for good the very same day.[4]

NOT SO QUIET FLOWS THE DON

Our last example involves the writer Mikhail Sholokhov, who after Stalin's death became the spokesman for a nationalist and conservative current, earning him strong enmity. But the events recounted here go back to 1933, when the Cossack region of Kuban, so dear to Sholokhov, was stricken by famine, like many other regions of Russia and the Ukraine.

Sholokhov wrote to Stalin to condemn the tragedy of the Kuban peasants, forcibly deprived of their harvest on the orders of the grain procurement agencies at the very moment when famine was setting in. Sholokhov was being bold, but Stalin tolerated the dramatic description of the results of his own policies. Why? In fact, it was calculated. Stalin literally forced himself to read Sholokhov's powerful denunciation of the mistreatment of peasants condemned to starvation, the arbitrariness of the local administration, and the provocative activities of the secret police. Once he had finished reading it, he ordered the region to be supplied with the quantity of grain that Sholokhov estimated was

---

4 Konstantin Simonov, *Glazami Cheloveka moego Pokoleniia: Razmyshleniia o Staline*, Moscow 1990.

required to prevent a calamity. He even protected Sholokhov from the enraged local authorities (including the secret police), who did everything in their power to discredit this direct communication between the two men, which was causing them so much trouble. The game here was utterly devious and Stalin played every role in it: he convened phoney 'confrontations', pretended to have checked the facts himself, and rehabilitated Sholokhov's friends in the local party apparatus. He did all this because he wanted something that Sholokhov possessed: prestige with the Russian public. The man was an authentic Russian Cossack – which Stalin was not – a powerful writer, and a good speaker – again, not Stalin's strong points. He therefore pretended to accept the facts and criticisms set out by the writer, even though he was intensely irritated by the whole business. Finally, however, he gave the game away. In one short passage in a supposedly friendly letter to Sholokhov, he vented his anger. It was pure Stalin:

> You only see one side of the story. But in order to avoid political errors (your letters are not literature, they are political), you have to see the other side. Your highly respectable cereal-growers are in fact conducting a 'secret' war against Soviet power – a war that uses famine as a weapon, comrade Sholokhov. Obviously, this in no way justifies the scandalous treatment inflicted on them. But it is clear as daylight that these respectable cereal-growers are not as innocent as it might seem from a distance. Well, all the best. I shake your hand. Yours, J. Stalin.

Setting to one side the question of who starved whom in 1933, what we read in this letter (and what Sholokhov read) is an expression of Stalin's real policy – a politico-ideological summons to arms against sabotage by 'respectable cereal-growers'. This war was launched by Stalin in similar terms at the January 1933 Central Committee meeting, when he called on the party and the country to mobilize against the hordes of shadowy enemies who were 'perniciously undermining' the regime's foundations. In his letter to Sholokhov, he even implied that a still greater enemy – the peasantry in its entirety – was engaged in a war of starvation against the system.

It is likely that Sholokhov appreciated the precariousness of his position. Stalin was actually accusing him of defending 'pernicious' enemies for whom Stalin had a visceral hatred. Sholokhov's prestigious correspondent was signalling that his life could be on the line at any moment. Stalin might have hated Sholokhov, but he needed his talents for his own ends at this point.

Stalin was unconcerned about the suffering of masses of people. Yet he knew that he was responsible for the calamity and that his image would suffer gravely if the peasant masses actually turned against him. There would be immediate repercussions in the army and the police, composed in the main of young people from the countryside who were never shy about protesting when they learnt that their parents were starving or suffering injustice at the hands of the authorities.

Constructing his own image was the name of Stalin's game. Standing on a pedestal above the fray was a better guarantee of his security and power than a host of bodyguards. And in these times of peasant star-vation and persecution, what better to serve his image than a public declaration by a defender of the peasantry like Sholokhov, to the effect that Stalin had personally ordered the dispatch of tons of grain to save lives? That was the heart of the matter and this was precisely what Sholokov supplied to the press, without even having to lie.

LIFE AT THE TOP (THE 1940S)

Another image Stalin liked to project – the thrifty farmer (*khoziain*) – was in part a genuine character trait. He was intolerant of personal weaknesses like drinking, extramarital relationships, or a taste for luxury, including among his closest associates. He made sure he was kept informed about such behaviour and ordered Politburo members to be spied on so that he could know about and, where necessary, exploit such weaknesses.

Aleksei Kosygin's memoirs provide an insight into Stalin's scheming in the late 1940s. A rising star at the end of the Second World War, Kosygin had to his wartime credit such achievements as the evacuation of industrial plant from territories about to fall to the Nazis and the organization of supplies to besieged Leningrad. Kosygin was unpopular with many at the top, envious as they were of his rapid rise. But he was also feared, because Stalin had taken him under his wing and assigned him the delicate task of making a list of the privileges enjoyed by Politburo members. As Kosygin subsequently reported to his son-in-law Gvishiani, Stalin had told him during a Politburo meeting that he possessed a list detailing everything that the families of Molotov, Mikoyan, Kaganovich and others were spending on themselves, their guards and servants, and was outraged: 'It's simply revolting.' At the time, while Politburo members earned a comparatively modest salary, they enjoyed unlimited access to consumer goods – hence their anger when Stalin instructed Kosygin to put the house in order. Obviously, they dared not blame Stalin himself and some of them, like Mikoyan, understood that this was a way of keeping them on their toes. But perhaps it was also a pretext for getting rid of some of them when needed.

In fact, Stalin was forever plotting such things. Kosygin also told Gvishiani that one of the accusations levelled against Voznesensky, head of Gosplan and Deputy Prime Minister until he was purged in 1950, was that he possessed one or more weapons. Kosygin and Gvishiani immediately searched their own homes and threw all the weapons into a lake. They also looked for listening devices and did find them in Kosygin's house (though they might have been installed to spy on Marshal Zhukov, who lived there before Kosygin). No wonder, then, that every morning in these years (1948–50), Kosygin – a candidate member of the Politburo – said farewell to his wife and reminded her what to do if he did not return home in the evening. They soon concluded, however, that he would not be harmed – Stalin felt some kind of sympathy towards him.[5]

He was lucky. But all the leaders, unless naive or too sure of themselves, very soon learnt from their own experience or that of their colleagues. After the assassination of Kirov in 1934, a sea-change occurred in their status vis-à-vis Stalin and they were immediately aware of it. It can be observed in the correspondence between Stalin and Kaganovich, then his number two. Hitherto self-assured and very direct, Kaganovich completely changed his tone, declaring himself immensely 'grateful' to fate for having vouchsafed him such a friend, leader and father: 'What would we have done without him?', and so on. It is obvious that at some stage Kaganovich had a 'revelation'. In particular, he realized that Stalin was informed of anything he might write to others. That such senior leaders should find themselves in such a situation is something unique in the annals of history. Nothing comparable occurred in Hitler's entourage after the Night of the Long Knives in 1934 (the SA were potentially political rivals). What we observe here is a highly elaborate despotic regime, launched in top gear, with an unchecked master of the art at its head.

In constructing his image, Stalin resorted to various methods. He

---

5   T. I. Fetisov, sost., *Prem'er – Izvestnyi i Neizvestnyi: Vospominaniia o A. N. Kosygine*, Moscow 1997.

personally selected the words to be employed in singing his praises in films, speeches and biographies. He ensured that his favourite superlatives were used, but censored others in order to demonstrate his modesty. He chose his decorations and titles. The rituals of congresses and other public occasions were perfected in minute detail. Finally, history was rewritten so that everything revolved around his person.

Stalin conceived himself as an autocrat and was determined not to share his place and image with anyone else, past or present. In his eyes, the other leaders were not in the same league. They did not really count: it was simply necessary to ensure their servility. From 1934 onwards, he turned them into something resembling temporarily reprieved inmates on death row. His spies supplied him with what he would need against them when the time came. In order to test and ensure their unfailing loyalty, he persecuted members of their families: Kaganovich's three brothers were killed and Molotov's wife arrested.

On various occasions, Stalin explained to gatherings at his dacha that what 'the people' wanted was a Tsar, a generalissimo. Everything in fact suggests that this is what he himself wanted and needed. Moreover, the spectacle of his oath to Lenin in 1924 had created a precedent for his own cult. Everything becomes clearer when we examine Stalin's relationship to his own revolutionary past. It is easy to demonstrate that he erased it and worked hard to create not only a different system, but also an entirely new pantheon and past. Stalin faced what might be called a historical alibi problem and needed to acquire legitimacy. Unlike Hitler, for example, he expounded his true strategy and programme only in snippets, as in his pronouncement on cadres in 1925. But we also know the grudges he harboured towards other leaders of the Bolshevik party, who had not given him the recognition he considered his due. In fact, the historical leadership, personified by Lenin, had rejected him. In the party's eyes, he did not belong to the category of founding fathers and did not deserve to belong to it. This had to be obliterated to justify the new self-image he was hard at work imposing on the country. And this he accomplished with considerable success.

9

THE PURGES AND THEIR 'RATIONALE'

The need to furnish himself with a new historical alibi was doubtless among the reasons that impelled Stalin to launch the purges of party cadres he had long been contemplating in 1937. He needed to erase a whole historical period and rid himself of those who had witnessed it and who knew who had done what in those heroic years. But this carefully nurtured, calculated revenge was not always cold-bloodedly conducted. At various stages, it unfolded in a state of extreme tension.

BUKHARIN'S CURSE[1]

The liquidation of a figure like Bukharin – politically weak, but intellectually greatly superior to Stalin, and guilty of having been (despite his young age) a 'founding father', 'the party's favourite' – sheds light on Stalin's approach and his state of mind. It unfolded in accordance with a precise script, beginning with a protracted phase of mental torture, proceeding to public degradation, and terminating in a show trial and execution.

The initial manoeuvring began in 1936. Anguished but defiant, Bukharin's reaction illuminates one aspect of the drama. At first, he thought he still had friends at the top and wrote a desperate letter to Voroshilov, asking for his help and support. He asserted his innocence, concluding: 'I embrace you because I am guilty of nothing.' Voroshilov

---

1 RGASPI, f. 56, op. 1, d. 198.

was not the right man to turn to. He immediately showed the letter to Molotov, who instructed him to return it to Bukharin with a note saying: 'You would do better to confess your vile deeds against the party.' If Bukharin did not comply, Voroshilov would consider him 'a scoundrel'. Voroshilov did as he was told.

Desperate, and conscious that he was the victim of a deadly plot, Bukharin then wrote to Stalin on 15 December 1936. Using his Georgian nickname, as in the good old days, Bukharin addressed him as 'Dear Koba'. He said that he had just read an article in *Pravda* against the 'Right' (i.e. against him) which 'knocked me off my feet'. The letter ended: 'I'm perishing because of scoundrels, human scum, loathsome villains. Yours, Bukharin.'

Supposedly directed against anonymous scoundrels, this curse-like tirade fitted Stalin perfectly. It is unlikely that Bukharin, however distressed, did not know who was pulling the strings. Stalin certainly understood that the expression 'loathsome villain' was directed at him personally. His vengeful response to Bukharin's appeals for help and indirect accusations came during a carefully planned 'spectacle' – the Central Committee meetings of February–March 1937. The way Stalin conducted these puts one in mind of a half-crazed actor, bent on driving a sane audience (the Central Committee members) into a state of collective insanity and forcing them to share his own fantasies. What he had to say was incoherent. But the aim of the meeting was not only to destroy 'his' enemy. In addition, it had a hidden agenda: to test Central Committee members through a barely concealed stratagem. Three versions of the resolution on Bukharin's 'guilt' were to be put to the vote. The first – 'arrest and consignment of the matter to the NKVD' – was clearly Stalin's preference (it betokened a death sentence, possibly preceded by torture); the second involved not proceeding to an arrest, but requiring the NKVD to pursue its investigation; while the third envisaged releasing Bukharin. This was a trap for Central Committee members, as most of them probably appreciated. No one dared declare for the third option, although several did choose the second – and paid with their lives for it.

This is just one small illustration of the incredible nightmare of the purges in 1937–8. 'Human scum' is the appropriate term to describe those responsible for this orgy of arrests, show trials, and sentencing without trial, conducted on an unprecedented scale. And there are good grounds for thinking that the events of these atrocious years had been being carefully prepared for a long time, possibly since 1933. As

Khlevniuk has indicated,[2] the supposed 're-examination of reality' on the agenda of the Central Committee in February–March 1937 is strongly reminiscent of a point addressed during the Central Committee session in January 1933. Then numerous speakers had said things they virtually repeated in 1937, in the hope of proving their lucidity and vigilance. It seems likely that Stalin was ready in 1933 to declare war on society and, one might add, the party, with the support of his acolytes and repressive apparatuses. But there were probably reasons preventing him (we have suggested some); and he opted for the 'interlude' despite his resentment at the 'termite-like' methods of his enemies – especially the 'respectable cereal-growers' of whom he had spoken to Sholokhov.

PREPARING THE VALIANT CHEKISTS

When it came to preparing the launch of the terror, certain measures were required apart from administrative spring-cleaning like checking the rolls of party members and validating membership cards. Above all, it was necessary to prepare the secret police, its leadership and personnel, for the gruesome task ahead. Ideological and moral inducements were applied along with material incentives. While propaganda extolled their valour, the new Interior Minister Yezhov increased the wages of NKVD functionaries at every level. An NKVD head at republican level received 1,200 roubles a month (as did other higher ranks), while an average worker's wage was 250 roubles. But the NKVD's top brass now received up to 3,500 roubles a month. Having previously had access to collective dachas and sanatoria, where they mixed with other party activists, they were now accorded individual dachas and significant bonuses.[3]

The infamous NKVD order no. 00447 of July 1937, approved by the Politburo on 31 July, contained the order to act and an action plan. It singled out two categories of victims and prescribed the punishment to be meted out to them: 75,000 people were to be shot and 225,000 sent to camps. There are different drafts of this order and the figures vary somewhat. But the documents in our possession demonstrate that in the event the 'norms' were fulfilled at least twice over. A budget of 85 million roubles was allocated for the operation. The pampering of the

---

2   O. V. Khlevniuk, *1937-oi*, Moscow 1992, pp. 20–1.
3   Ibid., p. 165.

NKVD reached an even higher pitch when, in a speech, Stalin bestowed upon his security apparatus the lofty status of 'armed detachment of our party'.[4] 'The cult of the NKVD,' writes Khlevniuk, 'the special extra-legal status of the secret police, attained its apogee.' Stalin used the heads of the NKVD and rewarded them for their services, while controlling them with an iron hand. He distributed material rewards and severe punishments with equal arbitrariness. Several authors have seen an analogy here with the way that Ivan the Terrible used the *oprichnina* (his militia) in his struggle against the boyars.

This dual attitude is Stalin all over. Chekists – the historical term of honour that is still used today – were now separated from other party members, including socially, since they had their own dachas, clubs and other leisure facilities. In December 1937, huge ceremonies were held throughout the country to celebrate the glorious tradition of the Cheka–GPU–NKVD. The Kremlin called on regional party commit-tees to organize public trials of 'enemies of the people' in agriculture and the NKVD was instructed to 'unmask' – in fact, supply – them. Likewise, on the third anniversary of Kirov's assassination (29 November 1937), Stalin telegraphed local party authorities and ordered them to 'mobilize party members mercilessly to eradicate Trotskyite–Bukharinite agents'. Khlevniuk concludes that the whole apparatus, as well as the wider society, was in the grip of a truly psychotic hunt for enemies, punctuated by the descent of the secret police, usually in the early hours, to knock at the door, seize their victims, and transport them in sinister black vans to meet their fate.

CRIME AND PUNISHMENT IN THE NKVD (1935–50)

As we have already indicated, the NKVD's symbolic incorporation into the party – in other words, its attachment to Stalin personally – elevated it above all other institutions. The party now possessed its own iron guard, its crusaders, on whom Stalin lavished favours and honours. The Stalinist party – especially its own apparatus – itself became a police agency, with the qualification that the secret police deferred exclusively to Stalin and no one else in the party. It was therefore above the party and a powerful weapon with which to bludgeon it. Here an impertinent

---

4 Ibid., pp. 164–7.

question is in order: if the chekists were a valiant detachment in the service of morality and ideology, why were its leaders paid ten times more than a worker? The real chekists of the Civil War, who risked their lives, were poorly paid. Was it really necessary to pay those charged with representing the country's ideological vanguard in cash, material goods and privileges? Lenin would have turned in his grave – had his embalming not prevented him...

The irony of history extends still further. Praised to the skies, the NKVD was a bureaucracy with its own routines. An internal inspectorate was assiduous in watching over its smooth functioning. Its reports reveal an institution characterized by innumerable irregularities, professional ineptitude, shortcomings and thievery; and we find long lists of criminal acts that had been investigated and reported to higher bodies, with demands for severe sanctions.

A few examples may shed light. In a memo to the head of the NKVD's cadres department, comrade Veinshtok, who held the rank of major of state security, inventoried the misdemeanours and crimes committed by NKVD agents in 1935. The data supplied by agencies at all levels (from republics to regions) for the first ten months of the year indicated a total of 11,436 offences and crimes. The memo also contained a list of the measures taken by way of sanctions. According to Veinshtok, something was wrong with the administrative policies of regional and local NKVD agencies and the problem should be discussed. The total number of criminal cases was 5,639, of which 3,232 were accounted for by urban sections. But what most worried the major was the fact that 2,005 of those had been committed by section heads themselves.

A breakdown of the punishments by rank indicates that all categories in every branch were committing offences and crimes – whether in the military or transport units – and at every administrative level (heads, their deputies, and junior staff). Thus, of the 3,311 leading personnel at the level of district and town sections, 62 per cent (2,056) received penalties. As Veinshtok commented, it had to be admitted that this was a very high percentage indeed. Sixty per cent of the sanctions against regional agents were for negligence, poor work, drunkenness, debauchery, and other acts bringing the NKVD into discredit. Of these, particular attention should be paid to the high percentage of penalties imposed for disobeying orders and instructions (13 per cent), for breaches of discipline (8.5 per cent), or for infringement of procedural norms (5 per cent). The list also contains cases of embezzlement and misappropriation, concealment of social origins (67 cases), 'anti-party and anti-Soviet' attitudes (17), suicides and rapes (78 in total), lack of the vigilance expected of a chekist and party member (76), as well as false statements.

Most of the penalties fell on younger agents, mainly from auxiliary services like signals. But the number of sanctions against the hard core of NKVD personnel with twelve or more years of service was also deemed too high (1,171).[5]

A further report from the cadres department for the period 1 October 1936–1 January 1938 provides information on 'departures' from the GUGB (an independent agency within the NKVD). Among the reasons for these 'departures', we find 1,220 arrests, 1,268 dismissals and 1,345 transfers to the reserves. To these must be added 1,361 cases of punishment for membership of counter-revolutionary groups, or contact with counter-revolutionaries (Trotskyists), right-wing nationalists, traitors or spies; 267 for 'workplace disruption'; and 593 for 'moral turpitude'. Finally, we have 547 individuals who were 'socially alien', or in contact with such people, or who had served in the past with the Whites. Among the other various causes for departures from the GUGB were illness (544), death (138), or transfer to other agencies (1,258).

The reports indicate that things did not change until after Stalin's death. The inspection agencies carried on doing their work and a separate branch, with responsibility for financial controls, also had a lot to say about the high frequency of theft and embezzlement, counterfeit receipts, and false accounting. It paid particular attention to what was going on in warehouses and storage facilities.[6] In addition, there are annual accounting reports for use by the authorities (and by today's researchers), for the Stalinist period at least. In short, in terms of professionalism, respect for the law, and honesty, the security services were no better than the rest. Efforts were made to improve the quality of the personnel by bringing in thousands of cadres from the NKVD's own schools. But it took a long time for positive results to emerge.

Such documents on the party's own security force, poised to save the country from the enemy within, highlight a further dimension of this dark episode: the security services were packed with morally and professionally dubious elements. Commanders were pampered, but were

---

5 GARF, 940, 8, 46, LL. 1 and 9–15: a report to the head of the NKVD's cadres department.
6 GARF, 9401, 8, 45, LL. 4–5.

nevertheless demoralized and disoriented by the very character of the task assigned them. They did not have to prove anything, they were simply required to fulfil quotas and, as throughout the USSR's planned system, to surpass them to obtain bonuses, promotions and wage increases. But the sword they suspended over the head of the country also hung over their own heads – and not for drunkenness or debauchery. All the security services, including foreign intelligence, constantly lived on the brink of a catastrophe lurking within their own regime – and which was much more dangerous than spying or catching spies, combating smugglers or bandits, or facing the other risks associated with their work.

'MAN HUNT'

Many details about the mass arrests and executions first became available from a committee headed by the party secretary, Pospelov, which was set up by Khrushchev in 1955 prior to his 'secret speech' of 1956. In fact, the policy of rehabilitation had already begun in 1954. It is worth starting with this committee's disclosures, if only in order to appreciate how little was known about these horrendous events not only by the wider public, but even by the political elite itself.[7]

The Pospelov committee received documents from the archives of the secret police, as well as depositions from many interrogators–executioners who recounted how they had obtained confessions from their victims. The Prosecutor's Office also supplied the committee with a wealth of material. Stalin's personal role was clearly documented. Other documents showed that the 'troikas' (composed of the local party secretary, the head of the secret police, and the local prosecutor), which were responsible for the terror at the local level, kept pressing Moscow to increase the 'execution quotas', knowing full well that it was disposed to do so.

When Pospelov presented his committee's findings to the Party Presidium, a 'terrifying picture emerged that shocked all those present'. We may surmise that this reaction was not feigned. Few people could fully have imagined the mechanics and scope of what were basically secret operations. The statistics supplied principally concerned party

---

7   Our source here is R. G. Pikhoia, *Sovetskii Soiuz: Istoriia Vlasti, 1945–1991*, Moscow 1998, pp. 138–9 and *passim*.

leaders accused of treason, as well as the broad category of people arrested for 'anti-Soviet activity', who were mainly party and state cadres. On the other hand, Pospelov said nothing of the enormous category of 'socially alien elements'. For the fateful years of 1937–8, the report gave the figure of 1,548,366 persons arrested for anti-Soviet activity, of whom 681,692 were shot. Leading personnel in the state and party had been decimated at all levels. Those who replaced them had succumbed in their turn, as had their replacements, and so on. The majority of delegates to the 1934 Seventeenth Congress (the 'Congress of the Victors') – 1,108 of them – had been arrested and 848 shot.

The report also cited NKVD orders instructing agents how to conduct the repression and provided an idea of its methods: the outright confection of all manner of anti-Soviet organizations and centres; gross violations of the law by investigators; phoney plots invented by NKVD agents themselves; a total failure by the Prosecutor's Office to exercise due oversight over the NKVD; judicial arbitrariness on the part of the Military Collegium of the USSR's armed forces, which condoned 'extra-judicial procedures'.

According to the report, the source of the whole venture lay in the Executive Central Committee's authorization in December 1934, following Kirov's assassination, of action outside the law. Stalin and Zhdanov's telegram to Kaganovich and Molotov preparing the ground for the February–March 1937 Central Committee plenum was cited as the direct trigger for mass repression. Stalin's personal responsibility for the widespread recourse to torture of the accused was stated in numerous testimonies, including those of officers from the Internal Affairs ministry (MVD) who were themselves victims of the repression, and by three documents appended to the report: a telegram from Stalin dated 10 January 1939 reaffirming the validity of 'physical methods'; a memo giving his approval for the execution of 138 high-ranking offi cials; and the letter he received from P. I. Eikhe (Politburo member) prior to his execution. Between 1937 and 1939, Stalin and Molotov personally signed around 400 lists of people to be executed (a total of 44,000 names).

The aim of Pospelov's report was not simply to take stock of the past. Its content was also a burning issue in debates about policy and strategy, which we shall study in Part Two. The overall toll of the terror was much heavier, since the verdict of the 1950s mostly dealt with victims from the party's ranks.

10

THE SCALE OF THE PURGES

A complete history of the purges of 1937–8 may very well never come to be written. But if we wish to grasp a phenomenon that exceeds the bounds of the imagination, we need to consider different data. We shall begin with the estimates made by various agencies, which are sometimes difficult to interpret because they are based on different sources, calculations, figures and dates, but which nevertheless permit a reasonable approximation. For the pivotal phase of the purges – 1937–8 – we can turn to a text written by an ad hoc commission appointed by the Central Committee Presidium in 1963, and chaired by I. M. Shvernik.

According to some sources, the years 1937–8 saw the arrest of 1,372,392 people, of whom 681,692 were shot. The figures given by Khrushchev to the Central Committee plenum in 1957 were somewhat different: more than 1,500,000 arrested and 680,692 shot (the differences stem from the criteria employed by KGB statisticians). Sources for 1930–53 indicate 3,778,000 people arrested, of whom 786,000 were executed.[1]

Other data are concerned exclusively with the category of 'administrative repression' – i.e. handled by non-judicial bodies: the NKVD's 'special concilium' in Moscow and its equivalents at lower administrative levels, the aforementioned 'troikas' responsible for most of the ravages of 1937–8. They virtually had carte blanche and, as we have seen, pressed the Kremlin to increase their quotas. The NKVD's special concilium, set up on 10 July 1934, was an exceptionally industrious body: it condemned 78,989 people in 1934, 267,076 in 1935, 274,607 in

---

1 E. M. Adreev, L. A. Karskii and T. L. Khar'kova, *Vestnik Statistiki*, no. 7, 1990, p. 44 (derived from the KGB and quoted in *Izvestiia*, 14 February 1990).

1936, 790,665 in 1937, and 554,258 in 1938. If they were able to do such a 'great job', it was because they dispensed with procedural niceties. In most instances, the accused was not even present. A case might be dealt with in ten minutes, resulting in sentences of between five and twenty-five years in a camp or even immediate execution. Most of the victims were accused of 'counter-revolutionary activities' – hence the brevity of the trials and the quantity of executions.

The data produced by NKVD researchers themselves afford another source. The 'historic' Central Committee decree of 2 July 1937, which we have already mentioned, instructed the NKVD to destroy 'enemy groups'. Quotas for arrests were fixed in advance and transmitted to administrative regions for fulfilment, just like grain procurement campaigns. These quotas were subdivided into categories of crimes, and the sentences likewise prescribed. Thus, category 1 included 72,950 people to be arrested and executed, the total being divided between the different regions. Category 2 numbered 186,000 people to be transported to camps. Additional forestry camps were to be opened for this purpose, but rapidly became overcrowded. The whole procedure was truly Kafkaesque: the number of enemies was stipulated in a quota, but it was permissible to exceed it. It only remained to name the culprits.

The figures for annual arrests are as follows: on 1 January 1937, 820,881; on 1 January 1938, 996,367; and on 1 January 1939, 1,317,195. Of these totals, the labour camps received 539,923 prisoners in 1937 and 600,724 in 1938. That year, the influx into the Gulag peaked. In fact, 837,000 detainees were released from camps and colonies following a re-examination of their cases under Beria's authority during a 'rectification campaign' ordered by Stalin. In 1939, however, the repression resumed afresh and on 1 January 1940 the number of inmates of camps and colonies reached 1,979,729, most of them common-law prisoners. Political prisoners, condemned under the 'counter-revolutionary' articles of the criminal code, accounted for 28.7 per cent of the total, or 420,000-plus persons. The number of inmates was also increased by the transfer of prisoners from recently annexed territories, to whom we must add the people arrested following these annexations. The application of the decrees issued in 1940 and 1941 punishing theft and unauthorized departure from the workplace also helped to swell the numbers.[2]

---

2 *Organy i Vojska MVD Rossii, Kratkii Istoricheskii Ocherk: MVD 200 let*, Moscow 1996 (with chapters written by MVD [Ministry for Internal Affairs] experts, some of them more 'liberal', others still 'Stalinist').

The havoc wrought by the purges, particularly among party and state cadres, is not easy to assess numerically. A valuable source on turnover among personnel in the Railways Commissariat in 1937–8 indicates that 75 per cent of managers and technical officials (senior and middle-ranking cadres) were replaced in the course of these years.[3] These data cannot be extrapolated to the whole machinery of government, but they permit us to speak of a haemorrhage of cadres, even in the strategically most sensitive agencies.

The consequences of the terror were felt throughout the economy, the bureaucracy, the party, and in cultural life. By mid-1938, the human, economic and political damage and its cost were such that a change of course was essential and almost predictable. A 'normalization' was indicated and was conducted in the usual fashion: someone had to be 'named' as the culprit responsible for the 'deviations'. This was not a problem, since there were no innocents in this affair. The turn was signalled by the dismissal of Yezhov from his post as NKVD head and his replacement by his deputy, Beria, on 25 November 1938. Yezhov was arrested in April 1939 and accused – as the standard formula dictated – of being 'at the head of a counter-revolutionary organization'. He was executed in February 1940, in accordance with the same script as that of 1936 when the then NKVD head, Yagoda, was eliminated. Those in the know could begin to speculate about the next occurrence of the same scenario.

In the context of the 'new line', several hundred thousand people were released from the Gulag, but these were primarily common-law criminals, not political prisoners.[4] After the Eighteenth Party Congress, some victims of the purges were rehabilitated. Once again, however, this cosmetic operation involved only a limited number of people relative to the scale of the purges – just enough for Stalin to be able to

---

3 *Zhelezodorozhnyi Transport v Gody Industrializatsii SSSR (1926–1941)*, Moscow 1970, pp. 309–10, document no. 91 (from TsGANKh SSSR, f. 1884, op. 31, d. 2546, LL. 171–3). This is a report, dated 17 November 1938, from the cadres sector of the Commissariat to the Commissar himself on the morale of leading cadres on the railways. Table A (length of service) shows that of the 2,968 leading cadres in this strategically crucial commissariat, 75 per cent (from managers to middle-ranking officials and specialists) had been appointed to their jobs between 1 November 1937 and 1 April 1938. Of those they replaced, most were certainly dismissed or were victims of the purges.

4 The data here are for the most part derived from O. V. Khlevniuk, *1937-oi*, Moscow 1992.

appear as the one who restored justice and punished the guilty. Such benevolence was further displayed somewhat later by the arrest and partial massacre for a change of numerous NKVD agents, accused of going too far by attacking party members and innocent citizens. Between 22,000 and 26,000 of them joined their victims in camps or graves. No one knows whether this cohort included the worst of them. Still, it must have reassured many people. Khlevniuk maintains that in the course of 1939 self-confidence inside leadership circles returned: salaries were increased and arrests were now subject to more stringent rules. Moreover, the perceptible downplaying of Yezhov's agency after his demise persuaded party cadres that they had regained ground from the security apparatus, even if a number of regional and city party bosses were purged together with unworthy chekists for having deviated from the right path.

Khlevniuk also surmises that the retreat from mass terror resulted from Stalin's sense that he had attained his prosaic objective: rejuvenating the party's cadres. (We might note that the pedagogy employed to bring on young talent was rather unusual.) At the Eighteenth Party Congress in March 1939, Stalin announced that between April 1934 and March 1939 more than 500,000 cadres had been recruited to breathe new energy into state and party administration, particularly at the top levels. At the beginning of 1939, of the 32,899 post-holders forming part of the *nomenklatura* administered by the Central Committee (from People's Commissar to party official assigned to important duties by the Central Committee), 15,485 had been appointed in 1937–8. This figure is interesting, for it involves the post-purge cohort: the so-called 'Stalin promotion'. The rapidity of their advancement was phenomenal, given that they had often not finished their studies. Among them were those who would lead the USSR after Stalin's death.

After the loss of human life, the heaviest losses were suffered by the economy. Appointed immediately after the terror, new cadres found nothing but empty desks and chairs in their offices: obviously, their predecessors were not present to introduce them to their jobs. Inexperienced, many of the new arrivals were afraid to take the slightest initiative. The purges had destroyed discipline and undermined productivity (even if many in Russia insisted on asserting the opposite). Government agencies were now full of all sorts of morally dubious types. To remedy this situation, some 'honest specialists' were rehabilitated (assuming they were still alive) and released from the camps. Among them were military figures – future generals and marshals, scholars, strategy experts, engineers – like Rokossovsky, Meretskov, Gorbatov, Tiulenev, Bogdanov, Kholostiakov, Tupolev, Landau, Miasishchev, and so on. The outstanding ballistic-rockets expert Korolev had to wait until 1944, and many others remained in detention until 1956. But those who regained their freedom in 1939 represented quite a contingent. Some of them were not in a fit condition immediately after their release to resume work and thus could not help repair the damage inflicted on the army by the destruction of the high command and many of the lower ranks. In the summer of 1941, 75 per cent of field officers and 70 per cent of political commissars had been in post for less than a year, so that the core of the army lacked the requisite experience in commanding larger units. That the Red Army was scarcely battle-ready was amply demonstrated by the disastrous war with Finland in 1940. The highly accurate analysis of this 'victorious defeat' conducted by military and political leaders laid bare lamentable shortcomings in leadership, training, the officer corps, and coordination between different army corps. Yet the main culprit – Stalin – was never mentioned.

The dementia of 1937–8 would never be repeated on the same scale, even if it continued at a more modest level. In 1939, the party recruited a million new members and everything seemingly returned to 'normal'.

This abrupt retreat from mass terror – signalled, as we have said, by the elimination of Yezhov, who took the blame – was never acknowledged as such. Thereafter, a whole series of manoeuvres sought to camouflage it. It was claimed that the bulk of saboteurs had been eliminated, as had those who were guilty of excesses in combating them. Even so, the propaganda against 'enemies of the people' persisted, clamorous and insidious by turns, for the regime did not want it to be thought that enemies had altogether evaporated. The state's terrorist machinery and activity remained veiled in secrecy, even from otherwise well-informed top officials. The Politburo was imposing a 'rectification', but in a manner that bordered on the absurd, since it did it clandestinely, while denying that it was doing so.

Some now declassified documents from the presidential archive lift a small corner of the veil.[5] In the minutes of its 9 January 1938 session, the Politburo instructed Vyshinsky to inform the Prosecutor General that it was no longer acceptable to dismiss someone from a job just because a

---

5 TsKhSD, f. 89 (various minutes and other texts from this file have already been published).

relative had been arrested for counter-revolutionary crimes. This was a move in a 'liberal' direction, putting an end to the unspeakable suffering endured by many. But even if the relative in question was 'rehabilitated' – in other words, even if the state admitted its error – no one was to know of the regime's admission. An example: on 3 December 1939, the Supreme Court suggested to Stalin and Molotov that the revision of sentences for counter-revolutionary crimes should be carried out via a legal procedure – a welcome change! – but dealt with by a tribunal sitting in some simplified format. In other words, even if the tribunals acknowledged that errors had been made, everything was to be done to ensure that public attention was not drawn to such cases. In a similar vein, on 13 December 1939 Pankratov, USSR Prosecutor General, suggested to Stalin and Molotov that relatives should not be informed of the revision of sentences in cases where the victims had already been executed.

The government was likewise fearful that the methods used during interrogation would become public. To avoid this, Beria wrote to Stalin and Molotov on 7 December 1939 to say that defence lawyers and witnesses should not be admitted during 'preliminary investigations' (instigated to review illegal proceedings), 'in order to prevent disclosure of the way in which these investigations are conducted'. Even in this top-secret document, however, Beria was resorting to a ruse. What he actually meant was this: in order to prevent disclosure of what the current investigations revealed about the earlier ones. The very fact that they had involved torturing people (as ordered by Stalin personally), and forcing them to sign 'confessions', was never mentioned even in the most confidential exchanges. To put that on paper was to run the risk of some official coming across it and blurting it out. In other words: do not tell anyone that the enemies and saboteurs, above all those who were executed, were innocent; do not disclose how their confessions were extracted; or the fact that someone just rehabilitated has already been shot.

Two further Politburo decisions point up the limits of the 'retreat'.[6] On 10 July 1939 it instructed those in charge of NKVD camps to abolish the reductions in sentence that common-law criminals, and some political prisoners, could receive for good conduct. Sentences were henceforth to be served in full. Similarly, when it came to political

---

6 TsKhSD, *perechen'* 73, doc. no. 1, PB-TsK, no. 56, 9 January 1938.

charges, there was no question of abandoning a hard line. The infamous Chairman of the Supreme Military Tribunal, Ulrikh, proposed to Stalin and Molotov that in cases involving 'right-wing Trotskyists, bourgeois nationalists and espionage', defence lawyers should not be allowed to see the files or appear in court. Those who had been selected for such categorization continued to be targeted and suffered the same treatment at the hands of investigators as before. Without such methods, how could a 'right-wing Trotskyist' be flushed out?

So the veil of secrecy was to remain tightly drawn. Lawyers were excluded from tribunals, even if the law required their presence. Nothing was to transpire concerning the regime's errors, methods, or targets − even if they were actually in the process of being reviewed.

The paradoxes are unavoidable: the much-bruited struggle against enemies of the people was in fact a conspiracy organized by a government that knew full well it was committing illegalities on a mass scale. And this government intended to keep secret the errors it had made. Some changes were, of course, needed to reassure the deeply demoralized and frightened elites. They were sometimes made in public, sometimes through more discreet channels. Not unlike the persecutions, however, the 'retreat' had to be controlled. Getting the balance right required great skill. Stalin's close lieutenants admired his mastery − or said they did.

Stalin had reason to be satisfied after the purges. Now that most of the old cadres had been exterminated, he finally possessed a new system: his own. Many of those who had failed to be transported by admiration for him, or who considered him a traitor to the cause, had been destroyed. The ruling elite had been almost entirely renewed; society as a whole now seemed subdued. All of Stalin's acolytes, old and new, were cowed; the Politburo as a ruling body was virtually stripped of power. As we have seen, Stalin henceforth worked with a small group of sometimes just four people. The others had no information about 'secret matters' − and most things were secret. The party's leaders, hitherto briefed on a whole range of issues by regular bulletins, stopped receiving them. And the Central Committee, although sometimes summoned to 'debate' questions that had already been settled, lost its importance as well.

II

THE CAMPS AND THE INDUSTRIAL EMPIRE OF THE NKVD

The documents we are now going to focus on should make the scope and character of the camps and forced labour, and their organic connection with the Stalinist system, more tangible. Here there was no 'retreat'. We shall try to outline what might be called the NKVD's 'economic empire', briefly summarizing its main features and trends.

Students of the justice and prison systems during the 1920s (the NEP period) know that camps were intended to be a more humane form of detention than the 'cages' in what were called prisons: labour in conditions approximating to a normal workplace was considered the best means of re-educating and rehabilitating people. At the time, conditions in the camps were far from rigorous, with the exception of those that held political prisoners – notably on the Solovki Islands on the White Sea, which was the sole camp under the jurisdiction of the GPU. Serious criminals were, of course, closely guarded, but some of those detained worked in the camp during the day and returned home for the night. Courts sought to limit prison sentences, opting instead for penalties of 'obligatory labour' (*prinud-roboty*) – sometimes mistranslated in the West as 'forced labour'. The expression in fact meant keeping the same job, but paying a fine deducted at source for the term fixed by the sentence. The penal system was being experimented with; and the literature and debates on crime and punishment were public and innovative.

However, the liberalism of the NEP period in penal policy suffered from an objective limit: too little meaningful work for the re-education of prisoners. The country had a high unemployment rate and the unemployed had to have priority in access to work.

All this came to end in the 1930s, even if liberal notions lingered on for some time. Judges and criminologists fought a losing battle against the camps becoming an instrument of punishment through labour (in fact, forced labour), thereby losing their original purpose of re-education through labour. The new trend was a 'side effect' of hyper-industrialization. The labour of prisoners was easy to mobilize, cheap to exploit, subject to firm discipline – and not too difficult to replenish. The erstwhile liberals – still present in the Justice and Labour Commissariats (the latter was soon wound up) – fought in the government and party to prevent the prison system from relapsing into penal servitude. But the centre was set on its course – even if it resembled a quagmire in these years. The respite of sorts occasionally offered by the government involved no change in policy, but simply its consolidation and coordination.

The NKVD and its secret police inevitably became interested in playing a key role in the country's industrialization and they spearheaded the transformation of the prison system into an enormous industrial sector under their administrative control. Obviously, convicts were to furnish the manpower, so they had to be supplied in the maximum numbers possible. Mere policing was not a source of glamour for the NKVD. But as soon as industrialization became the national ethos, the NKVD could hope to see its prestige enhanced by assuming an important role in economic development thanks to the Gulag. As for the Politburo, if it did not initiate this new line, it was certainly very interested in it. The Justice Commissariat lost its responsibility for penal institutions, which were gradually turned over to the NKVD. The process was completed in 1934.

Here we must go into some detail about a complex administrative situation. Officially, it was the NKVD that absorbed the secret police proper, the OGPU. But in these years, 'security' was never what it seemed. In fact, it was the GPU component – renamed the GUGB[1] –

---

1   The GUGB – *Glavnoe Upravlenie Gosudarstvennoi Bezopasnosti* (General Directorate of State Security) – was the direct heir to the Cheka and the GPU. It could at any moment be detached from the broader NKVD and become an autonomous secret police agency. At various points, especially during and after the Second World War, the GUGB became the NKGB (People's Commissariat for State Security), then the MGB (Ministry of State Security), before being reintegrated into the NKVD or MVD for reasons that are not always clear. The definitive separation occurred in 1953 with the creation of the MGB, which was subsequently renamed the KGB.

that took over the whole NKVD from the inside, with its head assuming control of the Commissariat of Internal Affairs. This complication serves to illustrate the confusing character of Soviet administrative practices.

To oversee the prison system – camps, colonies, prisons – a new administrative agency was created, called Gulag (*Glavnoe Upravlenie Lagerei*), or General Camp Directorate. It also ran prisons and colonies for petty criminals and juvenile delinquents. A separate agency within it was responsible for people sentenced to terms of exile and isolation in resettlement colonies – kulaks, for example. This is just the start of the story. Around and in conjunction with the Gulag, the NKVD created a sizeable network of industrial administrative agencies for the construction of roads, railways and hydro-electric dams, mining and metallurgical enterprises, forestry, and the development of the Far East region (the *Dal'stroi*). Research and engineering projects in weapons production, including atomic weapons, were set up in special prison camps – the so-called *sharashki* – containing top specialists, among them Tupolev (planes) and Korolev (rockets).

The first NKVD showpiece was the construction of the White Sea Canal, launched with much fanfare in 1931–2 as the feat of dedicated prisoners and their chaperons, the secret police. These odes to Soviet labour and the working masses concealed a quite different reality: the work was done by unpaid workers stripped of all rights – in short, by slave labour.

Around the same time, confidential reports informed leaders about the headlong growth of the still rather young Gulag and the significance of its major construction projects. In 1935 the total number of prisoners listed on the supply rolls reached almost a million. Among the major projects were the construction of railways (in the Trans–Baikal region, along the Ussuri River, on the Baikal-Amur line); a series of canals, one of which connected Moscow and Volga; and numerous factories, sovkhozy and sawmills. Over time, the reports became more elaborate. In 1936, a map of the Gulag was drawn up. It identified sixteen sites with the term *lager'* attached to their names (Dmitrovskii *lager'*, Ukhto-Pecherskii *lager'*, Baikalo-Amurskii *lager'*, etc.). Those were not actual prison units, but central administrative hubs with prison establishments – camps and colonies – mushrooming around them. Each such centre had a representative of the Prosecutor's Office attached to it, sometimes assisted by a few aides. But despite their substantial salaries, their presence made no difference to what went on in the camps.

What did count was the system's ever more numerous officials –

administrative and operational – at central and local levels. Like every other bureaucracy, this one displayed a strong appetite for growth. At the beginning of 1940 the Gulag's administrative structure was inspected by a brigade of officials from the Finance Commissariat, who concluded that the apparatus was excessively bulky.[2] The Gulag was therefore ordered to create a commission to review its structure and personnel, with the help of the inspectors from Finance. It emerged from this review that the Gulag's central administration contained 33 departments employing 1,697 staff, to which should be added ancillary units. In total, the Gulag had 44 directorates and departments, 137 sections, and 83 offices – some 264 structural units that were oversized and duplicated each other's work. The brigade proposed cuts, mergers and other organizational changes that would make it possible to abolish 511 posts or 30 per cent of the total. The supply agencies in Moscow and Leningrad were to effect similar reductions, cutting 110 posts. The brigade wished to reduce the current number of administrative units from 264 to just 143, and the workforce from 1,696 to 1,186. They also wanted the local structures, with their 4,000 administrators and operatives, inspected, simplified and slimmed down. The report's charts and lists indicate an enormously complex system. We do not know what, if anything, changed in the light of its proposals.

There is no doubt that had it not been for the outbreak of war, the Gulag's apparatus would have carried on growing. The number of prison camps contained in the major regional units, invariably referred to by a geographical term, stood at 528 at the beginning of 1941, justifying further expansion of the Moscow-based directorates and their officials and personnel in the field. Like any other administration, they found all kinds of excuses for creating new offices – supplies, finances, coordination – with the connivance of those who benefited from the labour camps. And there was a noticeable tendency to create new agencies in Moscow or some other desirable large city, 'where they would have a good time without bothering at all about the camps' – the words of a State Control commission rather bewildered by what it discovered. It added that all these functionaries had nothing to do in Moscow, where there were already plenty of them.

However gruesome its function, any administration can engage in

---

2 RGAE, 7733, 36, 331, LL. 55–65, January 1940.

business as usual. This administration wanted to be like any other. The fact is, however, that it found itself heading a gigantic industrial empire.

THE MVD AS INDUSTRIAL AGENCY

In 1940, the Finance Commissariat received reports and memos on each of its industrial and other branches of economic activity from the NKVD (which, like all the other commissariats, subsequently took the title of ministry and became the MVD, or Ministry for Internal Affairs). In its case, this was probably the first occasion. Here the complex administrative system we have just referred to becomes even more intricate. Forty-two agencies filed reports, but only two units pertained to the Gulag's camps and colonies. All the rest were industrial directorates (paper, timber, fuel, agriculture, etc.). The reports were composed in the habitual idiom of an industry ministry planning its finances, costs, budgets, labour force and, of course, output.[3]

This activity shrank during the war on account of a reduction in the number of prisoners – zeks – many of whom were mobilized, frequently in 'punishment battalions' assigned the most dangerous offensives. Those who survived joined the ranks of ordinary units and were 'rehabilitated'. Many were hardened criminals, and it is easy to imagine how they behaved towards civilians in territories liberated from the Germans and, a fortiori, in areas conquered from them. Not a few of them were condemned to death or returned to the camps.

As a direct producer or subcontractor, the Gulag began to boom again after the war (see Appendix 1). Here I shall simply summarize the NKVD's operation as an 'industrial agency', basing myself on the reliable source of Marta Kraven and Oleg Khlevniuk.

Once the decision was taken to use the labour of camp inmates for economic tasks, the NKVD (renamed the MVD) became a key component of Stalinism. In 1952 its investments, which amounted to 12.18 billion roubles (9 per cent of gross domestic product), surpassed those of the petrol and coal ministries combined. Gross output of MVD industry was estimated at 17.18 billion roubles in February 1953 – only 2.3 per cent of the country's total production. But it was the leading producer of cobalt and pewter and was responsible for a third of nickel production

---

3 RGAE, 7733, 36, 218, LL. 330–50 – a report delivered to the Finance Commissariat at the start of 1940.

and a significant percentage of gold, wood and sawn timber (12–15 per cent). The plan for the early 1950s enhanced its weight and one of Stalin's last orders related to cobalt output.[4]

Scrutiny of the meticulous and regular reports on production, finance and manpower leaves no room for doubt as to the prosperity of this booming economic complex. However, a few sentences complaining about ministries not paying up – making it impossible to feed inmates properly – set one thinking. In fact, this huge, peculiarly archaic industrial–police conglomerate was, despite some advanced branches, in deep crisis. The working and living – dying – conditions of *zeks* could not sustain genuine industrial expansion. Sooner or later, one way or another, the system would have to be abandoned. We can get a realistic picture of the camps' problems from a report by Beria himself to Molotov in 1940.[5]

According to this report, the camp labour force, employed in constructing enormous factories, railways, port facilities and 'special sites' (for defence needs), or logging and producing timber for export, was not used to the full because the inmates were fed too little and clothed too badly to face the difficult climatic conditions. As of 1 April 1940, 123,000 exhausted inmates were unable to work for want of sufficient food and some tens of thousands of others were idle for lack of adequate clothing. These conditions were creating tension in the camps and entailed losses. The reason was that party and government directives about improving food and clothing supplies were not heeded by the Trade Commissariat. Worse still, every quarter, food and clothing supplies were actually dwindling. Eighty-five per cent of the stipulated flour and cereals were supplied, but as for the rest only half materialized, and barely a third in the case of clothing. Hence the growing number of sick and idle inmates.

The norms themselves require examination. Daily expenditure per *zek* was estimated at 4.86 roubles, whereas the plan projected 5.38 roubles.[6] Evidently, then, targets were not being met. But had they been, what would they have amounted to? We can only make some indirect estimates here. The cost of an armed guard was 34 roubles a day

4   Marta Kraven and Oleg Khlevniuk, 'Krizis ekonomiki MVD – konets 1940kh– 1950e gody', *Cahiers du Monde Russe*, XXXVI (1–2), January–June 1995, pp. 179–90.
5   RGASPI, f. 56, op. 1, d. 900, LL. 25–7: the Molotov papers.
6   RGAE, f. 7733, op. 36, d. 442, L. 192.

– six times more than an inmate. Since we do not know the precise date
of this statistic, we can use a reference-point closer to 1940: a German
general who was a prisoner of war in a Soviet camp cost 11.74 roubles a
day in 1948 and he did not have to work.

Inadequate food and clothing, hard, unpaid labour, hunger and illness
– these rendered many *zeks* unfit for work. Some – the more daring and
desperate among them – refused to do so. To this must be added high
internal crime and mortality rates, not to mention the phenomenon of
dokhodiagi – prisoners at the end of the road who were now nothing but
human wrecks. Against this backdrop, the Gulag's administration
emerges as an utterly obscene complex. It was a rather opulent empire –
a state within a state – with its complicated economic interests, its secret
police, its intelligence and counter-intelligence agencies, its educational
and cultural activities. The MVD was also in charge of the regular
police, border guards, recording demographic data and population
transfers, and aspects of local government. In short, it was a classic
product of the Soviet administration's propensity for size and centralization. Viewed from above, the simplest way of running this highly
centralized system was to have administrative pyramids supervising a
plethora of agencies under the auspices of a single head, flanked by four
or five deputies. The idea would have made some sense if the agencies
had been less inflated, or if they had possessed simpler organizational
structures. As it was, the reliance on 'pyramids' was a very costly illusion,
threatening the power hub itself with paralysis.

In the given climate, it was well-nigh impossible to interfere with a
monster like the MVD. Yet at the same time, problems were piling up
in the Gulag's empire – notably in its administration. Theft, embezzlement, false reporting, criminal treatment of *zeks* (beatings, even
killings) – all these were facilitated by the remoteness of the camps and
the secrecy surrounding them. The plentiful supply of cheap labour
rendered the MVD careless about its efficient employment. The general
tendency to expand bureaucracy and the surplus of cadres bred irresponsibility. The MVD wished to be the spearhead of the 'building of
communism' vaunted by Stalin's propaganda, which consisted in covering the country with massive construction sites that were useless and
expensive in equal measure. But other central government agencies,
such as the Finance Ministry, Gosplan, the Prosecutor General, or
inspectorates (e.g. the Mining Inspectorate), were not blind. They kept
appealing to the government to eliminate the secrecy that shrouded so
much irresponsibility and inefficiency, and so many serious violations of

the law. Maybe they were aware of the report by Kruglov, Internal Affairs Minister, stating that the cost of a *zek*, however low, was still superior to the value of what he produced. According to the minister, the only way to achieve a balanced budget was to extend the working day and increase labour norms. Such a conclusion is comment enough on Kruglov's expertise.

The party and state leadership, the Prosecutor General, the presidency of the Supreme Soviet, and many other leading figures were by now well aware of how things stood. They, like numerous party and state institutions, received a flood of letters from *zeks* containing complaints, appeals, accusations, political criticisms and denunciations. And to cap it all, honest party members in post in the camps or neighbouring regions, and even some camp administrators conscious of their responsibilities, secretly forwarded desperate letters and reports about the terrible living conditions endured by inmates, their exhaustion, and the mortality rate. Thus the problem was not a lack of information: the government was informed of the situation down to the smallest details. At the top, however, the prevailing philosophy was 'So what?' Or worse still, the situation was contemptuously shrugged off: they're feigning it all, malingering . . .

As in other spheres, however, we observe a certain unrest heralding changes. Even at the height of Stalinism, it began spontaneously and surreptitiously in government agencies. Everyone knew that the low labour productivity of *zeks* was a major problem, discussed by the government. An extended, interesting analysis by a *zek* had reached the Central Committee. It demonstrated that prison labour was wasted and that the administration displayed not the least concern for productivity. Its author – a certain Zhdanov – proposed that camps be retained only for dangerous criminals; all other convicts should serve their sentences in their own workplaces as obligatory but free labour. Kruglov attempted to refute these arguments (and those of other letters cited in their support), but soon most heads of MVD production branches requested authorization to pay prisoners a partial wage in order to improve their productivity. In some camps, prisoners even began to receive a full wage. And on 13 March 1950 the government decided that a form of payment should be universally introduced.

While the MVD continued to trumpet its achievements as if nothing had happened, many economic officials realized that the camps were incapable of employing *zek* labour efficiently and that relying on such manpower was becoming a drain on resources. MVD 'planning' had an eerie quality to it: even though it paid the *zeks* next to nothing, it was in deficit. Given this anomaly, the economic system, in order to progress, had to acknowledge the superiority of civilian industry employing wage-labour. The police component of the industrial system was not only inefficient, it was moribund. Like its begetter, it was on course for self-destruction and threatened to take the whole edifice with it. This was evident to many administrators, economists and politicians, some of whom understood that lancing this boil was a precondition for reviving the system.

The search for ways to 'resuscitate' the forced-labour sector, by motivating its manpower, began even before Khrushchev's arrival in power. Different camp administrators had tried out modest changes with the utmost discretion, well before the gravity of the problem and the need to intervene had been acknowledged at the top by the Finance and Justice ministries, Gosplan, and their opposite numbers in the party apparatus. Some offered *zeks* a reduction in their prison terms – for example, one day in exchange for three days' productive labour. This practice had existed before the war, but was abolished in 1939. By 1948 it was being restored in many branches. And on 19 January of that year, the deputy head of Gosplan, Kosiachenko, deemed it worthy of consideration in a letter to Molotov.[7]

Whether as a consequence of this or not, a more radical reform was set in train. Prison terms were cancelled altogether and detainees were employed in their jobs as free wage-earners. In April 1952 the Council of Ministers studied these measures and issued a decree liberating some prisoners before the end of their sentences, on condition that they carried on working for MVD ventures as wage-earners. The MVD itself began to prefer to deal with relatively free manpower, thereby acknowledging the inefficiency of forced labour. Various partial changes were implemented in different sites with high numbers of *zeks*, and it became apparent that the next step was the total abolition of forced labour.

THE NEW 'DESIGNS' FOR *DAL'STROI* (NOVEMBER 1948)

One of the pilots for this was the enormous *Dal'stroi* MVD complex in the Far Eastern province, where 120,000 *zeks* worked. A wage, as well as

---

7 RGAE, f. 4372, 95, 672, L. 26.

other measures intended to stimulate productivity, had been introduced. Under pressure from the Ministry of Non-Ferrous Metals, *Dal'stroi* played a pioneering role in this transition. Those in charge of the Volga-Don Canal soon emulated them – unless they adopted the same approach at the same time. The *Dal'stroi* complex became fully self-financing and its procedures spread almost everywhere.[8]

According to Kraven and Khlevniuk, the 'thaw' of the Khrushchev period, already adumbrated in these moves, would have happened anyway, quite independently of the calculations and manoeuvrings of leaders at the top. The reason for the 'de-gulagization' (my term) was the crisis of the Gulag and its forced labour. By now, the MVD was finding it difficult to cope with the camps. The latest waves of arrests had brought with them many recalcitrant opponents – in particular, experienced military officers – in addition to hardened criminals. Refusal to work occurred on a mass scale and former officers were masters in the art of neutralizing informers and secret agents in the camps, undermining a proven system of espionage and making it increasingly difficult to recruit new informers. Moreover, there was a shortage of guards, at the very moment when acts of insubordination – even rebellion – were on the increase (the first of them occurred in 1942). The MVD sought to keep all this secret, despite the flood of letters of protest sent to Moscow, which it met with stubborn denials. But criticism and condemnation were now coming from guards themselves, as well as from prosecutors, at a point when the MVD was requesting more armed guards from the government in order to reinforce the camp regime – a confession of its inability to cope. In 1951, the number of 'refusals to work' climbed to a million days in 174 camps, colonies and other penal institutions. The bankruptcy of the Gulag, both as an economic and a penal organization, was irremediable.[9]

Immediately after Stalin's death, the changes were accelerated and the inevitable decision to destroy the very basis of the MVD's system of forced labour was finally taken. On 18 March 1953 the Prime Minister, Malenkov, transferred most of the MVD's industrial directorates to civilian ministries, while the penal establishments, with their inmates, reverted to the Justice Ministry, restoring the pre-1934 situation. On 27 March a further decree freed 1 million detainees out of a total of 2.5 million. During the same month, the order was given to discontinue

8   RGAE, f. 7733, op. 36, d. 2998.
9   Kraven and Khlevniuk, 'Krisis ekonomiki MVD . . .'

several major MVD projects: the Turkmenistan grand canal, the Volga–Baltic network of canals, several hydro-electric dams and major irrigation systems. These enormous construction sites – especially the canals – used huge quantities of forced labour and, in its reports, the MVD continually prided itself on its role in such chimerical wonders, which pandered to Stalin's penchant for the gargantuan. Khlevniuk surmises that higher governmental circles must have realized that such projects were ruinously expensive. And it was for the same reason that as early as 1950 Beria, responsible for the MVD in his capacity as Deputy Prime Minister, had envisaged reforming the huge ministry. But as long as Stalin was alive, no one dared put the issue on the official agenda. The only thing to do was to let factors inducing spontaneous decay do their work, as well as the courageous protests of unjustly imprisoned people. Only with Stalin's death were many of these glorious ventures liquidated as useless for economic development, dealing a decisive blow to the forced-labour system.

OMINOUS FIGURES

We now know a lot more about the number of Gulag inmates and other relevant data.[10] For a long time, wild speculation raged over the issue, sometimes giving rise to amazing exaggerations. We shall leave it to the authors of such hyperbole to explain what purpose they served. In addition to the human losses attributable to the camp system, we are now in a position to tackle another question statistically: namely, the number of political arrests per year for virtually the whole pre- and post-Stalinist periods, as well as the sentences imposed on the accused.

The toll in human life due to events such as the famines, the forced exile of the kulaks, and other calamities is more difficult to quantify precisely and uncontroversially. The best way of assessing it is via demographic studies that calculate excess deaths for the relevant periods. Such studies encompass all the events and political measures that might have caused such deaths. They also allow us to identify losses caused not by increased mortality, but by reduced birth rates. These are losses too.

---

10 I have published various tables in the appendix to my *Russia – USSR – Russia* (New York, 1995), compiled from reliable sources. Similar data have been published by Arch Getty, Gabor Rittersporn and V. N. Zemskov in *The American Historical Review*, vol. 98, no. 4, 1993, pp. 1017–49.

Yet the unborn cannot be directly included among the regime's victims, since they did not endure the terror. Readers can refer to the statistics and other data provided in the appendices.

I shall restrict myself to synthesizing the statistical material available for the period from 1921 to mid-1953 (the details can be found in Appendix 1).[11] Over the course of these thirty-three years, the total number of arrests for primarily political reasons (the charge of 'counter-revolutionary crimes') was 4,060,306 persons. Of these, 799,455 were sentenced to death; 2,634,397 were sent to camps, colonies and prison; 423,512 were banished – in other words, either forbidden to reside in some specified place (*vysylka*) or deported to a particular settlement (*ssylka*); and 215,942 fell into the category of 'others'. Given the enormous increase in the number of arrests from 1930 onwards, we may legitimately separate the figures for 1921–9 from the specifically Stalinist toll. In 1929, the number of arrests, already higher than in the previous year, reached 54,211 and included 2,109 death sentences. But it was not of the same order as the figure for the subsequent year, which leapt to 282,926 and included 20,201 death sentences.

We also possess other data, calculated by the KGB under Khrushchev, for the period 1930–53: 3,777,380 people had been arrested for 'counter-revolutionary crimes' and the number of death sentences was around 700,000 – the majority during the 1937–8 purges.

The intensity of the persecution, the criminalization of activities hitherto regarded as legal, and the inflation in the number of utterly fictitious crimes are no doubt good indicators of the degree of 'social peace' enjoyed by the system and the level of composure that prevailed in the state. Notwithstanding a surge in repression in 1928, and especially 1929, the total for 1921–9 is inferior – or just slightly superior – to that for 1930 alone.

In the first half of 1953, the repressive apparatus was suddenly checked and the figures become comparatively low: 8,403 arrests, with 198 death sentences, 7,894 prison sentences of various sorts, 38 exile or deportation sentences, and 273 'others'. At Stalin's death, 600,000 political prisoners were still detained in camps or prisons. By the end of 1954 the figure had fallen to 474,950. On Khrushchev's initiative, the regime had begun to review the Stalinist policy of terror.

According to some estimates, between 1934 and 1953 about 1.6

11 B. P. Kurashvili, *Istoricheskaia Logika Stalinizma*, Moscow 1996.

million inmates, including common-law prisoners, died in captivity. Mortality was somewhat higher among political prisoners, of whom half a million died in these twenty years. Thus, over a period of thirty-three years, around 4 million people were sentenced for political crimes and 20 per cent of them shot – the overwhelming majority from 1930 onwards.

Detailed calculation of Stalin's other victims is more difficult, but there are nevertheless reliable data. In 1930–2, some 1,800,000 peasants regarded as kulaks were exiled to the so-called 'resettlement areas for kulaks' (*kulakskaia ssylka*) supervised by the secret police. At the beginning of 1932, only 1,300,000 were still there: the remaining half a million had died, fled, or been released after review of their sentences. Between 1932 and 1940, these 'kulak settlements' registered 230,000 births and 389,521 deaths; 629,042 people had escaped, of whom 235,120 were caught and returned to their settlement. From 1935 onwards, birth rates exceeded mortality rates: between 1932 and 1934 there were 49,168 births and 271,367 deaths, but between 1935 and 1940 181,090 births were recorded as against 108,154 deaths.[12]

Without going into details, we might add that the great majority of kulaks did not perish. Most fled their villages and scattered throughout the country among Russians or Ukrainians. They got themselves hired on the major projects of the five-year plan, which were constantly short of labour and ready to accept anyone without asking too many questions. The exiles gradually had their rights restored to them and their case was closed. Some went into the army, while others were simply rehabilitated. By 1948 the kulak resettlement colonies under police surveillance had been closed.

We are thus dealing with a significant number of victims of the terror – a mass that there is no need to inflate, manipulate or falsify. It remains to add to the toll a further sad category: demographic losses in the broad sense. In order to sort out the complicated picture for the period 1914–45, we must turn to a specialist in historical demography: Robert Davies.[13] The figures here concern the history of the Russian population for the whole period. But the Stalinist phase within it is clearly distinguished.

In Russia–USSR, two world wars and a civil war occasioned greater

---

12 Ibid., pp. 161–2 and GARF, f. 9479, op. 1, d. 89, 205 & 216.
13 R. W. Davies, *Soviet Economic Development from Lenin to Khrushchev*, Cambridge 1998.

demographic losses (or population deficits) than elsewhere. These are measured both by 'excess deaths' – from violence, famine and epidemics – and by 'birth deficit', due to a temporary drop in birth rates. For the First World War and the Civil War, excess deaths are estimated at 16 million and the birth deficit at some 10 million. For the Second World War, the corresponding figures are 26–27 million and 12 million.

Stalinist industrialization also led to excess deaths in peacetime of the order of 10 million or more, many of them during the 1933 famine. Thus, total population loss for 1914 to 1945 from premature deaths and birth deficits amounted to 74 million: 26 million in 1914–22, 38 million for 1941–5, and 10 million in the peacetime years. Davies furnishes no figures for the birth deficit for this last period, but his work does aid us to have done with the fictitious body-counts in which anything goes as long as the record of 'communism' is drenched in ever more blood. When, for example, 80 million corpses are laid at its door, we might wonder: why not twice as many?

12

ENDGAME

At the war's close, the country was exhausted and the vast territories occupied by the Germans, or which had formed military theatres, were literally devastated. In the reconquered territories there was no economy to speak of and no government. The Soviet system had to be completely reconstructed, initially without an economic base and among populations that contained many former collaborators.

I shall restrict myself to one point about the reconstitution of the Soviet system in these regions. Finding cadres for the reconquered territories was an immense task, conducted in conditions of utter chaos. Newly appointed personnel often had to be replaced several times over, because they were incompetent, unreliable, or criminal elements who had penetrated the administration. Cadres assigned from areas that had escaped German conquest were often of poor quality and inclined to abandon a difficult job and return home. In the Ukraine, Lithuania and Latvia, strong detachments of nationalist insurgents fought Soviet troops and security forces, sometimes in pitched battles, with heavy losses on both sides. It took the regime time and effort to subdue these partisans. But work resumed, factories were rebuilt, and life slowly returned to normal.

Recovery and the restoration of social and economic indicators to their prewar levels – especially for agricultural output – had been achieved by the time of Stalin's death. But his disappearance from the scene was insufficient wholly to rid the USSR of his legacy – especially since postwar reconstruction involved restoring a decaying Stalinist model with its aberrations and irrationalities.

The return of peace confronted the state and party, hitherto wholly absorbed in the war effort, with unanticipated realities. The state bureaucracy – the main organizer of the war – now had to face the problems of reconversion. For the party and its apparatus, things were even more complicated. Whatever the propaganda, between 1941 and 1945 the party apparatus had been demoted to an auxiliary role. Certainly, Politburo members ran the war machine via the State Defence Committee, but they did so under Stalin's rod of iron as leaders of the state, not the party. The Central Committee was in abeyance and no party congress had been convened.

To put the party's house in order, Stalin brought in the well-known Leningrad party leader Alexis Kuznetsov, who had distinguished himself during the siege of the city as Zhdanov's second in command. He became party secretary for cadres, a member of the Politburo, and was thought to be being groomed by Stalin to succeed him. This was not an enviable lot for a beginner caught up in the complex power apparatus around Stalin. His prerogatives were considerable, but the task ahead was daunting. He was responsible for supplying high-quality, politically reliable leaders for all important state agencies. To do this, he was to supervise the work of the party's cadres directorate, which had been reorganized to tackle the job. The priority was to find qualified personnel for positions of responsibility in the most important branches of the economy throughout the country.

Reorganizing the party was another order of the day. If the personnel of the party apparatus were in a permanent state of flux, its structures remained more or less the same hereafter. This is why the new structure that emerged is sufficiently instructive to warrant us going into some detail.

It was now decided that the head of the cadres directorate would have five deputies and that it would contain twenty-eight departments (instead of the previous fifty), each of them responsible for overseeing a group of ministries or other government agencies. A single personnel department and a few sectional services were envisaged for the whole directorate.

Of the twenty-eight departments, one would deal with cadres for party organizations, another with the training and retraining of cadres, and a third with the cadres of Soviet institutions (armed forces, internal affairs and foreign trade). State security services, the Prosecutor's Office and justice came under the same department. Similarly, a department was projected for transport and for each branch of industry, as well as for agriculture, finance, trade, higher education and research, publishing, the arts, and so on. In short, the new directorate was a bulky piece of machinery, employing some 650 senior officials. Probably the largest of the Central Committee's apparatuses, it was organized on functional lines – until, two years later, it reverted to the older 'economic branch' structure. Meanwhile, the new secretary's position gave him sight of everything, including the most secret institutions, for they all needed the cadres his directorate supplied and controlled – or at least was beginning to supply and control.

Kuznetsov's (unpublished) speeches and conversations with his subordinates allow us to conclude that he was a man of considerable intelligence. His organizational abilities, and the ease with which he earned the esteem of the apparatus, attest to his calibre. The attempt to reconstruct and revitalize the party and its apparatus was, of course, coordinated with Stalin. When it came to organizational matters, Kuznetsov was clearly his own man. On ideology, however, he had to toe the line. Accordingly, before continuing our discussion of reforms in the party apparatus we must introduce these 'ideological questions', and especially a novelty that stemmed from Stalin's growing identification with Tsarist symbols during the war. The new ideological line directly concerned the party's central cadres, who were now subject to reindoctrination in common with various social groups and administrative bodies.

ZHDANOVISM AND THE 'COURTS OF HONOUR' (1946–50)

Zhdanovism – named after its chief proponent, Andrei Zhdanov, at the time party secretary – refers to an especially obscurantist chapter in the history of Stalinism.[1] Since this policy, which ravaged the country's cultural life, is studied in all histories of Soviet literature, we have opted to deal with it exclusively through unpublished documents from the party apparatus.

The main target of Zhdanovism was the professional intelligentsia, which was accused of 'fawning on the West' and taxed with 'cosmopolitanism' (a term that conveyed the regime's barely concealed anti-Semitism in these years). But its spirit profoundly marked the state and

---

[1] Good accounts of Zhdanovism can be found in histories of Soviet literature. A useful concise account is M. Slonim, *Soviet Russian Literature: Writers and Problems, 1917–1967*, New York 1967, chapter 26.

party apparatuses, which employed large numbers of people with higher education. An expression of extreme Russian nationalism, Zhdanovism attacked manifestations of nationalism in the non-Russian republics. The introduction into high party and government spheres of the archaic-sounding 'courts of honour' contradicted any minimally coherent administrative logic, and significantly frustrated efforts to raise the professional level of the party apparatus. These 'courts' were supposed to instil in apparatchiks a sense of patriotism and pride in the unique achievements of their (Stalinist) fatherland, by means of staged mock-trials in every administrative agency. The culprits were accused of all manner of infamies, but only their careers suffered (they escaped with their lives). In sum, these 'courts' judged 'crimes' approximating to treason, but which were not subject to criminal prosecution.

The practice was explained by Kuznetsov in a report to the full party apparatus on 29 September 1947. The target of such measures was individuals with higher education, including the growing number of specialists. The central apparatus was not considered immune from the relevant disease and the report was presented during a meeting convened to elect the 'court of honour' for the Central Committee's own apparatus – an election that gave the signal for similar elections throughout the country's administrative bodies. The professed aim was to combat behaviour displaying servility to the West.

A court was likewise established in the State Security Ministry (MGB). Its operatives were seemingly irked by being subjected to such a procedure, but Kuznetsov informed them that if such courts were required in the central party apparatus – the country's citadel – then there was no reason to exempt the MGB. Its members also had progress to make when it came to patriotism and 'spiritual independence' – the only things that could ensure recognition of the superiority of Soviet culture over that of the West.

Kuznetsov's argument ran as follows. In so far as the country's activity depended on the quality of the party apparatus, the 'courts of honour' had a decisive role to play. The apparatus harboured numbers of employees who engaged in anti-patriotic, anti-social and anti-state deviations. Hitherto, when such instances had been discovered, they had been handled internally with the utmost possible discretion. This stemmed from the widespread belief that once someone had become a member of the apparatus, there was no further need for vigilance or political improvement. But many officials seemed not to appreciate that their work in the central apparatus – that 'holy of holies' (the expression is used in the report) – was not a routine job, but a party duty. Dissolute behaviour was even to be found among leading figures, Kuznetsov observed – something that was absolutely inadmissible in the party's ranks, let alone the apparatus of the Central Committee. Drunkenness, debauchery, and negligence when handling confidential documents were among the most frequent misdemeanours cited. Such derelictions were highly dangerous, because the Central Committee received reports on all aspects of the country's activities, including defence and foreign policy. For this reason, any work performed in the apparatus, whatever the position held, must remain confidential. Vigilance was the party's best weapon against its enemies; it must form an inviolable principle of national life.

There was a disturbing but evident undercurrent to this policy. During the meeting, it was officially stated that the new line drew its inspiration from the methods of the great purges. Some of the key signposts of the latter were actually cited as useful reminders. Among them were the 'confidential' letters addressed to party members that had marked the launch of purges: the letter of 18 January 1935 concerning actions against 'Kirov's murderers'; the letter of 13 May 1935 on party members' cards; the 29 July 1936 circular on the Trotsky–Zinoviev 'terrorist bloc'; the 29 June 1941 circular to party and state agents operating near the front. All of these preceded or followed the unleashing of waves of terror against the population in general and cadres in particular. The shadow of this dark epoch was deliberately invoked to serve as a warning to a potentially disloyal intelligentsia. Stalin's speech on vigilance during the hallucinatory 1937–8 Central Committee sessions – another 'classic' on the best way to deal with enemies – was also cited.

Such was the spirit of a campaign gearing to inculcate nothing less than 'spiritual independence'. The foreign espionage factor was also employed. The apparatchiks were informed that Western intelligence services were seeking to penetrate the party and that their families were not immune: 'You tell your wife something, she tells a neighbour – and everyone gets wind of state secrets.' Anyone in the least familiar with Stalin's way of criticizing party officials and leaders would recognize his own inimitable style here. In fact, the condemnation of 'family chatterboxes' by members of the apparatus was based on a recent episode: in 1948, the government had decided in the utmost secrecy to raise prices, but the decision had become known to the population before its promulgation, resulting in a mad scramble for the shops.

The purges accompanying Zhdanovism never reached anything like the scale of 1936–9, but they nevertheless gave rise to such atrocities as the execution of the writers of the Jewish Anti-Fascist Committee, the assassination of the great actor Mikhoels (in a rigged car accident), numerous arrests and executions of cultural figures, not to mention careers ruined and artistic and scientific works destroyed. In 1950 came the 'Leningrad affair': all the old leaders of the Leningrad party and administration – including Kuznetsov himself and the Deputy Prime Minister and Gosplan head, Voznesensky – were executed and more than a hundred others perished or were sent to camps.

The ideology of the *zhdanovshchina* was Stalin's own, of course – the culmination of his ideological peregrinations. Stalin was by now fascinated by the 'glorious' Tsarist past. The 'courts of honour' were not the only thing he borrowed from its history. All the ministerial top brass now wore a uniform and their titles derived directly from Peter the Great's 'table of ranks'. Worse than the external paraphernalia was the extreme Russian nationalism, savouring of proto-fascism, typical of decaying Stalinism. Stalin wanted this spirit to survive him. To this end, he personally revised the new Soviet anthem, imposing on a multinational country a chauvinist paean to 'Great Russia'.

It is worth adding that the 'courts of honour' and the archaic titles and uniforms (with their ridiculous epaulettes) were abolished or abandoned under Khrushchev, to be quickly forgotten by an administration that had little time for such antics. And the putrid fumes of Zhdanovism largely dissipated.

All this is important for understanding the atmosphere that suffused the country when Kuznetsov tackled the important task of rationalizing the work of cadres, in the first instance in the party. His idea was to treat them firmly but fairly, and expect the appropriate response. The difference in tone and spirit between Kuznetsov's public explanation of Zhdanovism in 1947 and his frank and rational discussions with colleagues in 1946–7, is striking. It prompts the question as to whether he fully approved of Zhdanovism.

THE NEW APPROACH

New sources – in particular, the minutes of closed meetings of the cadres directorate, probably something unprecedented in the history of the apparatus – offer a sense of how the Politburo intended to put its own house in order. In the first place, this involved an attempt to redefine the functions of the whole apparatus, to clarify the division of labour within it, and – no less important – to change the way in which the central apparatus ran the economy. Astonishing as it might seem, the apparatus was to disengage from any direct involvement in economic management.

The functions and spheres of operation of party and state were henceforth to be redefined and separated. According to the new organizational doctrine, the Central Committee was a body charged with setting policy orientation, which it conveyed to the government. Through its personnel management, the party was responsible for the leading cadres of the state. Its mission consisted in the ideological education of the nation and supervision of its local organizations.

There was nothing inherently new about this, but the apparatchiks were surprised to learn that the Central Committee would no longer be dealing directly with economic questions. Its economic departments, such as those for agriculture and transport, were abolished. The main task of the apparatus was now to manage the party itself and supervise cadres in each domain, but without concerning itself with the details of their activities or the way in which they fulfilled their duties. The Central Committee would, of course, continue to issue directives, including on the economy, to the government. And in the context of its responsibility for supervising the cadres in government bodies, it did involve itself indirectly in monitoring economic policy. Finally, the party's local bodies, such as regional committees fulfilling 'executive functions', continued to supervise economic activity, as in the past. Their responsibilities were not a carbon copy of the Central Committee's.

To introduce some clarity into the ever more obscure division of labour between the two bodies situated immediately below the Politburo – the Orgburo and the Secretariat – it was decided that the former should take responsibility for local party organs. It summoned them, listened to their reports, and proposed improvements – though this was not how party statutes had previously defined its role. Its meetings were regular and their dates were fixed in advance. For its part, the Secretariat was a permanent body. It met each day, even several times a day, as and when required. It prepared the agenda and relevant materials for Orgburo meetings, and checked that the decisions taken by it and by the Politburo were properly implemented. It was also responsible for the distribution of leading cadres throughout the system via the appropriate departments.

Helping local party organizations to control state and economic bodies effectively; criticizing them; taking responsibility for political leadership of the masses: these were the main concerns of the top party leadership – and these were the terms in which they were defined.

The sources available to us shed light on the reasons for this disengagement from economic matters at the summit. The party's local bodies – all those below the Central Committee – were in a far from healthy condition; and even the Central Committee itself was in a spot of trouble. The main cause for anxiety was party officials' widespread dependency on, and submission to, economic ministries.

One aspect of this dependency was what has been called 'self-procurement' (*samosnabzhenie*), which covered various practices. Heads of government agencies, particularly those of economic ministries and their local branches, offered party bosses illegal inducements in the form of premiums, prizes, bonuses, valuable gifts, and services of all sorts – construction of dachas, house repairs, reservations in comfortable sanatoria for local party secretaries (and their families, of course). All of this was at the state's expense. According to our source, such economic cushioning of the party elite 'assumed vast proportions'.

Further information on this score derives from another Kuznetsov document, dating from late 1947. The Politburo had just issued a stern decree against the rewards offered to party officials by economic managers. During the war the practice had been generalized, and it was now ubiquitous, 'from top to bottom'. In these times of rationing and low living standards, the situation more closely approximated famine than simple everyday shortages. Many members of the party hierarchy actually engaged in illegal requisition – even extortion – of food and other merchandise from economic bodies. These were, of course, crimes. According to Kuznetsov, they were 'in essence a form of corruption that makes representatives of the party dependent on economic agencies'. The latter were prioritizing their own interests over those of the state they were supposed to represent. If the defence of state interests was to take precedence over private interests, how could party cadres ensure it when improvement in their own material situation depended on bonuses and benefits from economic managers?

Such cases of corruption, in which economic ministries 'remunerated' party officials throughout the country – some of them highly placed in the apparatus – had been uncovered and reported to Stalin by his right-hand man, Lev Mekhlis, Minister of State Control. Kuznetsov clearly had access to this information. Numerous documents which I have collected indicate that many local apparatchiks and their bosses expended much of their energy laying their hands on housing, goods and bribes – when they were not organizing profligate binges where the alcohol flowed, at the expense of local soviet or government agencies. Inspection authorities reported in enormous detail on the number of bottles of alcohol drained, their cost, the total bill charged by the restaurant that had supplied the food, and the name of the public institution that had paid for all this. Bribes were not simply offered; they were solicited, even demanded. The offices of the State Prosecutor were heaving with documents concerning cases against party bosses accused of misconduct or criminal behaviour.

Local party leaderships were manifestly in poor shape after the war. The central apparatus was perfectly well aware of the situation, but did not report it because it did not attribute much significance to such behaviour, which was so widespread that everyone had grown used to it. However, it was said that Stalin had declared such pillaging of national resources to be a crime. For Kuznetsov, bribes created cosy 'family' relations, making party organizations playthings in the hands of economic managers. 'If this situation persists, it will spell the end of the party', he declared: it was imperative for 'party organizations to recover their independence'. For those who regarded party primacy as firmly established, this phrase would have come as a surprise. It is clear that he was repeating what he had heard during a closed meeting of the cadres directorate in 1946, shortly after his appointment. A consultation of this kind, with all the ranks of the apparatus present, had possibly never occurred before. Kuznetsov had asked participants to be frank and had heard plenty: heads of department in the directorate itself were super-bureaucrats, inaccessible to their subordinates; they formed cliques and enjoyed special privileges; the hierarchy was very strict and did not allow for any party camaraderie; finally, the climate of secrecy was stifling. No less revealing was the apparatchiks' appraisal of important ministers: they were perceived as feudal lords who looked down scornfully on officials. Someone had interjected: 'When did you last see a minister come and visit us in the Central Committee?' And someone else added: 'Not even a deputy minister!'

It is interesting to note – and Kuznetsov himself was sensitive to this – how many of the criticisms, especially when uttered by younger, 'instructor'-level apparatchiks, were imbued with idealism and the bitterness they felt in seeing their expectations dashed. Kuznetsov had even heard a phrase he did not anticipate (and nor did a researcher like me, some fifty years later!): 'We [the party] have lost power!' (*my poteriali vlast'!*). All this is recorded in the minutes of the 1946 meeting. So it is scarcely surprising if a year later Kuznetsov declared that party organizations needed to regain their 'independence'. He did not even have to specify from whom. The party's 'economization' was the curse that was alarming its leadership as never before.

At stake was the very existence of the party as a ruling institution. During the war, its transformation into a ministerial appendage had accelerated, with a consequent loss of power. This was not surprising: the ministries had indeed been responsible for the war effort and its most glamorous activities. The party apparatus was being bought off and corrupted by managers, who increasingly dealt exclusively with the Council of Ministers and ignored the Central Committee and its *nomenklatura*. There is abundant data on such disregard for the '*nomenklatura* rules' (a term we shall return to).

Extricating the central apparatus from any direct involvement in economic affairs and agencies – from economics *tout court* – apart from general guidelines and oversight of cadres, seemed to be the remedy. But Zhdanovism was going to complicate matters. In the past, the cadres directorate had preferred to recruit people who already possessed technical training for party work. Now humanities graduates were to have preference, in order to avoid such ideological lapses as the failure to censor 'ideologically alien' passages in an opera, or the publication of an insufficiently expurgated biography of Lenin, and so on. 'Technicians' were regarded as incapable of exposing ideological subversion, let alone combating it. A threat like 'economization' – much more prosaic, but also less obvious – which was beginning to blur the party's ideological vision, was quite beyond their wit.

But what was the ideological framework that was supposedly losing its vigour? And what was to be counterposed to the influence of the capitalist West? Here we touch a sensitive point in the party's ideological armour. At this stage, Stalinism was characterized by an unwillingness – even an inability – to criticize capitalism from a socialist standpoint. As we have said, a virulent Russian nationalism had been opted for instead. This point will be taken up in Part Three, when we sketch a broader picture of the ideological history. As for the narrower practical problem of the party apparatus restoring control over the ministries and over itself, it was (to repeat the point) bound up with undue direct involvement in the economy, which had allowed managers to get the upper hand. Hence the 1946 reform of the apparatus largely consisted in terminating such direct involvement and halting the party's 'economization'.

In and of itself, however, this kind of 'line' could not replace the ideological cement that Stalinism had lost. Kuznetsov implied as much during the plenary meeting of the party apparatus. 'The party has no programme', he declared, stating that the only extant programmatic texts were the Stalin Constitution and the five-year plan. These words certainly possessed an audacious ring, for they implied that under Stalin the party had lost its original ideological vigour. They would have been suicidal had Stalin himself – we surmise – not said as much and Kuznetsov not simply been quoting him. When Kuznetsov referred to the party losing out to economic managers and needing to regain its independence, the sentiment was probably Stalin's – or approved by him, at any rate. As Stalin himself was aware, the erosion of most of the original ideology must have been a factor in the 'economization' of party cadres. Zhdanovite policies had been instigated at Stalin's behest, which tends to indicate that he was aware of the regime's ideological weakness and had decided to furnish it with a new ideological cement. We have seen what this consisted in. But it was part of the problem, not part of the solution.

At all events, for now 'the economy' was identified as the reason for the decay of the party's main apparatus. The measures adopted rested on the conviction that a better division of labour between the Central Committee and the Council of Ministers could remedy the situation. The Council of Ministers would continue to run the country, while the Central Committee would staff key posts and oversee the cadres departments in every institution. But this line – 'quit the economy and get back to party work' – would not last long. Less than two years later, the reorganization, which testified to a long-term vision (even if its goal was unattainable), was reversed.

RETREAT

A halt was called at the end of 1948. Let us now briefly analyse its consequences. In early 1949 the specialist sectors of the cadres directorate were converted into separate departments dealing with different spheres of state activity. Officially, they would deal only with the cadres in these various spheres, not with their professional field of activity. In fact, however, whether inadvertently or otherwise, these Central

Committee departments would continue to get entangled in the economy's managerial structures. The cause was the very character of the branch system – something the 1946 reform had sought to surmount. Thus the 'turn' turned into a retreat.

One document sums up the character of the new phase. Swings of the pendulum were recurrent in Soviet administrative practice, so this one was no novelty. Instead of the cumbersome cadres directorate, and specialist units in charge of inspecting party bodies, there was to be a new organizational structure. Henceforth the Central Committee apparatus, overseen mainly by the Secretariat and to a lesser degree by the Orgburo, would supervise the operations of ministries and other central government agencies. The task was assigned to new Central Committee departments – among them, 'agitprop', 'party–komsomol–trade unions', 'international relations', heavy industry, consumer goods industry, engineering (machine building), transport and agriculture, as well as a new, very powerful, 'administrative' department with responsibility for the security services and the cluster of agencies in planning, finance and trade. (The last three would soon be detached to form a separate department.)

In sum, the reorganization consisted in converting the structural units of the old cadres directorate into independent departments and distributing, more or less logically, the 115 ministries and all party bodies (republican and regional) between these departments. This was no easy undertaking. Each of the state agents to be supervised and monitored itself encompassed a multitude of local branches – in particular, a labyrinthine set of supply networks that were a headache for any inspection agency. This tangled web was even more complicated than the one we shall discuss when we deal with the state administration.

Each Central Committee department had its own more or less complex structure and personnel office. But there were also structures servicing the whole Central Committee apparatus, like the central statistical office, and coordinating departments such as the general-secretary's 'special unit', the encrypting service, and 'confidential matters'. In addition there were various 'groups' or 'special offices' unfamiliar to outsiders, including a service for receiving foreign visitors, a separate 'department of the Central Committee' (possibly an auxiliary secretariat for the Orgburo), a pivotal 'general department' through which all significant texts and appointments to and from departments passed, a 'business' department, a 'post office' for letters from the public, an office dealing with party membership registration, a 'commission for foreign travel', a special office for running the Kremlin, and a unit dealing with 'auxiliary farms' (probably part of the business department, which also had a cars and mechanical repairs service).

We still have one mechanism to investigate, and readers will hopefully not be discouraged by its complexity (simplicity often derives from a mastery of the details). In the final analysis, the Soviet tendency for administrative opacity is not as complicated as all that. And if a comparison between the Soviet and other bureaucracies can generate confusion, its results are invariably illuminating – and sometimes surprising.

THE *NOMENKLATURA* OF THE CENTRAL COMMITTEE

The endeavour in 1946–8 to reorganize the party's central apparatus can be encapsulated in the term *nomenklatura*, which refers to the mechanism used to keep leading cadres under party control. It was also the cause of problems and side-effects that plagued the regime to the very end.

The resuscitation in 1946 of the Central Committee's *nomenklatura* required considerable effort on the part of the cadres directorate and the three supreme bodies: the Politburo, the Orgburo (abolished in 1952), and the Secretariat. The Russian term *nomenklatura* means a 'list' of items, whatever they might be, that have to be 'named'. We are now going to examine this list more closely to figure out how it was supposed to work in practice.

A document signed on 22 August 1946 by Andreev, head of the cadres directorate, and his deputy Revsky, was sent to the four secretaries of the Central Committee (Zhdanov, Kuznetsov, Patolichev and Popov). It presented for their approval a version of the *nomenklatura* that contained 42,894 leadership positions in party and state apparatuses. (The precise number varied from one draft to another, but this need not concern us.) Let us underscore once again that this list was established and controlled by the Central Committee.

The text begins by stating the obvious: it is difficult to exercise control over cadres when more than half of the appointments to, and dismissals from, ministerial posts figuring in the current *nomenklatura* are decided without Central Committee approval. It was therefore urgent that the latter formally endorse the new list, which was only a draft but which was presented as better suited than previous versions to the requirements of the five-year plan for 1946–50. The directorate was also working on another much-needed list – the so-called 'reserve register' containing an auxiliary list of candidates for *nomenklatura* posts. In the event of rising demand for personnel, this would make it possible rapidly to supply the requisite cadres. The latest version of the new *nomenklatura* eliminated approximately 9,000 positions from the old rolls and introduced some new ones. These alterations were required to take account of economic and technological changes and concomitant alterations in the relative importance of various posts.

It took about three months for the first postwar '*nomenklatura* of Central Committee posts' to be approved in stages. At the end of November 1946 the Central Committee possessed a text that could serve as a basic grid for handling leading cadres. The general list of posts to be filled in accordance with *nomenklatura* rules was supplemented by a detailed record of the officials currently holding these posts. Referring to some 41,883 posts (and the names of their incumbents), it allows us to draw up a picture of the whole cohort that was considered pivotal to the system. The classification was extremely detailed. The enumeration of the posts that the Central Committee wanted on its own list began with 'posts in party organizations', classified by rank: Central Committee secretaries and their deputies, heads of department and their deputies, heads of 'special sectors', and so on. Next came local party officials at republican and regional level, followed by the directors of party schools and holders of chairs in Marxist-Leninist history and economics.

The list then proceeded to senior positions in the state apparatus, from central level via the republics to district level: ministers, deputy ministers, members of ministerial collegia, departmental heads. It went on down the whole hierarchy of administrative posts in government agencies, as well as the parallel apparatus of the soviets, until it reached the lowest rank that the Central Committee wished to have under its direct or indirect tutelage.

The text provides figures for each ministry, but examination of the data by hierarchical stratum is more illuminating. Out of 41,883 '*nomenklatura* positions', the top stratum (ministries and party) accounted for 4,836, or 12 per cent of the list. (Readers are aware by now that this 'excursion' into the *nomenklatura* leads us to a sketch of the whole Soviet administrative system.) To analyse what this represents, it should be read in conjunction with data from the Central Statistical Office, which provide details for the whole state apparatus. In sum, the *nomenklatura* represented around a third of the 160,000 top posts, of which 105,000 were based in the central government apparatus in Moscow, while

55,000 were located in republican administrative bodies (ministries and agencies). We might note that at this moment state administration numbered some 1.6 million managerial posts, 18.8 per cent of the total 8 million employees. (A more realistic calculation would reduce the latter figure to 6.5 million, by excluding from 'administration' categories like cleaners and other junior technical staff.) 'Senior managerial cadres' comprised officials heading up administrative units which lower ranks were directly or indirectly attached to. There we also find staff with the title (and probably the role) of 'principal' or 'senior specialist'.

Returning now to the Central Committee *nomenklatura* proper, we possess a breakdown by field of activity. The most important contingent was that of party and Komsomol officials: 10,533, or 24.6 per cent of the list. Next came industry with 8,808 posts, or 20.5 per cent; general administrative agencies with 4,082, or 9.5 per cent; defence with 3,954, or 9.2 per cent; culture, the arts and sciences with 2,305, or 5.4 per cent; transport with 1,842, or 4.4 per cent; agriculture with 1,548, or 3.6 per cent; state security and public order with 1,331, or 3.1 per cent; the prosecution service and justice with 1,242, or 2.9 per cent; foreign affairs with 1,169, or 2.7 per cent; construction enterprises with 1,106, or 2.6 per cent; procurement and trade with 1,022, or 2.4 per cent; social services with 767, or 1.8 per cent; trade unions and cooperatives with 763, or 1.8 per cent; state planning, registration and control with 575, or 1.3 per cent; and financial and credit institutions with 406, or 1 per cent.

Analysis of the professional profile of officials included on the list in mid-1946 reveals that 14,778 posts were held by engineers with different specialities. The fact that many of the rest had a lower educational profile was compensated for, or so it was claimed, by length of service. Seventy per cent of those who possessed only primary education had more than ten years' experience in leadership roles. This figure conduces to rather less optimistic conclusions. In total, 55.7 per cent of central *nomenklatura* cadres had more than ten years of service; 32.6 per cent had between six and ten years; 39.2 between two and five years; 17.25 per cent between one and two years; and 22.1 per cent less than a year. The *nomenklatura* also contained 1,400 office-holders who were not party members (3.5 per cent of the total). And last but not least, 66.7 of positions were held by Russians, 11.3 per cent by Ukrainians, 5.4 per cent by Jews, etc. (the 'etc.' occurs in the document itself).

Readers with a particular interest in bureaucracy will find plenty of food for thought here on supervisory methods, and the logic and illogic involved in such a centralized staffing policy. The complexity of the *nomenklatura* hierarchy raises the issue of the extent to which bureaucratic methods of controlling a bureaucracy are unrealistic. A more detailed examination would indicate that this list was in fact only one part of a larger system. The Central Committee controlled – or sought to control – the highest stratum of officials. But those at the top also had power over some lower-level nominations, though it had to be exercised in collaboration with the relevant party committee at each level, or with the lower echelon of their own hierarchy, which in turn performed the same function vis-à-vis the cadres of institutions under its control (alone or in consultation), and so on and so forth.

Thus, a system that seems clear when viewed from above turns out to be composed of different decision-making hierarchies, in which prerogatives are fluid and allow for numerous derogations. Endless complaints by the Central Committee apparatus against ministries demonstrate that the latter were not particularly diligent when it came to following *nomenklatura* rules. They appointed, transferred or dismissed job-holders without consulting the Central Committee; or only did so retrospectively. If they behaved like that, it was because the *nomenklatura* did not in reality operate as a one-way system. When a post became vacant, the Central Committee could look for a candidate in its reserve list, but it only did so if the ministry concerned was reckoned to be in a crisis situation. Otherwise, it asked the minister to propose the best candidate and would subsequently confirm the appointment.

At a later point in our study, in Parts Two and Three, the question of who ultimately controlled whom in this system will be posed once again – and answered. But we can already see that the logistics involved in controlling the machinery actually reveal dependency on it. And the dangers of 'economization' and losing control of the government machine and its administrative class were formulated in precisely these terms in internal party debates.

In conclusion, we would like to underscore two features of the Stalinist system. When dealing with Stalin's own governmental methods, we are in the realm of arbitrariness and personal despotism. When speaking of Soviet government, we are in the realm of bureaucracy or rather its two branches, one of them (the party apparatus) minor and the other (state administration) much larger.

13

AN AGRARIAN DESPOTISM?

In the aftermath of the war Stalin remained obsessed with constructing an adequate 'historical alibi' and thereby acquiring legitimacy. He needed something substantial in order to be fully absolved from his original political commitments. The war had seen the outline of the third panel of what was to form a veritable 'triptych', but it remained to display it to the full. The first panel corresponded to the elimination of Leninism and the taming of the party, the second to the extermination of the historical party via the purges and the rewriting of its history. The third would consist in dispensing with ideological liabilities and switching to a nationalist 'great power' ideology, comparable to Tsarism and adopting its attributes.

During these three phases, countless citizens had lost their lives, many of them valuable, independent-minded cadres. The whole society lived in terror. And yet Stalinism in its turn would be 'buried'. It would be a mistake to think that the dictator's death, eventually inevitable, was the decisive factor in this. After the end of the war, the system was in decline and Stalin, notwithstanding the impression of omnipotence he created, was in search of something to give it a new lease of life. The primary cause of the decline lay in the regime's internal contradictions. Its absolutist features, befitting another age, were profoundly incompatible with the effects of a forced industrialization in response to the challenges of new times. The government that had summoned these furies was unable to accommodate the emerging realities, or interest groups, or constraints embodied in the social structures and layers generated by the developmental process. The pathological purges attested to this: Stalinism could not live with the fruits of its own policies, starting with its own bureaucracy; it could not live without it, but could not live with it either.

Stalin's personal path was in a sense mapped out by his experience of the Civil War. The conclusions he drew about Russia's present and future needs were those to which his personality, intellect and experience predisposed him. But we should not ignore the decisive part played in this by the specificity of Russian history: it not only produced a Stalin, but allowed him to seize power and lead the country in a particular direction. Throughout its vast territory and the regions surrounding it (Middle East, Far East, and also Eastern Europe), the political system of old Russia had numerous ancestors, neighbours and cousins with experience of agrarian despotism. The transformation of Muscovy into a centralized state involved combining numerous separate principalities into a single political unit. On the one hand this betokened a form of 'de-feudalization', in the sense that parcellization was reduced. But on the other hand it meant the introduction of a new type of feudalism, with the conversion of peasants into serfs on the land offered to the nascent gentry in exchange for service to the state: the concurrent creation of serf-owners (servants of the state) and serfs. Expansion of the personal domain of Moscow's ruler coincided with the construction of an autocracy and the creation, over a huge territory, of a nation by means of colonization, which was the principal feature in the making of Russia. According to the term used by the nineteenth-century Russian historian Solovev, this process was 'drawn out' – in other words, it was extensive and repetitive. It dictated a highly centralized state under a sovereign who ruled by divine right.

In the eighteenth and nineteenth centuries the autocracy had sought with difficulty to shed its original agrarian mould, which had become an obstacle to its governmental methods and imperial image. The changes that had occurred over the centuries had rendered such a framework increasingly untenable, even if Tsar Nicholas II remained very attached to a model of autocracy that dated back to an era when the sovereign identified his state with a personal domain and ruled it like a family concern. In this connection, it is worth recalling that *despotes* in ancient Greek referred to the head of a household with many servants and slaves. But in the twentieth century, serfdom no longer existed and the patriarchal peasant system, where the master represented the equivalent of sovereign authority in the popular imaginary – something that could have served as the pillar of a *sui generis* popular monarchy – was changing rapidly. The head of the peasant family might have long supported

Tsarism, for as a mini-monarch he sensed an affinity with the great monarch – a 'little father' (*batiushka*) like him. But the base of this primitive rural monarchism was giving way as peasants began to question the analogy.

Stalin's growing tendency to identify with the imperial Russian past, and to tap its oldest traditions for the benefit of his regime, might seem puzzling in view of the fact that Tsarism had been in rapid decline. But it would be wrong to reduce the phenomenon to a device dictated by wartime mobilization against the German invader, or his repeated contention about the Russians to the effect that 'they cannot cope without a Tsar'. It corresponded to a profound political and psychological need: a radical redefinition of both his and his regime's political and ideological identity.

Stalin may have been aware of the historical evolution of the titles assumed by Russian rulers. Initially, a ruler was a *kniaz'* (prince), which was not particularly prestigious since there were numerous princes. Visilii III then adopted the term *gosudar'* (sovereign), but that was still too close to the title of other contemporary rulers. The title 'Tsar' – the Russian equivalent of the German *Kaiser* and the Latin *Caesar* – taken by Ivan the Terrible was more imposing; adopted by someone like him, it even sounded ominous. Finally, Peter the Great opted for *Imperator* as the most prestigious of all. His successors would retain the whole list of titles, beginning with *Imperator*. Stalin wanted to find his place on this ascending list. Given that there was nothing above 'emperor', however, he had to settle for 'generalissimo' – a title no Tsar had ever carried.

We would not be spending time on such ironies were it not for the fact that a taste for bombastic titles was not exclusive to Stalin; it was shared by other general-secretaries. The syndrome is indicative of the political vacuity that prevails when rulers do not know what to do with their power.

At the same time, the political and psychological calculations behind these borrowings from the past must not lead us to forget the main thing: the 'generalissimo' was now going nowhere. Asserting an affinity with the empire and especially its tsars, ruthless state-builders, allowed him to shed the liabilities entailed by the original promises to build socialism, which were impossible to fulfil. It thereby allowed him to close once and for all the chapter of Bolshevism, whose founders had turned against him. Lenin had characterized Stalin as a 'Russian bully' (a Georgian replica of the same), and requested that he be removed from the post of party general-secretary, which he was not fit to occupy.

Stalin was precisely set on becoming an authentic 'Russian bully' and, as such, endearing himself to the core Russian nationality – something that demanded a switch of ideological identity. Nothing is more instructive in this regard than the adoption of a new chauvinist anthem to the glory of a mythical 'Great Russia', offensive to all the empire's non-Russian nationalities, and of the worst kind of Russian nationalism, which was unleashed in the postwar campaign against 'cosmopolitanism'. These were constituent parts of Stalin's design to renounce the revolutionary past in favour of a different past. Eliminating Bolshevik cadres was insufficient. And the issue was not whether phase 1, 2, or 2.5 of some 'ism' had been reached (or was about to be): that was so much empty talk. Stalin's major success was the super-state he had created, unencumbered by promises to anyone – an agrarian despotism that may be counted as among the century's most amazing historical twists. The Stalinist system restored an old historical model (more like that of a Xerxes than Nicholas I or Alexander III), and actually reinvigorated it by means of a breakneck industrialization neither Xerxes nor Nicholas was capable of.

The term 'Oriental despotism' proposed by the Orientalist Karl Wittfogel comes to mind. It refers to a bureaucratic system with a central role for a priestly caste (the equivalent of the party?). At its head is a monarch with enormous powers, endowed *ex officio* with supernatural origins. The economic and social base of the system consists in a vast rural proletariat. The similarities are striking, especially in view of the despotic 'right' that Stalin arrogated to himself to determine policy as his frenzies dictated, as well as the need for enemies whom he 'nominated' before unleashing a completely depraved secret police against them.

Yet 'Oriental despotism' is in fact the wrong term. The old despotisms only changed their rural societies very slowly. In the case of the Stalinist system, 'agrarian despotism' is more appropriate. Even if it issued from, and remained rooted in, a rural past – the peasantry still accounted for 80 per cent of the population under the NEP – the regime's motor-force was industrialization, which induced enormous changes in society and ushered it into a new age. Initially, this marriage of two authoritarian systems – the old statist model and the industrial model – helped accentuate the regime's despotic and repressive character, for they compounded one another in a state-run, state-owned economy.

It is this amalgam of forms that allows us to reconstruct the institution of a personal despotism, focused on the cult of a supreme leader, with roots stretching back into a very remote past, which was temporarily strengthened by the injection of a novel feature: industrialization. In fact, a similar pattern, albeit on a much smaller scale, can be observed in Peter the Great's modernizing venture. Against this background and in this framework, we can make sense of the forced labour (the Gulag), a despotism that allowed free range to one individual's delirium (purges, forced labour, mass deportations), and a huge repressive apparatus.

It is appropriate here to recall that the great purges and show trials were personally prepared and supervised by Stalin (with the help of Vyshinsky and his ilk). Writing and directing a play requires great skill of a playwright. But someone who runs an empire in the twentieth century in the manner of a puppeteer is simply a primitive ruler.

The super-state Stalin had created was – and was bound to be – bureaucratic: it was a character trait genetically inscribed in a state that owned all the country's assets. This explains the enormous power acquired by the bureaucracy, but also prompts the question of whether Stalin could coexist with a power complex that eluded him. The response he hit on was as irrational as it was pathetic: mass purges to halt, or at least delay, developments that were ineluctable.

For Stalin, purges became his quintessential modus operandi and remained so until the very end. He regarded them as the most effective strategy. They acted like a drug, for they always seemed to succeed. Had Stalin been unearthing real enemies, the system, whilst still dictatorial, would have been very different. In 1953 new purges were still being planned; and it is likely that death alone prevented Stalin from having his closest acolytes – Beria, Molotov, Kaganovich, Mikoyan and several others – executed.

In a sense, the victory of 1945 'rehabilitated' Stalinism – even, to a large extent, on the global stage – at the very moment when the system and Stalin personally had begun a phase of marked decline. In fact, he had lost the capacity to rule the country effectively. He seemed to have achieved all his objectives, and yet the road ahead, quite independently of his state of health, led in only one direction: backwards! It will suffice simply to mention Zhdanovism to indicate where he was headed – and that he had nothing else to offer.

We can now turn to the last point in our inquiry: why was the cult of Stalin so successful? For notwithstanding all his aberrations, his cult, his legend, his aura and his personality were widely accepted in Russia and throughout the world as those of a *vozhd'* (guide) without historical parallel. And this cult persisted among many Russians even after Khrushchev's denunciation of Stalin and his atrocities. The reaction of the masses in Russia to the news of his death is well documented: an outpouring of grief and a sense of irreplaceable loss and despair in the face of the unthinkable – the death of an immortal.

There were many reasons for this, and they can be briefly summarized here. We can begin by returning to the old rural-patriarchal image of the landlord (*khoziain*), whose severity is accepted so long as he is just – a tradition with deep roots in Russia. Victory over Nazi Germany was a potent 'legitimizer', even though Stalin's regime was quite shaky. Skilful image-making was a further factor, to which not a few sophisticated minds succumbed. We shall have occasion to return to this image – that of awe-inspiring founder of a powerful empire – and the patriotic value placed on it, which was all the more resonant in that it did not altogether lack reality. A lack of information and the very immensity of the country compounded the mystery of its leader, whose every appearance was carefully staged: he knew how to reassure and charm, or how to terrorize. We must underscore the information deficit: when they were supplied, details were always wrapped up in powerful, effective propaganda. Many people were simply ignorant of the horrors that had been perpetrated and could not conceive that the state was directed by someone who invented enemies and massacred innocents. How could this incredible image be reconciled with the quite different one Stalin projected at the beginning of the war, with his unforgettable radio speech at a crucial moment? 'Brothers and sisters, I am turning to you, my friends. They came to enslave our motherland, but there will be another great holy day on our soil. The enemy will be crushed. We shall be victorious.' I am quoting from memory what I myself heard on the radio; and this is what Soviet citizens heard, oblivious of the raging Stalin who signed endless lists of those to be done to death.

Moreover, even if they had known more, what weight would such information have carried at a moment when the destiny of Russia and Europe hung in the balance? It is difficult to say. Finally, religious – 'Dostoyevskyan' – elements can be adduced in our search for an explanation, without stressing them unduly. At all events, many – if not a majority – of the most honest, brilliant and creative people went through Stalinism and accepted it, whether permanently or temporarily. The list of such cases is long. But we could also draw up a list of those who, while involved in the process, never accepted Stalin or his Russia.

I shall conclude on this subject by stressing an aspect of Stalinism that is implicit in what has just been said. I have spared readers none of Stalin's aberrations, but it must be appreciated that Stalinism rested on two historical imperatives: catching up with the West industrially as a precondition for constructing a strong state. The image and reality of a powerful state – in fact, a victorious great power (*derzhava*) that was recognized as such the world over – have to be underscored as a potent, even hypnotizing factor not only for many citizens but also for the political class, including those Politburo members who hated Khrushchev for removing from his pedestal the builder of a state of unprecedented dimensions in Russian history. The reasoning ran as follows: What need is there to concern ourselves with the irrationalities if the aim has been achieved? And such reasoning is not confined to Russia or its leadership. Insensitivity to the victims of atrocities committed by a strong state in the name of its strategic interests is widespread in government circles throughout the world. 'State power' is the highest value for many nationalisms and imperialisms.

Such qualifications in no way alter the conclusion to be drawn: Stalinism was riddled with irrationality that rendered it not only decrepit but abject. To exorcize it, a variety of shamanism was required; and this was what Khrushchev, following popular beliefs, supplied. When Stalin's body was removed from the mausoleum in Red Square to be reburied elsewhere, it was carried out feet first. In peasant demonology, this ensured that the evil dead would not return to haunt the living. Exorcizing the spectre, as Nikita intended, would offer Soviet Russia another, rather promising chance – even if it proved relatively short-lived.

PART TWO

THE 1960S AND BEYOND: FROM A NEW MODEL TO A NEW IMPASSE

14

'E PUR, SI MUOVE!'

My 1960s are as fluid as the 1930s, devoted to Stalinism, were; and will lead us via selected topics to the end of the regime. Having displayed considerable vitality in many spheres, from the early 1970s the Soviet Union entered into a downswing, before sinking definitively into 'stagnation' (*zastoi*). Leadership personalities are a good indicator of the system's variable health: Khrushchev and Andropov personified a certain dynamism, whereas Brezhnev and Chernenko epitomized decline. Such curves on the historical graph were nothing new in themselves. From the outset, the historical dynamic of the Soviet Union fluctuated. In this instance, however, we are dealing with the final phase of a descending curve that was novel and ominous – though not lacking in intriguing aspects.

This prompts us to reiterate what should by now be obvious: the Russia that went to war in 1941 and emerged victorious in 1945 was still only on the way to becoming an urbanized industrial power. Sociologically and, in many respects, culturally, it was still mired in its rural past – even when it came to the characteristic features of its modernizing state. 'Primitive' is the adjective that comes to mind to encapsulate the postwar period and Stalin's last years. All efforts were focused on two objectives: restoring prewar living standards and reconstructing a semblance of the Soviet system in the vast territories that had been occupied by the Germans.

The chaos that initially reigned over reconstruction is ineffable. Thousands of officials were dispatched to the reconquered territories, but were often unqualified for the task that awaited them. Of the thousands of others recruited locally, many were ex-collaborators. The regime faced numerous foes: in the Ukraine, Lithuania and Latvia, guerrilla units engaged the Red Army in pitched battles. Reconstruction of the system and suppression of the unrest took time and involved heavy casualties. Economic revival was launched and energetically pursued. But although recovery to prewar (1940) levels had been achieved in many spheres by 1953, this was not yet true of consumer goods. As far as food supplies were concerned, the USSR of 1945–53 remained a country whose population went hungry, or at any rate was very poorly fed.

The particular point we would like to emphasize here is this: reconstruction, however impressive in some spheres – beginning with arms production, and especially atomic weapons – coincided with the restoration of Stalinism, which was a degenerating, profoundly dysfunctional system. This included a return to wanton terror – the ageing dictator's main political instrument – and the promulgation of a retrograde nationalist 'great power' ideology. Openly adopted by the dictator during the war, it was now 'perfected' in the autocratic mould of imperial Russia.

The regime was the personal dictatorship of a man whose titles stopped just short of rivalling the Tsars', and who imposed a replica of Peter the Great's 'table of ranks and uniforms' on the senior bureaucracy. The reference to 'Great and Holy Russia' in the Union's national anthem, as the crowning symbol of the state and its ideology, rounded off this new–old rhetorical format. As for popular compliance, it was ensured by terror. Nothing is more characteristic of this aspect of the 'restoration', seemingly quite successful, than the figures for the Gulag. Having declined to 800,000 during the war, the number of inmates exceeded 3 million by 1953. And when we add the figures for those exiled and imprisoned, we arrive at a total of 5 million people – an all-time record. In the same year, however, the numbers did begin to fall again. Meanwhile, no policy switch of any significance can be identified. Stalin carried on plotting changes of personnel and none of the leadership knew where (or how) they would end up; Molotov and Mikoyan were convinced that they were going to be liquidated. Endless appointments and reorganizations – a replay of the constant ministerial musical chairs in Tsarism's dying days – are indicative of the confusion that prevailed at the top. In short, it cannot be said that the USSR was really governed in these years.

When Stalin was struck down by serious illness, Politburo members took turns at his bedside (or perhaps in an adjoining room). Once it was apparent that his condition was terminal, they turned to political matters. Most of them were already nurturing schemes and began manoeuvring for positions and allies. Whatever the outcome of these shifting combinations, the new rulers were inheriting a regime that belonged to a different – past – age. Changes began almost at once, and initially isolated measures soon gave way to successive waves of reform.

We shall discuss these reforms below. But for now it is important to appreciate that Stalin's disappearance opened various valves in the system, making it possible to form a leadership group capable of reviving the regime. Those at the top can all be characterized as 'Stalinists', so it is scarcely surprising that one of their first steps was the classically Stalinist deed of eliminating one of their number – Beria – as well as a significant number of secret police officials, who were shot or imprisoned on the basis of a tissue of hastily concocted, incoherent charges.

This affair is in part explained by the sequence of events. Stalin died on 5 March 1953. The same day, a session of the Central Committee plenum, the Council of Ministers and the Presidium of the Supreme Soviet decreed that the MGB (Ministry of State Security) and the MVD (Ministry of Internal Affairs) should once again be fused into one MVD, to be headed by Beria, who was also appointed Deputy Prime Minister. These decisions were made official by the Supreme Soviet on 15 March. That day, the Council of Ministers appointed people close to Beria and Malenkov to various posts: Kruglov, Kobulov and Serov became Beria's first deputies, Maslennikov was made MVD deputy minister, and all of them were named members of the MVD collegium (an internal consultative council present in every ministry). The precise whys and wherefores of these appointments remain obscure. But the fact is that Beria, under the auspices of his putative ally, Prime Minister Malenkov, retained a key role in government and kept a grip on the whole repressive apparatus and its military formations, totalling more than a million people.

Something in this rapid sequence must have alarmed Khrushchev. It is not clear to me how he managed to persuade Malenkov to dump his associate, but Beria was arrested on 26 June 1953 during a Politburo meeting and arrests of other MVD officials followed. It was decided to dismantle the ministry's industrial structures, and its extra-judicial 'special concilium' was abolished on 1 September. Further changes ensued.

However, the real story of Beria and co.'s misdeeds was not made public. Moreover, no one would have believed it. Instead, citizens were served up a classically Stalinist concoction. There is no way of knowing whether Beria really intended to eliminate all or some of his colleagues. Moreover, most – even all – of the leaders in post had signed or consigned orders for the execution of innocent people and thus risked being implicated. A single top leader – unquestionably a dangerous one – and some lesser figures thus paid for the crimes of all the other Stalinists, who had not yet stated what they thought about the whole bloody past. One fact nevertheless stands out: the nightmarish 'investigations', the fake accusations, and the trials currently in progress – notably the notorious 'doctors' plot' – were halted overnight. The victims were fully rehabilitated and the doctors returned to their positions in the Kremlin. Further rehabilitations and releases soon began, with less fanfare.

This was a clear signal that something significant was afoot. Il'ia Ehrenburg was to refer to these changes as 'the thaw' in a novel of that title, even though the leadership still contained figures who would remain faithful to Stalin, and utterly unrepentant about the past, for the rest of their lives. When, in 1956, Nikita Khrushchev launched his sensational attack on Stalin at the Twentieth Party Congress, Soviet society, and especially the intelligentsia, understood that the days of Stalinist show trials and arbitrary arrests and executions had gone for good. Yet the thaw was not initiated by that congress: its participants were as surprised as everyone else and the many Stalinists among them were in a state of shock. No one had anticipated such a bombshell – and so soon. The Stalinist riposte came a year later: assured of a majority in the Presidium, they attempted a palace coup against Khrushchev. But it was thwarted by an alliance between the military and a majority of Central Committee members; Khrushchev remained in power and consolidated his position. What happened next was unheard of: no death sentences – no prison sentences even – were pronounced against the plotters. They were simply relieved of their positions. One of them – Voroshilov – was even pardoned and retained a ceremonial post.

All this – and more that we have not mentioned – was quite unprecedented and remained the rule in the political class under Khrushchev and after his removal. Another decisive change occurred, which for the most part historians have not stressed sufficiently: imprisonment of countless people accused of 'counter-revolutionary crimes' ceased. The notion even disappeared from the criminal code, to be replaced by 'crimes against the state', directed at oppositional activities. Political opposition continued to be repressed, but (as we shall see) the repression was henceforth on a quite different scale and less brutal. Now – and this was not insignificant – the accused actually had to do something before being charged. Those who suffered repression certainly paid a heavy price, and comparisons with the past were small consolation, yet the fact remains that the changes in penal policy were meaningful. To engage in protest was no longer a suicidal step; people survived their sentences. Some public and confidential channels existed for protesting against the arbitrary use of power.

We can now turn to a survey of deeper systemic changes. These were ushered in by government policy, but also created by spontaneous transformations in Soviet reality. They concern the triad of social 'militarization–criminalization–mobilization' characteristic of the Stalinist regime.

Under the broad heading of changes in the prison system, we must mention the dismantling of a core component of the previous regime: the Gulag – a system of forced labour that we described above as being in an advanced state of decay. It lasted for twenty years. Yet many speak as if it had always existed, while others fail to register its disappearance. The reform began in earnest from 1954 onwards, although some key structures had been abolished the year before. Of crucial importance was the dismantling, already noted, of the MVD's economic industrial complex, which was the essential element in the Gulag's forced-labour empire. With the transfer to civilian ministries of most of its industrial agencies (road and rail construction, forestry, mining, etc.), this sinister repressive complex, deeply interested in a constant supply of unpaid labour, was significantly reduced. The labour force no longer consisted in slaves, but in paid workers enjoying the protections afforded by the labour code, which was substantially amended at the same time. With this large-scale 'expropriation' of the MVD went a step-by-step transformation of the whole Gulag structure into a reformed prison system with a new name, followed by a reduction in the number of inmates in the camps (now called 'colonies', 'prisons' and 'deportee settlements'). The number of detainees in these various institutions (excluding prisons) fell from 5,223,000 on 1 January 1953 to 997,000 on 1 January 1959; the figure for 'counter-revolutionaries' dropped from 580,000 to 11,000. From the early 1960s onwards, arbitrary persecution ceased to be widespread.

These reforms did not proceed smoothly, but public pressure to accelerate 'normalization' was supported by the Interior Minister and the office of the Prosecutor General. The latter were highly critical of the practices of the MVD's prisons directorate and pressured it to implement party and state decisions concerning the penal system. Two reports, separated by four years, are highly instructive in this regard. The first, dating from 1957, was written by the Interior Minister Dudorov (it was his second year in post) and concerned 'The Problem of the Camps and New Penal Policies'. The second was by the deputy Prosecutor General of the USSR, Mishutin, reporting in 1961. We shall begin with the latter, since it contains a survey of the steps taken between 1953 and 1956.[1]

Mishutin's main points were as follows. Until 1953, camp administrations did not bother about the 'correction and re-education' of prisoners. The prison population was predominantly regarded as manpower; and the MVD thus neglected what should have been its main duty. For years, legislation on penal policy was virtually non-existent. Access to penal institutions by representatives of society was barred and oversight of their functioning by prosecutors limited. On 10 July 1954, the Central Committee had adopted a resolution seeking to improve the situation in the MVD's camps and colonies. The MVD was criticized for concentrating exclusively on economic output, when its main task was to engage inmates in productive labour and thereby prepare them for their reintegration into society. On 24 May 1955, the Central Committee, followed shortly afterwards by the Presidium of the Supreme Soviet, promulgated a 'statute on prosecutorial supervision' in the USSR, chapter five of which dealt with the supervision of detention centres. Henceforth camp prosecutors had to refer to the territorial offices of the Prosecutor's Office, rather than directly to the Prosecutor General. This measure in itself was an improvement. But the situation in the camps remained unsatisfactory. On 25 October 1956, a joint decree of the Council of Ministers and the Central Committee was issued listing 'measures to improve the work of the MVD of the USSR' and its republican equivalents, which were accused of neglecting their re-education duties – the evidence for this was the number of re-offenders. The government now speeded up measures to reduce and abolish the system of corrective labour camps (*ispravitel'no-trudovye lageria* – ITLs), and to create supervisory bodies in conjunction with the executive committees of local soviets to oversee what occurred in what were now to be called 'colonies'.

Minutes of a session of the MVD Collegium from early 1957, under

---

1   GARF, 8131, 32, 6610, LL. 9196 – from a longer report by A. Mishutin, deputy Prosecutor General, 13 May 1961.

the chairmanship of Dudorov (former party apparatchik), give us some idea of the situation. Appointed to head the MVD by the party in order to improve its functioning, Dudorov was not at all content with the camps and colonies directorate in his own ministry, particularly when it came to the re-education and utilization of prison manpower.[2] Some 6 per cent of prisoners were not working because there were no jobs for them; and for those who were employed, the remuneration system was complete chaos. In 1956 the MVD had devoted much of its energy to dealing with police matters, and the minister hoped that 1957 would be the year when it would finally succeed in resolving the outstanding problems in the prison system, as required by the Central Committee. He continued:

> You know that the Central Committee and the Council of Ministers have decided to move from a system of *camps* to a system of *colonies*. Colonies do a much better job, but there is still work to be done on this system. At the moment, 35 per cent of prisoners are in colonies, while the rest are in camps where they work on a contractual basis with various economic agencies. The task before us is to transfer all prisoners to colonies. Over the next 4–5 years, that involves building some 370 colonies. All production work should be done by prisoners inside their place of confinement. [That, and a normalized pay system, was supposed to be the main difference between a colony and a camp. – ML] The 66 colonies already in existence are yielding good results as regards re-education – the key objective of incarceration – and labour is the main method.

In passing, the minister observed that 'colonies produce consumer goods (clothing, furniture, household utensils, some agricultural machinery). Thus, the *zeks* earn some money for themselves and their families.'

Dudorov was painting a rather rosy picture. Experience suggested (as he himself noted) that prisoners should not be paid in cash, because many of them tended to lose the money playing cards or being robbed by other prisoners. Some of the *zeks* themselves preferred payment in kind. Dudorov ended his report by stating that the directorate and collegium of the ministry hoped to resolve this problem in the course of 1957 (in the event, establishing the colonies was to take several more years).

Returning now to Mishutin's 1961 text, we learn that the initial liberalization had gone too far; that it was creating malfunctions in the

---

2 GARF, 9401, 8, 9.

system; and that adjustments were required (something we already gleaned from Dudorov's recommendation not to give prisoners too much money).

Local authorities were charged with finding employment for those being released. On 8 December 1957 the government approved a decree jointly drawn up by the Prosecutor's Office and the MVD on the 'correctional labour colonies and prisons of the Ministry of Internal Affairs'. The text required strict separation between different categories of prisoners, so as not to mix hardened criminals with first-time offenders. It ordered revision of procedures for early release based on a calculation of working days and sharply reduced the number of prisoners who were allowed to leave colony confines unescorted. It introduced non-cash payment, as well as other measures.

From 1953 onwards, the number of prisoners decreased regularly. Between 1953 and 1957, the Presidium of the Supreme Soviet announced several amnesties for different categories of prisoner – among them, one in 1955 for people who had collaborated with the German occupier. In 1957, the fortieth anniversary of the October revolution saw a new amnesty affecting a significant number of inmates. In 1956 and 1959, commissions were set up in the republics to review directly in prison establishments the cases of those convicted of crimes against the state, malfeasance and other economic crimes, as well as minor offences. The Prosecutor General of the USSR helped to draw up these measures and oversaw their implementation.

By January 1961, the prison population had declined significantly and its composition by category of crime had changed. In 1953, 10.7 per cent of prisoners were sentenced for organized crime, robbery, premeditated murder, and rape; in 1961 the corresponding figure was 31.5 per cent. This meant that a substantial percentage of prisoners was now composed of common-law offenders, with a hard core of recidivists and dangerous criminals. This is why the colonies and prisons statute issued on 8 December 1958 now seemed inadequate: it was insufficiently severe on dangerous recidivists and the fight against crime was suffering in consequence. So on 5 November 1959 the Central Committee enjoined the Prosecutor General's Office to step up the fight against such criminals and ensure an appropriate prison regime for them.

Two years later, the government was still not satisfied with the situation. On 3 April 1961 a new decree by the Central Committee and the Council of Ministers ordered the internal affairs ministries of the republics to do more for the prison systems they were responsible for, to analyse the condition of each institution carefully, and to reinforce the separation between different categories of criminal. It also abolished the liberal system of early release for a good work record. As our documents indicate, these and other measures had been under discussion for almost five years, but had not always been implemented. Liberal and conservative politicians and jurists had sparred over every point, and there were many. Another important measure was the creation on 27 February 1959 of the collegium of the Prosecutor General and republican equivalents, followed by numerous tours of inspection and training sessions by leading functionaries from the USSR Prosecutor's Office, with a view to reinforcing the fight against crime and improving prison administration.

We shall say no more about the way in which different government bodies tackled these issues. Specialist monographs would be required to tell the story in precise detail. But we can draw a few provisional conclusions. The Stalinist system of hard unpaid slave labour by prisoners – most of them convicted of common-law offences, but many of them 'counter-revolutionaries' who had committed no crime – was now a thing of the past. The same applies to mass exile settlements where more than 2 million people served sentences, often for life: in 1960, these were almost entirely emptied of inmates and such sentences were largely discontinued.[3] On the other hand, normalization of the prison and penal complex was not straightforward in a system that had inherited a strong inclination to punish without concerning itself unduly with proof of guilt. If that system had nothing to do with justice, the 1960s saw an attempt to create a proper justice system. This is what clearly emerges if we turn to the intensive drafting and redrafting of the criminal and prison codes by penal institutions and the government bodies responsible for them. The discussions and pressures for further change that began immediately after the war developed with Khrushchev's arrival in power, and continued almost to the very end of the Soviet system. A rapid survey of the legislation in force in 1984 provides a picture of the juridical principles that governed the treatment of offenders down to 1991.

In particular, we shall examine penal policy and 'prison labour law' as set out in the relevant codes and commentaries on them. This is a rather onerous exercise, but since the discovery of Hammurabi's code his-

---

3   This information derives not from the sources cited above, but from the appendix to my *Russia – USSR – Russia*, New York 1995.

torians have known how instructive legal texts can be – even if they are not always followed. The changes introduced by these codes should not be underestimated.[4] This particularly applies to the right now enjoyed by prisoners to meet with their lawyers, without time limits and with no guards present. This formed part of a broader definition of prisoners' rights, based on a premise to which the codes and jurisprudence devoted much space – namely, that imprisonment does not entail loss of the status of citizen and hence of citizens' rights. Punishment restricts such rights, of course, but prisoners continue to belong to the community of citizens. The restrictions were serious: a prisoner's wife could divorce him without waiting for his release, prisoners did not have the right to vote, they could not freely dispose of their own money, and so on. But they enjoyed the basic right to criticize and launch complaints against the prison administration. They could do so directly, in a letter to the administration, which was obliged to respond. They could also appeal to other instances (party and state) via the prison administration. The latter would probably seek to persuade the prisoner not to proceed with a complaint, but if he insisted the administration was obliged to submit it. Should it fail to do so, he could disclose the matter to visiting family or friends. The prison administration was not entitled to open prisoners' letters to prosecutors and had to forward them within twenty-four hours.

As pointed out, an important advance was the prisoner's right to see a lawyer with no time limit. Another source indicates that lawyers' visits to prisoners came under the section on 'visiting rights'.[5] But they were regulated by the 'correctional labour codes' of the republics, not by the All-Union code. Unless these codes specified otherwise, meetings with a lawyer were to be authorized following a written request by the prisoner, a member of his family, or a representative of a public organization. They were to be conducted outside working hours and the lawyer must be duly accredited. If so requested by prisoner or lawyer,

---

4   My main sources here are N. A. Struchkov, *Kurs Ispravitel'no – Trudovogo Prava: Problemy Obshchei Chasti*, Moscow 1984 and N. A. Struchkov and V. A. Kirin, eds, *Kommentarii k Osnovam Ispravitel'no-Trudovgo Zakonodatel'tsva SSSR i Soiuznykh Respublik*, Moscow 1972. Supplementary material derives from the highly competent British scholar, W. I. Butler, *Soviet Law*, London 1983, which offers a very balanced view of the Soviet legal system. Other references will be cited separately.

5   N. A. Struchkov, *Kurs Ispravitel'no – Trudovogo Prava: Problemy Osobennoi Chasti*, Moscow 1985, pp. 83–4.

the meeting was to be held in private. (I must confess that discovering these legal provisions in the texts of the late 1970s and early 1980s came as a surprise.)

There is plentiful evidence from prosecutors, courts and local bodies of the large number of complaints from prisoners received by the Ministry of Internal Affairs itself, government supervisory agencies (central and local), regional bodies and public organizations. They were more or less carefully investigated, or passed on to more competent authorities.[6] Legal power to monitor respect for the law inside places of confinement was granted to a number of bodies, of which the most powerful were the Prosecutor's Office and state control agencies (whatever their current title). The MVD also had an internal general inspectorate, equipped with real power and able to conduct detailed inquiries. It was quite legitimately suspected of bias, given that the prison system came within its ministry's domain. Nevertheless, there is no doubt that senior ministerial officials were well informed of the situation.

The control exercised by the higher courts over compliance with the law in the justice system had an influence on the bodies in charge of penal institutions. Such courts handled cases of violations by prison administrations and appeals, as well as cases requiring adjudication of the appropriateness of a sentence. Their activity certainly had an impact on the lot of prisoners and the atmosphere of the prison system in general. The right of social bodies to take an interest in the fate of prisoners had a similar effect, because it now formed one of a set of rights and possibilities of redress.

Political prisoners, including the better-known dissidents, were not entirely denied access to judicial review or channels for complaints. Protests by scientists and other members of the intelligentsia, addressed directly to the Central Committee or other high instances, or transmitted by confidential channels, are well documented. Some of them could be quite effective. International pressure also had an impact, prompting the authorities to prefer stripping dissidents of their nationality and exiling them abroad to keeping them in prison. We shall return to this subject.

The concern on the part of the authorities and judges not to have minor offenders mix with dangerous criminals – a principle adopted by

---

6   Ibid. The same author's *Problemy Obshche Chasti* (Moscow 1984), pp. 21–22 is more clear on many aspects.

democratic systems – led to the creation of institutions for different categories of prisoner with corresponding regimes. People serving a first sentence were separated from recidivists in all categories. There were separate institutions for women and minors. Finally, high-security complexes, isolated from the rest of the system, held those who had been convicted of 'especially dangerous crimes against the state', 'particularly dangerous recidivists', and prisoners condemned to death but whose sentence had been commuted by a pardon or amnesty. Foreigners and stateless persons were also confined in separate prison establishments. Republics had the right to demand the separation of other categories as well. In contrast, none of these distinctions applied in prison hospitals, whose regulations were determined by the Ministry of Internal Affairs in consultation with prosecutors.

In total, the system had four categories of corrective labour colonies, differentiated by their internal regime: general, 'enhanced', 'strict', and 'special' regimes. Added to this were the various categories of 'settlement colonies'. The 'strict' regime was intended for those convicted of 'particularly dangerous crimes against the state' and persons who had already served one sentence; while the 'special' regime applied to multiple offenders and women who had had their death sentence commuted. The 'settlement colonies' were for inmates well on the road to rehabilitation who had been transferred from other categories of colony.

Prisons comprised a sixth category, receiving those who had committed heinous crimes; especially dangerous recidivists were also sent to a prison if the court so specified. They also contained inmates transferred from colonies as a punishment for bad behaviour, as well as prisoners doing service work there instead of being sent to colonies. Prisons had two regimes: 'general' and 'strict'. A prisoner could not be subject to the latter for more than six months. Women who were pregnant, or accompanied by young children, were exempt from it. In the general regime, prisoners occupied collective cells, although if the prison governor so decided they could, with the prosecutor's consent, be transferred to individual cells. They were allowed one hour's exercise a day (30 minutes in the special regime). Those who served their prison sentence as auxiliary staff could keep their money, receive short-term visits and packages (as per the norms of the general regime), and buy food.

Two regimes were in force in corrective labour colonies for adolescents, which formed another important sector: 'general' and 'enhanced' – the latter for very serious crimes.

Finally, in the settlement colonies, where there was supervision but no guards, inmates could move freely from the time they awoke until bedtime. If their work or studies so required, this freedom extended to the confines of the administrative region. Inmates were allowed to wear civilian clothes, carry money and use it as they wished, and keep valuables. With administrative authorization, they could live with their family in the colony; they could acquire a house and cultivate a private plot. Once married, men and women could live together in the same colony, regardless of where they had separately served the first part of their sentences.

All able-bodied inmates were obliged to perform work in accordance with their physical abilities and, so far as was possible, their professional skills. The work was primarily done in enterprises located within the colony. Inmates might work for other agencies as well, but it was up to the MVD to organize its own workshops and factories. Economic agencies were obliged to help correctional institutions realize this objective.

In principle, the 'special' regime required inmates to do hard labour. In reality, they were given the available jobs in branches of the surrounding economy, which meant that the labour was not necessarily 'hard'. The physically handicapped had a lighter workload. Given that the professed objective was correction and re-education, the work was not supposed to entail physical suffering. Excessive toil would have contradicted the principle that work was not a punishment. It was up to a medical commission to assess each inmate's physical abilities, taking account of state of health, previous work experience, and so on. Work in the inmate's speciality could be refused only if the court's sentence expressly forbade it. The aim was for everyone to perform profitable labour and to keep work in the colony's internal services to a minimum.

We should indicate at this point that the issue of 'hard labour' under the 'special' regime was much debated. One senses from their reservations, which we have set out, that jurists were uncomfortable about it. When not seeking – indirectly – to challenge the very idea of 'hard labour', they attempted to water it down in one way or another. After all, these texts were studied in the law faculties where jurists were being trained. The latter certainly asked questions in the 1980s, or even earlier.

The vagueness of the category of 'hard labour' increases still further when we read the relevant paragraphs about feeding prisoners. Those subject to the special regime were entitled only to smaller, less varied rations. The suspicion arises that such prisoners were being punished by eventual starvation. The undernourishment of prisoners condemned to hard labour (or the mere power to inflict such punishment) was something that jurists commenting on the codes were vague about. However heinous their crimes (these were the most dangerous criminals), it left room for abuse. In contrast, pregnant women and sick people were entitled to better food. More generally, women (especially if they had young children), adolescents, and invalids were supposed to have special attention and better conditions. This prescription was probably followed: the death of a baby would inevitably have entailed an investigation.

LABOUR IN THE COLONIES

All prisoners worked an eight-hour day, except on Sundays and public holidays. But they were not entitled to a vacation and their years in prison were not taken into account when it came to calculating pension entitlements. Otherwise, health and safety rules and other provisions of labour law did apply to the colonies. People who became disabled during their confinement were entitled to a pension and compensation after their release. Prisoners' work was paid in line with civilian norms, minus the cost of upkeep (food, clothing) and, where stipulated, deductions ordered by the courts.

The research of W. I. Butler, a Western specialist on Soviet law, provides further information and some chronological clarification.[7] It was on 26 June 1963 that Soviet republics established the additional penal institutions known as 'settlement colonies', intended for prisoners who had displayed evidence of their aptitude for reintegration into society. On 3 June 1968 a statute on labour colonies for minors was enacted. Even though the texts were not published, such legislative measures helped shape the general development of penal institutions – in these instances, in the direction of reducing unnecessary severity in sentencing. Jurists exercised significant influence.[8] Among them we can identify a consistent school of thought that sought to push things in a positive direction, but which obviously needed support from above.

---

7 See Butler, *Soviet Law*, pp. 282 ff.
8 As documented in the work of Peter Solomon, *Soviet Criminologists and Criminal Policy: Specialists in Policy Making*, London 1978.

The MVD of the USSR determined the procedure for assigning convicted persons to one or other of the penal institutions or, in consultation with the Prosecutor's Office, to psychiatric institutions. Medical care in prisons and colonies was jointly regulated by the MVD and the Health Ministry. In 1977, 'Rules for Internal Order in Corrective Labour Institutions', valid for the whole USSR, were adopted by the MVD. Other rules defining the regime of a place of confinement could be issued by the USSR's Council of Ministers or that of the relevant republic, as well as by the Minister of Internal Affairs and his deputies. But Soviet jurists publicly warned against granting prerogatives to heads of internal affairs departments at intermediate levels or the directors of the institutions themselves. Their approach was a realistic one, but they would probably have also liked to reduce the MVD's prerogatives in determining prison regimes, because (or this is my hypothesis) many penal institutions were located far from Moscow and their administrations contained supporters of harsh methods. These jurists knew their country's history and the kind of people who worked in its law-and-order agencies.

Some of the principles professed by Soviet jurists under the banner of 'socialist humanism' did not aim only to guide interpretation of the law. While pressing for the law to be implemented to protect society from criminals, they also sought to promote a multi-faceted policy of reform, re-education and resocialization of prisoners, with a view to reintegrating them into society. Combining punishment with labour – a key part of their credo – was the best way of enabling a prisoner to return to normal life. Respecting human dignity, remitting sentences for good behaviour, combining coercion and persuasion, differentiating between punishments by separating categories of prisoner, and adjusting the severity of sentences to the gravity of the crime – these were principles they constantly invoked and fought for. Of the six categories of prison regime that we have listed, the two strictest involved only a relatively small number of inmates (unfortunately, precise figures are unavailable). Jurists also promoted the principle of 'individualization' – that is to say, adapting punishment and re-education to the personality of each prisoner, on the basis that everyone could be reformed.

It would certainly be reasonable to suppose that these 'principles' were unacceptable to conservatives of all hues, and even to some liberal-minded people who did not believe that prison warders or administrations could educate anyone and who were fearful that such measures might have negative consequences.

Other issues debated by specialists cannot be broached here. But one point that we have already discussed merits renewed emphasis: the basic premise that a prisoner remained a citizen. In itself, this challenged the deeply rooted Soviet tendency to repression. The very category of 'enemy of the people', and the special treatment meted out to those who fell under it, was implicitly – and often explicitly – condemned in numerous texts from the 1960s onwards. The provisions under which people were pursued for 'counter-revolutionary crimes' or as an 'enemy of the people' were removed from the criminal code, and the expressions disappeared from the terminology of law-enforcement. In 1961 they were replaced in the code by six paragraphs dealing with 'the most dangerous crimes against the state', which formed the basis for subsequent persecution of political opponents – unlike the furies of Stalinism, without providing for the death sentence. Several such crimes were punished by deprivation of Soviet citizenship and expulsion from the USSR (which was not in itself an atrocity). Guilt had to be defined in accordance with the Soviet codes. Sheer arbitrariness thus ceased to be the rule. But the very fact of pursuing political opponents, even citizens who were simply expressing criticism, was an embarrassment for the Soviet government, internationally and internally.

It is not easy to ascertain whether the letter and spirit of the legislation we have evoked were observed in practice. I have not come across a reliable monograph on the post-Stalinist prison system, except as regards the conditions of detention of political prisoners, particularly 'dissidents'. The latter were invariably held in high-security colonies in Mordovia and the Urals, and subject to the 'special' regime. Conditions were very strict and relations between prisoners – some of whom were combative and unyielding – and a brutal prison administration helped make camp life particularly harsh. Comprehensive research would be required to know the true state of these camps: their number, the sentences served, casualties, and so on. We have some information courtesy of Amnesty International,[9] and many of the rights that we have cited from juridical sources are not mentioned in it. Amnesty International refers to the limitations placed on the presence of lawyers during investigations (which we knew about), but says nothing about access to lawyers once convicted persons were serving their sentences. We can surmise that, having been convicted of an 'especially dangerous crime against the

---

9 See Amnesty International, *Prisoners of Conscience in the USSR*, London 1974.

state' and confined to high-security prisons with the strictest regime, political detainees had fewer rights than other inmates. For example, whereas a generally respected legal provision allowed most prisoners to be held in the region where their family lived, legal texts provided for the converse in the case of dissidents. In the absence of proof to the contrary, there is no reason to suppose that they were regarded as citizens with inalienable rights.

The situation of the broad prison population improved appreciably, but without additional information there is no way of knowing to what extent the reality corresponded to the new legislation. Because of the dispersal of the colonies over vast territories, the poor level of training of prison administrators, and the brutal habits of MVD prison staff – not to mention the obvious difficulty of handling hardened criminals – it is likely that actual conditions must have departed from legal provisions to varying degrees.

Even so, the existence of codes and powerful institutions responsible for enforcing them, public opinion, and prisoners' considerable experience in working the system and using the relevant provisions to their advantage, make it reasonable to assume that the reforms created a system quite distinct from that in force under Stalin, including for political prisoners – a subject we shall return to. At all events, this is the conclusion pointed to by the enormous quantity of material we possess, whether the complaints, appeals to prosecutors and judges, and demands for reviews from prisoners or their families reaching party and state authorities; or the various investigative committees (whose documents are sometimes available to Western observers). Appeals procedures, and the intervention of prosecutors or higher courts exercising their powers to review the decisions of lower courts, were important correctives in legal procedures and improved the lot of prisoners.

Another significant development, bound up with the rationalizing (should we say modernizing?) trend in penal policy, was the strong pressure from legal circles and their political allies to moderate the system's punitive bent still further, which – or so many argued – solved nothing and simply created new problems. W. I. Butler has studied the growing pressure for the application of types of sentence which, however harsh, were non-custodial. Thus he has analysed a whole range of 'conditional sentences', the harshest consisting in exile from a given place or banishment to some remote location. Others took the form of mandatory labour (convicted persons continued to work as before, but with a deduction equivalent to a large fine from their wages); aiding ex-prisoners with their reintegration; and sentences without mandatory labour (introduced into the legislation of the USSR and the republic by a decree of 15 March 1983 that regulated the status of such sentences, their supervision by prosecutors, and their execution). In addition to the fines that we have already mentioned, this type of penalty included proscription from holding certain posts or engaging in specified activities, confiscation of property, the loss of a military rank or a title, and public cautions in the workplace. Reforms in criminal justice in the 1970s and the early 1980s indicate that this was a growing trend, and non-custodial sentences became increasingly widespread among the judiciary.

It should be remembered that the number of political prisoners and dangerous criminals confined in prisons, or the two categories of colony with the strictest regimes, was relatively small. The great majority of prisoners served their sentences in the 'milder' categories, and this was the target population for the experiments defended among the higher judiciary, jurists and some government circles. The aim was a large-scale 'de-penalization' of a system traditionally inclined to impose predominantly custodial sentences. The fight to liberalize sentences had begun much earlier, in the immediate post-Stalin years or even before. But it became a serious – and largely successful – struggle in the early 1980s. The phrase 'in search of de-penalization', used by Todd Fogleson (from whom I derive this information),[10] perfectly encapsulates this period.

Data from the Russian Federation's Justice Ministry indicate that in 1980 roughly 94 per cent of defendants in criminal cases were found guilty, and nearly 60 per cent of them were imprisoned. In 1990 these numbers fell to 84 per cent and 40 per cent respectively. According to Fogleson, shifts of this magnitude are rare; and it is difficult to explain the phenomenon exclusively on the basis of the published material and interviews (the criminal justice archives for the late 1970s and early 1980s remain inaccessible). But he later surmises, not without reason, that labour shortages might have had something to do with it – a point we shall return to.

For now, we shall attend to an important discovery by Fogleson

---

10 See Todd Fogleson, 'The Reform of Criminal Justice and Evolution of Judicial Dependence in Late Soviet Russia', in Peter H. Solomon, Jr, ed., *Reforming Justice in Russia, 1864–1996: Power, Culture and the Limits of Legal Order*, Armonk (New York) and London 1997.

relating to the political sphere. In the past, judges had been supervised by party officials and justice ministries, whereas the higher courts essentially exercised their powers of judicial oversight. In the 1970s, the campaign to liberalize criminal justice was not led by the party, which had relinquished interference in this domain. The Justice Ministry was not a driving force either. It was the upper tier of the court system – i.e. the Supreme Court of the USSR and its republican equivalents – that took the initiative in pressing lower courts to 'de-penalize' their verdicts and make greater use of non-custodial sentences. To achieve this, it used its appellate or oversight powers, issuing criticisms and organizing training seminars for judges.

The first significant changes occurred in February and March 1977, when the Supreme Soviet 'decriminalized' a whole range of minor offences, which were henceforth punished by simple fines or two weeks' imprisonment (the minimum sentence had hitherto been one year). In cases they did not regard as 'socially dangerous', judges could now hand down suspended sentences, as well as penalties of mandatory labour for sentences of less than three years. In 1978 the Supreme Soviet broadened the categories of offences to which fines and non-custodial sentences could apply. Let us note that the arguments in favour of this reduction in penalties for minor offices derived from Soviet criminologists, who questioned the efficacy of short-term imprisonment. One of the most eminent among them argued from 1976 onwards that much of the increase in crime was caused by family break-up, disruption of social ties, lack of integration into broader social networks, and the increasing impact of social benefits. Isolation in prisons would only make things worse. Others, cited by Fogleson, maintained that non-custodial sentences prevented people thinking of themselves as criminals and hence actually becoming such.

Thus, in 1977–8 prominent jurists argued for 'greater economy in the means of repression' and changes in criminal law that would make it more effective in helping to realize the system's general objectives. Others insisted that their findings were scientific and that policy in the late twentieth century should be based on science. Some authors urged a move away from a punitive logic to a utilitarian philosophy: retribution should take second place to the achievement of social goals.

While the Supreme Court pressed lower courts to make greater use of differential sentencing, and to be more exacting about the conduct of criminal inquiries and proof of guilt, the overall results of this policy were a disappointment to its promoters. In November 1984, the Justice

Ministry concluded that some judges had not got the message and paid too little heed to the decisions of higher courts. The old policy was certainly more unproblematic and more acceptable to the repressive mentality that persisted widely in lower Soviet courts. Nevertheless, other changes were to follow, for the penal reform front was now broad and mobile.

The legal, judicial and ideological reasoning behind this impulse to break with punitive tendencies was not the whole story. The growing manpower shortage, which we shall discuss in more detail later, was a background factor in the de-penalization endeavour and the debates over it. In the Stalinist system, 'free labour' was no such thing, since workers were attached to their workplace by a whole series of legal and economic constraints. The actual situation was attenuated by an almost unstoppable spontaneous mobility of labour, which the authorities nevertheless sought to counter by legal and economic measures, and by campaigns of moral denunciation of shirkers and deserters.

Here we are dealing with a broader phenomenon – a natural development that could not be contained even at the height of Stalinism, and which ended up being legitimated and recognized during the post-Stalinist changes. This is what we might call the 'de-Stalinization of labour'. Reform of the penal system and the trend towards 'de-penalizing' sentences formed part of this broader process. The powerful waves of change that kept sweeping over workplace relations forced penal and social policy to follow suit. The survey of labour legislation and practices that we are about to undertake indicates how, in factories and offices, workers succeeded in acquiring *de jure* and *de facto* rights. These rights were written into legal documents, beginning with the labour code.

LABOUR LAW: A HISTORICAL SURVEY

From the very beginning of the Soviet regime, labour laws were a prominent part of the government's agenda: the eight-hour working day, two weeks' paid holiday, pensions, unemployment, sickness and disability insurance. On 9 December 1918 the Russian Federation's labour code was promulgated (but never published). All those between the ages of sixteen and fifty, with the exception of the disabled, had an 'obligation to work'. The principle of equal pay for equal work was proclaimed and various working conditions were subject to regulation.

According to Soviet experts, it was the Civil War of 1918–21 that dictated enlistment of labour in place of voluntary contractual relationships. A new code promulgated on 30 October 1922 came into force on 15 November. The 'obligation to work' was replaced by 'employment procedures': labour relationships were henceforth based on voluntary agreement. The 'obligation to work' was restricted to exceptional situations (natural disasters, urgent public tasks). A separate chapter dealt with collective agreements and individual work contracts. Labour and management could alter the latter, as long as certain key provisions were respected. Collective negotiations were conducted by trade unions; labour disputes were settled by people's courts; various ad hoc commissions on wages, conciliation bodies, and arbitration tribunals were established. The eight-hour day was maintained and overtime was regulated. In short, the 1922 labour code closely resembled those of Western countries, even if it favoured the state sector.

The transition to national economic planning in 1929 brought with it changes in several provisions. The state was now the sole employer and unions became a component of economic management. From 1934 onwards, they no longer drafted collective agreements, but administered social security and enforced regulations – something that had previously fallen to the powerful Labour Commissariat. In 1933 the latter was abolished: it was supposedly merged with the unions, but they did not possess the same authority as a Commissariat belonging to the government. Compulsory assignment of graduates to workplaces was introduced in 1930 as part of planning procedures. And in 1932, labour control was tightened – a single day's absence was immediately punishable by dismissal. Nineteen thirty-eight saw a further spate of disciplinary measures: arriving late for work, or leaving early, became an offence. A decree from early 1940 proscribed resignation from a job without the consent of management. Contrariwise, the state could transfer employees at will, without their consent. Collective agreements were formally reintroduced in 1947, but despite having been abolished in 1935 they had actually survived in various guises, indicating their necessity in workplaces. As for wage increases, they became ever more dependent on centralized decisions, with some flexibility permitted at local level. Thus, between 1930 and 1940 most of the 1922 labour code had been rendered obsolete; and the text was no longer published.[11]

---

11 Butler, *Soviet Law*, pp. 208–22 is my main source here.

In the post-Stalin era, some of the most draconian measures were rescinded. Workers recovered the right to resign or change jobs, and new texts (1957) relaxed the strict provisions introduced during the war. A new labour code was set in train. A first draft was published for discussion in 1959, but it was only enacted in 1970 and came into force on 1 January 1971.

Analysis of these texts, and the commentaries they prompted, allows us to track the development of labour legislation up to 1986. The right to leave a job, by cancelling the contract with one's employer, was set down as basic; management could not refuse it.[12] The 'work contract' became a serious procedure, with numerous guarantees for both parties and special clauses favouring workers. Managerial rights were clearly spelt out, including the power to impose sanctions for misdemeanours that are detailed in the code.

Cancellation of the contract by the employee (in the case of permanent contracts) was already included in article 16 of the 'Foundations of Labour Law' (replicated in the Russian Federation's labour code and elsewhere). Employees had to give two months' notice in writing; if they had valid grounds, the period of notice could be reduced to a month. A fixed-term contract (section 2 of article 10) could be revoked by a worker ahead of time in the event of illness, disability, infringement of the regulations governing individual or collective contracts, and for other valid reasons (as specified in the new versions of the relevant section drafted in 1980 and 1983).

The 1983 version also allowed workers to leave their jobs before the two months' notice was up. In all cases, management was obliged to return the employee's 'work record book' and pay any outstanding wages. These clauses were extremely detailed and one commentator even adds that the employee is not required to explain why he wishes to leave his job (this is in connection with a 1980 text which states that two weeks' notice is sufficient – a mere three days in the case of seasonal workers). Only those who wished to quit their job while serving a non-

---

12 Material on this, labour disputes and other problems derives from V. I. Terebilov, ed., *Kommentarii k Zakonodatel'stvu o Trude*, Moscow 1996. The general editor was chairman of the USSR Supreme Court. Labour disputes are studied in detail on p. 409 (paras 86–94 and 201–24 of the labour code). On the work contract and the worker's right to cancel it, see pp. 50–5, in particular para 29 of the Russian Federation's labour code: 'Grounds for cancelling the work contract'.

custodial sentence had to obtain authorization, from the body supervising their sentence.

LABOUR DISPUTES

Labour disputes take up a lot of space in the labour codes, central and republican. A whole system was established, comprising an array of institutions and rules, to handle every possible kind of complaint by workers (including work norms). Thus, every large enterprise and office was required to have a 'labour disputes committee', with equal union–management representation. In smaller enterprises and offices, a 'trade-union commission' was the competent body, and if it could not settle a dispute it was referred to a local (town or district) tribunal. Disputes involving senior employees and technical staff were a matter for the management of the enterprise concerned. If the judgement went in favour of the plaintiff, management was required not only to compensate him but also to take measures to eliminate the causes of such disputes. Where management was deemed guilty of having violated workers' rights, the case could end up in the courts.[13] In such instances, it was judged according to civil law. Prosecutors became involved and were authorized to accept complaints (in accordance with a list of very precise instructions); they even had the power to initiate proceedings if one of the parties broke the law. Employees involved in a dispute at a given level of an enterprise could simultaneously appeal to their senior management. They could go to the courts if they were not satisfied with the decision of their enterprise's union commission. Employers had the same right. Finally, in the event of dismissal, employees could turn directly to the courts – just as employers could sue them for any damage they might have caused – without going through either the union commission or labour disputes committee.[14]

The code was highly elaborate and extremely detailed. It indicates that employees could act as legitimate parties in court actions over work-related issues, though it might be wondered whether the legal

---

13 Decision of the plenum of the Supreme Court, 29 June 1979 on the tasks of courts, in the light of the Central Committee decision about improving ideological and political-educational work.
14 See Iu. A. Korshunov *et al.*, *Sovetskoe Zakonodatel'stvo o Trude: Spravochnik*, Moscow 1980, pp. 57 ff.

procedures were not excessively complicated for workers, whereas they were much more straightforward for employers. But the available statistics allow us to conclude that workers also learnt to use these procedures at different levels of conflict resolution, and turned in massive numbers to the courts, which were often more favourable to their cause than to the management's.[15]

At all events, the work contract committed both parties. And if management had a lot of power, employees possessed a more effective weapon than resort to the courts: they could defend their interests by changing jobs. The phenomenon of labour turnover was studied by Soviet sociologists and statisticians in detail. Administrators – not workers – formed the privileged class, but given that labour shortages loomed on the horizon, the bureaucracy was forced to arrive at solutions and accommodations to keep workers in their posts. Larger enterprises disposed of more means to do this, offering housing, clubs, crèches and other amenities, or squeezing the expenses for them out of municipalities that often depended on the presence of such enterprises (particularly with the proliferation of factory towns – a long-forgotten chapter in the history of Western industrialization).

The broader social phenomenon just mentioned – labour turnover – affected all sectors. Underlying and surrounding the provisions of the labour code was a quite different reality, with constant changes of employer, and migration to areas with new jobs and back again when working, housing and climatic conditions proved too exacting. These labour-force trends presented economic planning with serious problems. The Stalinist solution – mobilization, coercion and police methods – was now excluded. The system's rulers had to face what can legitimately be called a 'labour market' and the emergence of a tacit understanding between workers and the employer-state. It is encapsulated in the formula 'You get what you pay for' – or, in its surrealist version, 'You pretend to pay us and we pretend to work'. But the term 'labour market' captures this reality better than the 'surrealism' beloved of some intellectuals. What was actually occurring was the emergence and operation of an open, direct process – and/or, in part, an informal,

---

15 The last version of the USSR's labour code was published in 1970 (and that of the RSFSR in 1971). In my view, the best source on these codes and subsequent work-related legislation is V. I. Terebilov, 'Verkhsuda SSSR', in A. I. Startseva, M. E. Pankin, eds, *Kommentarii k Zakonodatel'stvu o Trude*, Moscow 1986.

indirect process – of economic bargaining, which justifies the use of this term. Increasing labour shortages exercised implacable constraints, because employers were not only badly in need of manpower, but also – by virtue of a paradox that hovered over the employment situation – had an interest in retaining a reserve labour-force. This created an interesting anomaly: workers leaving jobs in difficult areas with a labour shortage, on the grounds that the state had not fulfilled its contractual obligations to guarantee decent living conditions, could return to regions with a labour surplus – and still find employment.

The developments we have just described – in policing and penal policy, the abolition of the Gulag and mass terror, legal codes and labour rights – also affected the functioning of the state, its bureaucracy, and the party. A reinvigoration of conservative reflexes, and corresponding institutional changes (including in the KGB), were the leadership's response to what it perceived of the wider social world, particularly the world of work. Confronted with mounting social pressure for greater relaxation of the regime, some wanted to react, with the KGB's help, by tightening the screws. But it was becoming ever more difficult to find the 'screws' for the job.

15

THE KGB AND THE POLITICAL OPPOSITION

We can now turn our attention to one of the key law-enforcement agencies – the secret police – and the way it dealt with political opponents. As yet, we possess no authoritative history of the KGB and its archives are, at time of writing, still closed to researchers. We shall therefore have to make do with some of the information that has emerged.

In its various pre-Khrushchevite incarnations – Cheka, GPU, NKVD – the secret police had a chequered history that has been recounted by historians. From the creation of the Cheka (*Chrezvychainaia Kommissiia*) in 1917, its agents have always been officially referred to as 'chekists' (*chekisty*) – and still are in post-Soviet Russia. This unfailing attachment to a prestigious title, which is explained by the role of these agents in the revolutionary period, possibly served the tacit purpose of distancing the agency from the Stalinist period. Chekists fought for a great cause, risked their lives and died for it, whereas under Stalin NKVD operatives (*nkvdisty*) tortured and killed masses of innocent people. They too risked their lives, but not heroically: they might be eliminated by their patron to blot out the traces of the criminal deeds he himself ordered them to commit.

It is worth recalling that when, in 1934, the GPU was supposedly absorbed by the NKVD (Commissariat for Internal Affairs), it was in fact the reverse that occurred. The NKVD was taken over by the leadership of the GPU, which was kept intact inside the commissariat as the GUGB (General Directorate of State Security). In that way, the complex of political security and intelligence services, domestic and international, could at a moment's notice become an independent agency (of the MGB or KGB variety), or return to being a component of the NKVD–MVD. It should also be remembered that under Stalin the latter was headed by the chief of the security services, and that the 'part' was therefore in control of the 'whole'. Why such frequent, successive restructurings were required is a question for experts. For us, the key point is that the secret police and intelligence services remained substantially intact, even if the great purges took a heavy toll on them and numerous changes post-Stalin created agitation – sometimes chaos – in their ranks.

At one stage, the MVD – a bureaucratic 'superpower' – ruled over the Gulag, the whole intelligence complex and substantial military special forces, as well as border guards. In addition, it had all the usual functions of an interior ministry – public order, public records, local government supervision. After Stalin's death its power was seriously curtailed, and in 1962 it was abolished as a Union ministry. On 10 February 1954 the MGB (Ministry of State Security) once again became independent of the MVD – this time for good. It was placed under the authority of General Serov, previously MVD deputy minister, and several MVD functions were transferred to it. Serov was moved from this position on 8 December 1958, having been appointed head of military counter-intelligence (GRU) and deputy chief of staff of the armed forces. The MGB, which in the interim had become the KGB (K for *Komitet*), was entrusted to A. N. Shelepin, who had started his career in the Komsomol, before heading the Central Committee department responsible for supervising republican party organizations. On Khrushchev's instructions, Shelepin simplified the KGB's sprawling organizational structure and proceeded to substantial staff reductions. These changes have been seen by some historians as 'cardinal' and are summed up in Khrushchev's anti-militaristic phrase: 'tearing off their pompous epaulettes and trouser stripes' (it sounds more pithy in Russian: *raspogonim, razlampasim*). This was why neither Shelepin nor the new Interior Minister Dudorov was entitled to the military titles and uniforms so highly coveted by some leading figures.

Things fell slowly into place in the KGB's Moscow headquarters on the Lubianka. The secret police found its bearings once again, though not without some significant changes in its modus operandi (which fell far short of what liberal-minded citizens, jurists and intellectuals wanted to see). The KGB's internal structure remained unchanged from 1958 until the mid-1960s. At the same time, however, changes affecting the character of the regime – the growing importance of laws and legal codes, the considerable role of the legal professions, the diminished effectiveness of coercive measures in an increasingly urban society – were bound to have an impact on it. It is true that in this treacherous sphere there were 'natural' limits to change – notably because the same was true of the regime as a whole – and it is important not to forget them. Even so, the changes that did occur were substantial.

To begin with, curtailing the powers of Stalin's secret police was carried out in stages, but amounted to a thorough cleansing operation. Disbanding such extra-judicial bodies as the special conferences, the kangaroo courts operated directly by the political police, or the sinister local 'troikas', marked a decisive step, which was followed by obliging the KGB to hand over the results of its investigations to the regular courts. This move eliminated some of the most shocking potential for arbitrariness, which the security services had been instructed to exploit to the full. The abolition of the Gulag as an industrial labour pool for the secret police, and the latter's consequent disappearance as an economic actor, was another crucial turning point. The ongoing campaign against the venality and brutality of the police, whether secret or in uniform, tended in the same direction. In Part One we indicated how, as early as the 1920s, the GPU had bridled at supervision by public prosecutors – derided as 'legalistic hair-splitting' by the chekists, who preferred to have a free hand to pursue the regime's enemies. The prosecutors had lost out at the time, and many of them later perished. Now, the restoration of supervision of KGB investigations by prosecutors was in train, though it was not without its ups and downs.

Among the significant measures taken under Khrushchev to rein in the Stalinist monstrosity and change the climate in the secret services was the introduction of new people to lead them, selected from the party apparatus. In his autobiography,[1] Mikoyan, who in reality was second in importance in the regime after Khrushchev, approved of this move, but criticized him for the appointment of General Serov, who had been NKVD head in the Ukraine from 2 September 1939 until 25 July 1941, at the time when Khrushchev was Central Committee first secretary there. The new ruler in the Kremlin trusted Serov in a way no one else did – at least if we are to believe Mikoyan, who claims that Khrushchev was easily manipulated by skilful sycophants. When finally forced to remove Serov by irrefutable arguments (they actually derived

---

1   Anastas Mikoyan, *Tak Bylo: Razmyshleniia o Minuvshem*, Moscow 1999.

from opponents of Khrushchev), he still appointed him to an honorific position.

The MGB had been reconstructed in 1954 as an agency (the KGB) with jurisdiction over the whole USSR, and it absorbed a growing number of functions that had previously fallen to the MVD – border guards, among others. Unlike the MVD, however, it no longer ran an enormous prison system (that remained with the MVD) and operated only a smaller number of prisons for suspects under investigation. It is possible that it also possessed a larger camp or colony, but I have come across no clear evidence for this. On the other hand, the KGB constituted a formidable machine, concentrating intelligence, counter-intelligence and communications and transport security under one roof, and equipped with massive technical resources for surveillance, a typical detective service ('external surveillance' in its jargon), a whole host of other departments and subdepartments, and a large staff – not to mention *stukachi*, unpaid informers, recruited in any sector the KGB deemed sensitive. Such concentration of power was characteristic of the deeply ingrained Soviet belief in the virtues of centralization. It is yet more obvious if we round off this sketch by adding that the KGB was responsible for the security of Soviet leaders and, to a large extent, for what they knew (or what the KGB wanted them to know) about the USSR and the rest of the world. Hence the KGB was an administrative giant – but different from its predecessor under Stalin.

Finally, let us note that KGB chiefs were dependent on the power constellation at the top, and were doubtless tempted to support a preferred leader against some other figure. Thus, the KGB unquestionably played a role in the ousting of Khrushchev in 1964, as surmised by the well-informed R. G. Pikhoia. According to him, the ease with which the plot proceeded must have had something to do with Khrushchev's tense relations with the security services. After Beria's arrest in 1953, his deputy, S. N. Kruglov, had become head of the MVD, and many had interpreted this as a sign that Stalinist methods were on the way back – especially since various military industrial branches that had just been removed from the MVD were being restored to them. In fact, these ominous signs were generated by a partial and temporary short-circuit in the top leadership, and the purge of Beria's old accomplices continued. At the end of August 1953 the head of the MVD reported that the mopping-up operation in regional directorates was over (certain officials were condemned to death or lengthy prison sentences). Taxed with all the 'pogroms' of the 1930s, the MVD's influence was on the wane, while the future KGB's star was rising.

A year later, an MVD was created for the Russian republic, which had not possessed one since 1930, when an all-Union Internal Affairs Ministry based in Moscow was deemed sufficient. This presaged further changes. In 1956, Kruglov was replaced at the top of the MVD by Dudorov, head of the Central Committee's construction department. In 1956–7, many MVD cadres were dismissed as a logical prelude to the abolition on 13 January 1962 of the MVD of the USSR, whose functions were turned over to its republican namesakes. In Russia, even its name changed: it became MOOP (Ministry for Public Order). But the reader need not worry: it soon reverted to its old name, for in an authoritarian state such powerful traditions are not so readily blotted out.[2]

The KGB's so-called 'political' functions were defined by its statute, approved by the Central Committee Presidium on 9 January 1959. It was a 'political organ' responsible for defending the system from internal and external enemies. With Shelepin's appointment in 1958, a further thinning out of its ranks was conducted, extending the measures that had been taken since Khrushchev's arrival in power. In January 1963, Shelepin was promoted to the Politburo and replaced at the head of the KGB by Semichastny (an old Komsomol comrade). That same year, Semichastny reported that 46,000 officers had been dismissed (half of them before 1959), and that more than 90 per cent of the generals and officers in military counter-intelligence had been transferred to civilian jobs 'in the course of the last four years' (he probably meant 1959–63). New agents arrived with party and Komsomol references. On the other hand, many former KGB operatives were redeployed to work in the party, soviets, or in the Prosecutor's offices. Shelepin and Semichastny's KGB, strengthened by party cadres who were supposed to rekindle its ideological fervour, once again regarded itself as an 'armed detachment of the party' (Stalin's formula), and not necessarily as pro-Khrushchev. But many of the old cadres who survived must have been upset by the dismissal of tens of thousands of agents, the reduction in their salaries, and the elimination of several perks (free medicine, privileges for length of service).

---

2 My sources here are R. G. Pikhoia, *Sovetskii Soiuz: Istoriia Vlasti, 1945–1991,* Moscow 1998; T. P. Korzhikhina, *Sovetskoe Gosurdarstvo i ego Uchrezhdeniia, Noiabr' 1917 – Dekabr' 1991 g.,* Moscow 1995; and A. I. Kokurin and M. V. Petrov, sost., *Lubianka: VChK-KGB, 1917–1960, Spravochnik,* Moscow 1997.

The KGB could not but inherit a sinister reputation from the Stalinist NKVD. In the USSR and throughout the world, it 'enjoyed' the image of the repressive agency of a regime whose foundations largely rested on repression (it is enough to refer to the list of its duties). In reality, however, its activities in this sphere did not have much in common with those of the MVD during the Stalinist period. We now possess data on the number of arrests and types of sentence meted out to opponents in the broad sense. Not unlike the trend observed in other spheres, they were now on another scale, even though it should be specified that the level of repression was determined by the leadership decisions, not exclusively by the KGB. Horrified and fascinated by the absurdity of Stalin's repression, and amply supplied with data about it, Western opinion readily accepted the idea that it continued on the same scale and with the same means after his demise. In fact, however, the two periods are not comparable – if only because the secret police, however powerful, had lost the outrageous power to judge and punish their victims themselves. Their cases now had to go to court. As for KGB investigations, as with the Cheka at the beginning of the NEP, they had to be registered with the Prosecutor General or local prosecutors. Their results had to be communicated to the special department of the Prosecutor's Office that oversaw such investigations (the same applied at local level). The available evidence, albeit still scanty, indicates that these procedures were observed – although we may assume that the opening of the archives will disclose shortcomings in this supervision. Predictably, respect for procedures depended on the relative weight of conservative and reformist currents in the leadership. Moreover, the outcome of strictly political cases and trials, directly handled by the Politburo in accordance with the regime's interests, was a foregone conclusion: judges and prosecutors would simply act out a scenario decided elsewhere, and the professed guarantees were cast aside. Since persons accused of political crimes, notably the dissidents, no longer faced the death penalty, national and international public opinion could play a role. Debate within the regime and considerations of high politics would not infrequently introduce some important correctives. In the case of less high-profile individual and group oppositional activity, legal proceedings followed their normal course. We now possess a great deal of information about the number of such cases and the sentences handed down, appealed, reduced or dismissed.

OPPONENTS AND CRITICS

We shall start with the information supplied by the KGB to the government about anti-Soviet political activities. The KGB leadership was concerned about what it perceived as a growing mood of opposition in the country.[3] In the first half of 1962, it amounted to nothing less than an 'explosion of popular discontent with Khrushchev's policies' (this is Pikhoja's conclusion, not the KGB's own assessment). In this period, the number of anonymous anti-Soviet leaflets and letters in circulation was twice as high as in the first six months of 1961: 7,705 leaflets, produced by 2,522 authors, were seized. In the first six months of 1962, sixty anti-Soviet groups – invariably composed of only a few individuals – had been uncovered, compared with forty-seven for the whole of the previous year. After a lengthy interval, leaflets lauding the 'anti-party group' (Molotov, Kaganovich and Malenkov), which had been disbanded in 1957, began to appear. The chekists managed to identify 1,039 authors of 6,726 anti-Soviet documents: among them were to be found 364 workers, 192 employees, 210 students or secondary-school pupils, 105 pensioners and 60 kolkhoz members. More than 40 per cent of these authors had a secondary-school education; 47 per cent were younger than thirty; and some were party and military veterans. We leave it to readers to decide what conclusions to draw from these statistics. But other, more dramatic events were to jolt the Central Committee and KGB.

At the end of May 1962, reacting to a deteriorating supply situation, the government increased food prices and at the same time ordered factory managers to raise output norms without increasing wages. Given that kolkhoz members had just been prohibited from growing food on their private plots, Khrushchev's popularity was at its nadir. The KGB recorded signs of growing popular discontent. At Novocherkask, in the Rostov-on-Don region, things took an especially dramatic turn. Between 1 and 3 June 1962, protest exploded in an important factory and spread to the whole city: demonstrations, blockades of trains, attacks on party and KGB offices, beating up of policemen. The local administration, party and military were paralysed: soldiers fraternized with the strikers and their officers did not issue orders to open fire. For them, as for the KGB, the situation was unheard of. But when it threatened to get completely out of control, Moscow dispatched troops and the

---

3   As reported by Pikhoia, *Sovetskii Soiuz*, who uses material about events covered by other sources at my disposal, but who goes into more detail.

rioting was suppressed, at the cost of twenty-three dead and numerous wounded. Many arrests and sanctions followed.[4]

Events like this were worrying, because they demonstrated that the system could break down and lose control throughout a city: the soviet officials and party secretaries were arrogant, unpopular bureaucrats who collapsed when it came to the crunch. They often had no local roots and no popular following.

Thereafter, further disorders, varying in kind and importance, required the intervention of troops. Hitherto they had not been taken too seriously, but now they were followed with particular attention and measures were adopted to prevent any recurrence. The protest movement in Novocherkask had caught the KGB unawares and unprepared, and it was reeling from its failure. The Central Committee decided to strengthen the secret police. Perhaps Khrushchev had reason to regret his policy towards the KGB and even, more generally, his anti-Stalinism.

Various documents from the end of 1962 and the beginning of 1963 allow us access to the KGB's inner sanctum and to hear its chiefs talking, reasoning, organizing and acting. The new KGB head Semichastny reverted to the old-style repressive and aggressive attitude towards enemies. This approach, which his agencies tended to celebrate as authentically 'chekist', was in fact rooted in the ideology of the conservatives, shared by Semichastny when a Komsomol functionary. In July 1962 the Central Committee received a memo from a commission of seven senior officials (Shelepin, Semichastny, Ivashutin, Zakharov, Tikunov, Rudenko and Mironov – the last-named a party apparatchik with his eye on the KGB leadership). It offered a series of proposals for stepping up the struggle against anti-Soviet activities and possible mass disorder.[5] It was argued that there was no need for any new decisions; existing directives from the Central Committee and Khrushchev personally were adequate for the task. The commission of seven merely wanted to propose some supplementary measures relating to the activity

---

4 These details come from *Arkhivno-informatsionnyi biulleten'*, no. 1, 1993, pp. 110–36 – an appendix to *Istoricheskii Arkhiv*.

5 TsKhSD, f. 89, op. 6, d. 20, LL. 1–11 contains three documents dating from 1962. Two of them belong to the category 'Special file – Absolutely top secret: to be returned in 24 hours to the 1st sector of the General Department of the Central Committee'. The third pertains to the 'Special file – Top secret'. Among other things, it contains an extract from minute no. 42 of the 19 July 1962 session of the Central Committee Presidium.

of certain administrative bodies – measures that featured in draft orders drawn up by the head of the KGB and the Prosecutor General. It added that the MVD of the Russian Federation intended to create reserve units within its existing internal armed forces, to be used, should the need arise, to guard public buildings, communication centres, radio stations, banks and prisons (in case of riots), and which would be equipped with special weapons and communications systems. To this end, the MVD of the Russian Federation had presented a draft to the Central Committee office that handled the affairs of the Russian party.

This text did not wish to be alarmist. The same is not true, however, of one written by Semichastny personally and sent separately, which was much more 'activist'. His reference to the mass disorders occurring in different parts of the country possibly conveys genuine alarm. But it might also have been intended to present himself and the KGB as more indispensable than ever. In fact the few figures he provided were scarcely alarming – especially in a country as vast as the USSR.

The Presidium of the Central Committee approved the drafts of the decisions that Semichastny and Rudenko (the Prosecutor General) were to implement in their respective domains. The KGB was authorized to recruit a further 400 agents for regional counter-intelligence services. Parts of the text were to be communicated to party secretaries at regional and district level. But only key members of the Politburo and leaders of the MVD and KGB could have sight of the whole text; local officials were to be restricted to paragraphs 1 and 3, meaning that they were not to know that the KGB was recruiting an additional 400 agents (they did not always see eye to eye with the local KGB).

This text is followed by another document, marked 'top secret', containing the draft of an order by Semichastny to his agents enjoining them to 'intensify the KGB's struggle against demonstrations of hostility by anti-Soviet elements'. It begins with a report on the period between the Twentieth and Twenty-second Congresses (1956–61). According to Semichastny, links between the KGB and the population had been strengthened, allowing for an improvement in intelligence and 'operational activities'. 'Prophylactic' measures (a notion we shall return to) had also paid off. However, many KGB agencies had relaxed their guard in uncovering and suppressing anti-Soviet activities. Upright citizens were with the government, on the domestic and international fronts alike, but the fact that society still harboured anti-social elements was something not to be underestimated. Influenced by hostile foreign propaganda, they were spreading malicious slanders against the party and sometimes exploited temporary difficulties to incite Soviet citizens to riot. In recent years, such disorders had included the sacking of administrative buildings, the destruction of public property, attacks on state representatives, and other such excesses. The initiators or perpetrators were mostly criminals and hooligans, but all sorts of people hostile to the regime had also emerged from the shadows – former collaborators with the Germans, for example, or members of churches and sects. Having served their sentences, all these hostile elements were moving to the south, and they might have played a prominent role in the Novocherkask events. Dealing with the situation demanded both an intensification of the struggle against the subversive activities of foreign intelligence agencies and an improvement in KGB operations against the internal enemy. Moreover, in some KGB units, agents in leadership positions, or with responsibilities for operations on the ground, were guilty of a certain complacency and were not taking the requisite measures, which should include repression.

Semichastny mentioned other chinks in the KGB's armour. Thus, enterprises in the military–industrial complex had intelligence agencies. However, in many important enterprises deemed non-strategic, even though they were formally assigned to KGB officers, no one was actually doing the operative work. They had no secret agents and no reliable informers, with the result that the KGB received no timely information on matters of operational interest. The same was true of many higher education institutions. Furthermore, counter-intelligence units were falling down on what should be a constant preoccupation – i.e. surveillance of suspect individuals after they had served their sentences: foreign agents, members of nationalist and foreign organizations, former Nazis and their collaborators, members of churches and sects. In numerous instances, even the residence of such people was not registered, making surveillance impossible; and many of those on file had been lost sight of.

Semichastny also deplored the lack of cooperation with the MVD and the absence of common plans for action against anti-social elements (who 'live a parasitic existence'). The KGB had no information about where they gathered, and no measures were in place to deal with them in the event of them getting out of hand. This was one of the reasons why, in several cases, mass disorder had not been prevented, with far-reaching consequences.

These 'mass disorders' – a term and reality that were manifestly traumatizing for the KGB chief – had been the subject of KGB inquiries; in particular, to investigate how local chekists had dealt with them. What had emerged was that the latter were unprepared. As soon as the explosion occurred, contact between operational forces and intelligence agents was lost. The forces on the ground did not possess the requisite information and had no way of manipulating the rioters, because there were no agents planted in their ranks.

At this point we might pose a question: would the presence of plants have prevented the disorders? Only if the disorders were organized. But they were not – plants would not have made a difference. The disorders were provoked by the indolence of local leaders. The KGB chief did not raise such questions. His report was followed by a six-page order, beginning with the formula 'I am therefore ordering that', and containing thirteen points. Its general philosophy was this: without weakening the fight against foreign agents, it was imperative to strengthen the internal intelligence service and make it a priority issue. To the potentially dangerous elements he had already listed, Semichastny now added those who had been tried in the past for anti-state crimes, émigrés who had returned to the USSR, and any foreigners from capitalist countries. It was also necessary to make better use of technical services and the network of detectives; and to improve political training for secret agents and informers so that they were better equipped to identify people with hostile attitudes and intentions, potential fomenters of mass disorder and perpetrators of terrorist acts, as well as authors of leaflets and other anonymous material spreading provocative rumours and inciting people to riot. In liaison with party bodies, measures should be taken to isolate such individuals. It was also important to explain to cadres that preventive operations by the KGB should not replace or weaken the fight against enemies who had already been identified.

The KGB chief went on to list concrete organizational measures and plans for acquiring technical resources. He once again stressed the need to strengthen intelligence activity in higher education and special technical schools, as well as among the intelligentsia. This set of measures was aimed at preventing, with the party's help, political errors and dangerous ideological deviations, which could easily lead to anti-Soviet activity. The long order closed on a 'progressive' note: make sure that no enemy goes unpunished and that no innocent people are subject to unjustified repression.

The available data still do not allow us to answer this question: How serious were the 'increase in oppositional sentiment' and 'explosions of popular discontent' referred to by one of our sources (Pikhoia)? We know that in 1962 the KGB flushed out more authors of anonymous letters than in the previous year and that Khrushchev's policies were breeding widespread discontent. But that is not new. We also know of several mass riots that caught the KGB unawares (Novocherkask was the most dramatic). But we do not know how to interpret these events. In the third part of this work, we shall provide data that make it possible to compare mass riots under Khrushchev and Brezhnev. We shall discover that the system was never threatened, but that ideological hard-liners and the KGB may have had an interest in exaggerating the scale of the problem.

Conservative leaders like Semichastny, supporters of a hard line, painted a picture of a regime under attack: this was their way of thinking. But the kind of disorder he referred to was easily identifiable in advance and controllable, and its perpetrators were incapable of organizing politically. It is more than likely that his analysis was contested within the KGB itself. Semichastny himself may unwittingly have hinted as much when he confided that the recent influx into the KGB of a large squad of Komsomol and party officials (including himself) was not appreciated by older cadres. We know from other sources that these 'malcontents' regarded themselves as professionals and found the new arrivals from the Komsomol impertinent, unduly ideological, and incompetent. It therefore seems plausible that there were leaders, taxed with 'insufficient vigilance' by Semichastny, who had a different interpretation of the events and preferred different policies. Plenty of hints to this effect are to be found in the memoirs of ex-KGB senior officials. There were intelligent people in the KGB's ranks, particularly in the agencies responsible for analysing intelligence, and they had no difficulty in seeing that Semichastny's text lacked not only analytical content but also any self-critical reflection. It made do with a list of regrettable incidents, whose source could be traced to a few guilty individuals, and his response consisted in suggesting technical surveillance and intelligence measures – as well as the 'bonus' of 400 additional officers for the whole country.

This hard ideological–repressive line, which for Semichastny was self-explanatory, did not have to emanate from within the KGB itself. It came straight from the Komsomol, where opponents of Khrushchev's earlier de-Stalinization policies began to show signs of rebellion. We find similar refrains in conservative discourse everywhere – in particular, a tendency to regard 'immorality' as a direct prelude to criminality.

For Semichastny, 'vagrants' were potential enemies of the state and anyone without regular work was, by definition, about to engage in an anti-Soviet plot. Believers were also potential culprits, not on account of their religious faith but because of their tendency to create organizations, which virtually amounted to a conspiracy in the making. All this explains why Semichastny's KGB spied on citizens far beyond the remit of its statutes and at the expense of its actual tasks, which would have kept it fully occupied.

The background to the picture painted by the KGB chief suggested that the situation was more tense in the USSR than previously. Khrushchev was losing any sense of direction and vacillating. He had increased prices and work norms at a time of food shortages. Retreating from his initial anti-Stalinist ardour, which had proved too costly politically, he developed a more 'conservative' line just at the time when bold new initiatives were needed. (We shall return to these issues in due course.) Nineteen sixty-three was the year in which legislation against political opponents was reinforced by six articles in the criminal code redefining crimes against the state. This initiative led to a certain increase in the number of arrests, albeit a rather small one. From 1966 onwards, we even witness a clear decline in political persecution.

COUNTERING THE OPPOSITION: LAWS AGAINST CRITICS

Laws against political critics, targeted at 'especially dangerous crimes against the state', achieved notoriety during the Cold War when the phenomenon of dissidence emerged. Criminal prosecution of it was based on the following set of articles:

> Article 64: flight abroad or refusal to return to the USSR – act of treason.
> Article 70: anti-Soviet agitation and propaganda.
> Article 72: activity by organized groups leading to especially dangerous crimes against the state and participation in anti-Soviet organizations.
> Article 142: violation of the law on the separation of Church and state, including in education, punishable by a year's imprisonment or a fine of up to 50 roubles. In the event of a repeat offence, the maximum sentence was three years' imprisonment.
> Article 190: the circulation or composition of texts defaming the Soviet state and its social system (up to three years' imprisonment

or one year's mandatory labour, or a minimum fine of 100 roubles).

Article 227: infringement of citizens' rights under the guise of religious ceremonies (e.g. 'forced' baptism), punishable by three–five years' imprisonment or exile, with or without confiscation of property. Active participation in a group, or active propaganda in favour of committing such acts, could mean up to three years' imprisonment or exile, or a year's mandatory labour. Note that if the acts and individuals pursued presented no danger to society, methods of social pressure were applied instead.[6]

Most cases of a political character were brought for 'anti-Soviet agitation and propaganda', 'organizational activities', defamation of the state, or (in lesser numbers) violation of the law on separation of Church and state. According to the KGB, 8,124 trials were held for 'anti-Soviet manifestations' during the Khrushchev–Brezhnev–Chernenko periods (1957–85), most of them on the basis of the articles targeting anti-Soviet agitation and propaganda and the deliberate circulation of calumnies against the state – the two most widely used articles.[7]

POLITICAL ARRESTS AND 'PROPHYLAXIS' (1959–74)

For a period of twenty-eight years, the above figures seem 'disappointingly' low. Let us turn to a statistical table drawn up by an authoritative source,[8] furnishing data on repression in four four-year periods: 1959–62, 1963–6, 1967–70, 1971–4. The total number of cases is greater than that given by the KGB for the period 1957–85, because it includes all convictions for crimes against the state based on the six articles of the criminal code. For the four periods, the respective totals are as follows: 5,413, 3,251, 2,456, and 2,424. In the first period, an average of 1,354 persons per annum were charged; the figure drops to

---

6 Amnesty International, *Prisoners of Conscience in the USSR: Their Treatment and Conditions*, London 1975 and Butler, *Soviet Law*, pp. 7–8.

7 O. V. Edelman, sost., *58-10: Nadzornye Proizvodstva Prokuratury SSSR po Delam ob Antisovetskoi Agitatsii i Propagande: Annotirovannyi Katalog, 1953–1991*, Moscow 1999. This is also my source for the way in which the Prosecutor's Office supervised KGB investigations.

8 Pikhoia, *Sovetskii Soiuz*, pp. 365–6.

606 for the last period. The majority of the accused were pursued for anti-Soviet agitation and propaganda: 1,601 in the first period and 348 in the last. Readers will find full details in Appendix 3. But we should also add the category of those who were not charged or convicted, but made subject to 'prophylactic' procedures: 58,291 between 1967 and 1970 and 63,108 between 1971 and 1974. The trigger for a 'prophylactic' intervention by the KGB was suspicious contacts with foreigners, treasonable intentions or harmful political manifestations. 'Prophylaxis' could be carried on in the workplace and take the form of an official warning. In the event of recidivism, cases could be referred to the courts (this occurred in only 150 cases over eight years). Some publications supply different figures, using different timespans and recording the various alleged offences. But Pikhoia's data seem the most reliable (they doubtless derive from the presidential archive) and also provide information on categories of offence.

We know more about this curious procedure of 'prophylaxis' thanks to data from the KGB for the years 1967–72. Its then head was Andropov, and although its reports still bristled with the usual array of crimes despised by the regime, the emphasis on prophylactic work now became more pronounced. It consisted in 'measures to prevent attempts at organized subversive activities by nationalist, revisionist and other anti-Soviet elements' and to 'confine the potentially dangerous groups that tend to appear here and there'.

This method was not without ambiguities and surprises. Already in use under Shelepin, or even earlier, it took its name from medical terminology, implying that anyone entertaining political opinions different from those of the regime was in need of 'treatment'. Under Andropov it became a broader strategy, which was actually preferred to other means. We do not possess any sources on discussions about the validity of this option, but it is interesting to examine the report presented to the Central Committee by Andropov and the Prosecutor General Rudenko on 11 October 1972, which precisely deals with the way in which prophylaxis operated.[9]

It is described as being quite widespread. Between 1967 and 1972, 3,096 political groups had been discovered and 13,602 people belonging to them had been subject to prophylaxis. In other words, they had not been arrested, but summoned for an interview with a KGB officer who

9   TsKhSD, op. 25, d. 47, LL. 4–5 ('special file') from Andropov and Rudenko.

had explained the erroneous character of their positions or actions. Rather politely, but without concealing the danger they found themselves in, the officer had advised them to desist. In 1967, 2,196 people from 502 groups were 'interviewed' in this way; in 1968, 2,870 from 625 groups; in 1969, 3,130 from 733 groups; in 1970, 3,102 from 709 groups; and in 1971, 2,304 from 527 groups. Such groups, which typically comprised only a few people, had been uncovered in Moscow, Sverdlovsk, Tula, Vladimir, Omsk, Kazan and Tiumen, as well as the Ukraine, Latvia, Lithuania, Belorussia, Moldavia, Kazakhstan, and so on.

Thanks to these preventative measures, the number of arrests for anti-Soviet propaganda had fallen. The majority of interviewees left it at that, but others persisted in scheming that might induce them to commit a 'crime against the state'. In order to strengthen preventative action against people contemplating criminal activity, and to suppress manifestations by anti-social elements more actively, the authors of the report recommended that the KGB should be authorized, if necessary, to issue a written warning to such people requesting them to desist from politically harmful activity and spelling out the consequences if they refused to comply.

Andropov and Rudenko believed that such a course of action might increase the sense of moral responsibility of those so warned. If they did then commit criminal acts, they should be arrested, subject to preliminary investigation, and turned over to the courts for a 'character assessment'.

The authors appended a draft resolution for the Central Committee and a draft decree for the Presidium of the Supreme Soviet – the standard bureaucratic procedure when submitting a proposal – with a request that they be considered. Unlike the 1962–3 KGB texts deploring 'mass disorder', there was no suggestion this time that the system was threatened. The stress on 'preventative medicine', which sounded too soft to conservative ears, was quite liberal for a country like the USSR. A sense of imminent danger might certainly induce regression to the Semichastny-style line, but there was no question of it in the immediate future. Yet the longer-term prospects for the system's health were scarcely reassuring, as our later excursion into economic issues will show.

In one respect there was something troubling about this 'preventative medicine'. What did 'character assessment' actually mean? Among other things, it could lead to the person in question being sent, not to prison, but to a psychiatric clinic. This can seem like a fairly lenient gesture by judges anywhere. But abuses are possible and, in the case of the Soviet Union, there were numerous well-documented instances of the use of psychiatric wards to incarcerate perfectly sane people, whose political positions were identified as paranoid delirium or some such, and who were pumped full of harmful drugs. This was testimony to the ugly and reactionary mentality of some Soviet leaders.

There is an abundant literature on this subject in the West, but I have not as yet come across any satisfactory sources in Russia itself. We still do not know how long such practices persisted and how many people they affected. We do know that there were internal debates about the propriety of such methods, which were not unanimously supported within the government. It became public knowledge that figures from the academic community, and certainly legal scholars, had protested to the Central Committee – particularly in the case of the geneticist Zhores Medvedev, who was released. There is no doubt that the issue was debated within the KGB, by Andropov and people around him, and probably reached the Politburo.[10]

The actual number of people proceeded against (including by way of prophylaxis) does not in itself alter the fact that the Soviet system was politically retrograde, allowing its opponents' propaganda to score points. The regime possessed repulsive features that cost it dear in the international arena. But the scope of the repression we are dealing with for the post-Stalinist period – an average of 312 cases a year for twenty-six years for the two main political crimes (and in some cases, reduction or quashing of sentences by a higher court) – constitutes not merely a statistic, but an index: this was no longer Stalinism and it does not warrant description of the USSR as the 'Evil Empire', which was

---

10 Regarding psychiatric wards, a recent publication may be of interest. It is written by D. B. Dmitrieva and entitled *Alians prava i miloserdiia – O Probleme Zashchity Prav Cheloveka v Psikhiatrii* (Moscow 2001). Harshly critical of the Soviet system, its author is herself a psychiatrist and was a Yeltsin supporter and Health Minister in his government. She then became head of the State Institute of Social and Criminal Psychiatry – the well-known institution bearing the name of V. P. Serbskii that is alleged to have been the main culprit in supplying phoney diagnoses of psychiatric illness for perfectly healthy political critics. On the basis of research conducted in the Institute's archives of all the cases that passed through it, Dmitrieva argues that there was no widespread policy – and perhaps no policy at all – of using psychiatry for political ends in the USSR. There might simply have been instances of personal corruption or yielding to political pressure on the part of some psychiatrists. In any event, the jury is still out on this.

common in the West. Apocalyptic invective of this sort makes the Soviet Union seem rather innocent by comparison. Leaders should control their rhetoric, lest it rebounds.

Whatever their precise number, dissidents, of whom the most well-known were Solzhenitsyn, Sakharov, and later Sharansky, were aggressively followed and spied on by Andropov's agencies. Compromising materials were confiscated and hostile witnesses sought out and induced to testify, and so on. But we will arrive at a better understanding of the specific approach adopted by Andropov, KGB chief since mid-1967, if we compare it with what 'normal conservatives' would have liked to see him do in each particular case. It is true that the latter no longer demanded the death penalty. But they still sought criminal prosecution and sentences that would be heavy enough to remove culprits from the scene, by exiling them to a remote region where they could not be seen or heard. In each instance, Andropov pressed for the adoption of a more clement course – in particular, expulsion from the Soviet Union. Sakharov, for example, was exiled to Gorky – a city whose climate and living conditions did not greatly differ from Moscow's. The way that the West used each case (indeed, the whole dissident movement) for its own purposes, and the way in which different dissidents responded to the West's appeal, could not escape the KGB chief or be a matter of indifference to him, quite independently of the fact that excessive 'clemency' might bring his career to an abrupt end.

There is an enormous literature in the West on the dissidents. We shall restrict ourselves to a few points and, in the first instance, to the case of Solzhenitsyn, who together with Sakharov was the most famous of them (even though one cannot imagine two more different personalities). When discussing Solzhenitsyn, we shall also say something about the remarkable case of an opponent from within the system – namely, the editor of the literary journal *Novyi Mir*, the poet Alexander Tvardovsky. Sakharov, Solzhenitsyn and Tvardovsky constitute a 'typology' of political opposition and social criticism, even if they do not cover all its varieties and nuances, from open protest to silent 'internal emigration' via rejection through indifference and the pursuit of reforms from within the regime.

The Solzhenitsyn phenomenon has various facets. Viewed from afar (i.e. from abroad), he looked like a giant single-handedly taking on a dictatorial machine. The picture has become more complicated over time. Better knowledge of his personality would explain why he did not have only admirers in Russia. He also had many critics among liberal-minded oppositionists, probably because they did not regard him as a democrat. As long as he waged his battle from the inside, foreign observers assumed that he was fighting for democratization of the system: the cause he was defending – greater freedom for intellectuals, and especially writers – would help to expand political freedom for all citizens. However, once he was exiled in the West it soon transpired – as in many other cases – that anti-communism was not automatically a vehicle for democracy. Solzhenitsyn's struggle was in fact inspired by, and served, a profoundly anti-democratic ideology, combining elements of 'national-statism' with archaic traits of the Orthodox religion; it was hostile not only to the ills of the West but also to the very concept of democracy. In short, Solzhenitsyn harboured a deep authoritarianism of his own devising which, if not formulated when he first appeared on the public stage, developed in the course of his struggle – especially at the stage of his life when he sensed that higher powers were summoning him to 'slay the dragon', and single-handedly at that, by publishing his *Gulag Archipelago*.

Thrown in the face of the Soviet regime, a book like *The Gulag Archipelago* may be regarded as an act of literary–political revenge: condemnation of a system that had betrayed its own ideals and those of humanity by creating hell on earth for millions of people, including Solzhenitsyn. Yet he did not offer the slightest hint that by the time of its publication the Gulag as he had known it no longer existed. To have said as much would have been an act of political honesty and would have required of him a deeper critical analysis of the system, with arguments adapted to post-Stalinist Russia. But he did not offer one; and it was of no significance to him. It was much simpler to attack the Soviet Union for its Stalinist history and pretend that it still persisted – something that also fitted his self-image. For Solzhenitsyn considered himself the depository of higher values inherited from Russia's distant past, and it was with reference to that past that he sought to suggest remedies for twentieth-century Russia.

There were excellent reasons why his celebrated novel *One Day in the Life of Ivan Denisovich*, published in Tvardovsky's *Novyi Mir*, should have been unanimously well received in Russia. Resistance to a degrading penal system was identified with indestructible human values, personified by a simple working man, a peasant, who had the inner strength to resist the degradation inflicted on him by his jailers. But there were equally good reasons why *The Gulag Archipelago*, written and published when the Gulag had essentially been dismantled, was badly received by many internal critics, who regarded it as an apocalyptic exaggeration doubtless very useful to the USSR's enemies, but damaging for the democratic struggle against a system which, albeit modernized, remained quite primitive in many ways. Many critics of Soviet authoritarianism could not but reject Solzhenitsyn's alternative, as well as his pretensions to the status of liberator. A fine writer, but politically inept and with a highly inflated sense of his own importance, Solzhenitsyn lacked sufficient grasp of reality to think in political terms. In this respect, the contrast with such figures as Andrei Sakharov, Roy Medvedev or Andrei Sinyavsky could not be more pronounced.

His autobiography *The Calf and the Oak* supplies us with some of the keys to his personality – notably his sense of having been selected to accomplish a mystical mission, but also some of the other, less attractive characteristics that prompted him to engage in a vicious (and quite unexpected) attack on Tvardovsky and his colleagues at *Novyi Mir*. These were the people who had fought so hard for Solzhenitsyn and his work in the Soviet Union, and who launched him onto the national – indeed, international – stage. He accused the editorial board of cowardice, self-glorification, ineptitude and duplicity. The response by Tvardovsky's former deputy, Vladimir Lakshin – an outstanding literary critic and essayist – was powerful, indignant and devastating.[11] In his psychological portrait of Solzhenitsyn, Lakshin highlights the characteristics that helped him to survive the camps. In fact, he writes, Solzhenitsyn had assimilated the lessons of the Gulag only too well. He was a product of the camps, who identified with the *zek* and had always retained the *zek* mentality.

Highly relevant, this analysis will only briefly detain us here. The crucial question, already alluded to, is what Solzhenitsyn was fighting for. The *Novyi Mir* milieu was broadly socialist or social-democratic, and the battles they engaged in, however cautiously, were rooted in that ideology. This, more than anything else, was what provoked Solzhenitsyn's fury. Lakshin was highly dubious about the programme offered by Solzhenitsyn to his fellow citizens: 'Judging by his idyllic conception of our pre-revolutionary past, he seems to think that Russia's only future is ... her past.' This boiled down to advising the Soviet leadership to

---

11 Vladimir Lakshin, *Solzhenitsyn, Tvardovskii and 'Novyi Mir'*, ed. and trans. Michael Glenny, with additional contributions by Mary Chaffin and Linda Aldwinckle, Cambridge (Mass.) 1980.

renounce its ideology in favour of nationalism and Orthodoxy: 'What emerges from the fog of his verbiage is the triad proposed by Count Uvarov [in the nineteenth century]: Orthodoxy, Autocracy, Nation.' Lakshin does not deny Solzhenitsyn's great talent or his role in fighting evil, but he deplores that fact that he seems incapable of deriving anything positive from it:

> I cannot detect any sincerity in his faith, just as I find it hard to believe in Solzhenitsyn as a politician and a thinker — even though he has already acquired all the attributes of a familiar type of politician, with his insatiable urge to anathematize, to reject, and to demand of his supporters nothing less than an oath of total loyalty.

Lakshin's rejection of Solzhenitsyn's message becomes ever more bitter and adamant:

> I don't want to be in his paradise; I fear I would find myself in an ideally organized prison camp. I don't believe in his Christianity because no one with his misanthropic bent and such self-worship can possibly be a Christian. And I am fed up with his hatred and rejection of everything in present-day Russia . . . But had he not exploded the edifice of untruth? Yes he had. But he has become an infernal machine convinced of his divine mission, which has begun to blow up everything around it. I fear he will blow himself up as well. Indeed, he is already in the process of doing so.

The fury, bitterness and complexity of the battles over the Soviet system, and the drama lived by those engaged in them, are conveyed by these few quotations. No one won; everyone was right; everyone lost. Solzhenitsyn returned to his country liberated from communism and found it 'in a state of collapse' (such was the title of his book, published in 1998). The amazing journal *Novyi Mir* was progressively throttled after the Soviet invasion of Czechoslovakia in 1968. It fought on until the Writers' Union appointed a new editorial board without consulting Tvardovsky, thereby forcing him to resign (February 1970). He died shortly thereafter, a broken, bitter man who bequeathed a legacy of great poetry and personal nobility.

We have briefly dealt with some aspects of opposition and dissidence, after having mapped out the evolution of forms of political repression in the post-Stalin period. The sound and fury over dissidence at home and especially abroad, and the authorities' treatment of it, should not be allowed to obscure the systemic trends that were at work in the Soviet Union. It is one thing when a worker cannot leave his job or legally protest against injustice in the workplace; it is quite another when he can do so. A system denying all rights was supplanted by a system of laws, rights and guarantees.

Eliminating the notion of 'counter-revolutionary crime', and replacing it by that of 'especially dangerous crime against the state', might seem merely cosmetic and utterly irrelevant to those persecuted and prosecuted for such crimes. In this context, biography counts for more than historiography. But for historians, changes involve transition to another stage. We have already signalled the fact that the Soviet leadership had a justifiably poor reputation abroad for political repression. And yet, when a penal system amounting to arbitrary punishment and slave labour is transformed into one where slave labour is abolished, where judicial procedures exist, where prisoners possess certain rights and means of challenging the prison administration, where they can maintain access with the outside world, consult a lawyer, protest legally against their treatment, and when the system recognizes that it has an interest in establishing a modicum of legality in the penal domain – when all this obtains, we are dealing with a different kind of regime. To suffer a term of imprisonment for political opinions produces a legitimate sense of injustice, and the biographical experience eclipses the historical dimension: 'Why should I care if the punishment would have been worse ten years earlier?' For their part, however, historians cannot discount what would have happened to prisoners – and their families – ten years earlier.

The secret police, which had hitherto operated completely unchecked – running amok, arresting, torturing, imprisoning and shooting almost at will – was now brought under control: the KGB was no longer empowered to convict and sentence; and its investigations were subject to oversight by divisions within the Prosecutor's Office at all levels created for the purpose. The Prosecutor General now exercised this power at the very heart of a dictatorial system which, in Stalin's time, had also massacred a good number of unduly 'nosy' prosecutors. From March 1953 (and up until 1991), the department of the Prosecutor's Office responsible for oversight of KGB investigations had to be informed of any case opened by the secret police and would open its own file at the same time. It was also empowered to re-examine cases in the event of appeals by convicted persons or their relatives. They could then refer the case back to the courts (instances of a reduction in sentence were quite frequent), or initiate an appeals process for the rehabilitation of the convicted person or the amendment of the offence (on the basis of a different article in the criminal code from that of the original trial).[12]

These facts and trends, like many others, can be submitted to two types of comparison, requiring us to subject each phenomenon to two different interpretations. Thus, in the first instance the Soviet Union can be compared with other countries. Here the inability of the regime to accept society's increasing political differentiation, its fear and denial of independent opinions (a basic right in a modern civilized society), demonstrates the inferiority of the system, which had found ways of tolerating or professing more than one opinion, but generally of a rather conservative complexion. The Soviet Union paid a heavy political price for this in international opinion. And it may come as a revelation to some to learn that Soviet intellectuals were not the only ones concerned about this: such people were also to be found in the KGB's ranks.

So it is scarcely surprising if the Soviet authorities resorted to an 'active-reactive' policy, introducing or reviving a whole range of laws specifically designed to counter critics who explicitly or implicitly sided with the Western bloc. As regards the system's 'inferiority' (its dictatorial character), the laws against 'anti-state crimes' that were supposed to defend it from opponents were in themselves evidence of its failure – *testimonium paupertatis*. When its rulers wanted critics to be silenced, the various legal guarantees would be set aside and judges, secret services and prosecutors would operate hand in glove.

The second relevant historical comparison is with the country's own past. The anti-state crime laws were now on the statute books for all to see; and to be prosecuted, people actually had to violate them. The intention to commit a criminal act was no longer sufficient to justify such arrests, which were now illegal. The new version of an extensive criminal code and the strengthening of legal institutions afforded a marked contrast with the past, even if the overall framework remained undemocratic. This aspect of political repression was a subject of continual debate among the leadership, jurists, and the KGB; and it explains the protests from different, mainly academic circles when they judged that the regime was not respecting its own legal rules. Such phenomena were part of the political scene and should be perceived as such.

A further consideration comes to mind in the context of a historical reflection. We have stressed that historical changes were in train in all

---

12 O. V. Edelman, sost., *58-10: Nadzornye proizvodstva prokuratury SSSR.*

aspects of social existence, including the very character of the regime. Were it not for such phenomena, which attest to the system's accommodation to new realities, including in its repressive practices, we would be unable to explain how and why the regime disappeared from the historical stage without firing a shot.

A realistic approach, which does not shy away from unpalatable facts, is bound to admit that democracies which achieve the status of great powers do not always respect rights and are not always very democratic. Countries without a democratic system are not necessarily 'guilty' because they lack one. Democracy is not a plant that flourishes everywhere. Historical realities do not necessarily correspond to ideals or propaganda claims. The West knows perfectly well whose human rights are to be promoted and whose can be neglected or even curtailed. Ardour for democratic freedoms burns or dims according to global strategic considerations. Cold War pressures, and the whole complex put in place by the West (with the intelligence services playing a leading role) to identify the slightest crack in the other camp, were not invented by Soviet paranoia. And they did nothing to help the small groups or isolated individuals in the USSR who sought to liberalize the regime.

16

THE AVALANCHE OF URBANIZATION

The background to the changes we have sketched, particularly in the sphere of penal policy and what I have called the 'de-Stalinization of the workplace', was a momentous process of urbanization – the commanding factor in the history of the USSR. After the war – in stages, obviously – urbanization inevitably began to have a powerful impact on society, culture, mentalities, and even the state. An accelerated transition from a predominantly rural society to a mainly urban one involved, at halfway stage, a phase when the two types of society were basically intermingled. Frequently incompatible, they coexisted in an explosive mix and the historical distance between them remained very considerable. The Soviet Union became 'semi-urban' in 1960, but the Russian Federation had crossed this threshold earlier. Until 1958 there was no official definition of a 'town' or 'urban settlement' valid for the whole Soviet Union; each republic had its own. In 1958 the threshold was fixed at 12,000 inhabitants for a town and 2,000 for an 'urban settlement', provided at least 50 per cent of the population were not directly employed in agriculture.

So this intermediate phase could be considered a historical stage in its own right for the country and its regime. The rural population, which supplied the bulk of the new urban population, 'ruralized' the towns before the latter succeeded in urbanizing the rural folk. That would happen only in the post-Stalin period – and not without much friction and many 'side effects'. Although not without government input, these processes were basically spontaneous. They oblige us temporarily to distance ourselves from the idea of a rigid party-state dominating and controlling everything, and to reveal something passed over by most studies: 'spontaneity' (*stikhiia*, a term of Greek origin). In any serious general history of the USSR, *stikhiia* should be a legitimate – and sometimes central – topic, although it seems unacceptable to analysts with an overly politicized view of matters.

Scarcely a smooth process, urbanization was the crucial novelty of the twentieth century in Russian history and may be reckoned to have been completed by the mid-1960s. By then, the majority of the population was composed of town dwellers in Russia, the Ukraine and the Baltic states. Some of the towns were old, but most were of recent construction. One randomly selected index is revealing about the conditions of this urbanization: in Soviet towns in the 1960s, 60 per cent of families lived in state-owned housing with communal kitchens and toilets. Indicative of low living standards, this statistic also points to excessively rapid and, we might safely add, 'unplanned' urbanization. Likewise largely unplanned, the consequences were many and various. Whatever the specificities of the process in the USSR, some of them are common to cases of precipitous urbanization elsewhere. We shall return to this point when we consider other data, but we can already venture that at this juncture in its history the country embarked on a novel stage: it became a new society whose interaction with the state assumed different forms. The juxtaposition of these two themes will lead us to consider parameters that proved decisive for the system's vitality, longevity and mortality.

We have already dealt with labour mobility and an emerging 'labour market', which became an accepted reality. To extend the canvas to the whole society, we must signal an important manifestation of 'spontaneity' in action: namely, powerful migration flows, which the authorities could no longer control through the previous routine of sanctions and restrictions. In the new environment of massive population movements other strategies had to be conceived and applied. The following statistics for such population flows in 1965 can cut a long story short:[1]

---

1   RGAE, 1562, 44, 2598, L. 60, 19 March 1965: table from the Central Statistical Office.

All Towns in the USSR

Arrived from:

Other towns	Countryside	Unknown	Total
4,321,731	2,911,392	793,449	8,026,572

Departed to:

Towns	Countryside	Unknown	Total
4,338,699	1,423,710	652,478	6,414,887

Balance in favour of towns from:

Towns	Countryside	Unknown	Total
−16,968	1,487,682	140,971	1,611,685

If these numbers do not seem particularly high, a clarification specific to the Soviet Union should be introduced: the data include only those who registered with the police. Yet many came to the towns, sometimes stayed for long stretches, and left without registering, while others settled for good without reporting to any administrative authority.

Population movements for the years 1961–6 for the Russian Federation alone were imposing: nearly 29 million people arrived in towns while 24.2 left them, yielding a total of 53.2 million migrants. In Western Siberia the total was 6 million; in Eastern Siberia 4.5 million; and in the Far East 4.5 million.

Some worrying phenomena emerge from these figures. It transpires that few people set off for the east of the country with the intention of genuinely settling there. Streams of people returned from these regions where they were badly needed, in part because of housing shortages, and often because wages were too low. According to numerous local inquiries, 82 per cent of single people and 70 per cent of married couples left on account of often lamentable housing conditions (they were renting rooms – sometimes just the corner of a room).

This situation created a countrywide problem. Changing the direction of such population movements necessitated an improvement in the housing conditions in deprived regions. Yet despite sustained efforts, the housing problem remained critical throughout the country. In 1957, average availability of housing per inhabitant in the Russian Federation stood at 6.7 square metres; in the Far East, at 5.9; in Eastern Siberia, 6.1; in Western Siberia, 6.3; and in the Urals, 6.3. Thus, in the eastern territories of the USSR, whither the government wanted to attract labour, there was less housing, central heating and running water than the Russian average, and even than the average for central Russia, itself poorly equipped.

The Soviet leadership and elites were very preoccupied with the problem of inducing labour to migrate to the east and settle there. The problem was not that such population movements were impossible to control by police or 'totalitarian' methods – no one seriously envisaged any such thing. Given the new social conditions and realities, the situation seemed utterly inextricable. On the one hand, Siberia contained enormous wealth that could ensure the system's prosperity, and the requisite labour to exploit it existed in the populated regions of the country. On the other hand, it was impossible to attract this labour to the east and induce it to settle there. People from better-off European areas of the USSR would have to be guaranteed good wages and suitable supplies, while those from poorer regions with huge labour surpluses – e.g. the central Asian republics – would not move because of profound cultural attachments to their traditional environment.

We shall come across other such seemingly insoluble imbroglios, for they were to keep on emerging at a systemic level. For now, however, we shall stick to the problems bound up with urbanization, with particular attention to the issue of labour supplies between 1953 and 1968.

In the mid 1960s and for some years thereafter, the situation still seemed amenable to solution by better coordination and implementation of plans for manpower supplies – that is to say, correcting an excess here and remedying a deficit there by tapping the available reserves in some sector and place. The country was not as yet facing the generalized, acute labour shortage that we shall discuss in Part Three.

A good interdisciplinary institution, Gosplan's own research institute was perfectly capable of studying and forecasting complex situations and knew the planning system well. It sought to understand the present in order to prepare for the immediate future. Intellectually, its researchers were better equipped than other planners and politicians to grasp an intricate socio-economic constellation; and they announced that the clouds were gathering. In February 1965, at the request of Gosplan's leadership, they presented a report on the whole question of labour supplies and demography. The head of the institute, Efimov, had already ruffled feathers more than once and fuelled the ardour of economic reformers. But that was in internal, unpublished texts, which were often criticized by other planners and officials. Now, in a year already marked by a heated debate, Yefimov, who was probably a Kosyginite, produced a major report on Soviet industry, presenting weighty arguments in favour of change and offering a detailed view of the mechanisms involved in the complex business of managing labour supplies.[2] Efimov tackled the problems encountered by the centre and the regions, without concealing the looming tensions; and offered various proposals – sometimes clearly formulated, sometimes merely hints – about ways to confront them. The text is empirically and analytically very rich. It contains both a good diagnosis and a warning as to the dire consequences to be expected in the absence of reforms.

Here is the picture sketched by Yefimov. To start with, he drew attention to a growing imbalance between the available labour force and its employment. During the years 1959–63, the working population had grown by 9 million, while manpower supplies had increased by only 1.7 million. In other words, the requisite workers had been obtained mainly by drawing on those working at home or on their private plots. Eighty-one per cent of the shortfall (or 7.3 million additional workers) had been covered thus. But the number of those working at home was continuing to fall and this source would soon dry up.

The national picture indicated areas experiencing labour shortages and others enjoying surpluses. In Central Asia, natural demographic growth had risen to 27–33 per cent in recent years – twice the Soviet average. From 1959 to 1963 the number of people employed in the state-owned economy, or still engaged in their studies, had grown at the rate of 2.2–4.4 per cent a year; and the percentage of workers employed outside the state sector was between 20 and 26 per cent, compared with an average 17.2 per cent for the whole Soviet Union. In most of the central Asian republics, the bulk of those who did not work in the state sector belonged to the ethnic majority. Demographic growth in Kazakhstan had been lower, but there too the percentage of people working privately was very high: 21.8 per cent. In many regions, rates of population growth and economic development were diverging.

These major disparities lay behind the poor utilization of labour resources. The central Asian republics, Armenia and Kazakhstan were continuing to accumulate surpluses, whereas the Baltic countries – especially Latvia and Estonia – posted the lowest population growth and a high employment rate, and were obliged to look elsewhere for

---

2   RGAE, 4372, 81, 1091, LL. 1–44. On 6 February 1965, Efimov received from his deputy Korobov a report (commissioned on 26 December 1964) on 'the main problems related to rationalizing the use of labour resources in the key regions of the USSR in 1966–70'.

workers. Significant natural population growth was also evident in Moldavia, Western Ukraine and the Northern Caucasus, in towns and countryside alike. At the same time, there was a considerable influx of people from Siberia into regions that already had a labour surplus.

Employment rates also varied according to the size of towns – large, medium-sized or small. The report – and this was no trifle – deplored the fact that when the regional distribution of industrial plant and output was planned, labour availability was not taken into consideration, resulting in utterly aberrant situations. (This is my gloss: the report's author would obviously not have used such language when addressing senior officials.) Major labour-intensive industries had been located in regions where labour was scarce; while in other places where female employment could have been expanded, heavy industry with pre-dominantly male employment had been set up.

In small towns, there were some 2.3 million people in search of a job. The real figure was probably closer to 3 million, since large enterprises tended to maintain a labour reserve. Most of those seeking jobs had minimal education and few skills; they needed professional training. In order to encourage women to seek employment, crèches would have to be created, because otherwise they would not be prepared to work outside the home. In the central Asian republics, interviews with unemployed people in small and medium-sized towns had indicated that they did not want to work away from home, even when jobs were available. Most of these were young women with children who had no education or skills.

Special attention should be paid to the creation of youth employ-ment, not only for those who had reached working age (sixteen), but also for the many fourteen- to fifteen-year-old teenagers who had left school earlier for a variety of reasons. There was often no work for them and labour legislation prohibited the employment of young people who had just finished their compulsory education, when only 60 per cent of school-leavers went on to higher education. The Central Statistical Office had calculated that on 1 July 1963 some 2 million teenagers between the ages of fourteen and seventeen were neither at school nor at work. A further study conducted by the same body on 1 October 1964 had turned up an even higher figure.

The deteriorating employment situation of recent years was 'due in part to miscalculations by planning and economic agencies, and in part to errors in economic policy', concluded the report, which was not loath to identify the culprits. These shortcomings had reduced the effectiveness of investment, in particular as a result of faulty regional distribution of assets. Recent years had witnessed a major redirection of investment eastwards, into mining and electricity generation (particularly with the construction of large hydro-electric stations). But this policy had not been backed up by incentives to labour to settle in the east. At the same time, regions with surplus labour had experienced reduced investment – another mistake.

Job creation depended on capital investment, but the returns on the latter were falling because enormous quantities of material were 'frozen': uninstalled equipment and abandoned construction sites represented huge sums. Finishing such projects and starting up the new enterprises would alone create work for 15 million people, 10 million of them in industry. This was double the number of jobs created during the whole of the last five-year plan. Poor use of investment also stemmed from the fact that much of it was directed towards regional and republican centres, and what were already important industrial towns where spare labour was in short supply. The result was expansion of the latter at the expense of the countryside and small or medium-sized towns. The excessive growth of large towns entailed huge investment in infrastructure and housing, even though some towns with a lot of housing were not always in a position to maximize use of the local labour force or even squandered it.

The obstacles to a rational distribution of labour and employment had been compounded by Khrushchev's restriction of private family plots in the countryside, which had led to the loss of 3.5 million jobs in this sector (Central Statistical Office), as well as to serious food supply problems in towns and countryside alike. Estimates indicated that simply to maintain existing levels of consumption of meat and dairy products by kolkhozniks deprived of their private plots, kolkhozes would have to increase their production of milk and dairy products by two-thirds, of meat and lard by three-quarters, of eggs by 150 per cent, of potatoes by 50 per cent, and of vegetables, melons and gourds by two-thirds. These figures underlined just how important a source of food and income private plots were (approximately half of what people received from the kolkhoz). The restriction of family plots by administrative measures, especially in small and medium-sized towns where they were very common, was exacerbating the labour supply problem. People deprived of the income they had derived from them needed work to replace it, but jobs were not easy to come by in towns. (Khrushchev's reckless decision accounts for much of the popular discontent and instances of riot deplored by the KGB, which was ill-equipped to contain them.)

The unplanned, excessive influx of rural inhabitants into towns further complicated the state of the job market. Between 1959 and 1963, about 6 million rural inhabitants had arrived in towns. Most of them were young – under the age of twenty-nine. In itself this was a positive development, but not when it occurred in conditions of slow growth in output and labour productivity in the countryside. Most of these people from the countryside hailed from regions not where there was a labour surplus, but where it was in short supply and food production inadequate.

Another aberration: the spontaneous migration from countryside to town necessitated enlisting town dwellers to work in the fields, especially at harvest time. In some areas, this agricultural labour took the form of a 'sponsorship' of the rural zone in question; the phenomenon was becoming commonplace. The 'sponsors' (mostly factories) took on a significant share of the agricultural work in the farming units they were sponsoring – cultivation, harvesting, and so on. They supplied the state with its share of the crops and undertook the requisite construction and repair work. Industrial plants were therefore obliged to maintain a reserve labour force for this seasonal work. In some regions, the organization of such work was not increasing agricultural output, because the managers of kolkhozy and sovkhozy had grown dependent on outside help. At the same time, such collaboration was having a negative impact on industrial plants by hampering productivity improvements in them. In the final analysis, the consequences were negative all round.

The formation of labour reserves in urban enterprises for the purposes of agricultural work was promoting an abnormal process of labour exchange. Many kolkhozniks, accustomed to work in the fields, preferred to find a job in the factories of neighbouring towns. The reason was simple: the wages they could earn in industrial enterprises in the same region were 2.5–3 times higher than those paid by the kolkhozy.

One possible solution proposed by the Gosplan research institute is especially worthy of note. The central Asian republics, Kazakhstan and Georgia had high rates of population growth and possessed huge labour resources, but no economic assets – apart from agriculture, family plots and minor occupations. Moreover, their predominantly Muslim populations were reluctant to emigrate. This was where investment was required – not in more developed regions with low population growth and labour shortages.

Here a question suggests itself: What about the labour required to exploit resource-rich Siberia? The researchers probably assumed that their strategy of redirecting investment to central Asia and the Caucasus would generate enough economic growth to allow the state to offer the necessary wages to attract workers to Siberia.

One can image the debates that such a proposal must have sparked off. Just overcoming the opposition in Islamic areas to women working for a wage outside the home was far from straightforward. Language problems and professional training were additional major headaches. On the other hand, prioritizing the development of non-Russian regions, and postponing Siberia's exploitation until better times, would provoke strong reactions among Russian nationalists, defenders of the central state, and other analogous currents that would be difficult to counter. Nevertheless, unperturbed, the author of the report pursued his survey of all the regions, in each instance proposing specific solutions that formed part of a comprehensive policy – as if saying to the Soviet leadership: 'If you really want to plan, this is what you have got to do.'

Readers will by now have an idea of just how complex the labour issue was, as well as of the social and economic ramifications of the accumulating distortions. The whole venture demanded a set of coordinated measures, including material incentives, which were supposed to be the very essence of planning. Yet the Gosplan institute bluntly reported that 'the problem is not so much a lack of information, as the fact that the employment factor is still not genuinely integrated into the formation of the national economic plan'. In other words, Gosplan did not know how to plan employment, its distribution and stabilization; and therefore did not plan it. It remained stuck in an age when manpower supplies were plentiful and it sufficed to fix investment and output targets for the labour to follow – or be forced to follow. That period corresponded to a stage of economic development and was not a matter of chance. But times were changing and the complexity of the task was increasing.

At this point we may venture a provisional conclusion. There was no question as yet of an imminent crisis. However, the government had to opt for a different method of planning that was not confined to fixing quantitative targets, but which would coordinate, anticipate and correct the efforts of productive units, which themselves knew what they wanted and needed to do. Gosplan and the government had been put on notice: labour supply and demand was an urgent issue. If it was ignored, or assumed to be self-regulating, as had been the case, the economy would stagnate, Gosplan or no Gosplan.

Following this analysis of problems with labour supply in 1965, we can now supplement our picture with data and analysis first from 1968 and then 1972.

On 16 September 1968, three years after the Yefimov report, the head of the labour force department in the Russian Federation's Gosplan, Kasimovsky (who may have been attached to Yefimov's research institute), delivered a speech to a selected audience of government experts. His main points were as follows. The extraordinary concentration of the population in towns over the last twenty years had significantly complicated labour supply problems (availability and distribution). The fastest growth had occurred in large towns; the share of the population in small towns was declining. Between 1926 and 1960, the population of towns with more than 500,000 inhabitants had multiplied by 5.9 (the figure for the Russian Federation was 4.5). In many instances, smaller towns and urban settlements that could play a vital role for the surrounding population had been destabilized by the uncontrolled pace of urbanization. Instead of becoming centres of support for the whole area, they often turned into a source of employment and demographic problems.

The number of small towns was not increasing and their population had dropped by 17 per cent in Russia (and, to a lesser extent, in the USSR as a whole). In the Russian Federal Republic, the share of the population living in towns with fewer than 10,000 inhabitants had declined from 9 to 1 per cent between 1926 and 1960, whereas towns of between 100,000 and 200,000 had increased their share of the total. The USA had experienced a different pattern: the number of small towns and their share of the urban population had remained stable; medium-sized towns (10–50,000 inhabitants) had grown; and the largest towns had experienced a population decline. The US pattern was unquestionably preferable, because exploiting a hectare of land was much cheaper in a small town. In Russia, it cost 45–47 roubles, as against 110–130 in large towns.

In the country's twenty-eight largest towns, construction of new factories was banned. Yet in the current five-year plan, ministries, whether by obtaining exemptions or simply disregarding regulations, had set up enterprises there in order to take advantage of superior infrastructure, causing a serious labour shortage in those towns. Their population was growing fast, but the creation of new industries (and – I would add – not just industries) was outstripping it. In smaller towns, the reverse was true: enterprises were indeed being constructed, but there were still labour surpluses. This generated a set of related problems – in particular, the socially negative impact of imbalances between male and female labour.[3]

This complicated situation was analysed four years later in great detail by another labour expert. In small and medium-sized towns, worrying economic and social problems were accumulating, reflected in the use of the labour force. The imbalance between male and female employment was once again underlined.

In towns where new industries were located, the proportion of untapped labour was falling. In contrast, those that had not experienced economic development saw population outflows, to the point where some small and medium-sized towns were suffering from labour shortages. In addition, in many towns one-sided specialization led to predominantly female or predominantly male employment, resulting in imbalances between the sexes. In Russia alone, around 300 towns were experiencing more or less serious imbalances of this kind, impacting on the make-up of the population. The study referred to dealt with seventy towns in twenty large regions where this problem existed.

In towns where single-sex employment was prevalent, the other sex found itself without a job and turned to work at home or on a private plot. The impossibility of starting a family was fuelling labour mobility; a labour shortage was emerging, impacting in particular on the town's most important economic enterprises and disrupting the distribution of professional skills and qualifications. Research indicated that in towns with high female employment, the percentage of men among the unemployed was between 27 and 57 per cent, whereas the national average was 13 per cent. Labour turnover was much greater there than elsewhere, and automatically accompanied by an exodus and shortage of labour. Many textile factories had to import female labour – mostly women as young as fifteen. Fewer and fewer female workers were of local origin: no more than 30 per cent, as against 90–100 per cent for males. But these young newcomers did not stay long, on account of the unfavourable demographic balance. This was the main reason for instability in the female labour force up to the age of twenty-nine, as evidenced by a sociological study in the large textile centre of Ivanovo-Voznesensk. Another irrationality observed in towns with predominantly female employment was that skilled workers had nothing to

3   GARF, f. A-10005, op. 1, d. 248, LL. 51–5.

do except cultivate their private plot – work that required no skill. In the towns of the Vladimir region, 20–30 per cent of employees in commerce and the food industry were men, whereas the average for the Russian Federation was 15.1 per cent.

The sum total of these imbalances, particularly in the distribution of the generations and sexes, had a negative demographic impact: a low rate of natural population growth, high automatic population outflows, and a drop in overall population growth. Small towns had 125 women for every 100 men (118 for 100 for all the Russian Federation's towns). On average, the female surplus mostly emerged from the age of forty, but in small and medium-sized towns it was already evident from fifteen onwards.

A consequence of the slowdown in demographic growth was an ageing population: twenty- to thirty-nine-year olds accounted for only 30 per cent of the population of Russian towns. As a percentage of the total population of the republic, including the countryside, they represented 33 per cent. The report also dealt with the problem of starting families and single-parent families.

According to the report's author, the complexity of these phenomena was beyond the grasp of the republican authorities. The measures taken to rectify the situation had been found wanting. Among the obstacles cited were poor planning, a lack of incentives for ministries to locate industries in small towns, instabilities in their plans, and the weakness of their construction capacities. The government of the Russian Federation had tried to persuade the USSR Gosplan to help it eliminate these failures by a special plan for twenty-eight 'feminized' towns and five 'masculinized' ones – but to no avail. Gosplan had other priorities.[4]

As we can see, these complicated problems of labour supply and demographics attracted plenty of attention and anxiety; sociologists and a small team of social psychologists also joined in the debate. Their national and ethnic dimensions were further causes for concern.

Was the Soviet system equipped to deal with this kind of situation? It had certainly proved capable of determining priorities like the accelerated development of key economic sectors, defence (linked in numerous respects to the former), and mass education. But in each instance the specific task was fairly easy to define. What came to the fore in the 1960s

---

4   GARF, f. A-10005, op. 1, d. 249, LL. 244–53, October 1972 (report by the head of the RSFRS's state committee on labour resources to the Russian Council of Ministers).

were challenges of a quite different order, which required a capacity for articulating several plans. In other words, the task now was conceptualizing and managing complexity itself. Employment had become part of a social, economic, political and demographic puzzle and was regarded as such.

OTHER WOES OF THE ECONOMIC MODEL

After Stalin's death, important changes were made in the economy, with positive results. A sharp increase in agricultural investment (mainly in the 'virgin lands' of Kazakhstan and elsewhere), and an increase in the prices paid to agricultural producers, led to a doubling in the monetary income of collective farms between 1953 and 1958. Agricultural output grew by 55 per cent between 1950 and 1960; grain output alone rose from 80 to 126 million tons, with three-quarters of the increase deriving from the virgin lands. But the latter were not a stable source of grain in the longer run.

To improve living standards, investment in housing and consumer goods was stepped up. Between 1950 and 1965, the urban housing stock doubled and the gulf between investment in capital goods – priority of the Stalinist period – and in consumer goods narrowed.

Great improvements were made in health care. The mortality rate declined from 18 per thousand in 1940 to 9.7 in 1950 and 7.3 in 1965. Infant mortality – the best indicator of public health standards – dropped from 182 per thousand live births in 1940 to 81 in 1958 and 27 in 1965.

Educational levels also rose: the number of pupils continuing their education beyond the four years of elementary schooling rose from 1.8 million in 1950 to 12.7 million in 1965–6. As for numbers in higher education, they trebled from 1.25 million students to 3.86 million in the same years.

Extremely low in 1953, peasant incomes grew more rapidly than those of town dwellers. Within the urban population, a certain levelling set in: minimum incomes rose, as did pensions, while wage differentials narrowed.

But the old preference for heavy industry and armaments persisted, and in so far as an effort was being made at the same time to raise living standards and stimulate technological progress, problems were mounting. In these years, Japan caught up with Soviet growth levels and succeeded in both improving its living standards and modernizing its economy. By contrast, Soviet economists and planners knew and said – in secret but also in published works – that the country's economic model, which remained basically Stalinist, contained dangerous disequilibria. Nevertheless, the Soviet Union enjoyed some spectacular successes, especially in aerospace, so that (in R. W. Davies's words) 'by 1965 the Soviet Union faced the future with confidence, observed by the capitalist powers with considerable alarm'.[5] But as the archival material from Gosplan and other institutions indicates, the immediate future was much more complicated and worrying, and the planners began to grow seriously alarmed.

Regarding the targets of the eighth five-year plan (1966–70), certain failures were already evident. Gosplan's collegium had warned the government that these shortcomings would impact on the subsequent plan.[6] Although investment from all sources had increased by 1.7 per cent (10 million roubles), the central investment plan from which the bulk of new productive capacity derived (especially in heavy industry) had fallen short by 27 billion roubles (10 per cent). On top of this, an extra 30 billion had to be spent to cover increased construction costs for productive units, whose productive capacity had not thereby been enhanced. Thus, the plan's targets for the coming on stream of new units had been met only to the tune of 60 per cent for coal and steel, 35–45 per cent for the chemical industry, 42–49 per cent for tractors and lorries, 65 per cent for cement, and 40 per cent for cellulose. All this would impact on the construction of plant in the course of the subsequent plan.

Gosplan attributed the responsibility to government ministries, which had to find the reserves required to expand output. But most of them did not include proposals for improvements in their respective sectors in their plans for 1971–5 – and this despite numerous injunctions from government to do so and to find reserves.

---

5 With the exception of a few remarks of my own, this material is taken from R. W. Davies, *Soviet Economic Development from Lenin to Khrushchev*, Cambridge 1998, pp. 67 ff.
6 RGAE, f. 4372, op. 82, d. 1086 (undated but from the Gosplan Collegium in 1970).

CONTINUAL GROWTH IN EXTENSIVE FACTORS IN THE ECONOMY

A yet more revealing diagnosis was offered, again by Gosplan's research institute. On 19 November 1970 its director, Kotov, wrote to Gosplan's deputy head, Sokolov, and had this to say: in its directive for the ninth five-year plan (1971–5), the Twenty-fourth Party Congress had postulated that economic success was based on intensive growth and the introduction of new technology (this also applied to agriculture). But the relevant data indicated, in agriculture in the first instance, that the expenditure already committed in terms of labour, wages and social funds was growing faster than output. This trend contradicted the imperative of economic development – namely, achieving relative savings in social labour.[7]

The far from favourable prospects for the next five-year plan were primarily caused by the signal reduction in the productivity of capital assets. The existing indicator for measuring returns on investment was inadequate and economists in the agricultural department lacked a reliable instrument for assessing these assets and planning the requisite amounts of capital.

Kotov then produced a series of calculations that we shall not reproduce here, but which served as a basis for his warning to Gosplan and the government: 'Extensive factors are becoming stronger in the development of the Soviet economy, primarily because growth in basic capital assets is outstripping growth in output. This trend is even more apparent in agriculture than other sectors.'

If the experts were alarmed, it was because such a trend ran counter to modern industrial and scientific development. There is no doubt that some of the leaders involved in the development and implementation of economic policy were also aware of these trends and what they portended.

---

7 RGAE, 4372, 66, 3717, LL. 1–3.

17

THE 'ADMINISTRATORS': BRUISED BUT THRIVING

'BARGAINING'

We can now return to the Soviet bureaucracy, whose fate we tracked under Stalin. After his death, what happened to it can best be described, without the slightest hyperbole, as the 'emancipation of the bureaucracy'. Stalinism cost it dear, and even if administrators served as best they could, the system did not allow them to behave like the bosses they were supposed to be. Henceforth they did everything in their power to eliminate from the system all the elements of Stalinism that had spoilt things for them. To anticipate somewhat, we can say that the bureaucratic phenomenon was going to flourish as never before and that the Soviet system's modus operandi was to be profoundly transformed by it. Henceforth the decision-making process was 'bureaucratized' – that is to say, it no longer took the form of categorical orders, but of a complex process of negotiation–coordination (*soglasovyvanie*) between top political leaders and administrative agencies. This new modus operandi had already existed in many respects, but was always vulnerable to abrupt termination by sometimes bloody purges. That was now out of the question, even if a peremptory reform by Khrushchev abolished a large number of government agencies and offices with a stroke of the pen. But this had nothing in common with the way Stalin had operated. Moreover, the reform in question actually ended up failing, as we shall see in more detail later.

Two Russian terms are especially useful when dealing with the bureaucratic universe. The first, just mentioned, is *soglasovyvanie*, which perfectly encapsulates the interminable process of negotiation–coordination – similar to a variety of bargaining – between ministerial departments, as well as between government and party officials. The second is *upravlentsy*, referring to the administrative cadres engaged in *upravlenie*, which means something like 'managing–governing–commanding'.

Having registered the depressed state of the party apparatus after the war compared with the influence and arrogance of ministers – something bitterly resented by party apparatchiks – we are in a position to follow the policy initially pursued by Khrushchev. It aimed to reinvigorate the party and restore the status and power of its apparatus by strengthening its ideological role (this policy and the hopes it raised would subsequently fade). To this end, Khrushchev put much effort into his own reformulation, at once new and old, of socialist aspirations. He set particular store by such practical measures as raising the living standards not only of the population as a whole but also of the apparatchiks themselves, so that the latter could approximate to the level of material comfort enjoyed by top ministerial officials – the yardstick for party bosses and the ranks below them. It was not only a matter of wages, but in particular of an array of perks that were an intense object of desire among different upper strata. In their eyes, such perks were the only way of measuring their real status (something not invented by Soviet bureaucrats). The Central Committee had to do something urgently to satisfy the personnel of the party apparatus at central and republican levels alike, so that they did not remain a second-rate group composed of impoverished malcontents. As this was the only way of preventing an exodus of the brightest or cleverest apparatchiks to work for the 'competition', steps were taken to ensure that they once again felt themselves to be in the saddle and were seen as so being, as befitted a ruling party.

THE STATE ADMINISTRATION

In our sketch of the state administration, as in Part One we shall make a clear distinction between the *upravlentsy* on the one hand, and the apparatchiks of the Central Committee apparatus and party bodies on the other.

Predictably, in every sector the powerful state administration was, like the rest of society, highly sensitive to the transition under way to a different kind of social, cultural and, in some respects, political organization. The bureaucracy had to react to the spontaneous waves of change and, in so doing, exhibited a 'spontaneity' of its own – i.e. the various trends at work within it. It adopted new patterns of behaviour; its self-image and ways of conceiving its own interests evolved. Our inquiry will focus on this last point: the predominant orientation of the bureaucracy, especially in its upper echelons, to its own interests and its assessment of its position within the system.

The story of the Soviet bureaucracy remains little known. The complex, troubled history of the construction of the state's administrative structures and recruitment of its personnel, constantly on the agenda since Lenin first asked for an inventory of officials after the Civil War, contains a shadow history: the invention of new bodies to control this administration. Like the administrative structures themselves, these were constantly being disbanded and replaced by different ones. There is no need to go into the details. Suffice it to say that Soviet administrative history exhibited an astonishing tendency for 'bureau-creativity', replete with endless restructuring that finally subsided in the regime's last years. But by then, as wicked tongues had it, senior bureaucrats no longer retired: they died in their office chairs.

Whatever the supervisory agency in question (the first dated from 1921), its task was to define, classify, and of course inventory the numbers and cost of the monster. This in itself proved onerous. In the first two decades of the regime, there were numerous computations, inventories and classifications. But we shall pass directly to 1947, when the Central Statistical Office conducted a complete census of the various administrative strata and reliable figures were communicated to the leadership. Naturally, numbers were just the start of the operation. Assessing the cost of administrative agencies, establishing remuneration rules, working on organizational structures, handling appointments (the *nomenklatura* or rather *nomenklaturas*, for there were several) – this was a mammoth undertaking. Wages policy alone (assuming some order was desirable in it) required a huge amount of work: job definitions, pay scales (with special treatment for priority and privileged sectors), control over the use of the wages fund – not to mention the broader problem of how ministries actually managed the budgets accorded them by the Finance Ministry, after approval by the Central Committee and the Council of Ministers. Each of the tasks signalled here demanded considerable time and effort on the part of the supervisory agencies; and the top leadership also immersed itself in the matter. The 'circular' complexity of the venture (one apparatus controlling another apparatus) was such that no so-called 'state control' agency could effectively oversee a constantly expanding bureaucratic universe.

The first of the 'controllers' was the Finance Ministry, since it held the purse-strings. Next came Gosplan, which assigned ministries their economic tasks and therefore had to know the number, structure and cost of their personnel. The Central Statistical Office, whose services no one could dispense with, periodically conducted general or partial inventories. Then there was the 'state control' agency proper (frequently reorganized and renamed in the course of its history). It studied and investigated administrative bodies, uncovering a proliferation of agencies and officials. Its archives contain a wealth of data for researchers to delve into. Among other things, we learn from them that the state administration suffered from something like a propensity to 'parcellization' – that is to say, to the creation of multiple sub-units with overlapping functions and myriad malfunctions. Finally, the Prosecutor's Office, the police and the KGB had their hands full with cases of gross negligence, derelictions and criminal behaviour. Party organizations – particularly its own apparatus – made their own contribution to analysing the phenomenon with a view to formulating policy proposals. They frequently initiated investigations or created committees of inquiry to analyze the problems of the 'administrative system' in general or some particular agency. The Russian term for the whole bureaucratic phenomenon – *administrativno-upravlencheskaia-sistema* (command-administrative system) – is apt. But it covers both state administration and party apparatus. To round off our picture of a bureaucracy that was constantly being inspected, investigated and restructured, we shall mention in passing that each administrative body had its own inspectorate. Yet nothing could stop this ever more complex structure from expanding by its own momentum in a direction no one desired.

We cannot disregard the leadership's ability to wield its axe and launch anti-bureaucratic offensives. Stalin's purges are a case in point. But efforts to reduce and rationalize the administration, to make it more efficient, less expensive and more responsive to both the leadership and public opinion, had been as ineffectual as they were legion. This probably explains why the impetuous, cocksure Khrushchev opted for a frontal assault in order to settle the problem at one stroke, but as ever without having thought his strategy through. Initially, such shock treatment was highly impressive, because it was not wanting in plausibility.

KHRUSHCHEV'S ADMINISTRATIVE OVERHAUL (1957–64)

The aim was to replace the massive pyramid of economic ministries (mostly linked to industry), which were over-centralized and oblivious to local interests, by local economic administrative bodies. Their mission was to manage and coordinate the economy with a much clearer sense and knowledge of local conditions than remote bureaucrats based in Moscow could muster. Given that the bulk of economic activity occurred at local level, the move was intended to facilitate initiative and release new resources, remedying the failures of the previous pyramid structure. A joke captures the problem. Two economic agencies located opposite each other in a street in Kazan both possess merchandise in their warehouses needed by the other agency. But they cannot negotiate a transaction without calling their ministry in Moscow. When the latter gives its agreement, trains leave Moscow for Kazan loaded with the material already stocked in sufficient quantities in the local warehouses. This contained more than a grain of truth.

The unwieldiness of ministries made it imperative to bring management closer to production, by adopting a territorial rather than a branch principle. On 10 May 1957, the Central Committee decided that it was no longer possible to manage 200,000 enterprises and 100,000 construction sites spread across the country from ministerial offices in Moscow. The moment had come to enhance republican and local powers, and to dispatch management directly to the economic–administrative regions.

Mainly intended for industry and construction, the programme was also implemented in other sectors. In May–June 1957, the Supreme Soviet created 105 economic regions (70 in the Russian Federation, 11 in the Ukraine, and in some instances just one per republic). All in all, 141 economic ministries were abolished at central, central-republican and republic levels, shedding 56,000 officials, which represented a saving of 600 million roubles. They were replaced by economic councils (sovnarkhozy), which were responsible for several branches on their territory. Initially, their personnel was small – just 11–15 officials. In due course – 1960 – the managers of major enterprises and construction sites were co-opted and additional departments were created, containing sections responsible for branch management. Subsequently, technical councils were established bringing together experts, engineering staff, and so-called economic rationalizers.

In 1959 and 1960 the economic successes were beyond dispute, with annual growth rates of 8 per cent. In the largest republics, 'republican councils of the national economy' were instituted to coordinate the smaller local councils and handle material–technical supply issues. At the end of 1962 various sovnarkhozy were amalgamated and their number fell from 105 to 43. On 24 November 1962 an All-Union Council of the National Economy was set up in Moscow. Its task was to compile a national plan and a general supply system for raw materials and technology, and it managed things through the republican governments, sovnarkhozy, and individual ministries. Central government – i.e. the Council of Ministers of the USSR – dealt only with what was not included in the plan. Thus, even if it remained somewhat fragmented, a central level was being recreated. On 13 March 1963 the USSR Council of the National Economy was invested with dual union–republican status: a central body, it was now to have homologues in the republics. During 1963–5 it was assigned jurisdiction over Gosplan, the State Construction Committee, and the branch committees of the Council of Ministers in key sectors. Following the good results of 1957–60, the next four years were marked by a slowdown in economic growth, and the defects of the new system became apparent. The intention to decentralize and democratize management of the economy was a good one, but the sovnarkhozy proved incapable of ensuring the indispensable branch-level specialization where essential technological development occurs. They prioritized relations with the enterprises in their regions, neglecting the transverse problems peculiar to branches.[1]

Many had understood from the outset in 1957 that the territorial and branch principles needed to be combined. State production committees, under the Council of Ministers in Moscow, began to emerge for this purpose. Another anomaly in need of correction was that scientific research and development offices were cut off from production units. They did not come under the sovnarkhozy; and the state production committees that supervised them were not empowered to introduce their inventions into production – they could only make recommendations.

In addition, sovnarkhozy tended to prioritize local interests, aiming at a form of economic autarky where everything would be produced locally. This generated a certain 'localism' whereby everyone tended to their own business in the first instance. In these circumstances, the

---

1   See T. P. Korzhikhina, *Sovetskoe Gosudarstvo i ego Uchrezhdeniia, Noiabr' 1917 – Dekabr' 1991 g.*, Moscow 1995.

central government's branch committees (as their head, Kosygin, explained to the Central Committee in 1965) could not have any impact on technological progress: they were merely consultative bodies. Poorly conceived, Khrushchev's reform was coming apart at the seams.

The failure of the sovnarkhozy prompted a new wave of criticism of 'voluntarism' and a propensity to 'administer', which came down to issuing instructions. Such criticism had frequently been directed at the previous system. After Khrushchev's fall, however, the status quo ante was restored: the sovnarkhozy were disbanded and the vertical ministerial system re-established.

The restoration of vertical ministries in 1965, almost immediately after Khrushchev had been ousted, was no accident. The regime felt more confident about its ability to control centralized administrative pyramids than to deal with a system that combined both principles, but which had never been seriously worked out. The Central Committee plenum in 1965 drew the lessons of seven years of development and in a single stroke eliminated the different central, republican and local bodies of the 'sovnarkhoz' variety. At the end of 1965, thirty-five economic ministries were back at work, operating as before. As for Gosplan, which had had to endure an unhappy cohabitation with the National Economic Council, it recovered its previous powers, as did the powerful but notorious Gossnab (State Committee for Material and Technical Supplies).

This reorganization was not to represent a happy outcome, even if Kosygin had declared in favour of a return to the vertical pyramids of centralized ministries. Unlike other leaders, he did not idealize them and in the same year – 1965 – without fanfare he launched a new economic experiment – the regime's last – aimed at changing the system of economic incentives, but not directly the command-administrative system.

The rapidity of the reversion to the enormous complex of pre-Khrushchevite economic administration looked like a miracle. In fact, however, the old system had never really disappeared. Very soon after the creation of the sovnarkhozy, a system of substitutes had been established in the form of the industrial branch committees attached to the Council of Ministers, whose design actually corresponded to the former ministries. The number of officials in the various central industrial agencies reached 123,000 at the end of 1964, surpassing the figure for 1956. Moreover – something we have not yet mentioned – numerous branch supply committees, supplanting the disbanded supply super-ministry, sprang up quite incongruously in Gosplan. They employed many of the former cadres from the ministries, preserving their know-how, which meant that they were ready to restore the previous structures at short notice.

Some ministerial officialdom had been disadvantaged by Khrushchev's overhaul and even obliged to quit Moscow for the provinces, but this was no purge of any kind. It was well known in bureaucratic circles that administrators took care of their own: no sooner had they been removed from one post than they found another elsewhere – usually at the same level. The Moscow megacentre was a master in the art of this 'bureaucratic security system', even if those in the know were well aware that it was not necessarily the most effective personnel who were retained, but the best connected and most socially skilful – something, to reiterate the point, that is not peculiar to the USSR.

The re-establishment of the ministries, while a cause for rejoicing among many bureaucrats, also entailed the re-emergence of all the problems that had prompted the Khrushchev reform. A book by relatives and friends of Kosygin, who was the boss of the economy and intent on efficiency, affords us some idea of his scathing verdict.[2] Kosygin complained bitterly about the fact that so many things reached the Council of Ministers when they should have been resolved lower down by the numerous administrative bodies that existed to deal with them: 'Why should the government have to concern itself with the quality of the sand being supplied to the glass industry and other industrial branches? There are ministries and a state standards agency: why don't they meet and resolve the issue?' The State Construction Agency – a powerful body – came to see Kosygin to discuss its new housing designs, but these fell exclusively within its competence. All this, argues the author of the relevant chapter, attested to the inefficiency of numerous state agencies. Kosygin was unsparing in his criticism of them and sought to improve their functioning. One day, when the Finance Minister Garbuzov was talking to him about the expansion of the state apparatus, its multiple hierarchies, and the number of redundant departments, Kosygin answered him thus:

It's true, the productivity of our apparatus is very low. Most people don't do enough work and have no idea what they are going to do the following day. We've just abolished the Committee for Cultural Links with Foreign

2 T. I. Fetisov, sost., *Prem'er – Izvestnyi i Neizvestnyi: Vospominaniia o A. N. Kosygine*, Moscow 1997.

Countries. Did anyone notice? Nobody – anyway, I didn't. We are producing tons of paper, but in practical terms we actually do very little. With a
better organization of work, we could easily cut the number of officials by
half.

There is an audible note of despair here. Kosygin depicts a system
which, at the level immediately below the summit, is not doing much
and does not really care. For understandable historical reasons, the
system had been constructed 'from the top down'. But it remained stuck
in this mould to the very end. The reckless interlude opened by
Khrushchev was a legitimate attempt to alter this modus operandi, but
the former system returned like a shot. In essence, the bureaucratic
system remained the same; it was just temporarily split into local replicas
of the 'big brother'.

Did Kosygin have a clear idea of why things were going so wrong?
Had he pondered the deeper causes of the phenomenon? Without access
to his papers, it is impossible to say for sure. However, a provisional
response is perhaps hinted at by the reform of the 'economic mechanism', officially launched in 1965, which carries his name. This was the
largest economic reform since the war and it was initiated cautiously,
without official fanfare. Its main objective was to reduce the burden of
central planning indicators – a tentacular system that was difficult to
coordinate – and introduce new incentives from below into the system,
in particular by making funds available to reward managers and workers
for good results or technological innovation. The method was first of all
experimented with in a limited number of factories. Then, when it
yielded encouraging results, it was extended to a larger number of
enterprises and branches. However, it rapidly ran into obstacles that
could only have been overcome by taking other measures to bolster the
break with existing structures. These would have opened the way for a
'de-bureaucratization' and altered the relationship between the plan's
indicators (a veritable straitjacket) and material incentives inside production units and among consumers. Conservative critics were right
when they said that that would have amounted to transforming the
system beyond recognition. This was what was required. But the
political dynamic needed to push it through was lacking. Kosygin's
opponents managed to smother the reform, without even having to
proclaim it openly.

These 'opponents' comprised a coalition or, more precisely, a bloc of
the upper echelons of the state and party bureaucracy. The term

nomenklatura will serve to denote them here. They were all party members and some simultaneously occupied a high administrative position and a seat on the Central Committee. But there are good reasons for distinguishing between administrative cadres and party apparatchiks, and studying them separately. In Part One, we saw that during and after the war the two bureaucracies regarded themselves as distinct, competing categories, vying for power over one another. One of Khrushchev's first professed objectives had been to restore the pre-eminence of the party – in the first instance, of its apparatus – in order to make it an instrument of his own power. That is why it is worth returning to some key features of this apparatus.

THE PARTY APPARATUS

Some figures are a basis to start from.[3] On 1 October 1949 there were 15,436 party committees (or organizations) in the whole country. Excluding the Central Committee's own administration, full-time (i.e. remunerated) apparatchiks numbered 138,961, of whom 113,002 were 'political officials' and 25,959 'technicians'. We possess data on the staffs of local party bodies for the period 1940 – 1 November 1955, broken down into two categories (political officials and technicians), but also according to the position of the organization in the country's administrative structure (republics, regions, districts, subdistricts, and workplaces). Here are some annual totals for 1 January of each year.

	Political	Technical
1940	116,931	37,806
1947	131,809	27,352
1950	113,313	26,100
1951	115,809	26,810
1952	119,541	27,517
1953	125,005	28,710
1954	131,479	28,021
1955	142,518	27,830
1955*	143,768	27,719

*On 1 November.

---

3   RGASPI, f. 17, op. 75, d. 9.

A reliable source on party personnel on 1 December 1963 – the most recent that I have been able to obtain – gives the following figures for the apparatus, excluding the Central Committee: 24,290 party organizations, with 117,504 full-timers, of whom 96,909 were 'political officials' and 20,595 'technicians'. The monthly wages bill amounted to 12,859,700 roubles for the former and 1,054,100 for the latter. The relatively low proportion of technical personnel reflected pressure from above not to exceed budgetary limits. As a result, the political personnel lacked adequate support staff – notably secretaries and typists.[4]

In 1958, the personnel of the Central Committee – the Moscow power hub – numbered 1,118 officials and 1,085 technicians, or 2,203 people; as well as the officials of the party committee within the Central Committee (for like any other workplace, party members at the Central Committee had their own cell). As we can see, the Central Committee needed more 'technicians' and could afford them. The annual wages bill in 1958 was 57,039,600 roubles.[5] Five years later, a report refers to an annual wages bill of 65 million roubles – an increase justified by the recruitment of new apparatchiks for newly created posts and structures.[6]

Two thousand plus employees, 1,100 of them engaged in political tasks: such was the size of the workforce at Moscow's Staraia Ploshchad the famous square where the Central Committee apparatus was located, which constituted the seat of power in the Soviet Union. But these figures do not reflect the real configuration of central power. To them we must add the central administration of the USSR government and ministries, or some 75,000 people who were likewise based in Moscow (the party apparatus for Moscow and its region is not included in these figures, but belongs in the same category). Without adding more data, it is worth mentioning that the 'summits' of the republics and administrative regions – especially the wealthier ones – should also be included, since they acquired ever more power as the centre became submerged by an avalanche of seemingly insoluble problems.

This relatively small number of people making up the upper echelon is not to be confused with the much larger class of *rukovoditeli* (officials performing managerial duties), who were distributed throughout the country in economic, administrative and party positions and who numbered some 2 million.

4   RGASPI, f. 17, op. 75, d. 23, L. 67.
5   RGASPI, f. 17, op. 75, d. 23, LL. 62–7.
6   RGASPI, f. 17, op. 75, d. 22, L. 64.

The Moscow apparatchiks were certainly well paid. In the Soviet Union, however, wages were not an adequate yardstick for gauging living standards or the way in which merit was rewarded. Over and above the inherent satisfaction to be had from occupying high rank, as far as everyone was concerned the real rewards lay in the system of privileges and perks. It merits brief investigation.

PRIVILEGES AND PERKS

Access to priority medical services was an especially coveted privilege.[7] The list of beneficiaries was kept by a special main directorate – the fourth – of the Health Ministry, which was also in charge of the best medical centres. It managed three diagnostic centres and three top hospitals, as well as a special diagnostic and treatment centre reserved for members of the Central Committee, the government and their families. The first and second diagnostic centres, as well as the university hospital and an emergency centre, were reserved for the leaders of central and local party bodies, organs of the soviet, and economic agencies.

The list of the privileged grew with successive decisions by the Central Committee and Council of Ministers, which reflected the expansion of the national economy, social organizations and the media. It ended up including around half a million people. Thus, top-ranking officials (and their families), from the capital down to the districts, had access to the best medical facilities. The narrow circle of the Politburo and the Council of Ministers had its own health services in the Kremlin, supervised by the Health Ministry.

To provide proof of status (and take pride in it), it was enough to mention that one was entitled to the 'Kremlin's medical facilities'. Thus, in order to know precisely who belonged to the privileged few, the best source is the Health Ministry archives. In them we also find some interesting data on those who lost these perks – and not only because of their demise. But hospitals and medical facilities are only part of the story.

On 19 April 1966, the deputy head of the Central Committee's financial affairs department communicated to the Central Statistical Office, which had requested it, the list of sanatoria, rest homes and hotels it controlled. On 1 January 1966 there were twelve sanatoria, five

---

7 See M. Woslenski, *Les nouveaux secrets de la nomenklatura*, Paris 1965, pp. 441–50.

rest homes (excluding those for one-day visits) and two hotels. The document specified who was entitled to use them (adults and children), how many people per year stayed in them during the high season, and where they were situated. The Central Statistical Office had been instructed to keep tabs on these various perks. The file provided similar data for Defence Ministry and KGB establishments. Every self-respecting ministry possessed such recreational establishments, not to mention dachas for bigwigs.

Lower-level party officials in workplaces also had to be motivated in their work. Extraordinary privileges were invented for party, Komsomol and trade-union apparatchiks (i.e. paid functionaries not involved in production). In March 1961 the Central Committee decided that they were to share in the premiums accorded to engineers and administrators for introducing new technology into production (including in the arms industry). The premiums awarded by the relevant party body were not to exceed three years' wages, whereas administrators and engineers could earn bonuses worth up to six years' wages.[8] Even so, this represented a significant sum. The claim – or fiction – that the work of party secretaries was indispensable was thus bolstered by this remuneration of their 'contribution' to the technological innovation made by engineers in enterprises and research departments. In the absence of such devices, the pay and position of party officials in factories would have rendered them poor relations. And not to have granted them the right to these premiums would have implied that their work did not really count.

I have no evidence to prove for certain that this measure was ever implemented. It may be doubted whether it was the ideal way to restore the prestige of party functionaries in the eyes of technical personnel. At all events, it serves as a reminder – should one be needed – that most party secretaries were officials (and not people with a political mission) who wanted to receive their share like other people, even if their actual contribution to production was virtually nil.

PENSIONS: A DELICATE SUBJECT

We have not broached the delicate issue of pensions for top party apparatchiks. It might be assumed that they depended on the rank

---

8   RGAE, f. 7733, op. 36, d. 7242, LL. 10–11. This is the original draft of the decision sent to the Finance Ministry by the department of party organs.

people had attained by the end of their careers. Yet surprising as it may seem, in a bureaucracy obsessed with privileges pensions remained a weak point. Basically, the problem was evaded, for confronting it would have involved fixing a retirement age, which could have had unfortunate consequences. Retirement dates were largely arbitrary, dependent on the whim of superiors. This absence of regulation caused many difficulties for high-ranking officials who were retiring or being forced to retire. Despite their age, many regional secretaries glued themselves to their chairs, blocking the arrival of new blood. They feared an abrupt and drastic reduction in their living standards. Under Brezhnev, the size of pensions depended on connection with Politburo members, even with Brezhnev himself or members of his entourage. This legal vacuum only deepened the dependence of local leaders on the centre. Not infrequently, dedicated local leaders who had paid no attention to cultivating cosy relations with their superiors suffered when it came to retirement, unlike the toadies among them.[9] Our source here is Ligachev – a Politburo member dedicated to the party and known for his personal integrity. But he would have done well to ask if such behaviour was 'communist' and why he was so insistent on the term for his party.

To finish this section on a happier note, we can add that the Council of Ministers did finally issue a decree regulating pensions for leading state and party officials in 1984 – one year before Gorbachev's arrival in power.

A WELFARE STATE ... FOR PARTY AND STATE BIGWIGS

Even if there were surprising gaps when it came to pensions, the kinds of perks offered by the regime to its rulers – who were also party and state employees receiving a salary (though they were not the owners or co-owners of the units under their command) – mean that we can legitimately speak of a welfare state. Obviously, this welfare state also existed for poorer layers of the population, but in the case of the privileged it assumed luxurious proportions in the given Soviet conditions. In an economy constantly suffering shortages of every variety, a good wage was not enough. Special access was also required to products and services that were in short supply and available exclusively to the pri-

9   E. K. Ligachev, *Zagadka Gorbacheva*, Novosibirsk 1992.

vileged few. Hence the development of a perverse mechanism involving high-ranking employees, lobbying hard for perks as a condition of good performance, and their powerful employers (Central Committee, Council of Ministers, ministries) using these perks as a carrot (granting them) or a stick (withdrawing them). This threatened one day to exceed what the system could afford, for it revolved around the redistribution of existing resources, not the creation of new ones. Inevitably, it revealed new motivational realities on both sides. The appetites of administrators went on growing, beyond the system's limits. That some of the highest-level apparatchiks remained ardent partisans of their 'socialism' is readily explicable: no other system would have afforded them as much. We can judge for ourselves from some examples of the degree of material comfort extended to top apparatchiks as they climbed the ladder of the central apparatus.

Almost incredulous, a Central Committee secretary has recounted the perks offered him. We are in 1986, but the information is also valid for the earlier period. It comes from the former ambassador to Washington, Anatoly Dobrynin.[10] Dobrynin knew the leadership well, but had only a vague idea of the universe of the party apparatus. In March 1986 he became secretary of the Central Committee in his capacity as head of the International Department. The following day, he met a representative of the ninth directorate of the KGB, which was responsible for the personal security of leading figures and the material perks granted to Politburo and Secretariat members (it was frequently referred to as 'the Politburo's nanny'). 'I found myself in a world apart', Dobrynin writes. According to the current rules, he was entitled to three bodyguards, a Zil limousine, and a dacha near Moscow at Sosnovyi Bor – the 'Sosnovka' occupied by Marshal Zhukov until his death – with the following staff attached to it: two cooks, two gardeners, four waitresses, and guards. The building comprised two floors, with a large dining room, a living room, several bedrooms and a projection room. There was another building nearby, with a tennis court, a sauna, an orangery and an orchard. 'What a contrast with the Muscovite life I'd been used to!' And yet Dobrynin was simply one of several Central Committee secretaries, not a Politburo member, let alone general-secretary. What was a Politburo member entitled to? He does not say. More than a Central Committee secretary, obviously, but a lot less than the general-

---

10 Anatolii Dobrynin, *Sugubo Doveritel'no*, Moscow 1996.

secretary. In any event, it is worth registering the (doubtless sincere) astonishment of this highly placed – and hence already privileged – Muscovite.

Whatever the amenities they enjoyed, Politburo members could always demand more. But some of them – a majority, perhaps – were not really interested in luxury, and certainly not in ostentatious luxury, with the well-known exception of Brezhnev.

Ligachev's personal experience offers us a glimpse of the Politburo's working life in its twilight years in the early 1980s.[11] After Andropov's death, the Central Committee elected Konstantin Chernenko as general-secretary. He was proposed by Prime Minister Tikhonov and seconded by Gromyko – an unproblematic election. A year later, Chernenko caused some consternation by proposing that Gorbachev – Andropov's protégé – should chair Secretariat meetings, effectively making him the regime's number two. There was opposition from some quarters, but Chernenko, although not at all close to Gorbachev, insisted. The position of number two was not a formal one. Ligachev remembers that in 1984 there were people who sought to find compromising material on Gorbachev from the time when he was regional secretary of the Stavropol region, but does not name them. The use of compromising documents was a favourite weapon in leadership infighting: one side to a conflict would try to dig up dirt to dish on the other. Access to police material or information from the 'underworld' could be a precious asset.

Chernenko received detailed briefings on the state of health of other leaders from Tchazov, the Health Minister. But the health of the general-secretary himself was kept top-secret: even other Politburo members were largely ignorant. Such secrecy was fertile ground for rumours and allowed some members of the leadership, who had personal access to the sick general-secretary, to manipulate him to personal or group advantage.

The Central Committee building on the Staraia Ploshchad was itself a highly secret place. But those in the know would tell you that, traditionally, office no. 6 on the ninth floor was the general-secretary's. Office no. 2 was known as 'Suslov's office'. It was from there (I think) that the Central Committee Secretariat was managed.

The Politburo convened every Thursday at 11 AM precisely, either at

---

11 Ligachev, *Zagadka Gorbacheva*, pp. 26–7.

the Kremlin or Staraia Ploshchad. In the Kremlin, on the third floor of the old part of the building, the general-secretary had an office as well as a reception room. This was also where the 'nut-tree hall' was located, with its large round table around which leaders discussed problems informally before the Politburo session began. While candidate members and Central Committee secretaries attended the latter, they did not participate in the informal discussions.

Under Brezhnev, Politburo meetings were short. It took an hour, or even forty minutes, to approve decisions that had been prepared in advance. Under Andropov, the Politburo's work was more serious and deliberations could last hours. The Politburo had to decide on important appointments – something it did rapidly under Brezhnev and more attentively under Andropov.

A brief passage in Ligachev's memoirs adds an interesting note to this collective portrait. One day – probably in 1983 – one of the most powerful partisans of the conservative wing, the long-time defence head Ustinov (who died in 1984), said to the newly arrived Ligachev: 'Yegor, you are one of us, part of our circle.' Ligachev says that he did not understand what was meant by this. In fact, Ustinov was giving the provincial newcomer to understand that there were factions in the Politburo. His own comprised the conservative 'state patriots', and after his death, the lack of Ligachev's support for 'us' was sorely felt. By then, Ligachev was already in Gorbachev's camp. Subsequently, during perestroika, he rejoined the conservative faction. In his memoirs, Ligachev comments that Gromyko, Ustinov and Chernenko – the figures from the previous generation – can be taxed with a whole variety of failures: they were responsible for the fact that the state was 'on the verge of collapse' in the 1980s. However, he adds that it was to their credit that they opted not to pursue Brezhnev's line but to back Gorbachev instead. In this respect, they proved superior to all the last-minute turncoats who abandoned politics to concentrate on their own personal interests. Gromyko had been the first Politburo member to propose Gorbachev for the post of general-secretary, which had secured him unanimous endorsement not only in the Politburo but also from the Central Committee secretaries. According to Ligachev, things could have turned out quite differently.

As for the modus operandi of the Politburo in Gorbachev's time, there is some interesting information in Dobrynin's memoirs. It remained pretty much unchanged. The main difference stemmed from Gorbachev's personal style, which was more modern than that of the figures described by Ligachev in a period when, with Chernenko ill, the atmosphere had more in common with the priesthood of a mystical cult than the leadership of a modern state.

As a Central Committee secretary, Dobrynin participated in Politburo meetings. He had the right to express his views, but not to vote. The Central Committee secretaries were invariably in attendance. From time to time, Gorbachev convened special sessions. Votes on contentious issues were rarely taken: Gorbachev would forestall them by stating that the issue merited further attention and would be discussed at the next meeting. He would use the intervening period to prepare the decision he wanted to see adopted. Gorbachev liked to talk at length, and sessions would sometimes last until 6 or 8 PM. But he also allowed his colleagues to express their opinions; and in this respect, the atmosphere was more democratic. During the lunch break, which lasted an hour, everyone sat together at a long table in a small working hall. They could choose between two very plain menus, without alcohol. At lunch, discussion was more freewheeling and no stenographic record was made, although Gorbachev's personal assistant did take 'private' notes.

Officially, only Politburo decisions were recorded in writing and transmitted to a short list of officials to be implemented and supervised. The most important decisions were kept in a special folder. The agenda was drawn up by the general-secretary, but Politburo members were entitled to supplement or amend it – something they rarely did. Papers for each meeting were sent out a day or two in advance by the 'general department', the Secretariat's main executive body. This department occupied a special place in the party apparatus. It was always headed by the general-secretary's right-hand man: Chernenko under Brezhnev, and Lukyanov, followed by Boldin, under Gorbachev. Lukyanov was a well-educated, measured person, while Boldin was a narrow-minded bureaucrat who held sway over Gorbachev. This was a cause of bewilderment to many, especially when Boldin showed his true colours by turning out to be one of the instigators of the plot against Gorbachev in August 1991.

The international department run by Dobrynin had nothing to do with foreign affairs. Its 200 officials dealt with Communist parties and other left-wing movements abroad, but not the parties of the popular democracies, which were handled by a separate department. Dobrynin had asked Gorbachev to reverse an old decision, dating from the time of the Comintern, and let his own department handle foreign affairs. He had his way on 13 May 1986, when Gorbachev also authorized the transfer of some experts from the Foreign Ministry to the international department to aid Dobrynin in his new duties.[12] We should add that these moves involved some internal politicking. As we can see from his memoirs, Gorbachev was trying to eliminate Gromyko's influence over foreign policy and even remove him completely from political life. Henceforth, with Dobrynin's professional input, the general-secretary monopolized foreign affairs.

In the context of this brief sketch of the Politburo's functioning, it is important to realize that, for all his 'modern' style, Gorbachev remained a 'classical' general-secretary. His career in the party apparatus had shaped his conception of power, and particularly of the role of general-secretary as superior to other Politburo members and subject to its own rules. Even if Dobrynin does not explicitly say as much, his description confirms it: Gorbachev manipulated his colleagues through rather transparent stratagems in order to get his own way. Gorbachev was incapable of shedding the 'general-secretary syndrome', and it took him time to realize that a system of power which generated this kind of 'disembodied' central position was already moribund.

---

12 Dobrynin, *Sugubo Doveritel'no*, pp. 652–3.

18

SOME LEADERS

Let us now pursue our investigation of the country's problems and woes through a different optic: that of the men at its head or in charge of a key sector. The figures selected here are not typical Politburo members – Brezhnev, Kirilenko, Suslov, Chernenko, and their ilk – some of whom were skilful operators, but political and intellectual mediocrities who ultimately prevailed. They can be tagged as 'the swamp', and the very fact that they held power is a symptom of the system's decay. We have instead singled out personalities who proved capable of reflecting on the system – or their own domain, at any rate – and who were ready to attempt change. Many of them may have shared our opinion of the 'swamp' that was primarily responsible for the period of 'stagnation'.

We only have space here to discuss a few figures – in particular, Khrushchev, with whom our period opens, and Andropov, with whom it closes.

ANDREI GROMYKO

Andrei Gromyko was a figure of considerable stature, but with a seemingly unimpressive personality – an unusual combination of incompatible characteristics. He was at the hclm of Soviet foreign affairs for twenty-eight years. Although not known to have been involved in reformist initiatives, he was nevertheless a pillar of the system in this crucial sphere. Many found him utterly boring and sour-faced, but if we turn to the Western diplomats who dealt with him, like Henry Kissinger, we are given to understand that he was probably the 'number one' of international diplomacy, renowned among his peers as a glutton for work: 'If you can face Gromyko for an hour and survive, then you can begin to call yourself a diplomat', said Kissinger. One of the 'survivors' was President Reagan. Having spent an hour with Gromyko, he returned all excited to the White House, where the event was duly celebrated: the meeting was in a sense his graduation. What he did not know was that Dobrynin had briefed Gromyko on Reagan and advised him to go easy on him for diplomatic reasons. The heads of the Israeli UN delegation (including David Horowitz) never said anything in their memoirs about Gromyko's 'sour' face at the time when he was Soviet ambassador there and the creation of the state of Israel was on the agenda. Each day he would ask them: 'What can I do for you today?' Times change.

Whatever one's assessment of Gromyko's personality, Soviet diplomacy and the performance of its experts and senior ambassadors were mostly of a high quality under his intendancy; and this was largely attributable to his own perfectionism. A reading of his briefs, analyses and recommendations on the world situation confirm his in-depth knowledge. Whether his Politburo colleagues listened is another matter. But the general quality of the information available to the leadership was constantly improving – and not only in the diplomatic sphere – which was no doubt testimony to the system's 'modernizing' aspect. It is sufficient today to meet any Russian diplomat formed in this school – he will invariably speak several foreign languages well – to see how proud he is of his *alma mater*. The Soviet ambassadors to key countries were always highly respected – particularly their doyen, Dobrynin, or the special envoy Kvetsinsky, famous for making progress in negotiations during his 'walk in the woods' with his American counterpart, Paul Nitze.

Gromyko's main characteristics were his complete identification with the interests of the state and his faithful service to it. They explain his personal self-effacement and mastery of his ego – things extremely rare for someone who was the linchpin of international diplomacy for twenty-eight years. The West German politician Egon Bahr, who was in charge of foreign affairs from 1968 to 1972, does not conceal his critical admiration for Gromyko. Commenting on the latter's memoirs, which disclosed so little about his life and work, Bahr remarked:

> He has concealed a veritable treasure-trove from future generations and taken to the grave with him an inestimable knowledge of the inter-

connection between the historical events and major figures of his time, which only he could offer. What a pity that this extraordinary man proved incapable to the very end of evoking his experience. As a faithful servant of the state, he believed that he should restrict himself to sober, concise presentation of the bare essentials.[1]

We can round off this rapid sketch of Gromyko with reference to a decisive political intervention of his. Having been one of the senior statesmen in the Politburo under Brezhnev, Andropov and Chernenko, he played a crucial role in the election of Gorbachev to the post of general-secretary, knowing full well that it would entail a reformist course, probably in the direction mapped out by Andropov. As Ligachev intimated, the outcome of that Politburo meeting might have been very different.

NIKITA KHRUSHCHEV

Nikita Khrushchev was endowed with a unique mixture of character traits. I still do not know how he survived Stalin and whether he ever entertained doubts about him when making his career under him. His folksy side, and his ability to perform a *gopak* (a popular Ukrainian dance) during one of Stalin's banquets ('when Stalin says dance, you dance!', he reminisced), may have fooled the chief as to the ambitions and intentions of this 'simpleton'. One cannot imagine two more utterly contrasting characters.

He certainly became a sensation on the world stage, and not only as a result of such behaviour as banging on his lectern with his shoe during a session of the UN (not terribly diplomatic!), or exclaiming 'We shall bury you' to the Americans – a statement that was in fact distorted by a poor translation (*My vas pokhoronim* also means 'We shall outlive you'). He knew how to take enormous risks, especially in 1962 during the Cuban episode, when he neither won nor lost. He was also a genuine supporter of peace on the international scene. Those who dealt with him directly in international summits never claimed that he was not master of his brief. But he had a tendency to talk too much, to the point

---

1   E. V. Nesternko, ed., *A. A. Gromyko – Diplomat, Politik, Uchenyi*, Moscow 2000, p. 222: the papers of a conference to mark the ninetieth anniversary of Gromyko's birth organized by Moscow University (with contributions sent from abroad by foreign political figures).

of sometimes disclosing state secrets even when sober – much to the despair of the KGB. Khrushchev was a reformer, not a state-builder; an impatient, impetuous leader with a propensity for large-scale – and sometimes risky – panaceas. On occasion, he could be truly bold. The 'secret speech' against Stalin at the Twentieth Congress was his own initiative; he stuck with it and imposed it on recalcitrant colleagues without regard for the rules or niceties. And thus the Congress suddenly learnt that the icon, the idol, the glorious symbol of the country's superpower status was a bloody mass murderer. For the anti-Stalinists, it was a shocking revelation. As for the Stalinists of various hues, they were more than embarrassed and claimed that the picture was exaggerated, when in fact it was very incomplete. For inveterate Stalinists, the most embarrassing thing was to see so many high-ranking leaders evince their astonishment: how could they pretend that they knew nothing about the scale of the atrocities? In fact, only a few insiders were aware of the true scale of things: Stalin's personal secretariat, a handful of Politburo members, and the MVD chiefs who had conducted the operations.

The denunciation of Stalin and his cult was preceded by a wave of rehabilitation of innocent victims, who were subsequently restored to party membership. This made the Stalinist terror a crucial issue for the first congress to be convened after his death.[2] Even before the 'secret speech', by a Central Committee decision of 31 December 1953 the Presidium created a committee of inquiry, including Pospelov, Komarov, Aristov and Shvernik (it became known by the name of its chairman, Pospelov). Its brief was to determine how the mass repression had struck members and candidate members of the Central Committee elected by the Seventeenth Party Congress in 1934. It was assisted in its work by KGB chief Serov and by a group of departmental heads from the same body: secretariat, personnel, archives and special inspection. The Prosecutor's Office was represented by the deputy of the chief military prosecutor. Naturally, all of these were party members. On the eve of the Congress the Presidium of the Central Committee heard the testimony of the prisoner Boris Rodos, who had been the investigator in some highly sensitive cases and a key figure in the political trials of the late 1940s. In his affidavit he testified that Stalin had directed matters personally. He (Rodos) had interrogated victims and constantly

---

2 See R. G. Pikhoia, *Sovetskii Soiuz: Istoriia Vlasti, 1945–1991*, Moscow 1998. Pikhoia has examined the relevant documents in the Politburo archives and reconstructed the unfolding of the Twentieth Congress in detail.

demanded higher execution quotas. Khrushchev insisted on fore-grounding Stalin's personal responsibility and demanded that the issue be raised during a session of the Twentieth Congress. During the debates in Presidium meetings, Molotov, Voroshilov and Kaganovich argued for stressing Stalin's greatness despite his crimes. But Mikoyan and Saburov argued against this: 'If all this is true, it cannot be pardoned' (Saburov). On 8 February 1956, the committee presented to the Presidium a terrifying picture of the systematic extermination of countless party and state cadres by Stalin.

With the eviction of Khrushchev in 1964, a more conservative line re-emerged. Reformist circles were anxious lest Stalin's rehabilitation was envisaged. But notwithstanding some efforts in this direction by members of the new team, neither the spirit of Stalin nor Stalinism ever returned. Following Khrushchev's bold moves, the term 'Stalinism' ceased to apply to the Soviet system. His decision to remove Stalin's body from the mausoleum and rebury it elsewhere did prevent the evil spirit from returning – proof that popular beliefs sometimes count. Even if there were still Stalinists at the summit of power harbouring secret hopes, and even if some pernicious features of the old system endured, Stalinism as such belonged to the past.

The shock therapy applied by Khrushchev cost him dearly politically. But he survived the various after-shocks of de-Stalinization, if not without difficulty and even if it may be that he had second thoughts about the whole enterprise. In any event, the denunciation of Stalin was not restricted to words, but was preceded and succeeded by deeds: a large-scale process of 'rehabilitation' and the dismantling of the MVD's industrial complex which, as we have seen, was the core of the Stalinist machinery of repression.

Khrushchev's style and passion can be explained by the authenticity of his populism, but also by an emotionalism he did not always control. But over and above the joke about his 'goulash socialism' (he actually did say that goulash was preferable to empty phrases about popular well-being), he was convinced that an improvement in living standards was more than a political imperative: it was a matter of justice and 'social-ism'. His folksiness was authentic. He was proud of his working-class origins and even his rural roots. He had been a shepherd's apprentice prior to his industrial career as a metal-worker and miner. There was a direct connection between this past and his language, his aversion for the military, his loathing of bureaucrats, and his preference for production-oriented secondary schools. If he tried to promote such a reform, it was (he said) because the existing secondary schools were educating wimps who knew nothing about physical labour in factories or fields. The reform was abandoned under pressure from public opinion – that is to say, from the better off, the better educated, and bureaucrats, who were indignant and lobbied against this 'industrialization' of secondary schools. As it happened, they were right. But we may assume that this was a crowd of people for whom Nikita had no time: they had never held a pick in their hand!

The same mentality was at work in his turbulent relations with the creative artists. He liked *The House of Matrena* and *One Day in the Life of Ivan Denisovich*, and allowed their publication. Both novels depicted profoundly moral characters from the countryside: Matrena, a peasant woman, has a strong, impressive personality; Ivan, also a peasant, preserves his human dignity despite the humiliating reality of the camps.

Here we must once again mention Tvardovsky, the editor of literary journal *Novyi Mir*, who had published Solzhenitsyn's first two novels and fought to publish more. The friendly relations between Khrushchev and Tvardovsky were literally based on common ground. Tvardosvky was the son of a dispossessed, persecuted kulak. He knew the rural world well and had remained in touch with rural realities despite his elevated position in Moscow's intellectual elite. It is likely that Khrushchev could accept political criticism if it was presented in a down-to-earth manner by people of popular extraction – but not when urban intellectuals said the same thing in their sophisticated idiom. He was also capable of crude, even indecent outbursts against works he did not understand or artists whom he suspected of being hostile to the regime.

Tvardovsky was different in Khrushchev's view. During the war, he had written a long poem about the adventures of a soldier of popular extraction, Vasilii Terkin. After the war, he returned to his now demobilized hero in a poem entitled 'Terkin in Heaven'. In it, Terkin is sent to heaven, where he observes (and endures) the celestial bureaucracy, before deciding to return to earth: at least the bureaucracy down there is breathing. As soon as he learnt of the existence of this scathing satire of the Soviet bureaucracy and hence of the system, which was also turned into a play, Nikita called his son-in-law, who was editor of *Izvestiia*, to tell him to publish it forthwith. Had it been written by a modish intellectual, he would probably have dialled a different number.

Here we might insert a symptomatic detail. The famous film director Mikhail Romm and the no less celebrated sculptor Ernst Neizvestny had both been subject to Khrushchev's irascible outbursts; and both had reacted sharply and uncompromisingly. Later, however, they both referred to him fondly, defending his historical role. Khrushchev's tombstone was sculpted (free of charge) by Neizvestny – against the will of those in power. Romm's later assessment was likewise warm. Manifestly, Khrushchev emitted contradictory signals, but both these artists accentuated the positive ones. Similarly, as we shall see, Anastas Mikoyan, after weighing up the pros and cons, ended up judging Khrushchev 'a somebody'.

Here we must restate two important historical facts discussed in Part One. First, in 1945 Soviet Russia was a mighty state, but in reality a shaky one. It was hungry, devastated, exhausted, terrorized, ruled by a decaying power complex: a needy, ailing superpower. Under Khrushchev, the Soviet Union experienced dramatic improvements in the 1950s and early 1960s. Whatever experts might say about not exaggerating the results given the low starting point, Soviet citizens felt the difference in their lives. Russia succeeded in recovering its great power status, while healing the wounds of the Second World War and overcoming the ravages of Stalinism. It found the reserves to ensure its future growth and the functioning of its institutions at all levels. Thus the regime possessed reserves and muscle: to recover from such ruination demanded enormous vitality.

The second fact is that, while undoubtedly talented, shrewd, and capable of learning, Khrushchev was still a 'non-modern' leader – a new version of the *khoziain* ('master'), rather than a contemporary statesman and political strategist. The *khoziain* model was still widespread among the leadership, with its sense of owning the state in rather the same way that one owns a farm, meddling in every detail. Khrushchev and most of the other leaders were products of a deeply ingrained patriarchalism – as is indicated, for example, by their impatience with other people's opinions. This is confirmed by observers like F. M. Burlatsky, who spent many years in the Soviet press and apparatus. Although the impetuous populist ruler was no despot by comparison with Stalin, he too had a tendency to want to run everything personally – institutions and people alike. After all, Stalin was the only big chief Khrushchev (and others) had known; and he must have served as a model, even if Khrushchev rejected many of his practices. Unlike the generalissimo, for example, he deeply disliked the military and their pompous uniforms. He enraged them, and especially the KGB's top brass, who were so attached to their uniforms and titles, with his 'We are going to tear off their epaulettes and trouser stripes' – a threat he actually began to implement in the case of KGB generals. Some of his ideas were very dangerous for the apparatchiks, especially the proposal to introduce mandatory rotation of officials at all levels after a certain age. Some say that the Brezhnevites ousted him on account of this. For others, the 'conservatives' never forgave him for 'de-Stalinization', and the loss of prestige and disorientation it occasioned in the communist world and elsewhere. Both these factors were at work, together with others – particularly the new 'hare-brained' ideas he was entertaining, and which the 1964 plotters nipped in the bud.

ANASTAS MIKOYAN

Anastas Mikoyan was a quite remarkable personality – a veritable résumé of the Soviet regime, or rather of its leadership. A Politburo member for something approaching forty years, he was known for being 'unsinkable'. A master in the art of survival, he proved capable of retaining a degree of humanity and a sense of reality, despite his participation in many atrocities that were not necessarily down to his initiative. In his memoirs he emerges as a Stalinist from the very beginning. His reflections on his early years as a leader are deeply and naively indulgent towards Stalin, hostile to all the anti-Stalinist oppositions, and utterly ignorant of what was really at stake.

As a member of the Politburo, Mikoyan would not have survived had he not signed the death sentences circulated by Stalin or made the requisite speeches about 'counter-revolutionary traitors'. In his memoirs he claims that he was once forced to co-sign arrests and death sentences because convincing 'proof' had been presented. In charge of trade issues in the Politburo, in a country suffering constant shortages, he accomplished remarkable feats in a domain which, though vital, was not a real priority for the regime most of the time. His talent as an organizer is beyond dispute, but he was also a skilful politician. While considerable flexibility on his part was to be expected, his steadfast support for Khrushchev's de-Stalinization comes as a surprise. He even claims to have initiated it. At any rate, it was he who supervised the work of the rehabilitation commission in his capacity as President of the Supreme Soviet. He was also the only person to support Khrushchev during the Central Committee session that deposed him: a lone voice among the howling pack. Reading his personal file reveals that the conservatives resented him well into the 1970s. But he was too strong for them.

Mikoyan's book has a wealth of detail on Stalin's final days. Stalin had decided to eliminate – and probably execute – Molotov and Mikoyan: both were sure of it. This might help explain the anti-Stalinist ardour of the post-Stalinist Mikoyan. While Stalin was dying in March 1953, the Politburo's main players were almost permanently in touch, meeting in the Kremlin or in attendance every day at Stalin's home. Discussions occurred and alliances began to take shape. Initially, Mikoyan was not a prime mover. The Malenkov–Beria–Khrushchev trio took the lead. Mikoyan's sketch of how things played out in the room used for Politburo meetings is worthy of Ionesco. The whole Politburo was present, but the heavyweights – Khrushchev, Malenkov and Beria, who were respectively General-Secretary, Prime Minister and Deputy Prime Minister (Beria was also head of the secret police and a massive industrial–military production complex) – huddled together in a corner of the room to discuss the agenda for the meeting that was due to be held. The lesser figures were reduced to observing, not without some disquiet, the formation of a new clique that would decide their fate. The suspense was to continue for some time, because the clique did not last: Malenkov and Khrushchev allied with Molotov to remove Beria. And that was only the beginning. Shifting alliances were endemic and manifestly inherited from Stalin's modus operandi.

Mikoyan describes Khrushchev's turn against Beria approvingly, as well as other alliances, realignments and coalitions. His narrative illuminates a further feature of the way the Politburo functioned: its inability to establish fixed rules, with genuine debates in which disagreement could be expressed, followed by a majority decision, before proceeding to the next item on the agenda. Once again, this was part of Stalin's legacy. Engaging in an argument and losing it could be lethal under Stalin, who deliberately kept everyone in a state of permanent insecurity. When the Politburo finally found itself liberated from his sinister tutelage, it had no idea how to construct a working arrangement – i.e. the very 'collective leadership' it proclaimed. Everything continued to revolve around the general-secretary (still called chairman of the Presidium of the Politburo), and no political measure could be adopted without the approval of the general-secretary and his followers. Before Stalin, leadership bodies – and especially the Politburo – definitely did have a constitution (written and unwritten). Depending on the issue, majorities could switch. The then leader (Lenin) was used to being in a minority and yet pursuing the business in hand: an altogether different set-up. We shall return to the absence of any constitution for the Politburo.

The main problem posed by Mikoyan's memoirs lies in his argument about Stalin and Stalinism. He was a staunch supporter of the man, his ideology and policy. He was on good terms with him, deemed him a highly able leader, and often argued with him (mostly on economic policy). But when Stalin began to eliminate the people around him, and particularly after Kirov's unexplained death, he began to ask himself questions. He pleaded with Stalin on behalf of arrested people whom he knew personally, or would say to him: 'But you know very well that he couldn't have been a spy.' Stalin would then show him alleged 'confessions' or sometimes accede to his plea for clemency. When it comes to the great terror of 1937–8, Mikoyan's text strikes a disingenuous note: 'We other members of Politburo did not know the truth [they were always shown the documents adduced as "proof"], or the scale of the repression.' He claims to have learned the true facts only from the rehabilitations commission he supervised. Even more troubling is that Mikoyan proceeds to no critical reflection on this type of rule or 'party' (which had actually ceased to be one). He argues that Stalin had displayed rationality and greatness during the war, but had become 'unpredictable' again thereafter, refusing the democratization expected by a victorious people. Without pressing his critique any further, he merely declares that after Stalin's death he constantly hoped for a democratization that never occurred.

It may be that such criticism is misplaced in the case of a politician who was no political thinker. It may be more relevant to identify character traits that serve to distinguish one type of Stalinist from another. In other words, 'structural' Stalinism was not common to all Stalinists. Thanks to the high position he had attained, the young Mikoyan adapted to the system well before the definitive triumph of Stalinism. Subsequently, he had no difficulty shedding Stalinist practices and attitudes and genuinely adopting a different perspective, even a different world-view. 'Structural' Stalinists like Molotov and Kaganovich were completely identified with the Stalinist model and Stalin personally, and they never reneged on their commitment. A third breed of Stalinist might change – or pretend to have changed – allegiances, while remaining Stalinist in their make-up and behaviour. Dogmatism and the habit of exclusion, absolute condemnation, rigid argumentation and the perception of conspiracies everywhere were integral parts of their personality. Mikoyan was not of this stamp.

What Mikoyan has to say about Khrushchev is revealing (we shall pass over his all too predictable assessment of Brezhnev). Reviewing the

changes introduced by Khrushchev after his assumption of power, he
endorses some of them but criticizes many others. Naturally, he also
challenges what Khrushchev had to say about him in his memoirs,
where Mikoyan's merits are ignored and he is even attacked. Even so,
Mikoyan's appraisal of Khrushchev's personality and activity is measured, offering a veritable balance sheet of his qualities and faults.
Khrushchev often irritated Mikoyan, who lists his errors meticulously.
But he ends up with a positive assessment. In fact, Mikoyan supported
Khrushchev on many crucial issues and in difficult situations. But he
draws a portrait of an inconsistent, disloyal character who more than once
lost his sense of reality. As other witnesses have also testified, his rule was
a story of reckless initiatives and an incomparable capacity for turning
everything upside down. Mikoyan offers a good inventory of Khrushchev's zigzags. He understood full well that Khrushchev had antagonized
just about everyone and was heading for a fall. And yet he defended this
chaotic general-secretary because he had numerous things to his credit
and the alternative was unappealing. His conclusion is that the irascible
Nikita was 'someone' and that after he had been sacked his abilities
should have been utilized in a different post. This judgement relates to a
little-known episode. Some time before his removal, Khrushchev, who
had become disillusioned with the party, had mused about revitalizing
the Supreme Soviet, transforming it into something like an effective
parliament. The first step would have been for Mikoyan to become
President (not merely Chairman) of the Supreme Soviet and then seriously to empower this body. Khrushchev had made some initial moves
in this direction and the prospect enthused Mikoyan, but Khrushchev's
fall signalled the burial of the project. This episode clarifies Mikoyan's
closing remarks. At all events, if this final initiative petered out, other
irreversible changes had been introduced thanks to Khrushchev.

One point in Mikoyan's critique merits separate examination. He
criticizes Khrushchev for having yielded to the conservatives (or his own
misgivings) by abruptly terminating the policy of rehabilitating the
victims of Stalinism, which Mikoyan supervised by virtue of his position
in the Presidium of the Supreme Soviet. Mikoyan and liberal public
opinion wanted to cap the process by rehabilitating the victims of the
show trials: Bukharin, Kamenev, Zinoviev, and so on. But Khrushchev
balked, despite Mikoyan's insistence. For the latter, all the accusations
were false and the executions belonged in the category of Stalin's
crimes. However, for as yet minimally de-Stalinized party stalwarts,
those accused, even if it was on the basis of false charges, were the

leaders of an 'anti-party' opposition. In an earlier chapter of his book, Mikoyan himself refers to them scornfully and does not conceal the fact that he supported Stalin's moves against them. In his fervour for de-Stalinization, Mikoyan seems not to appreciate that to have rehabilitated the victims would have been to restore these oppositionists – erstwhile 'Trotskyists-rightists' – to the status of critics of Stalin and Stalinism.

Here we can 'sympathize' with Khrushchev. He had encountered enough problems with the de-Stalinization he had launched. Reviewing the show trials would have been too much for him. After all, he never envisaged the possibility of open factions and debates within the party.

19

KOSYGIN AND ANDROPOV

ALEXEI KOSYGIN

Alexei Kosygin was never a central political player and not a flamboyant one either. Moreover, he never wished to be in the 'race' for the post of general-secretary. Nevertheless, his remarkable administrative skills made him indispensable. It was known in top circles that the economy rested on his shoulders – and that nobody else possessed such broad ones.

The career of this phenomenal administrator reads like a history of Soviet government, from junior jobs to the highest posts, and contains some genuinely heroic chapters during the war. Among the latter, as has already been mentioned, were evacuating industry from territory about to be overrun by the Germans and breaking the Leningrad blockade by organizing the construction of a supply route and pipeline on the bottom of Lake Lagoda. But he was also sometime Finance Minister, head of Gosplan, Deputy Prime Minister, Prime Minister, and Politburo member; and admired and envied by general-secretaries because he knew better than anyone else how to make the administrative machinery work. The people around him really did work! But he was also known in government circles for having challenged Brezhnev over the right of the general-secretary to represent the country abroad – a function which he believed should fall to the Prime Minister, as in every other country. This was actually implemented for a period until Brezhnev, who could not have been very fond of such a figure, put an end to it. Kosygin was also known for the interesting economic reform he launched, which was scuttled by the conservatives, who continued to hold it against him.

The book edited by his son-in-law, Gvishiani, offers a glimpse of Kosygin's thinking.[1] Dedicated to the system, he was also well aware of the need to reform it; and around 1964 everything still seemed possible. He believed in semi-public companies and cooperatives. He was conscious of the West's superiority and the need to learn from it. He believed in initiating gradual changes, setting in train a transition from a 'state-administered economy' to a system in which 'the state restricts itself to guiding enterprises'. He was in favour of a multiplicity of forms of property and management – something he tried to explain to Khrushchev and then Brezhnev, but to no avail. Khrushchev had fully nationalized the producers' cooperatives and Gvishiani was present on an occasion when Kosygin tried to convince Brezhnev to elaborate a genuine economic strategy and discuss it at a Politburo meeting. As was his wont, Brezhnev used delaying tactics, which amounted to burying the idea. Kosygin emerged from such conversations completely demoralized: 'He warned against a blind faith in our power and the danger of incompetent policies.' He was strongly opposed to hare-brained schemes for 'reversing the course of Siberia's rivers', and was against the interventions in Czechoslovakia and Afghanistan. He said out loud that massive military expenditure or the aid to 'friendly countries' was beyond the USSR's means. However, the Politburo refused to tackle these real problems and 'instead busied itself with all sorts of nonsense'.

Under Brezhnev, many important questions, including foreign policy, were dealt with on the Staraia Ploshchad. But it was difficult to find anyone there with a good intellectual education. The role of grey figures like Suslov and Kirilenko was 'considerable', says Gvishiani, who was present at numerous meetings or commissions of the Central Committee when nobody spoke. They all just sat there obediently in silence, until a document appeared stating: 'The Politburo (or Secretariat) considers that . . .'

No one would dream of attributing a role in some 'intellectual effervescence' or 'renaissance' to an austere, non-flamboyant person like Kosygin. However, something like that actually did occur with the economic reforms of the mid-1960s (in fact, from the late 1950s). The cautious Kosygin, who had never uttered the least heterodoxy in public, promoted, supported and protected a real renaissance in economic

---

1   T.I. Fetisov, sost., *Prem'er – Izvestnyi i Neizvestnyi: Vospominania o A. N. Kosygine*, Moscow 1997.

thinking and publishing. A genuine economic literature, accompanied by a wealth of data, was published, including utterly subversive texts parading under innocuous titles. This brought about an explosion of creativity in the social sciences, which coincided with the economic debates by challenging various 'sacred cows' and their political implications. All this occurred under the prime minister's protection.

The debate took apart, bit by bit, all key aspects of the economic system. In 1964, academician V. Nemchinov published a powerful indictment in *Kommunist* of the whole system of material and technical supply, demonstrating that it was the main obstacle to economic development. Many well-known economists participated – Novozhilov, Kantorovich and Yefimov among them – as well as a group of mathematical economists. They all attacked Gossnab directly, showing that it was merely an outgrowth of an administrative planning system that handled the economy in terms of physical units and fixed prices arbitrarily. The capital required for investment was offered cost-free – hence the enormous pressure from ministries, enterprises and local government for ever more investment, but without any constraints on them to use it productively.

This in itself was a barrier to an expanded reproduction of capital at a higher technological level. Over-investment lay behind falling growth rates and had a further inevitable consequence: permanent shortages. In such conditions, planning ultimately amounted to perpetuating a routine.

The lively debates of the 1960s extended to numerous publications. Even though many authors avoided drawing direct political conclusions from their analyses, they were implicit. Everyone knew that there was a political 'owner' in charge of the economy and the system, and that there was no way to keep the genie in the bottle. A letter to the Central Committee from three dissidents – A. D. Sakharov, V. F. Turchin and Roy Medvedev – reached *Le Monde*, which published it in its edition of 12–13 April 1970. It warned of the dangers looming on the horizon if political reforms were too long delayed. The production situation was critical, as was the plight of citizens; and the country was doomed to become a second-rank state. At least one book – V. P. Shkredov's *Ekonomika i Pravo* (*The Economy and Law*), published in 1967 – engaged in a powerful, head-on critique of the state and its ideological underpinnings, which was all the more remarkable in that it defended a Marxist perspective. According to Shkredov, the state – a politico-juridical institution that claimed ownership of the economy – was forgetting that the politico-juridical aspect (however important in economic life) came second to the actual state of the country's socio-economic development. Consequently, the owner's claim to impose its vision on the economy, to plan and run it directly as it wished, would inflict great damage if the level of economic and technological development did not yet (if ever) allow for administrative planning. The relations of production were not to be confused with legal forms like ownership. That would be Proudhonism, not Marxism. An usurper state, hiding behind its right not to conform to economic reality, could only breed bureaucratization and constituted a major obstacle to economic development. Shkredov stressed that basic property forms had not changed for long stretches of history, whereas forms of production – as Marx had shown – had evolved in stages into developed capitalism.

The book received a positive reception in *Novyi Mir* (no. 10, 1968) from V. Georgiev, a Kosygin supporter. The reviewer praised Shkredov for having directly tackled what was now the country's central task: 'overcoming voluntarism in managing society's system of production', by integrating it into the framework of a broader theoretical problem – 'the correlation between objective relations of production and the subjective, voluntary activity of human beings'. No one was naive enough not to read in these words the message that the state, by running the economy as it currently did, was doing enormous damage.

Economics was not the only science to flourish in this period. Other fields of knowledge were in a state of effervescence, uncovering new dimensions of social and cultural life, asking pertinent questions, and verging dangerously on the political. The journal *Novyi Mir* had become the outlet for critical thinking in many areas, not just literature. Its 150,000 monthly copies, which were distributed to the farthest reaches of the country, were eagerly awaited. It carried plenty of information on and analyses of the West and an embryonic social-democratic vision for the Soviet Union. Its initial sponsor had been Khrushchev, and Kosygin protected it as best he could, at least until 1968. As we have seen, Tvardovsky was removed as editor in 1970 and died the following year. He was buried in the Novo-Devichii cemetery in Moscow, with a small, inconspicuous grave stone amid a profusion of sumptuous ones for highly decorated nonentities.

Sociologists were also knocking at the door with studies of labour, youth and many previously neglected topics – especially urbanization (migration, families, women). They raised the problems of a new society in the making, which required novel approaches and novel solutions.

The legal world, particularly criminologists and jurists, pressed for reform of the criminal law and the abrogation of purely punitive elements. A commission was appointed for this purpose, comprising three authoritarian ministers and six liberal judges and scholars (including Strogovich), who were thus assured of a majority. It can safely be assumed that someone high up had taken care with the commission's composition. In 1966, the same Strogovich – one of a small but combative group – published his *Fundamental Questions of Soviet Socialist Legality*, in which he argued strongly in favour of the rule of law with no exemptions or exceptions. The book contained powerful arguments, supported by numerous concrete examples, for protecting citizens' rights against arbitrary infringement. Much remained to be done in this domain. He came out unequivocally against a retrograde, essentially repressive legal system – one more inclined to punish than to seek solutions, and indifferent to the many other avenues open to courts when it came to fighting crime. In effect, prison served only to transform inmates into hardened criminals.

The flourishing of econometrics and cybernetics, and the creation of a Ministry of Scientific and Technological Development (assigned to Gvishiani), mainly staffed by reformers and enjoying considerable prestige – these were so many signs of the times, with its news ideas and hopes. We may assume that Kosygin was not antipathetic to all this, even if he never openly challenged the status quo with provocative statements. Others could speak out without mincing their words in the official media. Thus, academician Nemchinov declared that 'a system which is so harnessed from top to bottom will fetter technological and social development; and it will break down sooner or later under the pressure of the real processes of economic life'.

So we can see that it is false to claim that 'no one' predicted the collapse of the system, as has often been maintained in recent years: Nemchinov's declaration dates from 1965.[2] Readers will already be aware that the years ahead became known as the 'period of stagnation'; and now they know that they were preceded among the elite, and possibly ordinary people (but this requires research), by a ferment of

---

2   It comes from Nemchinov's *O Dal'neishem Sovershenstvovanii Planirovaniia i Upravleniia Khoziaistvom*, Moscow 1965, p. 53; quoted in my *Political Undercurrents in Soviet Economic Debates – From Bukharin to the Modern Reformers*, Princeton and London 1974, p. 157 (reissued as *Stalinism and the Seeds of Soviet Reforms*, Armonk (New York) and London 1991).

considerable intellectual and practical import. It was attributable to the 'men of the 1960s', who many hoped would one day assume control of the party and transform Russia. But all this came to an end with 'Brezhnevism' and its debilitating 'maturation'. When Gorbachev launched perestroika, the 'men of the 1960s' were already worn out.

YURI ANDROPOV

Yuri Vladimirovich Andropov, who closes the period we are studying, remains little-known. Here we shall touch upon various aspects of the regime's history that are directly bound up with his personality. Then we shall sketch his short stint as general-secretary, even if the relevant archives remain closed. In May 1967, when he left the leadership of one of the Central Committee's international departments to head the KGB, Andropov became the system's shield. His biographers say that the scenes he had witnessed in 1956 during the uprising in Budapest, where he was ambassador, haunted him. It would also appear that the Hungarian leader, Janos Kadar, was an important influence.

Under Andropov, the KGB's status attained its zenith. A year after he took over the agency, on 5 July 1968, the KGB became a state committee directly attached to the USSR's Council of Ministers – something that elevated it above other committees and ministries – and its chairman became a member of the government. A candidate member of the Politburo since 1967, Andropov became a full member in 1973. The jurisdiction of the KGB, based in Moscow, extended to the whole of the Soviet Union; and it had its equivalents in all republics. Its statutory duties were espionage, threats to state security, frontier guard, the protection of official secrets and confidential documents, investigating acts of high treason, terrorism, smuggling, large-scale currency crime, and the defence of all lines of communication against electronic espionage. Which of these many tasks consumed most time and resources is not as yet clear, though intelligence and counter-intelligence may be a safe bet.

From the 1960s to the 1980s, the KGB acquired considerable influence in all spheres of life. It watched over the whole state apparatus, the uniformed police, and churches; it ran military counter-intelligence, initiated legal proceedings against opponents, and fought against the intelligentsia. These activities earned it an appalling image and reputation, as they did its master, who managed to tame the dissident movement – an issue at the heart of the propaganda war fought by and against the West. Andropov was a loyal Brezhnevite, but what else could he have been? We should add to the picture the abusive recourse to psychiatric asylums – probably the regime's most reprehensible act.

Nevertheless, rumours and attested characteristics complicate our image of Andropov. Why was it that this rampart of an ultra-conservative system was also constantly reputed to be a 'liberal'? To fool people? Maybe not. For a start, unlike other KGB chiefs he was first and foremost a politician, not a product of the firm. When still in charge of one of the Central Committee's international relations departments, he was described by his aides (he had recruited some very bright ones) as someone who was very open to discussion, a great reader, with a gift for analysing foreign and domestic affairs. For his principal lieutenants (Arbatov, Burlatsky, etc.), working with and under Andropov was an unforgettable experience. In the midst of that bastion of dogmatism, the Staraia Ploshchad, Andropov's office was the 'free world'. They discussed all subjects with him with absolute freedom and openly expressed their disagreements. If he disapproved of one of his aides' viewpoints, it entailed no sanctions. He himself had told them: 'Remember that in this office we can say what we want. But don't get carried away: once you're out the door, don't forget where you are.'

Such a statement from a politician interested in intellectual issues, but who was also a realist, attests to the presence of a second persona – intelligent enough to talk freely, but also to act cautiously. Much can be gleaned about this 'other' Andropov from the memoirs of Markus Wolf, the former secret service head of the German Democratic Republic, who knew and admired him.[3]

During the 1950s, the KGB played a sinister role in the countries of the Eastern bloc. But things changed radically for the better when Andropov became its head, argues Wolf: 'Here at last was a figure I admired, unbound by protocol and aloof from the petty intrigues that had marked the tenure of his predecessors.' Andropov was free of the habitual arrogance of Soviet leaders, who considered their empire invulnerable. He realized that the interventions in Hungary and Czechoslovakia were signs of weakness, not strength. In his political and human qualities, he was entirely different from his predecessors and successors. His expansive horizon of interests and his ability to grasp the

---

3 Markus Wolf, *Man without a Face – The Autobiography of Communism's Greatest Spymaster*, New York 1999.

major problems of international and domestic politics convinced him that reform of the Soviet Union and its bloc, albeit risky, was imperative; and he intended to get down to the task. During official visits to East Germany and the banquets given in his honour, Andropov was relaxed and courteous, and a few drinks never altered his demeanour. In conversation on political matters like Czechoslovakia or relations with West German Social Democrats, he rejected any purely ideological approach. He implied that the Czechoslovak communists had been slow to realize the extent of discontent and to remedy the situation. He also favoured a dialogue with social-democrats and was unperturbed that this clashed with the East German leadership's hatred of the SPD. Wolf appreciated such candour 'in a forum where flattery and rhetoric were otherwise the order of the day'.

Andropov's ideas about foreign intelligence methods, and the greater accountability and new managerial structure he introduced into the KGB, are of less interest to us here. However, we should perhaps mention his disapproval of the arrogance of KGB agents towards their own diplomats or government agencies in Eastern bloc countries: he had sharp words for the 'imperial manner' of some of his officers.

Andropov's numerous conversations with Wolf demonstrated his awareness that the Soviets were lagging behind the West. Excessive centralization, obsessive secrecy and the total divorce between military and civilian sectors deprived the Soviet Union of the huge benefits that Western countries derived from advances in military technology. The two men discussed ways to overcome this damaging compartmentalization. Observing the stagnation all around him, Andropov mused about a social-democratic 'third way' led by Hungary and certain factions in the GDR, and about forms of political as well as economic pluralism.

The conversations between Andropov and Wolf confirm one key point: in the light of the mass of information on the West and the USSR at his disposal, Andropov had arrived at the conclusion that his country was in need of profound restructuring. According to one of his deputies, Bobkov, even the propaganda war strengthened his conviction that change was the only course. We do not know when he began to think that it was up to him personally to assume this mission. But his mind was engaged and, within the context of his KGB and Politburo duties, he prepared for such an eventuality.

The KGB was a complex organization, sometimes sloppy and undisciplined. But Andropov turned this 'conglomerate' into a highly effective instrument. There is much evidence to this effect, though I am not in a position to make a definitive judgement. Andropov had his own views, but shared them only with close associates and people like Markus Wolf. Those who knew and worked with him are unanimous in their view that he was a convinced anti-Stalinist – an important trait in view of the forces around Brezhnev. This was reflected in his style and working methods. In transforming the KGB and its methods of repression, he demanded 'professionalism' above all. He was always extremely curious about the Western world – particularly the United States – and his knowledge in this area earned him the admiration of the best Soviet diplomats and even some of the system's critics.

For Andropov, a policy of repression had to be conceived as a way of resolving a problem. Faced with Solzhenitsyn, Sakharov, Medvedev and other dissidents, the approach he adopted aimed to limit the political damage they could cause – and not to destroy the persons themselves, as a Stalinist or any species of *derzhavnik* would have done. Andropov was an analyst, not an executioner. Whereas the hard-liners wanted to isolate Solzhenitsyn by dispatching him to Siberia, he opted to exile him abroad. I do not know what their preference was in the case of Sakharov, but Andropov's solution – exile to Gorky – threatened neither his health nor his pursuit of his intellectual work.

It has often been said that Andropov was simply the old system's policeman – a conservative, a supporter of repression, and hence a KGB boss like any other. However, this is to miss the point. Of course he was the system's shield and put political opponents in jail. How else should he be expected to have behaved, given that he was under close surveillance by hawks in the Politburo and his own agency? Andropov performed his duties faithfully and carefully. His country's security was certainly of concern to him and he believed that its enemies, who were often allies of the Western world, should not be tolerated. The fact that his own position and safety were at the mercy of Brezhnev's whims was another aspect of the rat-trap he found himself in.

Nevertheless, his analytical mind and the politician in him made him an unusual KGB chief. For his predecessor Semichastny, there was a list of threats on the one hand and of enemies on the other: the latter were automatically guilty as charged. They had to be repressed: full stop. Andropov asked himself: What is the nature of the threat? What are its causes? How is it to be guarded against, given that serious problems, if left unresolved, become open wounds? He sought to come up with a political solution and reforms. Because he was regarded 'on high' as a hard-line defender of the system, he was in a strong position, affording him the possibility of neutralizing certain influential supporters of a hard line, or even enlisting their support, and thus dividing their ranks. (This was the case, for example, with his good relations with the ultra-conservative Ustinov.)

His option for analysis, as opposed to a repressive approach, emerges from two reports on the situation in student circles that he submitted to the Politburo, the first on 5 November 1968 and the second on 12 December 1976. They contain very different messages.[4]

The first report, containing an extended analysis of the 'group psy-chology' – the mentality, aspirations and political attitudes – of students in the city of Odessa, had been produced by a student who was working for the KGB. Andropov recommended that members of the Politburo read it carefully because, notwithstanding some naivety on the part of its young author, what it had to say was important. Its main message was the total, abysmal failure of the whole party structure and its politico-ideological arsenal among the student body. The argument was straightforward: students knew their city very well and were perfectly well aware that local leaders were accumulating material privileges, they were shocked by the cynicism with which the latter exploited power for personal advantage. Documents, data and quotations were adduced to demonstrate the stupidity of Komsomol and the party in higher educa-tion institutions. The author pointed to the complete intellectual disarray of party functionaries, who gave standard 'idiotic' lectures and were unable to answer questions logically and cogently. The level in the social sciences was very low – hence students' preference for the natural sci-ences and technology, which enjoyed prestige. The social sciences were held in disdain – of interest only to those set on a career in the party. Students' preference for anything Western was scarcely surprising given their lack of respect for those whom they heard criticizing the West.

So this is what Andropov, shortly after his appointment, wanted the Politburo to hear. A few years later, he would know better. We do not know how long it took Andropov to realize that his first deputy Semen Tsvigun, who was appointed at the same time as him with the rank of general, was in fact a Brezhnev plant, charged with keeping an eye – and reporting – on him (such were the habits of the time); and that he was not the only one.

---

4 Intelligentsia i vlast', *Istoricheskii Arkhiv*, no. 1, 1994, pp. 175–207.

The second document, eight years later, was produced by the fifth directorate (dealing with ideological subversion), headed by Bobkov. It was signed by the latter and likewise dealt with students' state of mind. It began by maintaining that Western intelligence and propaganda agencies targeted Soviet youth in particular (which was not wrong), before proceeding to a statistical analysis of 'events' of a political nature in the student milieu in recent years: distribution of leaflets, small demonstrations, and so on. According to Bobkov, the most alarming thing was the number of young people sanctioned for heavy drinking and other 'immoral' habits. Some KGB observers noted that such behaviour led directly to political opposition. We do not know what Andropov thought of this document or why he had agreed to extend the fifth directorate's remit well beyond the realm of counter-intelligence. In any event, this move was certainly to the taste of the hard-liners.

The difference in approach between the two texts is striking. Not unlike Semichastny, Bobkov lays the blame on the West and the culprits themselves; he says nothing about the system's responsibility. Andropov submitted the report without any recommendations, listing the names of its five recipients (first among them Suslov, the 'grey eminence' of the Politburo). He simply attached a note indicating that the KGB intended to employ its usual methods ('prophylaxis' and arrests in the case of actual clandestine organizations). And the five recipients merely appended a 'Yes' to the document, probably indicating nothing more than 'Yes, I have read it.'

If Andropov forwarded the report without comment, it was because its contents did not meet his wishes. However, in the book he wrote after the fall of the regime, Bobkov maintains that the KGB and the fifth directorate were often opposed to all kinds of 'persecutions' attributed to them by 'uninformed' critics.[5] They were simply obeying orders from the Politburo or party apparatus. His key argument – often heard from Andropov himself – was that, faced with the West's intense anti-Soviet propaganda, there was a better way of responding than by simply turning the accusations back against the United States. The battle could have been won by instead recognizing the system's weaknesses and failures and seeking to correct them. Analysts from the fifth directorate had often argued along these lines, but the leadership had brushed them aside, as if the KGB was sticking its nose in business that was none of its

---

5   F. D. Bobkov, *KGB i Vlast'*, Moscow 1995, p. 4.

concern. According to Bobkov, Andropov was the only leader who actually undertook to change Soviet domestic policy radically. Fully apprised of the other side's strategy for undermining the system, he proposed a broad strategy of counter-measures developed by scientific researchers (psychologists, military specialists, economists, philosophers). The plan was radically to alter the character of propaganda, to adopt an entirely different attitude to religion and political heterodoxy, to step up the fight against corruption and nationalist tendencies and, above all, to tackle the most urgent economic problems. The fifth directorate had carefully prepared the arguments deployed in Andropov's report to the Politburo, 'which could have led to a democratization of the party and state'.

Andropov presented the report at a Politburo meeting. Brezhnev, Kosygin, Mazurov, Shelepin, Shcherbitsky and even the main ideologue Suslov pronounced themselves in agreement with this dual programme of reform and a propaganda counter-offensive. Bobkov confides that he does not know whether the Politburo was serious about this, but the fact is that nothing actually happened, despite the fact that the text circulated by hand inside the apparatus. Thus it was that the only remaining card was squandered.

It is unclear why Bobkov does not date this meeting. Yet it seems unthinkable that an experienced KGB general would simply have invented such an episode. The report must be sitting in more than one archive. If true, the manoeuvre was an elegant one: table proposals for reform while making them palatable to conservatives by indicating that they also represented powerful propaganda counter-measures, in a phase of the Cold War when the Soviet Union's position was fragile. Gorbachev's phenomenal popularity on the world stage at the beginning of the perestroika indicated that a reforming Russia could score a big success with world opinion.

Yet either the idea was too clever given the intellectual level of Politburo members; or they were too shrewd to accept their own suicide. At all events, the KGB's fine strategists saw their hopes vanish, leaving Bobkov to deplore the fact that those who held the trump card did not know how to play it. This event, which proved to be a non-event, confirms the uniqueness of Andropov's profile. But it would be more convincing if we could read the famous report for ourselves.

ARRESTS AND DISSIDENTS

We now possess data on the repression of political dissidence for most of the 1960s and '70s, and we cited some of it in chapter 15. The number of arrests and type of punishments meted out are revealing. Under Andropov, the key method was prevention: he favoured 'prophylaxis'. This affected many people, but mass arbitrary arrests were a thing of the past. And many Russians confirm that from the 1960s onwards, the fear of the secret police and its arbitrary intrusions, familiar in Stalin's day, had mostly faded. This in itself made dissidence and other forms of political activity more feasible.

Andropov, who knew some of the dissidents (including Roy Medvedev) personally, studied their characters, read their work, and often appreciated it. As head of political security, however, his agenda ranged far wider. His agencies had to be in a position to provide a precise map of sources of possible trouble. According to his estimates, the number of people with a potential for active opposition was in the region of 8.5 million, many of them ready to spring into action when the circumstances were right. The existence of such a potential offered some leading dissidents the chance to play a catalysing and unifying role. As far as Andropov was concerned, police methods were indispensable in confronting this – all the more so because not a few dissidents openly identified with the 'other side'. Even so, the performance of the system was the key for him. The discrepancy between its growing needs and its ever scarcer means (not just in material terms, but also in the limited intellectual resources of its leadership) was widening. And this was true not only of the economy, but also of the system's political foundations.

THE NEW BOSS

Paradoxically, to have stood a chance of success in 1982–3, the leader (or leaders) would have had to recognize not only that the system was ailing (that had been clear to an Andropov or Kosygin for some time), but that several of its vital organs were already dead.

As early as 1965, the economist Nemchinov had foreseen dangers ahead when he castigated 'an ossified mechanical system in which all the key parameters are fixed in advance, so that the system is paralysed from top to bottom'. When an individual is pronounced dead, we know he cannot be resurrected. But when what is involved is a mode of government, dismantling and rebuilding remain an option. This may sound puzzling, but governmental models have been rebuilt using a significant number of old components.

As has already been indicated, it is clear that Kosygin and Andropov knew the situation better than any Western historian, thanks to the reports they read, which only became available to us twenty-five years later. Among them was a solid, unpublished work, commissioned by Kosygin when Prime Minister, from the economic section of the Academy of Sciences. Three years after Nemchinov's warnings, the academicians presented a systematic comparison between American and Soviet economic structures – productivity, living standards, technological progress, incentive systems, the direction and character of investment. Their unvarnished verdict was as follows: the USSR was losing on all fronts, except in coal and steel. The latter was the pride of the regime, but it attested to the country's backwardness, for this sector had been the benchmark in the previous century. The message was clear: it was that of the old Aramaic inscription on the walls of Belshazzar's palace in Babylon – only now it read differently. The threat no longer came from God, but from the United States. There was not a minute to lose.

Underlying the stagnation – but also constituting its main symptom – was a deadlocked Politburo around a brain-dead Brezhnev: a humiliating impasse exhibited before the whole world. It was impossible to remove Brezhnev, for contrary to the case of Khrushchev no majority could be mustered in favour of a new leader. The other aspect of the picture, which was blatant enough to be widely known throughout Russia, was the spread of a tentacular corruption. Members of Brezhnev's family were ostentatiously involved in it – a subject poor Leonid did not like to hear spoken about. Mushrooming mafia networks, with which many highly placed party officials were associated, were something else the country (if not certain leaders) was aware of. Nothing on such a scale had been known before. No doubt the KGB had all the information it required.

Just as the country learned of a major drive by the KGB against this scourge, and even as the noose around the Brezhnev family and other heavyweights was tightening, a shot suddenly rang out on the political stage: on 19 January 1982, Andropov's first deputy, Semen Tsvigun – Brezhnev's shadow over Andropov – committed suicide. Other such shots were to follow. A few days later, the second most influential conservative in the party – the grey eminence Suslov – died of natural causes. This conjunction of events was the key to the altered balance of forces within the Politburo, to the detriment of the 'swamp'.

If it reads like the screenplay of a political thriller, so be it. Inside the KGB, Tsvigun (under Suslov's supervision) was in charge of the main files on corruption – those involving people in high places, including Brezhnev's family. Personally beyond reproach in this respect, Suslov nevertheless forbade him to use these files or to show them to anyone. Thus, Andropov supposedly had no access to them. When the two men died, Andropov got his hands on them and began to dig further. Tsvigun himself, it turned out, was involved in several corrupt transactions, along with various people connected to Politburo members.

We shall pass over the details (there are many). Brezhnev died just in time in 1982. The anti-corruption drive had broken the capacity of the 'swamp' to maintain a favourable balance of forces within the Politburo and Central Committee. And thus it was that the unusual KGB chief Andropov became general-secretary, almost by accident. He was only in power for fifteen months – another accident – but this brief period raises interesting problems that can only be treated tentatively, and partly as an exercise in counter-factual history ('and if . . . and if . . .').

The various characters I have sketched were dynamic and capable. The obtuse and inept ones who comprised the 'swamp', or the sheer dead weights, have been omitted. But it is worth lingering for a moment over one aspect of internal manoeuvrings in the Politburo. The general-secretary had power over all nominations: he could co-opt or exclude whomever he wished. It was up to his supporters to ensure approval of these decisions by the Politburo and Central Committee. Another scenario, which had a precedent, indicates that a group which wanted to select a new general-secretary could oust the incumbent on condition of obtaining sufficient support in the Central Committee and being able to count on the army and KGB. In fact, the army would suffice even against the KGB, which was no match for it in such circumstances.

Conversely, and paradoxically, weak leaders like Brezhnev or Chernenko could block the situation if there was a majority of mediocrities at the top who depended on an enfeebled general-secretary for their position. Thus Brezhnev, a cunning but not a malicious figure, became the cement and guarantor of the status quo: he was not a threat and the dead weights felt safe. The situation became even more paradoxical when such a general-secretary was still in post, but in practice completely absent because he had been ill for years.

When Mikoyan criticized Khrushchev's 'erratic' policies, he was factually accurate. But they were not exclusively attributable to his character. Khrushchev's shortcomings were in part made possible by the absence of constitutional rules within the Politburo, which was supposedly the all-powerful summit of a hyper-centralized system. In the absence of a proper constitution, a general-secretary intent on acquiring or regaining the ability to pursue some particular policy, or simply retaining his position, had to plot to obtain total control of power with the help of his personal following (which was never wholly reliable). The old model of personal dictatorship just popped up again as if the institutional vacuum could only be filled by one man. This prompted members of the Politburo to support an autocratic position, or to aspire to it personally, as if no other modus operandi was conceivable. This is what made possible the 'impossible' Khrushchev, who could have been an important player in a genuine team in a constitutionally regulated system. This quasi-structural weakness, which pushed the general-secretary into behaving like a dictator, or at least allowed him to, was a congenital feature bequeathed by Stalin – part of his legacy that was not eliminated.

However, not everything was fixed on the chessboard of power at the summit (Politburo, Central Committee, ministries). The top position could certainly be filled by a mediocre or weak figure (Brezhnev or Chernenko). But it could also fall to a strong, dynamic character (for better or worse) – a Stalin, Khrushchev, or Andropov. Ousting a mediocrity and changing course proved impossible for quite a time, until the appropriate moment arrived: such, to my mind, was the occasion when the tentacles of corruption extended to various members of the 'swamp', rendering them vulnerable and malleable.

Thus, if the system was prone to paralysis, with no one really at the helm, this did not prevent the emergence of a real pilot capable of imposing a change of direction, starting with a shake-up at the top. Sheer chance unquestionably played a role at the outset. But once that chance had been seized, it was possible rapidly to drain the 'swamp' by means of a vigorous purge of its supports in the party apparatus. With the arrival of new leading cadres, new initiatives became possible. And this is precisely what happened with Andropov.

One of his close associates in the KGB, Viacheslav Kevorkov, a high-ranking official in counter-intelligence, adds to our picture of him.[6]

---

6 Viacheslav Kevorkov, *Tainyi Kanal*, Moscow 1997.

Kevorkov carried out various international assignments – in particular, running a 'secret' channel with West German leaders. In this capacity, he frequently met with Andropov and is thus a primary source. According to Kevorkov, Andropov reflected on the possibility of coming to an agreement with the intelligentsia whereby it would aid him to reform the system. His model was manifestly Lunacharsky who, under Lenin, had known how to communicate and cooperate with this social group. A highly intelligent man, Andropov was acutely conscious that the party suffered on account of the low intellectual level of many of its top cadres and leaders. The frequent sneers about his 'pro-Brezhnevism' are disingenuous: his job was in Brezhnev's gift. My claim that Andropov appreciated the true worth of the top leadership is confirmed by Kevorkov, who quotes his chief's opinion: 'Virtually none of the party or state's current leaders belongs in the class of talented politicians who could confront the problems the country is facing.' For Kevorkov, Andropov did belong to this class, and he concludes his book with this sentence: 'Andropov was no doubt the last statesman who believed in the vitality of the Soviet system, but not the system he had inherited when he came to power: he believed in the system he intended to create by carrying out radical reforms.'

From this and other accounts, it seems clear that an intelligent politician like Andropov understood that the system was in need of reconstruction, because its economic and political foundations were by now in a parlous state. Reconstructing it could only mean replacing it in a phased transition. Did he really think in these terms? Even though his personal archives remain inaccessible, the decisions he took (or was intent on taking) permit us to answer in the affirmative.

He took over power rapidly and smoothly. He started off very cautiously, but the country soon learned that something serious was afoot in the Kremlin. The first steps were predictable: restoring discipline in the workplace. But this extended beyond the workers to re-educating the elites, who were not a shining example when it came to their work ethic. He scoffed at their addiction to dachas and other amenities (he was known for his rather austere lifestyle). As soon as this became common knowledge, his popularity grew. The country had a boss – visibly so. Reforms required preparation and time: task forces and commissions were set up. Some measures were temporary; others were irreversible – notably, a rapid purge of a whole layer of powerful, backward-looking apparatus officials that had been the linchpin of the previous leadership. The account given by one of those nominated to replace them furnishes some details.[7]

The dismissal of N. A. Shchelokov, a Brezhnev protégé running the Interior Ministry, was widely acclaimed. In the Central Committee apparatus, the heads of departments like 'business organization', 'party organizations', 'research and academic institutions' and the 'general department', who formed what was called the 'small working cabinet' (or sometimes the 'shadow cabinet'), prepared many of the most important policies. Andropov put an end to their omnipotence.

The intelligentsia was delighted by the pensioning off of Trapeznikov, another Brezhnev protégé who considered himself the ideological luminary of the party. A grand inquisitor and inveterate Stalinist, he pursued writers and academics whose statements displeased him. Such people were the hard core of the party leadership: eliminating them at one stroke sent a very powerful signal.

Under Andropov, Gorbachev's role carried on expanding. New people arrived in key positions in the party apparatus. Andropov invited Vadim Medvedev to head the 'research and academic institutions' department. Medvedev had been violently criticized by its previous head for his 'insubordination' in trying to make the party's Academy of Social Sciences, of which he was the director, a serious research institution. Andropov told him that new approaches were needed to accelerate technological and scientific progress and to improve the situation in the social sciences, which had been given a hard time by Trapeznikov. The Academy should engage in serious research, rather than producing utterly empty ideological texts.

V. I. Vorotnikov, Deputy Prime Minister of the Russian Federation, was appointed its Prime Minister and a member of the Politburo by Andropov in 1983. In the private diary he published,[8] he adds to our picture of Andropov. He was very impressed by his intelligence, which was evident from their conversations. His notes, taken during Politburo meetings, disclose a vigorous, incisive Andropov, not reluctant to broach ever more complex problems, from workplace discipline to the functioning of the economy and the search for a new model. The way he approached change was highly pragmatic: he wanted to proceed by gradually enlarging the scope of the reforms. The first important step in the economic sphere consisted in allowing factories to operate on a fully

---

7   Vadim A. Medvedev, *V Komande Gorbacheva: Vzgliad Iznutri*, Moscow 1994.
8   V. I. Vorotnikov, *A Bylo Eto Tak – Iz Dnevnika Chlena Politburo TsK KPSS*, Moscow 1995.

self-financing basis – that is to say, taking account of costs and profits. However, Vorotnikov – a novice who was not as yet fully integrated into Politburo practices – says nothing about the high-ranking commissions set up to prepare such moves and was not in the know as regards Andropov's plans for reforming the party. For that we shall have to look elsewhere.

As Andropov's first modest initiatives began to unfold, he was preparing others and alluded to them: 'We have to change the economic mechanism and the planning system.' A task force, which may have existed before he became general-secretary, set to work. In the meantime, private plots, which Khrushchev had reduced or outlawed, were rehabilitated. And the state administration was put on notice: ministerial departments had not given a good example of efficient organization and had failed to create the conditions for a 'normal, highly productive work atmosphere'.[9]

These initiatives were significant, if rather predictable, and more seemed in the offing. But excerpts from the minutes of Politburo meetings that have become available cast new and surprising light on the emerging strategy. As the campaign for the re-election of party bodies approached, accompanied by the reports habitually delivered on these occasions, Andropov suddenly declared in an official party resolution in August 1983: 'The party's electoral assemblies are conducted in accordance with a pre-existing script, without serious and frank debate. Candidates' declarations have been edited beforehand; any initiative or criticism is suppressed. From now on, none of this will be tolerated.'[10]

This was a bombshell. Criticizing sloppy, self-interested party bosses, and making it clear that they could be removed just as the re-election campaign was opening, created an absolutely novel situation for the whole ruling stratum. Most of them were *ex officio* members of 'elected' party bodies at all levels, from party offices and committees, via regional committees, to the Central Committee itself. Changing this set-up would be a momentous step. It would create an entirely different atmosphere from one in which 'election' simply meant 'nomination'. Andropov openly stated that he wanted to see real elections. This meant

---

9   Here we follow the findings of Professor R. G. Pikhoia (who had access to presidential and other archives denied to common mortals): *Sovetskii Soiuz: Istoriia Vlasti, 1945–1991*, Moscow 1998.

10 This quotation and other material are taken from Pikhoia, *Sovetskii Soiuz*, pp. 434–5.

he knew that the so-called 'party' was in fact a corpse, that it could not be resurrected and must be destroyed. And the incumbent rulers understood this full well. The notorious 'security of cadres' (security of tenure regardless of performance) was about to disappear – and, with it, the impunity of the 'good old days'. The cosy, parasitic power of the class of party-state bosses was nearing its end. Genuine elections inside the party betokened the re-emergence of political factions and new leaders; and this could mean the advent of a new party, whatever its name might be. Such a party, still in power but planning reforms, could have served to steer the country during the difficult transition to a new model.

Of course, this is all counter-factual history. Andropov, who suffered from an incurable kidney disease, soon departed the stage in 1984. He was replaced by another very sick man, Chernenko – a faceless appa-ratchik who lasted only thirteen months. Thereafter, the 'party' was headed for some spectacular novel experiences. First, in 1985, came a young general-secretary, Gorbachev, who was Andropov's heir, had many of the right ideas, and was destined for a downfall that was as pitiful as his rise had been meteoric. Next, the state-party (or party-state) would disappear, without any blood being spilt, with its formidable security forces still intact but receiving no orders to shoot. This was another of Gorbachev's merits, but it did not prevent him from sinking into impotence and losing power. In fact, there was no one to shoot at, since the system had not been toppled by enraged masses. There then ensued the slide into 'reforms' that have plunged Russia into a new form of underdevelopment.

DIAGNOSTIC NOTES

Terms like 'paradox' and 'irony' are wholly apt for characterizing Russia's historical destiny. But so is the image of a heavy burden borne by its people, in the manner of the bargemen of the Volga who hauled heavy barges while singing: 'Those smart English have an easy time of it; they use machines to haul their loads.' For their part, the Russians had only their song to give them courage.

This troubled history, with its twists and turns, has induced a deep existential anguish in many Russians (or, more precisely, inhabitants of Russia), which is best expressed by the term *toska*, with its wealth of nuances from melancholy, through sadness and anguish, to depression.

We may add to it *unynie* (despair), as well as a touch of self-pity of course. This is a powerful brew of sorrows — one that could perhaps only be drowned by another brew ... These sentiments, plus an unbearable dose of cynicism, are to be found in popular songs about the underworld, with their sentimental attachment to the knife — a tool for settling scores and the symbol of a whole way of life. Prior to perestroika, singers like Okudzhava, Galich and Vysotsky rarely sang cheerful songs: they expressed a mood — theirs and their country's — poised between rejection, commiseration, entreaty and despair. Not because people knew no gaiety in the USSR (there was plenty of it), but because these artists perceived that the country was on the wrong track and that history would not treat it kindly. In times of decline, decay and stagnation, the rich party and the bards despair.

Our data are drawn from the archives of Gosplan and the Central Statistical Office, which were unavailable when the songs of the bards were reverberating in Russia. Yet putting these two types of 'source' together, we find that they were telling the same story after all.

PART THREE

THE SOVIET CENTURY: RUSSIA IN HISTORICAL CONTEXT

20

LENIN'S TIME AND WORLDS

In the Introduction, it was pointed out that the polarization of opinion and the powerful impact of Cold War propaganda had squeezed out the 'contextual reflection' indispensable to historical inquiry in favour of other objectives and priorities, to the benefit of the media, ideology, and emotion.

Scholarly work on the Soviet Union has to confront widely held and fervently defended opinions – a highly structured 'public discourse' that does not exist in other fields of knowledge. This discourse rests upon a series of methodological errors that are paraded in the various media as obvious verities. The first error consists in focusing on leaders, actors and ideology, depicted as independent agents abstracted from their historical context. Neither the circumstances that shaped and conditioned them, nor the past, nor the surrounding world are taken into account. For many, everything began in 1917 – the moment of the 'original sin'. For others, it occurred even earlier, in 1902–3, with the publication of Lenin's *What Is to Be Done?* Thereafter, events unfolded as if they had been genetically programmed, and the sequence Leninism–Bolshevism–Communism is constructed as a fatality. I exaggerate somewhat, but the irony is justified when we recall that *What Is to Be Done?* was written at a time when Russian Social-Democracy in its entirety, Lenin included, was absolutely convinced that the coming revolution in Russia would be a liberal one ('bourgeois-democratic' was their term) – something that precluded the Left taking power. In those years, Lenin regarded Russian capitalism as a triumphant force, rushing full steam ahead and already visible under every bush . . .

Whenever a determinist perspective is adopted, historical research takes a back seat; and whenever a 'party line' (left, right or centre) is adopted in historical research, one only gets out of the piggy-bank what has already been put in it – not a penny more.

In the case of historiography about the Soviet Union, an additional impediment is the common tendency to discount the social changes it actually underwent. The failure to study the society over the longer *durée*, and the almost exclusive focus instead on the power structure, is sometimes justified by the formula 'There was no society, only a regime': the Kremlin, the Staraia Ploshchad, the Lubianka – three addresses, and nothing else. More recently, the term *nomenklatura* has been presented as a great discovery, without noticing that in the absence of a detailed study of what it denoted, it is only another word.

This is just one example among many of the propensity of numerous commentators for not noticing the obvious gaps in our knowledge of the country. Knowing that such gaps exist and wanting to fill them stems from an old piece of epistemological advice: *scio ut nescio*.

The 'contextual' approach also requires paying attention to the general European scene, its dramas and their aftermath. There the situation changed rapidly, with one crisis following another. From 1914 to 1953 we witness a veritable cascade of cataclysmic events, which impacted very heavily on Russia's population. And the leaders, before engaging in any action, had to confront this series of crises – many of them not of their making. Lenin did not cause the First World War, or engineer the fall of Tsarism, or even the failure of democratic forces to control the chaos in Russia in 1917. Action or inaction, folly or reason – these cannot be understood without taking account of a period that was confused, crisis-ridden, and laden with the past: it engulfed people and set their agendas. A political strategist par excellence, Lenin was only reacting to what he perceived and understood of the crises he was living through. It is therefore imperative that we broaden the canvas and situate people and movements on it.

Historical complexity is composed of countless factors that can converge, diverge, or collide. It is always much more than the action of a leader, a ruling group, a dominant class, an elite. To arrive at a better understanding of these factors, broader parameters are indispensable. Even the history of a regime as brutal as Stalin's is not one-dimensional. We have to pose its whys and wherefores, distinguish between its different phases, and determine when it was in – and when it was out of – touch with reality.

Whatever the regime's degree of isolation and autarky, the external environment cannot be ignored. Not only were foreign radio broadcasts monitored, but systematic studies of Western economic performance landed on the desks of Soviet leaders. The intelligence services, diplomats, and officials from the Foreign Trade Ministry were so many sources of information about what happened abroad, even though it was reserved for the elite. As to the broader Soviet public, we should not underestimate the importance of foreign literary works in translation. However selective, they were numerous: they included many masterpieces of world culture and the quality of the translations was excellent. Soviet citizens became renowned for being great readers of quality works, not to mention their passion for poetry and its specific political role. Today, these qualities have almost entirely vanished.

I have already alluded to another set of problems, which are just as complex and difficult to disentangle. The Soviet and Western systems impacted on and influenced one another, the repercussions varying in form and intensity with the fluctuating international situation. The image the USSR wished to project of itself – as a country building socialism – was at the heart of this process. A closer look at this theme will allow us to clarify some of its aspects, both in the history of Soviet ideology and in its interaction with the outside world – notably in the images and self-images of 'socialism versus capitalism' that the two camps projected at one another at different historical stages. How and why so many left-wing critics of the Western world were led to see in the Soviet Union something it was not, and could not have been, is a complicated issue that belongs here. At the same time, we must not forget the use made by the Right of the Soviet Union's claim to be what it was not, in order to strengthen its grip on Western societies and try to undermine democratic institutions.

The Soviet claim to represent a counter-model and alternative to capitalism helped the USSR mobilize not only its own people, but also considerable external support. It was used after the war to justify the existence of a 'socialist camp' and to deck it out in what seemed like natural finery. But if the voice was Jacob's, the hands were Esau's. Looked at more closely, the reality had nothing idyllic about it, but was a phenomenon in its own right – much like the Chinese system, which today is a power to be reckoned with.

The last of the impediments worth mentioning here is the massive use of concepts like 'totalitarianism' (I shall return to it) that have greatly contributed to ignorance of the significant changes which occurred in the Soviet system. The blatant disregard for the social dimension was proof positive of the conceptual inadequacy of the ideology of totalitarianism. Its concentration on the regime, as if society was by definition so much putty, contributed to the neglect of the deep structural changes in society that were crucial for understanding the regime's achievements, internal changes, crises and downfall.

These omissions, encouraged by the aridity of ideological confrontation and propaganda warfare, are themselves legitimate subjects for historical inquiry, as of course is the damage the Soviet regime inflicted on itself by banning free inquiry and debate. Ideological arguments and postulates, wherever they come from, cannot be a guide in research; they can only be one of its topics, with a view to unpicking unwarranted claims and understanding their source and purpose. But the important task is to fashion conceptual tools and research strategies in order to clarify what the Soviet system really was, how it evolved (ideology included), and where it is to be situated on the map of political systems.

Let us reiterate the point: the past – in fact, several pasts – were (and are) active, because in Russia realities (not merely relics) inherited from earlier centuries coexisted simultaneously. Unlike periods when the pace of change is slow, in crisis-ridden periods social strata and phenomena pertaining to different epochs collide violently, and in the utmost confusion they shape and reshape political behaviour and institutions. Tsarist Russia experienced its fair share of upheavals in the twentieth century, and these continued well into the Soviet period, exhibiting a whole range of phenomena bound up with political and social changes: 'crises', 'revolutions', 'civil war', upswings, 'decline', and then collapse. This spectacle is not necessarily tedious, even if it is somewhat depressing. We also need to hit upon the right terms for each phenomenon, because we cannot use the same ones for the prewar Stalinist phase of breakneck industrialization, combining social development and a 'cancerous' political pathology, and the postwar Stalinist period of rapid economic recovery and retrograde political and ideological campaigns. Finally, we must not lose sight of the swing of the pendulum specific to Russia. An important European power in 1913, it was a devastated country by 1920. Mobilized in an impressive war effort from 1941 to 1945, it was a victorious superpower in 1945 and yet once again ravaged. Ten or so years later, it was a superpower with Sputniks and intercontinental missiles, and the sequel was no less surprising. This is a very dense set of hectic historical processes – and a vast field for students of social change.

We are not going to play the role of counsel for the prosecution or for the defence. Any historical study deserving of the name strives to state what was the case. Where there is something positive – progress – it should emerge clearly; and where there is a pathology (history is full of them), it too should emerge.

We have seen that widespread opinions in political circles, the media and popular perception are so many obstacles to serious study of the USSR. The scholarly works devoted to this country and its system belong in another category altogether; they must be approached quite differently, even if some academics contributed to the confection of a standard 'public discourse' on the Soviet Union. Spread over many countries, academic research has generated a wide variety of studies that certainly reflected the biases of the 'great contest' in some respects, but which were nevertheless the product of serious, sometimes impressive work. In the absence of access to Soviet sources, they adopted a multiplicity of approaches and formed into various schools of thought. Today, given easier access to the archives, but perhaps also in view of the sad state of contemporary Russia, many colleagues would probably concur that a more balanced approach to the Soviet era, warts and all, is not only possible, but indispensable.

The Soviet Union was an integral and intricate part of the twentieth century. It cannot be 'decoded' without a clear grasp of the role it played in that century's dramas. This brings us back to a virtual truism: the impact of world events on Russia was constant and formative.

The 1905 revolution and the First World War strongly influenced the programme of the Russian Social-Democrats, including the tendency led by Lenin (it was established as a party in 1912), and guided their expectations and strategies. Let us reiterate that this political movement had been created with a view not to exercising power or leading a revolution in the short term, but to participating in it and propelling it in the direction of the prescribed historical stage. However, when the attempt at a 'bourgeois-democratic' revolution in 1905–7 failed, Lenin began to doubt the validity of his own and the Social-Democratic Party's assessment of the extent of capitalist development and its impact on Russia. He had hitherto seen capitalism at work everywhere; now he discovered that the leading force ready to topple the Tsarist regime was not the liberals, but rather the peasantry. Accordingly, Lenin began, rather tentatively, to search for a new perspective and a new strategy. And it was only during the First World War that his initial conception of the coming revolution (in fact formulated by Plekhanov) began to change, although it remained valid for most members of his party.

It is important to stress that many members of the Russian Social-Democratic Party, including Lenin himself, had lived in the West and participated in the activities of Western social-democratic parties, while continuing to follow Russian affairs very closely. It might be said that they possessed political 'dual nationality' or, more precisely, that they lived in two different worlds politically. Lenin was a case in point. He was a Russian-German social-democrat and a member of the Executive Committee of the Second International. There is no reason to doubt his commitment to that side of the equation; and as with so many others, it was where he had acquired the conceptual tools he used to think about the world. However – and it was no secret to anyone – he was also moulded by Russia, which remained at the centre of his concerns. But this Russian universe was quite distinct from the West. As Lenin had discovered, notably by reading historians of Tsarist Russia, it was a multi-faceted conglomeration, whose components coexisted in the same space without moving at the same pace. Both his worlds were now entering into a long period of turmoil, beginning with the First World War and continuing in crises and revolutions. These events overtook the whole of Central and Eastern Europe – an economically under-developed, largely agrarian region, run or about to be run by dictatorial or deeply authoritarian regimes (with the exception of Germany and Czechoslovakia, whose democracy was actually more stable than the Weimar Republic). All these factors have to be encompassed in the matrix of the Soviet system. A further crucial point should not be forgotten: German Social-Democracy (in a sense, Lenin's ideological *alma mater*) had rallied to its country's war effort and aims, as had other socialist parties in their respective countries. The Second International, seemingly so powerful in 1914, split apart – a disaster from which European socialism never really recovered. The unprecedented slaughter and economic devastation produced by the war created expectations in many left-wing circles that it would be followed by a revolutionary crisis throughout Europe. They threw themselves into a search for prognoses and strategies that would lead to a revolutionary government in Europe. The role of Russia, and its own historical potential (as a backward country), was deemed of secondary importance.

An exchange of letters in 1915 between two Bolshevik émigrés, Lenin and Bukharin, in which they argued about revolutionary prospects and strategy, offers a flavour of their high hopes and their thinking. At the time, Lenin, like Bukharin (a young, romantic revolutionary ten years his junior), was completely immersed in the prospect of a future revolution in Europe or even on a world scale. Often young, the Bolsheviks were preparing to play a decisive role in it. In all seriousness, Lenin and Bukharin discussed the possibility of resorting to a 'revolutionary invasion' of Germany to defend the revolution, but disagreed as to whether the backing of the German Left should be sought. Bukharin considered it indispensable: otherwise, he argued, there was a risk of nationalist unity being created in Germany and 'our invasion' failing. In this European revolutionary perspective, revolution in Russia seemed a secondary issue to Lenin, and Bukharin's 'our invasion' referred to any revolutionary force in Europe – not some invasion from Russia. Lenin and Bukharin wondered whether the impossibility of establishing socialism in Russia (a hitherto commonly accepted idea) was still a problem. According to Bukharin, that would be the case if only some countries were affected by revolution. But if the revolution was to be pan-European, Russia would become just one part of a much broader entity; and in any case, national identities would dissolve.[1]

It emerges from this exchange that revolutionary strategy, and not just in Russia, would be imposed by ... 'Bolsheviks' – a term that now seems to refer to European revolutionary parties, united in a new international organization, since the Second International was dead and its leaders bankrupt. What was occurring was a shift to the Left, with such 'Bolsheviks' taking the lead.

The thinking here is rather utopian and might seem to imply a 'red imperialism'. But since the stage of current and future events was global, it was not about Russia (which, as everyone agreed, had no socialist potential), and certainly did not situate Russia at the centre of events and speculate about any expansionist advantages it might draw from them. Lenin's orientation towards the revolutionary potential of Europe was to persist until the launch of the NEP in the Soviet Union. With the recession of revolutionary prospects in Europe, the feverish search for allies in some crisis-torn country, which was motivated not by the strength but by the extreme vulnerability of the new Russian regime, was abandoned. A very different Leninism then took the place of its predecessor.

---

1   Bukharin's letters to Lenin in 1915 are published in *Voprosy Istorii*, 3/94, pp. 166–9.

1917: THE MAIN CAMPS

With all this in mind, we may jump forward to 1917 – a year that experienced a glorious spring, but a very harsh autumn. The brevity and intensity of these two seasons, and the contrasts between them, are striking, though there were of course more than two chapters in this highly compressed slice of history.

The exhilarating revolution that broke out in Russia in February–March 1917 was full of unusual features. Tsarist autocracy was not actually overthrown by anyone: it faded from the scene in the middle of a war, without any obvious alternative to take its place. The Duma, which enjoyed zero prestige, was incapable of taking over. It simply produced a provisional government and then retired from the public political stage. The government was not accountable to it and did not last. Thereafter, a new government was formed every two months. Since we are only concerned here with the bare essentials, we must underline the appearance – and then the disappearance – of three main players. First, there were the soviets, whose leaders – Socialist Revolutionaries and Mensheviks – became (with or without the liberals) the central figures in successive provisional governments from May 1917 onwards. Next came the Bolsheviks, who initially played a merely subsidiary role in the soviets, but whose strength grew rapidly. Finally the future 'Whites', almost entirely absent at the outset, began to assemble their forces and soon became the third central protagonist. As for the liberals, they had their own agenda and switched allies accordingly.

The soviets – a unique phenomenon that had first emerged in 1905 – were in fact the only structure resembling something like state power. However, their leaders did not push them to assume power because, according to their analysis and ideology, the future regime was to be a liberal one. The two socialist parties gained a place in government thanks to the soviets, but were almost embarrassed by the fact. For example, the Mensheviks – most of them orthodox Marxists – based their whole strategy on the impossibility of socialism in Russia. For them, the only route ahead was capitalism and democracy; hence the sole indispensable ally was the propertied classes (the middle classes in current terminology). As Ziva Galili has shown, the Mensheviks were divided into various currents. Once in government, some of them revised their pre-revolutionary positions. Others worked in the soviets or stuck with their earlier views. There was also a minority led by

Martov – the 'internationalists' – that preferred a purely socialist government supported by the soviets. It was opposed to socialist participation in the Provisional Government, which it considered too heavy a price to pay.[2]

The Constitutional Democrats (the Cadets), led by the historian and politician Pavel Miliukov, initially wanted to preserve the monarchy in order to avoid a revolution. From May onwards, however, they 'withdrew' (as Miliukov put it) – renounced any responsibility for developments as a party and sympathized with General Kornilov when he attempted a coup against Kerensky's government. They longed for a strong government capable of containing the chaos that threatened to engulf the country. Miliukov stressed that this should not be a military dictatorship, but proposed that Kornilov should take the place of Kerensky, whom he deemed ineffectual. Thus the Cadets banked on a monarchist general to restore order and proceed to a democratic republic when circumstances permitted. The key point here is that the liberals (or at least those who shared Miliukov's views) believed a strong hand was required – but not, of course, from the Left. They did cooperate with the Provisional Government in lukewarm fashion, not as a party but in the shape of individuals accepting ministerial portfolios in order to counter the Left, which was linked to the soviets. The latter represented the only force the Provisional Government could count on. But because they sought the support of the Cadets, the democratic left-wing parties had to pay the price of participating in the government and forsaking the support of the soviets. Such were the contradictions in which, on account of their political and ideological orientation, the Cadets on the one hand and the leaders of the soviets on the other found themselves trapped. These issues must be treated in more detail, since they allow us to understand the kaleidoscope of events that filled the first ten months of 1917.

The political opinions and options of Miliukov and his supporters among the Cadets are highly illuminating. The most heavily criticized aspect of Lenin's revolution – his programme for a one-party dictatorial regime – started out from a sense of what was possible and what was inevitable that was shared by other forces in the political arena. It is scarcely a revelation to indicate that the Whites (mainly monarchists)

2   Z. Galili, 'Mensheviki i vopros o koalitsionnom pravitel'stve: pozitsiia "revoliutsionnykh oborontsev" i ee politicheskie posledstvia', *Otechestvennaia Istoriia*, no. 6, 1993, pp. 15–26.

intended to install a military dictatorship which would restore an autocracy. They loathed such institutions as the Duma – even the fairly impotent one that existed under the Tsar. And there is no doubt that they were not fond of Miliukov's party, even when, in response to their attacks, Miliukov insisted that he had done everything in his power to save Tsarism – it was not his fault if it had turned out to be irredeemable. But although they were supporters of a constitutional monarchy, the Cadets – the liberal party – believed that even that degree of liberalization was excluded in Russia for the time being; and for this reason, they defended a dictatorship. This was also the case with the third main actor: Lenin and the Bolsheviks. This unexpected parallel between Miliukov and Lenin in assessing the Russian situation may prove illuminating.

Miliukov's description of the final days of the monarchy in his 1927 book, *Rossia na Perelome* ('Russia at the Crossroads'), is as sombre as that subsequently offered by the Soviet historian Avrekh in a remarkably detailed volume on the twilight of Tsarism. Miliukov sets out his thesis of a lack of 'cohesion' between the various classes – peasantry, nobility, middle classes – and between Tsarism and the rest of society.[3] Hence the enormous fragility of the Tsarist system, which found expression in the indolence of the state, a propensity for rebellion among popular strata, and the utopian thinking of the intelligentsia. Miliukov's views – including his formulas about the primacy of the state over society (which amounted to making it the sole bulwark against the danger of fragmentation) – were influential in Russian historiography. Even if they used a different terminology, Lenin and Trotsky's ideas about Russia's social structure exhibit some affinity with Miliukov's. His pessimism about the prospects for a democratic outcome to the events of 1917 onwards was grounded in a historical perspective: military dictatorship or chaos.

Some older, unpublished texts by Miliukov, recently discovered in the archives, explain why he hoped to save the monarchy.[4] It is clear that it was the absence of any alternative acceptable to him, in circumstances where the door to democracy was barred, which justified this card in a game of historical poker, as far as he was concerned.

The 'democratic forces', which corresponded to the non-Bolshevik

---

3   An excerpt from volume 1 of *Rossia na Perelome* (Paris 1927) is reproduced in *Svobodnaia Mysl'*, February 1997, pp. 103–13.
4   N. Miliukov, 'Pri svete dvukh revoliutsii', *Istoricheskii Arkhiv*, nos 1–2, 1993.

or, more precisely, anti-Bolshevik Left – the Mensheviks and Socialist Revolutionaries – were in principle committed to a democratic solution. Confronted, however, with the reality of a disintegrating country, some within their ranks, particularly ministers in the Provisional Government, were forced – hesitantly at first – to resort to measures associated with a state of emergency: price controls, rationing, compulsory grain purchases, dispatch of police and military units to quell unrest in the countryside. Inadvertently to start off with, but soon quite deliberately, many of them became champions of a strong state, in outright contradiction of their previous orientation and ideology. Moreover, although they approximated most closely to a genuine democratic outlook, and adamantly refused the diagnosis of Miliukov and Lenin, they never stopped 'yearning for Miliukov' – which was a mirage, given that Miliukov was yearning for the 'iron fist' of a monarchist: another mirage. No wonder nothing seemed feasible.

The government was headed for financial bankruptcy. The Finance Minister, Shingarev, depicted the approaching catastrophe as follows. Before the war, the money in circulation had amounted to 1.6 billion roubles in paper notes and 400 million in gold. During the war, however, instead of the projected 6 billion roubles, 12 billion had been printed – hence the very high inflation that he characterized as a 'sweet poison'. The revolution had unleashed enormous expectations among the population. Everyone's wages had been increased, as had pensions. Expenditure went on rising, but the state treasury was 'empty'. Thirty million roubles were being printed daily (something that required 8,000 workers). How was this chaos to be brought to an end? It was impossible to print more than a billion roubles a month, and yet it cost 1.5 billion because of inflation. Ten million people were enrolled in the army: 'Blood is flowing on the front, but in the rear we are having what might be called a feast during the plague. The country is on the verge of ruin. The fatherland is in danger!'[5]

Police reports coming in from all over the country attested to the growing unrest in the countryside, a deterioration in food supplies, and the piteous state of the army. In this sombre context, the Provisional Government, mainly composed of Socialist Revolutionaries and Mensheviks (with the symbolic participation of some property owners), realized that it was no longer in control of anything, that its legitimacy

---

5 A. I. Shingarev, *Finansovoe Polozhenie Rossii*, Petrograd 1917; undated speech.

was dwindling with every passing day, and that it was running out of room for manoeuvre. The need for a new, reinvigorated coalition led it to convene on 14 September a 'Democratic Assembly', which was to elect an informal 'pre-parliament' charged with negotiating the make-up of a new, strengthened provisional government with (or so it was hoped) some prestige. But everyone observing the debates and man-oeuvring within the pre-parliament elected by the Assembly had to conclude that the political will and ability to build a state were alto-gether absent from it. All it had to offer was interminable talk.

SEPTEMBER–OCTOBER 1917: THE PRE-PARLIAMENT

The reality of the pre-parliament is clearly described in the memoirs of Nikolai Avksentev, one of the leaders of the right wing of the Socialist Revolutionaries.[6] From February 1917 he was president of the executive committee of peasant soviets; in July he was appointed Interior Minister; and in September he became president of the provisional soviet of the Russian Republic (the pre-parliament).

His narrative offers the impression of a solemn session in some lux-urious palace – in fact, an utterly sterile gathering united only by hatred for the Bolsheviks – when on the outside a quite different system was already being conceived. With much bitterness, Avksentev vividly describes the internal divisions within each group (all the parties were fissiparous). The situation possessed the typical features of a case of stalemate and impotence, a glaring example of which had been the meeting in Nicholas II's headquarters at the front a year earlier, when he had proved incapable of doing anything except endlessly reshuffling his government while everything around him was collapsing. Further examples of such paralysis could be cited. The screenplay is different on each occasion, but the spectacle is the same: the political impotence of the key players of the moment. The efforts in September–October 1917 to regain control of events are a classic of the genre.

Avksentev and his associates tried to stabilize the situation by calling on the representatives of the soviets to accept a minority position in the 'pre-parliament' that the Democratic Assembly was about to constitute. A majority position was offered to 'property-owners' – that is to say, the

---

6   Published in *Otechestvennaia Istoriia*, no. 5, 1992, pp. 143–55.

organizations and parties representing the middle classes. The Democratic Assembly met in mid-September in Petrograd. The Bolsheviks,
who participated at the outset, wanted to exclude the property-owners
completely and to create a purely socialist government, which they
declared themselves ready to support. This position was of interest only
to a small left-wing group in the Menshevik Party, led by Martov. The
Democratic Assembly proceeded to elect 250 members according to
their party's relative strength in the Assembly; and 250 other persons
were added from various middle-class and business milieux. These
representatives were supposed to provide political and moral support for
the government. According to Avksentev, this was necessary because
'the government enjoyed no other support whatsoever'.

The situation described by Avksentev is one paradox wrapped up in
another. The democratic camp offered the property-owners a majority
in order to secure legitimacy for the government, without seeing that
the soviets (which they led) were the only source of legitimate support.
Thus, they sought support from elements who possessed nothing like
the power of the soviets. Avksentev understood this very well: he
extolled the efforts made by the heads of the soviets to organize the
bourgeoisie and bring it into the political fray, and yet he noted· 'this
only served to highlight the weakness of the bourgeoisie' – something
for which neither the Bolsheviks nor the democratic forces were
responsible. In the coalition government, the democrats (i.e. the
socialists) had mass support (in the soviets), while their bourgeois allies
had none. Yet the democratic forces continued to offer parity – even a
majority – in the Assembly to bourgeois elements who had nothing to
offer except their weakness, but who demanded a high price for it.

Avksentev stresses the debilitating character of the whole process of
trying to establish an utterly artificial coalition. It yielded only petty
squabbles, failing to produce unity or the kind of succour the government needed.

The remaining Provisional Government ministers – Kerensky, Ter-
eshchenko and others – then embarked on negotiations with different
protagonists in the Winter Palace. All sides were aware that the country
was on the road to ruin and that unity was urgently required. Yet each
of them stuck to their sacrosanct 'formula', fearful lest the masses on the
outside cry treason if their magical terms were abandoned. The bickering focused on minor questions of dogma, even simple points of
grammar. While the nitpicking proceeded within the palace walls,
outside a storm was brewing that would soon sweep them all away.

In the meantime, a coalition government was formed and another body – the Provisional Council of the Republic – set up. The latter was to be inaugurated at the beginning of October, to give the Cadets and property-owners enough time to select their representatives. Negotiations continued on the composition of its presidium. Avksentev recounts them in great detail and finally brings us to the solemn meeting of the Provisional Council on 7 October, at 3 PM, in the Marinsky Palace – the very hall where the Tsar convened his Grand State Council. The hall was full; the diplomatic corps was present in its loggias; applause greeted Kerensky, who opened the session. Yet as Avksentev recounts, 'one did not sense any real conviction that a great new beginning was under way ... A unitary institution had been created for the democrats and the bourgeoisie, but there was no unity in it ... and the contradictions remained just as potent'. People were more concerned with words than deeds. The Left insisted on peace and the agrarian question, whereas these were things the Cadets would not countenance. Avksentev was in agreement with the latter, and sought to persuade the Mensheviks to exclude contentious items from the final document that was to be adopted. According to Avksentev, it was the soviets – in other words their Menshevik and Socialist Revolutionary leaders – who demonstrated their impotence at a critical moment and failed to support the government. So much for Avksentev's account.

Avksentev accused the 'democratic Left' of programmatic inflexibility. In fact, it had no independent political programme corresponding to its actual strength. Its representatives placed all their hopes in the Cadets and other bourgeois elements, while the Cadets only had eyes for the monarchists. Like the Socialist Revolutionaries, the Mensheviks were divided, and neither party could offer anything clear of their own or accept anything proposed by other forces. When Martov called for a purely socialist government based on the soviets, his position at least possessed the merit of clarity – but it commanded only a small minority of his party.

As everyone argued against the Bolsheviks, there was no prospect of socialism. Here the Mensheviks and others were perfectly right. However, while they already possessed considerable power, this did not fit their 'formula'. The latter required that they persuade the middle classes to opt for a democratic system. But the bourgeoisie was in disarray and did not wish to participate in such a government. So this raises the question: What were the Mensheviks right about? As Miliukov clearly understood, the 'middle classes' whom everyone was counting on were a phantom army politically; and the liberals who should have been their political leaders dreamed only of taming the beast and finding someone with an iron fist. The country was falling apart and there was no central government available capable of averting total chaos.

The monarchist Right saw no other way of resolving matters than through military force and recourse to terror; and they made no secret of it. But what system were they planning to establish once the rioters had been hanged from the lampposts? Many of the White generals looked to the past for a model – a return to the monarchy that they still believed feasible. In the first months of 1917, these stalwarts of the old regime seemed to have been shown the door. Yet Kornilov's abortive coup in August and the fact that the liberals supported him should have rung alarm bells. Kornilov's target was not just the Bolsheviks but the whole of the Left, the Provisional Government, and the forces behind it. For the military and other right-wing circles, the leaders of the soviets were guilty of perpetrating a crime – the equivalent of what the German Right was to denounce after the defeat of 1918, or the myth of the 'stab in the back' by the enemy within. The introduction of soviets into the army on the initiative of the leaders of the civilian soviets was an affront to the officer corps and, in its view, undermined the troops' fighting ability. The future White forces (including many 'Black Hundreds') needed time to regroup. They dreamt of then retaking Moscow, having the bells of its hundred of churches tolled, and then restoring the empire with a Tsar at its head.

For the time being, though, from September 1917 onwards the country was not governed and looked ungovernable. Only a movement that supported the construction of a strong state could save it. But one candidate for the task – the democratic Left – was in decline. It had no armed forces at its disposal and took no initiatives. Having been certain that the country was ready for a liberal democracy, and nothing else, and having failed to realize that the liberals themselves did not believe in this prospect, it refused to acknowledge its error or pose an obvious question: What was Russia ready for? For their part, the liberals were very weak and saw no alternative to making common cause with the Whites, for only an iron fist could save the country.

My intention is not to denigrate these people, most of them honourable men caught in a historical cul-de-sac. Many of the future victors would also crack their heads (sometimes literally) on all these problems, starting with the same dilemma: What was Russia ready for?

The pre-parliament's inability to come up with anything was chronic.

It offered a foretaste of what would happen in the Constituent Assembly after its inaugural session on 19 January 1918, under the presidency of V. Chernov, who was completely discredited even in his own party (Socialist Revolutionaries), let alone outside it. The forces that had supported the Provisional Government were no more capable of producing a new leadership team in January 1918 than they had been in September 1917. By then, their political potential was completely exhausted and they had also lost any support among the military, especially after the disastrous results of the July 1917 offensive ordered by Kerensky. When they convened the following January in the Constituent Assembly elected in October, they were already a spent force. Yet such an assembly, which was something completely novel in Russia, was incapable of effecting a historical turn without the combined support of the popular masses and the troops. It did not enjoy the support of the soviets (including the military soviets), and those who had elected it in October had already forgotten all about it by January, so fast did the scenery change on the stage of history. The Bolsheviks were not the only ones who wanted to send this Constituent Assembly packing. Had they represented a unified force at the time, the Whites would have done the same. And the Cadets, the supposedly quintessential 'bourgeois-democratic' party, had no use for it either: they held only 17 of the some 800 seats and the divided Left that dominated the Assembly was of no interest to them.[7]

In January 1918, the central committee of the Cadet party adopted a resolution stating that it was 'neither necessary nor advisable' to demand the restoration of the dissolved Constituent Assembly, because it was incapable of discharging the duties assigned it and hence of restoring order in Russia.[8] Such was the logic of those who longed for a 'strong hand'. The Cadets looked for such a figure among the right-wing military, because they did not believe in a democratic solution at this

---

7 O. N. Znamenskii, *Vserosiiskoe Uchreditel'noe Sobranie*, Leningrad 1976, pp. 337–8. According to calculations made in the 1920s, the Constituent Assembly contained 370 Socialist Revolutionaries, 175 Bolsheviks, 40 left-wing Socialist Revolutionaries, 86 representatives of national organizations and parties, 17 Cadets, 2 national socialists, and one independent. The Bolshevik strongholds were in the industrial regions and among soldiers, where they often commanded a majority of votes. The countryside predominantly elected Socialist Revolutionaries. For their part, the Mensheviks were not mentioned: they had only 17 delegates.

8 See *Istoricheskii Arkhiv*, no. 2, 1993, p. 168, n. 121.

stage, at a time when Russia must continue to fight alongside her allies
and in any event was not ready for real change. Thus their response to
the actual needs of a country in danger of disintegrating was to set off in
search of a promising general.

As has been indicated, the background to this analysis lay in Miliukov's ideas about Russia's structural weakness: its socially composite
character made it prone to crisis, which threatened it with disintegration. But this analysis should have led its author to dwell on the causes of
the fall of Tsarism and be more sceptical as to the potential of a right-
wing military dictator. One of Miliukov's reasons for trying to keep
Nicholas II on his throne in 1917 was that 'we cannot afford to change
national symbols in times of turmoil', but the Tsar had disappointed
him. His subsequent decision to opt for a right-wing dictator was based
on an incorrect socio-political analysis of what such a figure implied:
dictators do not usually float above social reality for the duration of their
restorative mission. The social forces behind each of the generals on
whom Miliukov successively pinned his hopes were already basically
spent. Miliukov later described the predicament his party found itself in
when cooperating with the Whites: some of its members felt out of
place, whereas others were perfectly at ease in this camp – an obvious
reason for them to renounce their allegiances and split the party.

In September 1917, some Bolshevik leaders believed that the situation
was desperate and that the Provisional Government was bankrupt. But
the line of action to adopt was still a matter of debate. After some
hesitation, in September 1917 Lenin adjudged that Russia was experiencing a 'revolutionary situation' which was not be missed. This
concept – i.e. Lenin's definition of this type of crisis – was crucial in his
thinking. In the absence of visible symptoms of a revolutionary crisis,
seeking to take power was sheer adventurism. Assessing such situations
accurately is not easy, and Lenin had erred on several occasions: when
the whole of Europe was tottering on its foundations, 'revolutionary
situations' could be detected at will. But Lenin admitted his errors and
sought to rectify them. In the autumn of 1917, things seemed clear in
Russia: the formula for a revolutionary crisis – that is to say, a situation
where the ruling classes can no longer rule and the popular classes will
no longer tolerate their lot – obtained. The growing power vacuum
could only be filled by a left-wing force or forces (a conclusion categorically rejected, as we have seen, by the Mensheviks and Socialist
Revolutionaries); otherwise, the monarchist Right might step in. A

sizeable group of Bolshevik leaders, led by Zinoviev and Kamenev, agreed with the characterization of the crisis, but was in favour of a coalition government containing the parties active in the soviets. For them, this was a *sine qua non* of any takeover of power by socialists. But they were no more successful in securing the cooperation of the Mensheviks and Socialist Revolutionaries than the latter had been in their overtures to the elusive bourgeoisie.

Lenin and Trotsky did not believe that all they had to do to establish a post-capitalist regime was to proclaim a socialist revolution. The starting point of Trotsky's theory of 'permanent revolution' was the premise that Russia on its own was far from ripe for socialism. For Lenin too, the prospect of socialism could only be envisaged on a European scale. After October, he left open the issue of how to characterize the new regime and how it might – and should – evolve. At all events, what is certain is that following his initial disillusionment with the prospect of rapid capitalist development in Tsarist Russia, he switched to a much more sober thesis about Russia's 'combined development' (Trotsky's term), with the coexistence of 'the most backward agriculture, the most uncouth countryside – and yet also the most advanced industrial and financial capitalism'.[9] Obviously, this was not a good starting point for any socialist project: even after the bastions of financial and industrial capitalism had been seized, the bulk of the population would remain historically too remote from the first steps leading to post-capitalism. Lenin's second, more realistic assessment of Russia's socio-economic system as 'multi-layered', which may have been inspired by Miliukov's historiography, did not make the task any less complicated: the prospect of socialism remained just as remote.

Thus the proclamation of a 'socialist revolution' in October meant above all that socialists were taking power and that they believed the international situation to be revolutionary. In the case of Russia, it was a statement of intent, referring to a distant future in a different international environment. Although utopian, the declaration possessed genuine political force: presenting the seizure of power as a socialist revolution (even if fraught with difficulties for the future) played a decisive role. It foregrounded the Leninist notion that backward Russia could serve as a trigger or catalyst on a very troubled international stage. The prognosis was not confirmed, but at the time there was nothing absurd about it.

---

9   Lenin, *Sochineniia*, vol. 13, p. 406.

The second crucial advantage of this utopian vision stemmed from the fact that 'socialism' signified a commitment to social justice and equal rights for the various nationalities: an essential ingredient in the credo, with a strong resonance among the latter. The absence of a Russian nationalist orientation proved a powerful weapon against the Whites, who espoused a traditional Great Russian domination – a fatal weakness in a multinational country.

The socialist vision also allowed for an appeal to the peasantry; class terms were familiar to them. Moreover, the slogan 'Seize the land from the landowners and the rich' was not an incitement to do it, but retrospective acceptance of the fact that peasants were already in the process of doing precisely that and that no one could stop them. The peasants thereby eliminated the landowners, who constituted a class, and the richer peasants – the kulaks – who were also regarded as a class (though this was not unproblematic in a more rigorous class analysis). The Bolshevik approach thus expressed a reality that was familiar to the peasants and contained demands for social justice that were very close to their basic interests. The term 'socialist' made sense to them, without having to read Marx. This was another considerable advantage over the Whites: in the territories they conquered, they restored the land to the nobility and landowners – a fatal but far from accidental blunder. However powerful militarily, the Whites were doomed to failure politically, as was Russian monarchism in general.

At any rate, a few months after October and the Bolshevik seizure of power, the alternative facing Russia was crystal-clear. On one side were the Reds, a radical camp with considerable appeal and the ability to fashion a state; on the other were the Whites, who knew how to fight but who were incapable of (re)constructing a state – precisely as Lenin had predicted.

Because it was oriented to the poor peasantry, soldiers and workers, this revolution that could not be socialist could be a distant relative of the same: a 'plebeian' revolution. And that was the key to its victory: it allowed the Bolsheviks to mobilize vast armies hailing from the popular classes. The composition of the Red Army is very revealing. The soldiers were mainly peasants and the NCOs workers who had served in the Tsarist army; others, like Khrushchev, had undergone rapid training courses for young commanders. Many members of the intelligentsia were in military or political-military positions. The picture was complicated by the presence of tens of thousands of former Tsarist officers, some of them issuing from the nobility. While some of the latter deserted to the Whites, a majority remained loyal to the soviets. It was a winning combination!

The revolutionary phase in the strict sense (late 1917–early 1918) saw little bloodshed. But the situation became ever more tense and when full-blown civil war broke out in July 1918, it was a savage, bloody confrontation for very high stakes. It would determine who was to hold power in a country that had been plunged into indescribable chaos. No compromise was possible between the two camps: it was a struggle to the death.

These events drastically changed the Bolshevik Party's modus operandi, which no longer had anything in common with the pre-October situation. Not only was the organization completely remoulded, but membership was renewed by successive waves of adhesion – each of them bringing different ways of thinking and acting. With the approach of peace, there was a further influx of new members who wanted to contribute to a wholly novel task: constructing a state, administering a country, fashioning a strategy for the conduct of international relations. For a time, the principal cadres were recruited from among those who had joined the party during the Civil War, which had formed them politically. This explains why many of them were supporters of an authoritarian line even in peacetime. From 1924 onwards, a new recruitment would alter the membership once again, filling its ranks with what some of the old guard regarded as completely 'raw' elements – that is to say, people with no political experience who, unlike the Civil War veterans, had not demonstrated their commitment to the regime. For the old Bolsheviks, whose surviving number generally held high positions, the party was no longer recognizable: it was no longer a party of revolutionaries totally devoted to the cause of socialism. The newcomers shared neither their values nor their past. They would all now be moulded into an organization that was altogether different from the earlier one, even if was still called 'the' party.

Let us note that the broadly plebeian orientation of this recruitment remained a source of strength throughout the 1920s. The policy of comprehensive industrialization in the 1930s brought the party additional popular strata who had a stake in the regime and were also instrumental in the victory of 1945.

A clarification is in order here: there is all the difference in the world between a privileged person who acquires an additional privilege and someone at the bottom of the social ladder who suddenly has access to what was previously beyond her, however modest it might be.

Although power did not belong to the 'plebeians' as a popular class, they and their children (many of them) now had the chance of attaining positions that had previously been out of their reach. For the regime, this influx of popular elements into the lower and middle levels of the bureaucracy and technical professions remained a constant source of strength and popular support. But because 'plebeian' meant low educational levels and a propensity for authoritarianism, an old Bolshevik, who was often highly educated and who had studied *Das Kapital* (frequently in a Tsarist prison), could feel swamped by a milieu where (to borrow a witticism from industrial Birmingham) they would not know the difference between Marx and Engels and Marks & Spencer.

In fact, this predominance of plebeian origins and attitudes, combined with the pride of place given 'technicians' (often trained on the job or crash courses), had a darker potential: it could serve as the social background for the politics and ideology of Stalinism, during the NEP to start off with and then massively during the subsequent decade. For those who had experienced such upward social mobility (and who had such attitudes), the power of the state and its head were not only acceptable but necessary. Even so, the social base of Stalinism, which accounts for the apparent mass support it enjoyed in the 1930s and thereafter, was not the only source of the phenomenon. As I argued in Part One, the seeds of Stalinism lay in the peculiar brand of 'statist' ideology that emerged in the ranks of Civil War combatants who gravitated towards Stalin as the NEP was unfolding.

21

BACKWARDNESS AND RELAPSE

We have established a link between the Russian revolution and the general European crisis unleashed by the First World War. Some have argued – even categorically so – that without the war, the Tsarist system would have survived. This line of argument is strengthened if we recall that the 1905 revolution seems to have been triggered by Russia's defeat at Japanese hands. We do not know what would have happened in Russia had there been no world war, or had Russia been able to stay out of it. The latter scenario is of course utterly counter-factual, and the only thing that can be claimed with certainty is that wars, whilst not the only determinate causes, accelerate the collapse of regimes that prove incapable of winning them. The Tsarist regime had already lost wars in the nineteenth century and its defeat in 1905 by Japan – a seemingly much weaker power – was immediately followed by a revolution. Examination of the causes of these defeats leads to the conclusion that Russia was in a state of crisis that could only deepen before and during the major cataclysm of 1914–18. After 1905, nothing had been done to redress the situation and no adequate preparations were made for any subsequent war. Social problems were left to fester and the regime itself (its way of governing) was in an advanced state of decay and had lost contact with reality. If this diagnosis is correct, then it was not the war that toppled Tsarism. It was already undermined by a crisis, and it was this that led to its military defeats and subsequent decomposition. The fact that other, more modern parties and social groups, which should have been able to assume control, failed to prevent the regime's collapse is further proof of the existence of a grave systemic crisis. This condemned to impotence the narrow Tsarist establishment, the elites who represented alternative middle-class and inter-class sympathies, and also the still embryonic multi-party system brought about by Russia's development since the beginning of the century. In circumstances of military defeat and an ever more feeble government, the disgruntled soldiers and humiliated officers of a defeated army played a decisive role in the Civil War and the victory of the Reds. This was one of the key features of the whole upheaval of 1917–21 – not to mention the fact that those soldiers were overwhelmingly peasants.

It is important to stress the impact of the military factor in these years. The effects of the First World War and the Civil War were the subject of a roundtable discussion by scholars in Moscow in 1993, which unearthed new data in the archives. Its conclusions are of interest.

A first paradox is that the war, which was initially a unifying factor among considerable sections of society, was also something in whose absence February 1917 would not have occurred. At the outset, the war kept millions of soldiers in the trenches, but as it unfolded it increasingly fractured society. By creating 2 million deserters and arming the nation, it supplied the fuel without which the Civil War would have been impossible. In this respect, pointing the finger at the Bolsheviks makes no sense: they contributed to the downfall of the old regime, but the objective conditions of its collapse were not of their making. More than 15 million soldiers served on the eastern front, around 3 million of them in auxiliary duties – more than the French and British armies combined. They represented the bulk of the nation's workforce, people aged between twenty and forty and hailing from all social groups – in a word, the country's lifeblood. On the eve of February 1917 there were 10 million soldiers in the armed forces, 7.2 million of them in the regular army. This means that in two and a half years of war, about 5 million of those mobilized and active had died in combat or as a result of their wounds, or had been taken prisoner, fled, or been invalided out. Almost one in three! These were staggering losses – much higher than anything suffered by the other belligerents.

Russia's soldiers paid with their blood for their country's technological backwardness and lack of preparedness. They had to hump heavy loads; they had to toil hard; and they were poorly fed: amid a dramatic shortage of all kinds of supplies, the army received no more than between 30 and 60 per cent of its peacetime requirements. The enormous military losses profoundly altered the socio-political situation in the country. Masses of people now had access to arms and their psychology was that of front-line troops. A large number of regular army officers and category one reservists perished. They were replaced by second and third category reservists, and by men who were over the age for military service and who were not really fit to serve or ready to risk their lives. The highest losses were recorded in the elite units (Cossacks, imperial guard) and among regular officers and sergeants – the army's backbone. Wartime ensigns and reserve officers had also been hard hit. This was how Tsarism lost its main prop: the army. The monumental mistake made by Kerensky in July 1917, when he threw the troops into a new offensive, contributed still further to the demoralization of this mass of armed peasants, who were soon going to disperse throughout the country with their weapons. They would swell the ranks of all kinds of bands, whether of 'greens' (neither red nor white) or mere bandits, while providing the peasantry with the weapons and leadership it needed to seize the land from the landowners and redistribute it. This was a major contribution to turning the crisis into a deepening catastrophe.[1]

These are important points. Nothing is more dangerous and devastating than a demoralized army collapsing into banditry, and it was on these masses of deserting soldiers that the two sides would draw to conduct the Civil War. If, as we have seen, the NCOs were workers and the soldiers predominantly peasants, the officers derived from the middle classes, the intelligentsia and the nobility. The Whites rallied to their cause officers, cadets, and what remained of the Cossack units; the Reds counted on party members, factory workers, a sizeable contingent of NCOs from the Tsarist army, and even – more surprisingly – many officers.

The fact that defeated soldiers played such an important role in the decomposition of the old regime and the creation of a new one is further evidence that the result of the war was attributable to the regime's dilapidation, not to misfortune. It also confirms the plebeian character of the revolution. It is puzzling that the authors I have drawn on here refer to the 'soldiery' without mentioning that they were peasants. In the introduction to his *History of the Russian Revolution*, Trotsky describes it as a predominantly peasant phenomenon, involving the rural masses whether in or out of military uniform.

---

1   See 'Grazhdanskaia voina v Rossii - kruglyi stol', in *Otechestvennaia Istoriia*, no. 3, 1993, pp. 102–15. The discussion is very interesting: here I have used only the contributions by Iu. I. Igritskii and L. M. Gavrilov.

RUSSIA'S BACKWARDNESS AND LENINISM

The picture of post-revolutionary Russia we sketched in Part One (Marxist intellectuals, an enormous mass of semi-literate party members and even cadres, breakneck industrialization, and a leadership cult straight out of an old political repertoire) brings into focus the issue of Russian backwardness.

The key syndrome in this underdevelopment was the chasm (i.e. the historical gulf) between the elites and the bulk of a still rural population. In itself a cause of crises, this distance, which was deeply rooted in Russian history, could only exacerbate the socio-political crises that did occur. The tendency of a state to respond to problems with repression rather than flexibility and compromise is a familiar scenario, and it is not impossible that Stalin reasoned thus.

The other dimension of the same problem was the historical distance between an underdeveloped empire and the developed countries. In such a situation, the problems to be resolved are defined both by the 'advanced' countries and by those that have to catch up with them. The more powerful the imperative to quicken the pace, the more crucial the state's role becomes – especially when this scenario has long been operative in the country's history. In Russia, the problem was especially acute because of the lack of 'cohesion' (*tseplenie* – a term used by Miliukov) between the various social strata, who geographically inhabited the same territory, but who did not live in the same century economically, socially and culturally. Lenin had clearly identified this problem when he distinguished between five socio-economic strata (or structures), ranging from the landless peasant who still used a wooden plough to the ultra-modern financial and industrial groups in Moscow or Petrograd. These structures (*uklady*) were used in the USSR itself by critical historians to challenge the thesis defended by party conservatives in the 1960s – namely that the 1917 revolution was a socialist revolution and the system a bona fide developed socialism. These historians, who advanced a different interpretation of 1917, started out from Lenin's 'structures' to show that the Russian revolution was not and could not have been socialist, implying that the ruling conservatives were making false claims. This debate occurred during a conference at Sverdlovsk, and readers will not be surprised to hear that the historians lost their jobs, under pressure from Trapeznikov, whom we have already encountered.

If we regard it as a central feature of Russian economic and social reality in 1917 that the overwhelming majority of the population had not yet entered into the industrial age, we are bound to assign great significance to the surplus dose of backwardness and underdevelopment occasioned by the Civil War. In conditions where merely staying alive was difficult enough, it was normal that the most sophisticated forms of human organization should have been the most vulnerable, while the most basic forms of activity, providing at least some food and fuel, had the best record of survival. As regards economic, demographic, political and cultural indicators, the regime's starting point in 1921 was in fact some fifty years in arrears. Many landowners and businessmen had been killed during the Civil War; many more had emigrated. The land-owning class (about 500,000 people, including family members) and the *grande bourgeoisie* (125,000 people) had disappeared. A mere 11–12 per cent of former landowners – most of them small ones – remained in the countryside, working in the manner of peasants. The losses in the ranks of the intellectual professions were also heavy. On the eve of the First World War, 136,000 people with a university education were employed in the economy, and an even larger number of semi-professionals. They were mostly hostile to the new regime and it is assumed that a high proportion of them emigrated, although we do not possess precise figures. It is known, however, that a majority of doctors remained and continued to work. But the ravages of war, revolution and civil war were even greater than the numbers betray. As a consequence of the war and the events of 1917, about 17.5 million people (more than 12 per cent of the population) were displaced and lived a precarious existence. Several million more were uprooted in the course of the next few years. Large towns lost many of their inhabitants. Between 1917 and 1920 the combined populations of Petrograd and Moscow fell from 4.3 million to 1.96 million (more than 2 million people emigrated). During the 1921–2 famine, many of those who stayed became refugees in search of food.

Some 3 million soldiers were killed in combat or died of their wounds or disease. Some 13 million civilians died prematurely, mainly because of the 1921–2 famine and a series of epidemics that gripped Russia (particularly the Spanish flu that struck the whole of Europe). In January 1923 the population of the USSR hit its lowest point – some 6 to 9 million below the January 1914 total. The combined events of 1914–21 plunged the Russian population into misery and inflicted colossal losses. Naturally, the economy was also devastated. The output of large-scale industry was only 13 per cent of the 1913 total (iron and steel a mere 4 per cent). Grain output was no more than two-thirds of the 1909–13 level, and that was a miracle which can only be explained by peasant vigour and endurance. Foreign trade had collapsed, and at the beginning of 1921 a disastrous fuel, transport and food crisis supervened. Protest and unrest spread among industrial workers, who were regarded as pillars of the regime.[2] Never had the country touched such a nadir. The political effects of this enormous regression generated an 'archaicization' of society, with the destruction of many elements of civilization accumulated in the past. The consequences were momentous. There can be no doubt that such conditions were conducive to the formation of a primitive autocracy. In the short term, however, they triggered the New Economic Policy, which in many respects was successful and dictated a redefinition of the regime's strategy.

In 1917–19, Lenin, who belonged (as we have said) to two worlds, reacted to the crisis of socialism in the West as a disappointed member of the Second International by creating the Third International (1919). Two years later he was facing a West that had begun to recover its strength and a Russia that was more backward than ever and scarcely the site from which to direct a world revolution. Moreover, it was now saddled with the challenge its revolutionary slogans and the creation of the Comintern presented to the West and East. One way or another, everything had to be rethought and placed in historical perspective. True to character, Lenin recognized the depth of the changes in Russia and the world and began to reconsider many aspects of the previous strategy, mapping out an entirely new one. Forced to react to dramatic historical developments, he switched perspectives and strategy. This rules out imputing any inflexibility to his 'ism', despite a widespread view to the contrary that is itself utterly inflexible.

LENINISMS AND THE LAST REVISION

The relevant 'ism' was largely shaped by abruptly changing historical conditions. The prewar period, when the forthcoming revolution was supposed to be a liberal one; the crisis unleashed by the First World War; 1917 with its very different perspectives; the Civil War and war communism; and finally the NEP – each involved sufficiently divergent

---

2   The data on Civil War losses are taken from different sources, in particular R. W. Davies, *Soviet Economic Development from Lenin to Khrushchev*, Cambridge 1998, pp. 21–2.

conjunctures to require in each instance a change not just of diagnosis but also of strategy and the very goals to be pursued. It may well be that the essence of 'Leninism' consisted in Lenin's ability to conceptualize and initiate these turns. If so, there were at least three different Leninisms, the last of which is especially interesting.

In 1921, with the advent of a period of domestic peace, the revision and adaptation Lenin engaged in involved all aspects of the system to be constructed, including its ideology. On 27 March 1922 he declared to the Eleventh Party Congress (the last one he participated in) that 'the car is not travelling in the direction the driver thinks he is headed in'. This was a 'classic' Leninist declaration – especially when he added: 'We need to rethink our ideas about socialism.' This was followed by other public utterances of the same tenor in the course of 1922 and up until May 1923, in what became known as his 'testament'.[3] But already at the Eleventh Congress, frail as he was due to illness, Lenin had advanced a set of new ideas that paved the way for a substantial revision of previous concepts and practices.

Lenin now made a general recommendation: 'We must learn from anyone who knows more about something than us' – whether it be national and international capitalists, humble employees in a commercial firm, or even former 'white guards' if they were competent. For the important thing was to demonstrate to the peasantry that the new masters of the country were willing to learn; that they knew how to run the country and to do so to the peasantry's advantage. This was followed by a stern warning: 'Either we pass the exam of competition with the private sector, or things will be a total failure.' Not unexpectedly, he then reverted to the idea of 'state capitalism' that he had already toyed with in 1918, and which seemed to him the best solution as long as it was kept within certain limits by the new state. This was a concept that allowed for a degree of realism while retaining a socialist perspective, even if it was postponed to a distant future. In his speech to the Fourth Congress of the Comintern on 13 November 1922, Lenin reminded his audience that he had already raised this idea in 1918 (it had been inspired by the German war economy operated by Walter Rathenau). But it now had to be geared to the needs of a social alliance. He still saw Russia's socio-economic system as composed of five structures, from private peasant farms to state-owned firms (dubbed 'socialist'). The issue

---

3   These texts are published in volume 45 of Lenin's *Sochineniia*.

he now raised was whether 'state capitalism', which came second in the scale of progressive socio-economic formations, should not take precedence over socialism in the immediate present and future.[4]

The subject was a complex one, but the aim was clear: Lenin was trying to map out a different long-term perspective in the framework of his appeal to 'rethink our ideas about socialism'. Given that the party was socialist, whence the need for this line of thought? What existed was a still primitive patriarchal peasantry with some isolated socialist forms at the summit. Although not socialist, 'state capitalism' would manifestly represent a real advance for Russia: 'We have made a revolution, but it is preferable to achieve the state capitalist stage first.' Lenin returned to the term when explaining the reasons for the introduction of the NEP: 'state capitalism' was the best way of establishing an alliance between peasants and government, by offering the peasantry a state that played the role of a major producer and merchant. Russia was not modern enough to proceed directly to socialism; commencing with 'state capitalism' was the right course.

Lenin sought feverishly for a non-utopian way of preserving a long-term socialist perspective and ideals, while embarking on a transition towards realistic objectives, whereby the state would become a kind of collective capitalist with the aid of a private sector. In sum, this was a form of mixed economy of the same variety as Trotsky had proposed in late 1921 at a session of the Comintern (or its executive committee), but without using the term 'state capitalism'. Trotsky explained to his audience that socialism was a distant prospect (several decades away) and that there was only one way for state-owned factories to become socialist: it led through the school of the market economy. Lenin had read this text, published by Trotsky in a small print-run. He found it 'a superb pamphlet' and wrote to Stalin and Molotov to request that they publish it in an edition of 200,000 copies. Naturally, they did not.[5]

The central feature of this thinking was the attention paid to the peasantry and the development of a corresponding strategy. In the texts that make up his 'testament', Lenin argued that while a radical policy had been appropriate in the context of the Civil War, it had to be seriously moderated in peacetime: 'no communism in the countryside', 'no summary executions', socialism is a system of 'civilized cooperation'

---

4 Lenin, *Sochineniia*, vol. 45, p. 280.
5 For the relevant sources, see my *Russia – USSR – Russia*, New York 1995, pp. 156–7.

– itself a task and a challenge, given that the bulk of the peasantry was barely literate. But such a declaration also signified that the state was looking for a genuine alliance with the rural world, which would respond to its vital needs and induce the countryside to understand and accept its policies. It also implied a significant rectification of the character of the dictatorial system. Dictatorships are not all established for the same reasons and the differences between them can be enormous – as 'no summary executions' attests.

Thus, all the elements were assembled: Lenin was ready to redefine the concept of socialism in accordance with Russian realities, to switch strategy towards the peasantry,[6] and clearly to indicate the type of state he hoped to see. His plans for the functioning of the party, and the institutional set-up required to guarantee the ultimate primacy of the party Congress over its elected bodies (starting with the Politburo), are another crucial dimension of his new doctrine. And in this context we should not forget his dramatic call, albeit as yet secret, for Stalin to be removed from his top post.[7]

Fully to appreciate the scope and depth of the rethinking, we need to return to something that has already been discussed in Part One in connection with the conflict between Lenin and Stalin over the making of the USSR. We saw that it involved a clash between two political camps: between what was still 'Bolshevism' – a radical branch of Russian and European Social-Democracy – and a new current that emerged from the Bolshevik Party and which would become known by the name of 'Stalinism'. It was a decisive battle in which the very nature of the new state hung in the balance: either a variety of dictatorship that rejected autocracy and addressed itself to society as it was (predominantly peasant), negotiating with it as it were, or an autocracy that prioritized violence.

The two currents seemed to be one and the same. In reality, however, there was a deadly antagonism between them, as is demonstrated by the fact that the victor set out deliberately and systematically to

---

6 This notion was formulated in Lenin's article 'Better Fewer, But Better'. The adjective 'civilized' is my translation of the Russian term *gramotnye* (literate or educated), because I believe that Lenin regarded this term as the one most appropriate to socialist aspirations and ideals in the given historical circumstances.

7 These points are treated in more detail in my *Lenin's Last Struggle*, originally published in French in 1967 and subsequently translated into English and other languages.

destroy his opponents. 'Bolshevism' remained part of the party's jargon, but not of its substance. We must therefore dwell for a while on this political organization before it exited the historical stage.

WHAT WAS BOLSHEVISM?

The question can be answered by briefly examining the political turns effected and methods of action adopted, including their capacity to produce the programme we have just evoked.

We shall set aside the Bolsheviks' pre-revolutionary activity underground (to the best of my knowledge, there is no recent monograph on this subject). But it was nevertheless an organized political party at the time and continued to operate as such during the Civil War and thereafter. The substance of 'Bolshevism' cannot be understood without a close examination of the way it functioned. A comparison between the texts of the early congresses and those of later ones indicates the profundity of the metamorphosis. Leninism was a strategy (or rather, a series of strategies) for transforming society. Bolshevism was a party organization, possessing various structures that ensured its functioning as such. It sought to preserve the popular character of the state in the making and excluded any regressive affinities with earlier forms of despotism. Policy discussions were a normal procedure; the exchanges were often sharp and decisions taken by majority vote. Virtually all the leading figures, and also many lesser ones, had crossed swords with Lenin, often vigorously, on key questions of political strategy. Ideological debates were a normal feature of inner-party procedure, which occurred not only in the restricted circle of the Politburo, but also during sessions of the Central Committee and, more widely, in party congresses and conferences.

Characteristically, even during the Civil War, when party cadres were mobilized and had to come straight from the front for meetings, congresses and conferences were yearly events, as required by party statutes. The minutes offer a clear picture of these gatherings: people not just discussing policy, but battling it out, with reports and counter-reports; the chair silencing a speaker from the majority so as to allow a representative of the minority to exercise his right to express his views or rebut the majority position. However highly respected, Lenin was frequently subjected to strenuous attack and could react irascibly. But that was it: such were the rules. A few years later, these procedures had disappeared without a trace. In view of future developments, it bears repeating that Lenin was not the object of a 'cult', either before or after the revolution. But if the term 'charisma' can be used without meta-physical connotations, then Lenin possessed it. It took a specially staged operation for his body, notwithstanding the protests of his wife and family, to be embalmed and thus 'beatified'. This rendered him more dead politically than if he had been given a normal burial.

Founder and leader of the party and the state, Lenin never behaved as a despot or dictator in his party. He enjoyed genuine authority, but so to some extent did other leaders who found themselves in disagreement with him on many occasions, without losing their positions as a result. In the one well-known instance in 1917 when he did want to expel two leaders (Zinoviev and Kamenev) from the Central Committee, he was quietly told by the chairman of the session, Jakov Sverdlov: 'Comrade Lenin, we do not act like that in our party.' This is a revealing snapshot: in the course of a meeting where taking power was under discussion, Lenin, who was agitated and conducted himself in a emotional manner, was called to order by another influential leader who was in the chair. This modus operandi, which was constitutive of the Bolshevik tradition, persisted after the revolution. Lenin always operated in the framework of party procedures: he debated and protested vigorously, but accepted that all important decisions should be voted on, as required by party statutes, and was not infrequently outvoted. He was a leader, not a despot. He was a top leader of his party, not its proprietor. He cannot therefore be treated as 'Russia's dictator', and even less so when we recall that during the Civil War the leadership was hyphenated to 'Lenin-Trotsky' in the eyes of the world and Russia itself – an inter-esting phenomenon given that the party's founder was Lenin and him alone. But Trotsky was a co-leader of the revolution alongside him, and this was accepted by the party and by Lenin himself.

Bolshevism was a party, but it was also an ethos. Discussion could range far and wide. We shall offer a few examples of the issues debated in party bodies and in public. Thanks to the publication of the Central Committee minutes from August 1917 until February 1918,[8] the debate about whether to take power in 1917 and, if so, with or without allies, is well known. Another example: in December 1920, Osinsky-Obolensky – a leader of the 'democratic centralist' oppositional current – published

---

8   These remarkable minutes are available in English in *The Bolsheviks and the October Revolution*, trans. Ann Bone, London 1974.

an article in *Pravda*. The party was still militarized and he himself was performing military duties at the front. However, victory now seemed assured and Osinsky believed it was time to tackle impending difficult issues. According to him, one of these was the task of reviving the party as a political organization once the military phase was over. He therefore proposed constitutional rules that would enable majorities to pursue their chosen policies, while allowing minorities the right to criticize and take the helm if the previous line proved a failure. Otherwise – and this was a warning to the leadership and ordinary membership alike – the party would perish as a political organization. Even though a paper shortage often reduced the main party daily to a single sheet, the article was published in *Pravda*.

A further example of debate on sensitive subjects was the post-mortem on the failed push on Warsaw, conducted during a party conference in late 1920. Part of the debate occurred in closed session (and there are no published minutes). But the other part was staged in public, and it was here that a party leader like Radek could taunt Lenin (the minutes confirm it) with a 'We told you so'. Along with other leaders, he had warned that Polish workers would not rally to the Russian troops and that the counter-offensive on Warsaw was an error. I do not know who the main instigators of the Polish adventure were, but Lenin had endorsed the idea in the hope of rousing the German Left. He certainly did not enjoy Radek's taunting remarks, but was obliged to listen to them. Trotsky too was opposed to the operation (this probably accounts for Radek's 'we') and made it known at the Eleventh Congress without anyone contradicting him – something that was entirely acceptable in these years. In short, the left wing of the party had been against the operation and Lenin had erred.

Even graver issues were aired in open public discussion or broached in the party press: the evidence is available in the minutes of party congresses and conferences. Lenin was not alone in reacting to the problems that plagued the party. It was a poorly organized ruling party, acutely aware of its weaknesses and the low level of its cadres and press. It was also debilitated by a proliferation of internal squabbles and 'cliques', particularly in ruling circles at local and central levels. A major issue was the development of a growing, deeply resented gulf in power and privileges between those at the top and those at the bottom. This was an especially disquieting phenomenon in an egalitarian party of 'comrades', most of whom suffered material poverty. The problem was openly debated in party organizations and the party press; and the leadership, conscious of the depth of the malaise, sought to do something about it.

But an outcry from the base was not the only source of the debates forced upon a sometimes reluctant leadership. They themselves raised political and social problems and discussed them publicly, pointing to the dangers the party was exposing itself to. Witness the reflection by Zinoviev, a Politburo member, at the Eleventh Congress. Shortly before, Lenin had sounded the alarm about the disappearance of the 'working class' during and after the Civil War. According to Zinoviev, this was no longer the problem: the working class was being reconstituted, was leaving the countryside where it had sought refuge, and was ready to join the party. What worried him was the influx into the party of barely literate workers and many candidate members from other classes. He supported a temporary suspension of recruitment in order to exorcize the dangerous spectre of a process of degeneration – a kind of Thermidor from within (my term). Menshevik émigrés were forecasting this as an imminent prospect and Zinoviev cited them to this effect – something unthinkable a few years later.

Increasing social differentiation within the party, on account of the influx of new members, was leading to the emergence of various ideological and political trends. This was the thesis defended by David Dallin, a Menshevik leader, in a book he had just published in Berlin.[9] To his mind, there was no political and social life in Russia outside the party and army; and he therefore reckoned it impossible to eliminate Bolshevism from without. Contrariwise, this could happen as a result of spontaneous processes occurring inside the party. Dallin anticipated all manner of splits, plots and intrigues. Elements of the peasantry and various groups of workers and petty bourgeois were slowly acquiring a sense of their own interests. The intelligentsia was reacquiring its natural capacity for generating ideological currents (democratic, imperial, revisionist). All these would surface in due course 'and political history will be full of their political battles'. All of this was cited by Zinoviev and features in the congress proceedings. Dallin mocked the naive idea that a purge (in the traditional sense of expulsion from the party) could alter anything when it came to the inevitable expression of the centrifugal forces in society. Zinoviev would not appear to have disagreed

---

9 D. Dallin, *Posle Voin i Revoliutsii*, Berlin 1921 (the author was the father of our deceased colleague Alexander Dallin, himself an eminent Russian scholar).

with him. He declared himself convinced that 'there is, in fact, a molecular process in the party, which is not simply a reflection of internal struggles, but echoes everything that is occurring in the country more widely – the whole spectrum of the ongoing class struggle'. All manner of elements foreign to the world of work were penetrating the party, but he still hoped that the 'proletarian core' would endure, maintain the party's original ideological commitment, and prevent alien elements getting the upper hand.

Zinoviev also reckoned that at this juncture preserving workers' democracy would have a healthy influence on party life. The 'workers' opposition' (composed of party trade-union leaders) deplored its absence and made it a central plank in its list of demands. It even demanded that such a 'workers' democracy' should be strengthened by purging white-collar elements and muzzling the intelligentsia – a rather problematic way to create a viable party! These positions were not acceptable to the party leadership. The cultural level and class consciousness of workers at the time was too low to base party-building exclusively on them.

In fact, the party had no compelling answers to all these questions in the short term. What it could do was make the switch to the NEP without losing control of the process; improve the work of the party and its administrative apparatus; and undertake patient educational work, while excluding dubious elements. All this assumed an increased dose of central control and authoritarianism. Whatever the good intentions, democratic objectives were manifestly unattainable even within the party. Even so, the party's old guard still hoped to maintain a democratic spirit and modus operandi in its upper echelons.

Members of the old guard remained committed to the pre-revolutionary ethos. For them, party membership was not the route to a cosy career. They had burnt themselves out in the party's service during the revolution and Civil War and amid the ruins it left behind it. Many leaders were in poor health and their doctors warned them that they could not continue at the same pace. In several cases, they had to be forced by government decision to take leave and seek treatment, often in Germany or elsewhere abroad. It is true that many thousands who joined during the Civil War did not belong to the old guard in the strict sense, but they were still people who were ready to pay a high price for the cause. For the most committed members, in itself power was not a major concern. Membership was a commitment that exacted a personal price – not something that brought a reward.

All these debates occurred just before or during Lenin's radical rethink, which lasted as long as he could think, speak and dictate. During his dramatic last appearance, at the Eleventh Congress, he vehemently criticized supporters of authoritarian methods – a point that we have not as yet mentioned. In these years, party members participated in numerous public meetings in clubs that existed throughout Moscow and probably elsewhere – meetings where party policy was freely criticized, if not roundly denounced. Some party conservatives railed against such 'disloyal behaviour' and appealed to Lenin to put a halt to these infringements of party discipline. During the Eleventh Congress, one of the 'undisciplined elements' – Riazanov – was present in the hall and the supporters of a hard line, hoping for Lenin's backing, reminded him that he had banned political factions within the party in 1921, at a point when it was splintering into different groups and subgroups. Lenin's lengthy response was unambiguous. He did not refer to the 1921 episode, but offered many past examples of fundamental discussions in the party and asserted that, in the absence of free debate, it would not have survived – and would not now survive.

The key point we are seeking to stress here is the following: Bolshevism was a political party that offered its members the right to express their opinions and participate in the development of its political line, and Lenin was eager to preserve it as such. In his speech to the same congress, he also declared that the party must free itself of administrative tasks and concentrate primarily on political leadership, leaving administration to professional bureaucrats, the forces of 'state capitalism', and cooperative organizations.

Such were the essentials of the last version of Leninism. There is no question but that the situation looked alarming to Lenin. In his last appearances, statements and writings, he countered the style and substance of the policy pursued after his death with a firm, lucid 'No'. And this cannot be erased from historical memory.

As we know, the programme of this major figure, who had led a radical revolution but pleaded for moderation now that power had been conquered, was not implemented. The possibility of reflecting freely on the party's problems, the currents it contained, or the threats it faced, was the prerogative of the historically specific political formation that called itself 'Bolshevik'. As long as its various bodies functioned and the decision-making process followed the rules that stipulated the division of authority between them, there was no personal dictatorship either in Russia or in the party. The dictatorship was in the hands of the party, not Lenin. When it did fall into the hands of an individual, the party's party would soon be over.

A ONE-PARTY SYSTEM?

The bulk of old party cadres were still members and continued to regard themselves as such. But they sooner or later discovered that they were now actually somewhere else. Soon after Lenin's death, they no longer recognized the party and reacted by leaving it, adapting to the new line, or joining one of the opposition currents (and perishing as a result). We know that the system was kept in one piece, but – as it turned out – at the price of its wholesale transformation, which involved mass terror against the party and a profound change in the spinal column of the party and system alike, which were henceforth dominated by classes dependent on the state.

Mensheviks (from abroad) and a number of internal party critics continued to advance the idea that political monopoly was bound to come into conflict with the inevitable social differentiation occurring inside and outside the party. Dallin anticipated an implosion in the more or less short term. And it might be said that something of the sort did in fact happen under Stalin's absolute dictatorship. But it was not an 'implosion' consequent upon inner-party contradictions. Describing it in the terms and categories of the inner-party controversies of 1902–3, or the beginning of the Soviet period, makes no sense. The political scene had changed utterly. Terms like 'party', 'Bolshevik', 'socialist', and even 'Leninist' were still used – but had a quite different content. The pathological character of the top leader and the consolidation of his autocratic power – phenomena foreign to Bolshevism – now defined the essence of the political order. Rapid industrialization and population movements towards the towns generated massive changes, and increasing social differentiation was accompanied by the emergence of new social trends and interests. All this complicated the rulers' task. Stalin detected a constant threat in these developments and natural differentiation, which were in fact positive phenomena. And throughout his long rule he waged a war rooted in terror against the cadres and broader layers of the population. This was the irrational core of his policy, exacerbated by the paranoiac dimension of his personality.

The Twelfth Congress of March 1923 may be regarded as the last one where the party could still legitimately use its revolutionary name, and the year 1924 as marking the end of 'Bolshevism'. For a few more years, one group of old Bolsheviks after another was to engage in rearguard actions in an attempt to rectify the course of events in one fashion or another. But their political tradition and organization, rooted in the history of Russian and European Social-Democracy, were rapidly swept aside by the mass of new members and new organizational structures which pressed that formation into an entirely different mould. The process of the party's conversion into an apparatus – careers, discipline, ranks, abolition of all political rights – was an absolute scandal for the oppositions of 1924–8. But their old party was dead. People should not be misled by old names and ideologies: in a fluid political context, names last longer than substances.

That Russia was not ready for any form of Marxian socialism was a self-evident truth to every Marxist. However, the mass of new members set no store by such theoretical considerations. They joined the party to serve the cause offered them, including that of thoroughly erasing the original Bolshevism. For a while, the impossible socialism served as a fig-leaf. Yet the events and trends we are studying cannot be described as the 'failure of socialism', because socialism was not there in the first place. Devastated Russia was fit neither for democracy as Miliukov understood it, nor for socialism, as Lenin and Trotsky knew full well. In these conditions, the original cadres found themselves flooded by masses of newcomers who shared neither their ideology nor their ethos. The ruling party, denounced throughout the world by the enemies of socialism and Bolshevism, reinvented itself for new tasks and realities, while retaining the original labels.

Viewed in this optic, Lenin's last writings represent an attempt to refound Bolshevism in order to prevent the emergence of a totally different creature. Lenin realized that his opponents were inspired by the pre-capitalist forms of an absolutist state; and that Russia's political culture, the character of the cadres formed in the Civil War, and the influx into the party of poorly educated new members with little or no political experience conduced to this regression. The country's backwardness and the imperative of accelerating its economic growth likewise afforded fertile ground for the construction of a no-nonsense 'strong state' – something that could win over, or even serve as an ideal for, people dedicated to their country, whatever its current policies. This is even more true when the backwardness is hampering a country with an imperial past and potential and the pressure being exercised on it by more advanced countries is strong, prompting a commensurate popular mobilization in its defence. In such an atmosphere, the formation of a 'despotic regime' was not immediately perceived as altogether different from the construction of a 'strong state'. Lenin had grasped the difference, called it by its name, and identified the real culprits. To put it mildly, however, most of his erstwhile companions from the heroic years did not get the point. And Bolshevism exited the stage soon after the death of its founder.

22

MODERNITY WITH A TWIST

We have dwelt on the institutional decay of what was supposed to be the system's mainstay. This chapter will be entirely given over to social dynamics, change, and progress. Here too we shall encounter conflicts and will consider them in due course.

We have already stressed the extent to which the depth of the inherited backwardness and the complexity of the task were dramatically accentuated by the serious regression consequent upon the First World War and the Civil War. In a country already in the throes of a crisis, such regression made the task of reconstruction and recovery that much more difficult and increased the pressure for recourse to the big stick – i.e. the state. However, this assertion must be qualified somewhat in view of the NEP, its vitality, and the interest in its possible retention for a much longer period – an expectation shared by Lenin and Trotsky alike when it was launched. The short-lived NEP still continues to fuel discussion about the alternatives open to Russia at the time (during perestroika, some even believed that it could serve as a model for the post-Soviet period). Evidently, one of the readily available alternatives was a hypertrophied, despotic state, which (as we keep on stressing) found fertile ground in the country's history – ground rendered even more fertile by recent catastrophes. In 1921, the country was poorer than it had been before the First World War, and it lagged even further behind the West – something that was painfully felt. The 'historical distance' between rural, urban and bureaucratic components widened. Those who embarked on modernization after Lenin's death began by emasculating the original political organization of the revolutionaries who, having arrived in power in 1917, had constructed a state, saved the country from disintegration, and planned great things for the future. They now prioritized their own methods, which combined accelerated economic development with an accentuated form of political archaism, leading some commentators to use the term 'agrarian despotism' to characterize the Stalinist state. At all events, we are dealing with the phenomenon of a non-modern modernizing state, creating a conundrum that would influence the country's destiny for decades.

This line of thought also proves useful when attempting to understand the Soviet phenomenon in its historical trajectory as a whole. The contradiction involved in the category of 'non-modern modernizer' endured and manifested itself in a variety of guises after Stalin's death. The modernizing aspect of the state's activity (industrialization) generated a series of developments (urbanization, education, upward social mobility) that were broadly emancipatory for the masses of people involved, even if this emancipation was constrained by some powerful checks. One of the keys to the Soviet riddle lies in the interplay between emancipation and the factors fettering it.

Development in the standard sense of the term could not occur without bringing millions of peasants into the towns and partially closing the gap between privileged minorities and the broader mass of the population. Such a dynamic accorded with the plebeian spirit and character of the revolution. Soviet social development was in fact very broad and profound, with momentous effects that varied depending upon the period – the 1920s, under Stalin, and thereafter. Often used and sometimes criticized, the term 'modernity' is applicable here so long as we stick to the bare facts and steer clear of its ideological undertones, which are sometimes present in the sources we use below.

INDICATORS OF MODERNITY IN THE USSR

One of these sources is the two-volume social history of Russia recently published by B. N. Mironov, a Russian historian and statistician.[1] His approach is based in the main on anthropometric data, although he also assigns considerable space to social factors. The book contains a wealth of analysis and information. Yet readers must be attentive to the highly subjective and metaphorical character of some of Mironov's statements,

---

1   B. N. Mironov, *Sotsial'naia Rossia*, St Petersburg 1999, pp. 341–56.

which we shall occasionally react to but mostly allow to speak for themselves.

Mironov's adoption of 'the West' not simply as a model, but as an absolute yardstick for measuring historical development, is disarmingly naive. Readers can judge for themselves as I recount his findings. In sum, what it boils down to is informing us that Russia was not the West. But it is not enough merely to cite what the East lacks when compared with the West. Over the centuries, 'the East' (in fact, there are several of them) founded states, resolved problems and produced cultures; accordingly, we must also examine things from within and not simply refer to the non-existent.

Even so, Mironov's general view of the USSR's actual advance towards what can be called 'modernity' is realistic and competently argued. Russia, he maintains, differed from the West in the way an adolescent does from an adult: it was emotional, hyper-active, lacking sufficient self-control and prudence, tending to experimentation, naive, and absolutist in its demands – but at the same time endowed with an innate curiosity and an ability to assimilate novelty. After all, an adolescent is not a 'backward adult'. Russians did not produce Western institutions, not because they proved incapable of so doing, but because they did not feel the need for them. Everything of value in the West reached Russia sooner or later – if not at the beginning of the twentieth century, then at its close.

Mironov highlights the secularization of social consciousness, which comfortably exceeds what we observe in the West: the Russian value-system became fully secular and temporal. A demographic revolution occurred that liberated women from the heavy burden of giving birth to children who were condemned to die young. The social structure acquired a modern aspect: social mobility attained high levels and social classes became open. Society as a whole became more receptive to the influence of Western values and behavioural norms. A nuclear family model emerged, with children receiving greater attention and women achieving legal equality with men and higher social status. Urbanization progressed: the country became basically urban and its inhabitants reoriented themselves to urban patterns of consumption. They automatically switched from rural–communitarian forms of social organization to different, more complex ones, including in the countryside itself.

Thus, by the end of the Soviet era modernization had progressed quite far towards Western models. A robust social welfare system had been created (pensions, health care, benefits for pregnant women, family allowances), and the list can be rounded off by noting the remarkable development of education and intellectual culture as a whole. In addition, the empire became a *de jure* confederation and the non-Slav nations experienced genuine development. Only in the Soviet period did a 'disciplined' society (Mironov uses Foucault's term) emerge in Russia, which made it possible to avoid any revolutionary explosion during the transition to a post-Soviet regime. In broad terms, the distance between Russia and the West had thus been reduced, and the country was no longer part of the developing world. Mironov is, of course, aware of the means used at the outset to effect this modernization. But he is right to stress that the outcome was remarkable. I would add some more features: personal physical security, libraries, a broad reading public, interest in the arts in general and poetry in particular, the importance of science. For reasons unknown to me, Mironov does not register the fact that since 1991 all these developmental indicators have regressed appreciably, when such knowledge is indispensable for a better understanding of the Soviet phenomenon and its legacy.

Mironov then turns to a method borrowed from Western researchers: the use of anthropometric criteria – e.g. the height of conscripts during their compulsory military service – which, he believes, offer a good indicator of the country's fluctuating socio-economic state. Thus, we find that the average height of men began to fall from the 1850s (on account of the Crimean War) and went on dropping after the emancipation of the serfs. The crisis lasted thirty years and its main victims were peasants, on the verge of exhaustion as they bore the brunt of warfare and taxation. In the 1880s, the biological condition of the population improved somewhat. Various data (which are not altogether reliable) suggest that nutrition worsened between 1850 and 1890, but improved thereafter up to 1910. Mortality was high and unstable between 1850 and 1890, but declined from 1890 onwards thanks to medical progress. After Alexander II's reforms there was much talk of the degeneration of the Russian people, based precisely on the physical condition of young recruits. Such complaints continued until the end of the century, although improvements began in the 1880s. P. R. Gregory's estimates for national income for the years 1885–1913, quoted by Mironov, indicate a growth in per capita consumption from the mid-1880s onwards.

In 1927, as we know from reliable data published subsequently, the population had recovered from the ravages of the First World War and the Civil War. In the towns, the average height of recruits was 1.676 m; in the countryside, 1.675 m. Their average weight was 61.6 and 61.9 kg, respectively. Hence the body mass index (the weight–size ratio) was 22 in the former case and 22.54 in the latter, indicating what Mironov calls a 'good bio-status'. Thus, contrary to what might be expected, the height of the newborn continued to grow between the end of the Civil War (1920) and the late 1960s (and even between 1985 and 1991) – meaning that the 1930s and the Second World War did not have an impact in this respect. Beginning with the 1936–40 generation, the increase in average height was as rapid in towns as in the countryside. In the space of a quarter-century, it rose on average (according to different categories) between 47 and 61 mm – an unprecedented rate of growth. This means that during the Soviet era the 'biological status' of town dwellers, and probably that of rural inhabitants as well, went on improving.

How was this possible when we know that the state was constantly depressing living standards?, asks Mironov. His hypothesis is that in the 1930s–1950s per capita family income rose thanks to internal resources, and in part to external resources, in four ways. Birth rates decreased sharply, and with them the cost of rearing children. Medical expenses likewise declined, for the population in general and children in parti-cular. Many women who had not previously worked were now able to do so, because they had fewer children, there was a huge demand for labour, and the state supplied crèches and kindergartens. Finally, a better distribution of wealth also conduced to this improvement in 'biological status'. We might add that this is a fascinating but under-explored topic.

All this has to be seen in the framework of the demographic revolution that occurred in Russia between 1920 and 1961 (later than in the West, where it had already been achieved by the beginning of the century). It was marked by a sharp reduction in birth rates (in accordance with parents' own wishes), by greater success in the fight against infectious diseases, and by a reduction in infant mortality – in sum, a more modern, rational and economic pattern of population reproduction.

Some reduction in birth rates had already been observed following the 1861 reforms. A further reduction was attributable to the ravages of two world wars and a civil war. By the mid-1920s, prewar birth rates had been restored. The second half of the 1920s exhibited a downward trend that continued into the 1930s. In 1941, the rate was 25 per cent down on the 1925 figure. The Second World War further aggravated the decline. Peace did not, however, restore prewar rates. After some increase in 1949, a sharp, irreversible reduction set in. Two figures illustrate the scope of the phenomenon: Russia went from a birth rate of 206 per thousand in the 1920s to 29 per thousand in the 1960s. The main cause was the desire of Russians to limit the number of children they had, in particular by abortion (the highest rate in the world). Some importance must also be ascribed to the tendency to postpone marriage, the divorce rate, and the increase in the number of unmarried women.

This downward trend in birth rates was counterbalanced by an extraordinary decline in general mortality (39.8 per thousand in the 1880s, 30.2 in 1900, 22.9 in the 1920s, 7.4 in the 1960s), with a corresponding increase in life expectancy (28.3 years in 1838–50, 32.34 in 1896–7, 44.35 in 1926–7, 68.59 in 1958–9) and a commensurate growth in the number of pensioners. In 1926, for every 100 able-bodied persons we find 92 not belonging to the active population (including 71 children and 16 pensioners); in 1959, the figure for the non-active population was 74 per 100 (53 children and 21 pensioners). In the years 1926–59, the average figure fell by 20 per cent per family. And since most non-able-bodied people received pensions, the family was aided correspondingly. All in all, society and families thus benefited from the decline in mortality and the increased length of working life. Mironov concludes that everyone gained from the demographic revolution, which he calls a 'rationalization of the process of reproduction'.

This kind of modern reproduction rationalized the whole life-cycle of families and individuals – especially women. The procreative functions that had demanded such enormous effort from them in the past, from the onset of nubility to the menopause, were henceforth confined to a narrower span of their life, allowing them to work and help increase the family income. Women in fact became an important component of the workforce in all key branches. By 1970 they were broadly well educated, were well represented in the technical professions, and had a strong presence in scientific research. Mironov is right to insist that 'no other country in the world has experienced such a high level of female participation in the world of work and culture'.

We might halt here for a moment to point out that, while basically accurate, this strikes an unduly triumphant note. Numerous Soviet sociological studies have demonstrated that the very real emancipation of women was marred by two limits: their purely symbolic presence in the power structure and a tenacious patriarchal system, including in urban families. The latter was aggravated by an inadequate supply of household appliances. Women still returned home after a hard working day to a good three hours of household chores, contributing to widespread chronic fatigue. In the 1960s the state made 'heroic' efforts to increase the production and supply of household appliances and obtained satisfactory results. But this was not enough to eradicate a sizeable obstacle to women's equality.

Despite these qualifications, the indicators of female emancipation are undeniable and we are indebted to Mironov for a better appreciation of the changes that occurred in the country's social structure and the formation of what I call a 'new society' – and this in record time and despite past cataclysms. The demographic data will detain us further in the next chapter, for whilst they indicate a genuine emancipation, they also reflect some darker realities.

For now, we shall make do with mentioning in passing a phenomenon described by Mironov, which is specific to Soviet society and well known, but never really studied in depth, and whose importance has also been underlined by the prestigious sociologist Tatyana Zaslavskaya of the Academy of Sciences. Mironov argues that the 'equalization of incomes for the broad mass of the population around a certain average represented a further internal reserve that Soviet society could mobilize'. He makes an even stronger claim to the effect that reduced income inequality between social groups contributed to the improvement in the population's 'biological status': the poorer a society, the more prone its 'biological status' to inequalities. We do not possess any reliable assessment of this inequality in the USSR, but the state worked hard to reduce material inequalities and it unquestionably succeeded. Significant population mobility and mixed marriages between people from different regions and cultures also impacted positively on such indices as the height of conscripts, as did the phenomenal rate of urbanization (from 15 per cent in 1921 to 50 per cent in 1961). Even if the system offered its citizens a much lower standard of living than that of Western countries, it remains the case that the height of men went on increasing in Russia, until the 1980s at least, at about the same tempo as in developed countries.

From Mironov's work we shall above all single out the idea that the improvement in 'biological status' (and the set of factors that produced it) was the system's 'secret' – a secret it might not have been aware of itself. And given that the population's 'biological status' is no doubt on the decline in the post-Soviet period, this probably accounts for the nostalgia felt by many Russian citizens for the defunct Soviet system.

23

URBANIZATION: SUCCESSES AND FAILURES

Our constant attention to the changing social landscape – bureaucracy, politics, economics and law enforcement all belong to this landscape – offers an analytical framework enabling us to distinguish between what was urbanized *and* modernized, on the one hand, and what urbanized without really modernizing itself, on the other. The important issue of income equality merits further research. But relative equality, and the concomitant reduction of class differences and barriers among broad swathes of the population, were incontestable facts, fondly remembered even among many Russian émigrés to, say, the USA, where economic inequality forms part of the system's ethos.

Mironov's positive assessment of this phenomenon contradicts his own conception of modernity, defined in terms of conformity to the Western model. Moreover, it leads him to regard the fading of the old Russian 'community spirit' (*obshchinnost'*), inherited from the rural past, as a sign of the country's 'maturity'. But what was the sense of equality and neighbourliness that had such a positive impact on the health, physical growth and moral well-being of Russian citizens, if not the 'non-modern' spirit of community? Is it really a good thing for modern societies to be rid of it? The common phenomenon of solitude amid milling urban masses is an unhealthy product of social atomization that can only be remedied by a 'community spirit'.

If we have thus far dwelt mainly on 'mechanical changes' – i.e. continuous waves of migration, which are a complex phenomenon in their own right – it is important to appreciate that urbanization imparts a novel content to the term 'mobility'. It does not merely involve changing address or workplace, or moving across space. In what was now an urban environment, we are dealing with social, cultural, economic and psychological mobility, which is best understood when juxtaposed to the traditional spatial sense of the term.

The complexity of urbanization and its transforming power consisted in generating masses of ideas that circulated via new channels of communication, exposed the population to a flood of information, put a premium on inventiveness, education and intellectual creativity, and, finally, engendered new conceptions of existence and new needs in people's personal lives. All this was light years away from the rural rhythms of traditional Russia, where change was slow and the social world often just a village – hence easily mastered (everyone knew the details of their neighbours' lives), offering a profound sense of familiarity with social reality and inducing fatalism about the vagaries of nature. Clinging to tradition, limited mobility and narrow horizons (frequently in the literal geographical sense) – these were the rule. Without proper schooling and transitional stages, this rural civilization was not equipped to face the large towns and urban settlements, where it was indispensable to have an education, to improve one's professional skills, or to switch professions. The newcomer was exposed to a bewildering variety of creeds, personalities, fashions, information and values, which constantly disrupted traditional familiar social arrangements of all kinds. Atomizing influences, as well as incentives to enter into all sorts of networks of new and different relations – social, political, economic and cultural – challenged the traditional socio-cultural universe, wearing down its sometimes stubborn resistance.

But it was not just the rural world that came under challenge. Urban society also exercised enormous pressure on the state – to begin with, simply because it presented a new, utterly different entity to be governed. Moreover, this society was still rather young, inexperienced in the ways of self-regulation, and carrying quite a freight of older traditions. It is therefore appropriate – and maybe by now rather obvious – to regard the urbanization process as tantamount to the formation of a new society. For as long as the transition period made it possible to speak of a halfway stage, old rural and new urban worlds coexisted, earlier traditions and mentalities mixing with the commotion of capitals and the complexity of 'scientific towns'. The state and its principal institutions were governing 'different centuries' simultaneously and under ideological and political pressure from utterly heterogeneous groups. The complex interplay of culture and mentalities, which at this stage was reflected in the sphere of politics and the state, yielded a mix of religious and secular elements that could be detected in the state's symbolism and the way it exercised power, but also in the population's reaction to state power. The cult of Stalin, the explosion of popular grief at his death, the acceptance deep down of an authoritarian government, the phenomenon represented by Nikita Khrushchev – not only the manner of his leadership, but also the widespread protests it elicited from the populace and the intelligentsia: all this indicated a social and cultural landscape undergoing massive changes. Urbanization was progressing and urban society was becoming the dominant way of life.

Whatever the survivals from past traditions and practices, urbanization transformed society and forced the government to adapt to this new entity, since otherwise the country could not be governed or developed. In other words, the state and system of government had to acquire a mobility of their own and respond to a quite different historical agenda. The changes we have already pointed to – particularly in the sphere of repression – were a reaction to the complexity of the tasks imposed on the state by new realities. The old methods of coercion and mobilization were no longer suitable: new means were required and novel, more thoughtful strategies had to be adopted. Problems often developed spontaneously and their resolution dictated flexibility and an ability to negotiate with the population. But the bureaucratic authorities were still neophytes when it came to handling the urban maze, which was often independent and intractable. Urbanization, which went hand in glove with modernization, generated new trends in social behaviour and a wealth of specific 'resources' that largely eluded state policy. This huge concentration of dynamic energy could not be controlled with the methods and apparatuses that had been employed to manage a predominantly rural population and a relatively small urban sector. In this particular instance, the 'call of history' required the state to adapt to the new reality and alter itself sufficiently to give rein to the dynamic forces of urban society and concentrate on the domains where it was actually competent.

In this regard, the changes made at the beginning of the Khrushchev period in the spheres of penal, labour, educational and social policy – surveyed in Part Two – were promising moves in the right direction. They betokened the system's recognition of the transformation under way in society as a whole and gave rise to new forms of relationship between society and the state apparatus. This process proceeded in tandem with a 'de-militarization' of society and the regime. The imbrication of social and economic factors became extremely complex and the state strove to respond to it by adapting to new needs and moods. The relationship between the world of work and the state was often summed up from the workers' standpoint by a quip we have already cited: 'You pretend to pay us and we pretend to work.' Some people took it for the literal truth, and although it was only a witty remark it did contain a grain of truth – i.e. the existence of a tacit social contract, never signed or ratified, whereby the relevant parties arrived at an understanding about running a low-intensity, low-productivity economy. Its consequences were multiple. The first was that it made for a relatively small number of conflicts in the workplace, and perhaps even in society at large. But it also meant a rather low standard of living, which encouraged people to find ways to supplement their income in various private activities, whether legal or semi-legal (private plots, part-time second jobs). And this in turn had consequences that were not necessarily negative for all concerned.

For their part, the administrative strata, who were now better edu-cated and more firmly in the saddle, used a whole range of initiatives, whether tolerated or illegal, which were indispensable for the success of the official side of the operation. Sometimes they veered towards plainly criminal acts of corruption and black-marketeering. In order to get anywhere near meeting the targets fixed by the planning authorities, ministerial agencies and the management of firms learnt to protect themselves with a whole array of defensive measures. In fact, they established a system based on informal rules: building up unauthorized reserves of stocks, means of production, and labour; using *tolkachi* ('pushers', expediters) and other intermediaries to obtain the requisite supplies from outside official channels; sabotaging or disregarding official investigations and policies; and, finally, creating powerful networks of allies and lobbies at the top. These administrative bodies eluded any real control by the party (or any other instance) and were not far from being the actual holders of state power.

The reality of an urban society and a nationalized economy also accounts for the changes in the modus operandi of the party, which was supposed to be the system's forcing house, and in its relations with upper echelons of the bureaucracy. Its lower ranks ('employees') were part of society at large, as well as of the administrative network they were employed in. As such, they were both a source and a recipient of social opinions, moods, practices and interests. Bureaucratic interest groups (the managers of economic branches, the military–industrial complex, the scientific community, the military), as well as the interests, opinions and rights of lower bureaucratic layers (trade-union members all of them), were de facto legitimized. Similarly, the right of specialists to bargain hard over terms and conditions was de facto recognized in a 'specialists' labour market'. The de jure and de facto existence of a labour market became part of Soviet reality, as did the complex relations between management, workers, unions and party.

Concern about public expectations and a desire to respond to them now frequently featured on the government's agenda and altered its modus operandi to a degree that was unprecedented since the end of the NEP. Party and state documents published at the time, or subsequently discovered in the archives, contain ample information and warnings about the moods of different social strata: party or government bodies express their anxiety over some particular policy (or lack of policy) that risks creating discontent. Workers' attitudes were a major concern for the authorities and were often discussed by the apparatus, especially when reports indicated that workers were not attending party meetings, were not opening their mouths, or were booing speakers – not to mention the more determined forms of action and different forms of protest they resorted to (the number of strikes was on the increase).

Trends and opinions among students, intellectuals and administrative cadres were likewise reported and widely discussed. Low morale among these strata was issuing in poor performance and, not infrequently, in hostility to the party. This was why when a policy did create massive discontent it was moderated, officially withdrawn, or effectively abandoned. If women refused to accept jobs unless there were crèches for their children, the authorities responded: they admonished those responsible for this state of affairs, reorganized things, took steps to improve social policy, and offered concessions. This amounted to de facto – even de jure – recognition of various rights on a massive scale. Taking account of public opinion and negotiating with citizens were henceforth part of the socio-political scene. And when this was interrupted by rash policy decisions (as occurred under Khrushchev from time to time) there was an immediate political price to pay.

Given the efforts undertaken to improve the civil and criminal codes and modernize the judicial system, can we speak of a *Rechtsstaat*? No. For this category to be appropriate, legality would also have had to apply, at least partially but unambiguously, to the top leadership. The system would also have had to extend rights to critics, or at least grant oppositionists the right to a fair trial. This was not the case. On the other hand, we certainly may speak of a vastly increased role for the law and legal system following the abolition of secret extra-judicial procedures and arbitrary executions.

'Mass disorder' of the Novocherkask variety haunted the KGB, because it did not know how to deal with it: in that particular instance, military intervention had produced a considerable number of casualties. A recent book based on archival research provides data about events of this kind, which were of such concern to Semichastny.[1] In the Brezhnev period, there were nine cases of mass rioting, seven during the first two years. Under Khrushchev, the figure was two and a half times higher. Between 1957 and 1964, weapons were used in eight cases; under Brezhnev, in three (all of them in 1967). Under Khrushchev, the number of dead and wounded among the rioters totalled 264, as against 71 under Brezhnev. The total number of casualties during riots in the space of twenty-five years amounted to 335 – most of them wounded (but the number is not specified). Thus, the annual average was 13.4 wounded or killed (although many years witnessed no riots). It would be useful to have details about instances of rioting in other countries (incidence and casualties). Was the Soviet figure – 335 casualties in twenty-five years – exceptional, given the huge size of the country and a non-democratic regime?

The panorama of changes, innovations and reforms we have provided hopefully makes it possible for readers to appreciate the difference between the Stalinist and post-Stalinist models. The elimination of mass terror as a means of governing forced the authorities – and the party, in the first instance – to engage in what I have called 'negotiation' with the main social and bureaucratic actors, increasing the regime's dependency on them.

'Over-Stalinizing' the whole of Soviet history, by extending it backwards and forwards, is a common practice that serves a variety of purposes – but not that of historical inquiry. We have no reason to ignore the extent and significance of the changes in the social structure, the strategic weight of particular social groups (large or small), the fusion between the state apparatus and the party, the end of mass terror – unless, of course, we are pursuing some ideological hypothesis, as opposed to trying to unravel a complex historical reality.

That said, we must not forget that this society and regime were not

---

1   V. A. Kozlov, *Massovye Besporiadki v SSSR pri Khrushcheve i Brezhneve, 1953 – Nachalo 1980-kh godov*, Novosibirsk 1999, p. 402.

insulated against the emergence of reactionary ideological and political currents, including from within the state and among party leaders. Here we shall tackle this huge subject exclusively with respect to the difficulties of de-Stalinization and the pressure for a rehabilitation of Stalin. The continuing internal debates among the post-Stalinist leadership, and the opposition to Khrushchev's de-Stalinization, were focused not on the continuation of Stalinism as such, but on the image of Stalin as state-builder and head of a 'great power' (*derzhava*); and a readiness to use drastic methods when state interests were at stake. Unquestionably, and not surprisingly, some among the leadership of a dictatorial regime defended this attitude. Nevertheless, it is important to note that, despite all sorts of trial balloons and half-measures towards restoring Stalin's image as a great leader, rehabilitation did not occur because it no longer made sense. Even among the Stalinists, no one any longer defended the idea of bloody purges. Political arrests certainly continued. But they involved actual critics and real political activities, not imaginary or hallucinatory crimes that people were forced to 'confess' to. This did not have much in common, whether in character or scope, with the Stalinist period.

But this verdict on what the system no longer was would remain suspended in a vacuum if we did not offer a broad picture of what it had become. Seen from below, it was a veritable maze: masses of people and agencies acted as they saw fit, while a significant number of decrees and laws issued by the Central Committee or, more solemnly, jointly by it and the Council of Ministers, were not observed or were followed only half-heartedly. Mass phenomena like labour turnover remained just as pronounced. Officials did not actually lose their jobs even if they were sacked. Judges who disagreed with the severity of some laws sought to reduce charges when they felt that punishment made no sense; others did exactly the opposite, in the belief that the new policies were too liberal. What all this indicates is that a history restricted to government policy would be misleading. The historical events we are observing took the form of processes that depended on policy measures only in part. In fact, they mainly – even completely – derived from spontaneous developments (the *stikhiia* we have already encountered).

'Those above' were not just promoters of a voluntarist politics. The Politburo governed with the help of a 2–4 million strong layer of *nachal'niki* ('bosses' in the broad sense): around a million of them in top positions, a million in administrative positions of lesser importance, and a further million in charge of industrial enterprises. This amounted to a broad social stratum with its own history and sociology. Its members were conscious of their own interests – just like the workers, peasants and intellectuals who worked under their authority. Thus we find the managers of industrial enterprises setting up their factories in well-developed areas even if it was formally prohibited, and maintaining labour reserves and hoarding other stock – schemes that were also proscribed and, what is more, not financed. (So where did the money come from? Secret funds?) Even *nomenklatura* rules were circumvented to offer good positions and promotions, making it possible to constitute a network of cronies around a boss, with its attendant coteries, cliques and clienteles, as any sociologist would have expected.

Such spontaneous developments involve every social group, whatever the regime: the higher ups concentrate on their own affairs, while their subordinates do everything they can, licit or illicit, to further their own interests. Consequently, when a broad range of factors is involved, we can make out several interacting dynamics that render reality more complex than is portrayed by official clichés. The social changes that occurred during the hectic phase of urbanization ushered in a new stage in social complexity, expressed in the increased momentum of the 'social factor' (greater freedom of movement for labour, creation of a labour market for specialists which helped enhance the role of the intelligentsia). This degree of complexity was bound to test the limits of the political system severely.

Attending to the 'social factor', as we have done throughout this book, aids us in appreciating a complex social reality and the profound changes that accompanied it. The existence of the Soviet regime in the post-Stalin period was relatively short, but it was characterized by a historical experience of exceptional intensity. After Stalin's death, we witness not only the abandonment of mass terror, but also the disappearance of other features pertaining to the 'enserfment' of the population. The changes consequent upon the end of this state of serfdom were especially significant: they marked an expansion in personal freedom that should be acknowledged, and not dismissed with contempt on the grounds that a democratic system offers much more. The subsequent fate of the regime would be unintelligible without this increased breathing space for popular and other classes. The improvement in social conditions, the greater attention to safety at work, the shorter working day, longer holidays in more readily accessible holiday resorts, higher wages (albeit not spectacularly so) – all these must be factored into our reflection on the system. Thus, as we indicated in Part

Two, labour relations were now based on the labour code and legal guarantees granting workers the right to switch workplaces. The rights of workers and employees were more clearly defined and better protected: legal dispositions made it possible to challenge management decisions and pursue cases in tribunals or special chambers created to settle work disputes – tribunals where workers had a good chance of winning.

This was all certainly aided by the improvement in workers' educational levels, due in part to an influx of secondary school graduates into factories. The latter put considerable social pressure on management and government when they realized the gap between their level of education and aspirations and the still relatively primitive working conditions in industrial and other concerns, which were slow to introduce the technological innovations young workers expected to see. Whereas many workers from the previous generation had adapted without difficulty to a low-intensity system, this educated section of the workforce was certainly disappointed. Dissatisfied with the monotonous, archaic and often even non-mechanized character of their work, they were ready to look for more interesting jobs elsewhere and now had the right to do so. To retain them, the technological level of enterprises had to improve. But for this to happen, the whole incentive system in industry (and the economy in general) had to be revised – a prospect that raised immensely complicated economic problems and became a real headache for the leadership.

The term 'sociology' is shorthand here for the set of interests, interactions, and practices of social groups, and also applies to the production and circulation of ideas, ideologies, political trends and moods, which were now of considerable intensity. This was bound up with the enhanced role of the intelligentsia, the growing weight of public opinion, and the attitudes that now pervaded the bureaucratic class, the party apparatus, the young, and the working population. Some seem to think that there can be no political history – let alone ideological history – in a country that does not recognize the right of other political opinions to exist, express themselves, and take organized form. However, ideological and political trends did indeed exist in the USSR and found ways to make themselves heard, even if they did not assume an organized form and seek to overthrow the regime. Those who pursued that course risked the attentions of the secret police, but the latter, however powerful, proved helpless when it came to ideas diffused among youth and large segments of the general population, the bureaucracy, the army or the intelligentsia. When such diffuse ideas emerge, history (or, if one prefers, political sociology) takes over, and the police are powerless, especially when these opinions are widespread among leading strata, even in their own ranks.

The party, too, was not only helpless, but succumbed to these ideas and trends: varieties of (sometimes virulent) nationalism or 'statism', deeply rooted in these circles, were almost openly expressed with impunity, even though they helped undermine the regime that tolerated them. But directly anti-regime forces were not able seriously to threaten it. The regime was not toppled: it died after exhausting its inner resources and collapsed under its own weight – a special case in the history of the fall of empires. Nuclei of individuals and forces who wished to overthrow it certainly existed, but they lacked sufficient popular support. We have seen that Andropov's agencies put the number of potential opponents and plotters at some 8.5 million people, mainly located in south-east Russia and among the intelligentsia of the capitals. But these elements never managed to combine into a coherent political force.[2]

The presence of police controls and informers (*stukachi*) is insufficient on its own to explain the regime's robustness. Citizens must have found something in the system to desire or appreciate, be it the country's international status, the relative social homogeneity of its population, the considerable openings for social promotion for disadvantaged strata, or the relative novelty of the liberties that were granted, de jure or de facto, during the revitalization of the system after Stalin's death and even in its declining phase. All these freedoms were bound up with a new urban reality that was probably still too young to allow for the crystallization of new, clear-cut political aspirations, with the capacity to attract broad popular support.

In the context of an expanding urban society, the emergence of sociology as a field of scholarly knowledge is a natural and yet highly significant development. Pressure to develop a hitherto banned discipline derived not only from academicians, but also from various officials and analysts at Gosplan, the Finance Ministry, the Central Statistical Office and the State Labour Committee – so many bodies

---

2   Identifying and assessing potential 'sources of trouble' is one of the tasks of any secret service, whatever the means and methods of surveillance employed against groups or organizations.

whose sphere of activity was not restricted to a single branch, but involved the whole economy, society, and the machinery of government. Not to be outdone, the KGB, with the help of the Academy of Sciences, created an institute for the sociological study of various milieux – the student world, in particular – with an emphasis on behaviour that was anti-social and actually or potentially hostile to the regime.

Sociology underwent rapid development. Whether wittingly or otherwise, sociologists became a pressure group (supported by academic institutions and their members) and rapidly seemed indispensable for a better knowledge of society, workplaces, youth and its aspirations, the condition of women, and so on. Sociologists' articles, and particularly their field studies, offered an image of reality that had little in common with the clichés and rhetoric of official ideology. They forced this reality on the consciousness of ordinary people, but also of party and state officials, attuning them to new realities, new tasks and new approaches. Government agencies soon began to commission sociological studies. Various sociologists stood out (Tatyana Zaslavskaya and her colleagues at the highly innovative academic centre in Novosibirsk, others in Moscow and Leningrad). Without mincing their words, they produced realistic studies on living conditions in the rural world, factories and offices. Economists from various centres, particularly those at the Central Institute of Mathematical Economics, engaged in intensive research, circulating studies, whether or not they were published, which were communicated to the government. Some of these were commissioned; others were carried out on the initiative of the researchers. Political scientists also gave their opinion, even when they had not been asked for it. They sent unsolicited memoranda to the leadership protesting against some particular policy (for example, the intervention in Afghanistan).

The government and party apparatus selected academic experts as permanent or occasional advisers. These academics formed the branch of the intelligentsia best attuned to urban reality in all its complexity and sought to develop a new type of analysis – one that was remote from official ideological discourse or conservative agitprop. In this respect, government circles were sometimes much more open than the party apparatus, which was packed with Brezhnevites, even if their influence was counterbalanced by the tendency on the part of some departments and secretariats to have their own brains trust. Andropov, who probably initiated this trend, introduced some very bright, forward-looking people into his department.[3] Following the fall of the regime, many of them were to demonstrate an intellectual and moral capacity that imparts credibility to their accounts of the past.

This educated urban society harboured much more than the encouraging phenomena we have just referred to. Politically, it produced not only enlightened reformers but also reactionaries and hardliners of various hues. But we have chosen to focus here on the novelty and complexity of the urban reality that the regime had to confront, and not on any particular political current – especially given that such currents can readily switch direction.

WHAT DID THE ECONOMY 'SAY'?

The functioning and performance of the economy was becoming ever more of a problem. A fatal dichotomy seemed to be operative: as the new social structure expanded, economic growth rates went on declining. It suffices to indicate that the rate of growth of national income (according to Western estimates), having reached a respectable 5.7 per cent a year in the 1950s (almost as rapid as during the first five-year plan), dropped to 5.2 per cent in the 1960s, 3.7 in the first half of the 1970s, and 2 per cent in 1980–5.[4]

Robert Davies has confirmed this picture. From the mid–1970s, the Soviet growth rate fell so low that for the first time since the 1920s GNP was increasing less rapidly than in the USA, and much less rapidly than in several newly industrialized countries. Behind such data lay an ever more intricate reality that eluded all economic or political regulation. Economic agencies and scholars knew that the situation was becoming increasingly acute.

No wonder, then, that the man in charge of the whole edifice, Prime Minister Kosygin, had already asked the Academy of Sciences in 1966 to assess things from the standpoint of competitiveness with the USA. The Academy had a section responsible for 'competition with capitalism',

---

3 Based on the memoirs of some of his collaborators – among them, Arbatov, Shakhnazarov, Burlatsky, Cherniaev and Beketin (editor of the outstanding political review, *Svobodnaia Mysl'*).

4 See E. J. Hobsbawm, *Age of Extremes*, London 1994, p. 400, citing Gur Ofer, 'Soviet Economic Growth, 1928–1985', *Journal of Economic Literature*, vol. XXV, no. 4, December 1987, p. 1778.

and thus could be asked to do this without irking Gosplan or the Central Statistical Office, which regularly supplied the government with comparative data on the development of the Western economies. The report in question, commissioned by the Council of Ministers, was probably finished at the end of 1966 and presented to the government at the beginning of 1967. The study, which was wholly in the spirit of Kosygin's economic reforms (officially launched in 1965 and the focus of heated debate), sought to impart a sense of urgency that might strengthen the reformers' hand. The picture of the economy offered to the government and Gosplan was stark. Lack of access to Kosygin's archives means that we cannot tell what he thought of the situation, but the text is the best clue we possess as to his own anxieties about the system's vitality. Moreover, the report did not breathe a word about the burden of military expenditure, which was blocking economic development. It made do with arguing that higher wages and expanded production of consumer goods were a precondition for the whole economy embarking on a course of accelerated technological progress.[5] But Kosygin certainly knew all this already from other sources.

We know that the Academy's economists demonstrated that the USSR was lagging behind on all key indicators, except in what were regarded as the leading branches at the end of the nineteenth century. Conservatives hostile to Kosygin's projects probably claimed that improving economic management would suffice to eliminate waste and increase resources, without interfering with the system. This was a way of suggesting that the waste was attributable to Kosygin ... But if Kosygin was absorbed with the problem, he was not responsible for it: waste was the effect – not the cause – of the malady. Investigating its breadth and depth would help to identify the blockages more clearly.

---

5 Academician Yevgeny Fedoseev, who presented the findings of this inquiry into the 'essential problems and perspectives of the competition between the USSR, the United States, and other important capitalist countries' on 5 August 1966 (as instructed by the Council of Ministers in April 1966), explained that the study was conducted by the Institute of the World Economy and International Relations of the Academy of Sciences of the USSR, with the collaboration of Gosplan's director, Baibakov, who received the following instructions from Kosygin on 15 March: (1) discuss the Academy's report at the session of Gosplan's collegium, in the presence of representatives of the Academy, so as to include the relevant conclusions and recommendations in the text of the next five-year plan, currently in preparation; and (2) present the relevant texts to the members of the Presidium of the Council of Ministers.

The task was entrusted to a Commission for the Elimination of Waste equipped with considerable powers, and certainly with Kosygin's support, even if his opponents were also interested in such a commission (it might actually have been their initiative).

Appointed in 1966, after having been renamed the Commission for Economizing State Resources, it was composed of the heads of the inter-sectoral ministries and agencies (Gosplan, Finances, Statistics, Labour and Wages, Gossnab). With the help of other agencies, its task was to study the system's key sectors (we do not know whether its remit extended to the huge military–industrial complex). The Commission's labours yielded an enormous report examining the work of administrative bodies in most areas (including research, investment, economic branches, culture and public health). It almost resembled the medical examination of a gigantic body that was ailing all over, conducted by a hospital's staff in its entirety. The facts and figures were surely known to Kosygin, but it may be (as we have suggested) that the initiative was a double-edged sword. Moreover, the 'doctors' had nothing to say about how to cure the patient.

Among other data, the commission had used material supplied by the State Control Commission, which detailed, for example, wastage and loss of raw materials; the enormous amount of damage suffered by materials as they were being transported; the waste of fuel and electricity; the accumulation of non-saleable products; the production of goods that were too heavy and/or too primitive on account of obsolescent production techniques and methods; and the costly use of coal from very remote regions when it was readily available nearby at much lower cost.[6]

Here are just a few examples. The importance of pipes and pipelines in the economy was enormous. Yet the Soviet economy was continuing to produce metallic pipes rather than reinforced concrete pipes (e.g. for water mains), even though the latter were between 30 and 40 per cent less expensive even taking account of the investment required to switch to this type of production. In addition, using them would make possible a saving in metal of 80–90 per cent and their lifespan was three times greater. Yet the 1966 plan anticipated the production of only a small quantity of modern pipes, as opposed to the requisite 1 million cubic metres.

6   RGAE, 4372, 66, 670, LL. 31–53, 54–66, and LL. 67–91.

Another costly anomaly was factories accumulating reserves of materials (raw materials and finished products) greatly in excess of authorized norms. These were often stored in unsuitable premises, sometimes in the open air, where they were vulnerable to bad weather and pilfering. Enterprises refused to sell them on to others in need of them, even though they had the right to do so. In defiance of the regulations, factories also often used considerable resources to pay wages for exceeding production targets in the case of goods for which there was little demand. Measures had been proposed to compel managers to reduce reserve stocks to an acceptable level.

Another problem was growing distribution costs, which represented 5.31 per cent of retail price sale in 1958 and 6.25 per cent in 1965. Furthermore, the cost of work canteens had risen sharply in the same period, on account of the loss of goods while they were being transported or stored, low-quality packaging, and the overpayment of personnel (and also because of the payment of high fines).

Many enterprises offered wage increases that outstripped improvements in labour productivity. In the first half of 1966, 11 per cent of industrial, commercial and transport enterprises had acted thus, running up a wage overdraft of 200 million roubles.

Because of the illegal dismissal of workers, the government was incurring serious costs. In 1965, in 60 per cent of the cases brought before them, tribunals had ordered the reinstatement of sacked workers; and paying the wages they had lost cost 2 million roubles every year, while the officials responsible for the illegal dismissals went unpunished.

Losses attributable to shortage of stock and misappropriation of goods in commercial organizations and the food industry were estimated at 300 million roubles. The culprits were referred to the courts, but the cases were long-drawn-out and the payment of damages very slow. Many enterprises were in no hurry to sue the culprits.

The situation in commerce was repeated in the fields of research and culture, where facilities were underused and heavily overstaffed. Moreover, enterprises took a considerable time to apply technological inventions to production. The report provided a list of products and equipment that had been developed years ago, but which were still not in use. Once again, the losses were staggering.

For its part, the Popular Control Committee had investigated a large number of industrial enterprises and added its contribution to the litany of complaints. In particular, it had discovered that the production costs fixed by the plan were invariably exaggerated. The determination of these costs did not take account of the fact that the costs in previous years, which served as a base-line, had already been overstated on account of waste, mismanagement, overproduction, and poor use of productive capacity. The Committee did not skimp when it came to listing inefficiencies and waste, but we should note the 'gentility' of its recommendations to the ministries that swallowed up resources. It merely drew 'the ministries' attention to the need to plan a reduction in production costs more carefully'. But what incentive did they have to do that?

As ever when a control commission or task force was appointed to look into a problem, it presented a picture of utter chaos where nothing worked. It must therefore be made clear that many enterprises functioned reasonably well: otherwise, the whole economy would have collapsed long ago. But the system was approaching the critical point where 'waste' was going to render it a historical aberration: a system that produced more costs than goods.

If it continued to limp along, it was because the country possessed immense resources. Hence another paradox: a very wealthy country with very low consumption. In sum, the commission suggested that everyone had to learn to be more thrifty. In fact, the problem did not stem exclusively from wastage. No less amazing was the fact that the planning system perpetuated, even exacerbated, inefficiency and waste in the production process, when by definition it should have prevented them.

By now, purely economic and technological measures would not do the trick. Some experts thought that reserves for economic development were to be found in the costly arms sector, since, according to Gosplan's calculations, 40 per cent of all new machines manufactured in the USSR were intended for 'special projects'. Was it not time for them to help revive the civilian sector? But this was another pipe dream. In the military–industrial complex itself, technological progress was rooted in waste and utter disregard for costs. Excessive secrecy (and the excessive power of this complex) aggravated the situation. Whatever the achievements (and they were numerous, but remained in the notorious 'closed cities' that took a lot without giving anything in return), the economic spin-off for civilian industry was non-existent.

On the other hand, the Soviet 'planning' system, whose targets were almost exclusively quantitative, failed to establish sufficiently well-thought-out correlations between these targets and the incentive system; or to ensure an overall balance between the main socio-economic factors conducive to scientific and technical progress and to the satisfaction of social needs that were changing and growing. Soviet planners knew full well that the most advanced Western economies established these correlations successfully – most of the time, at least. A formula for outperforming the West existed on paper in Gosplan's offices; and things seemed to have worked out in the regime's early years and during the war. But that simply meant that pathologies could be tolerated for a time. With the economy growing and changing, unaltered planning methods were becoming a fetter: they only perpetuated – even exacerbated – the pathologies. The planning system was in disarray and decaying together with the whole politico-economic statist model.

That is why, as far as Kosygin was concerned, the task was much more complicated than squeezing savings out of each agency (industrial, commercial, etc.). The real task was nothing less than Herculean.

24

LABOUR FORCE AND DEMOGRAPHY: A CONUNDRUM

A good indicator for assessing and understanding both the growth of the 1960s and the decline of the 1970s is to be found in the complex of factors which, astonishingly enough, created a growing labour shortage.

As we saw in Part Two from Gosplan's own research, in 1965 the main problem stemmed from a distorted geographical distribution of labour: some areas had a surplus, and yet it was difficult to persuade workers to move; others experienced shortages that were difficult to make good.

As the years passed, it became ever more clear that planning methods had not progressed sufficiently beyond the original 1930s model. This consisted in allocating investments in abundance, while relying on the system's ability to mobilize massive labour reserves when and where required. Everything was different now. In the first place, the planning and education systems had to train large numbers of qualified personnel – technicians and high-level specialists, as well as scientific researchers – and this was a task they acquitted rather successfully. But from 1968 onwards, an entirely new problem arose: the spectre of an outright labour shortage (not just of certain categories) – and without any real prospect of remedying it.

How are we to explain such a situation in a country of 270 million inhabitants, a higher population than the USA's, but with an economy and national income that were much smaller? In the previous chapter, the report we summarized at some length revealed that 'waste' was absolutely central. The factors underlying it also hampered productivity and allowed for growth exclusively through an injection of huge sums of investment, which issued in quantitative expansion – a formula that could only lead, in the more or less short term, into a dead end if nothing was done. Some had grasped this logic at a time when the Soviet economy still seemed to be in reasonably good shape. The plan was unable to ensure a fit between investment targets, output, and an adequate supply of labour. Numbers for the quantity of labour required did exist, but there were no coherent policies and measures for guaranteeing its supply. That in turn would have required appropriate social policies. In the past, labour requirements had been met by the spontaneous gravitation of labour or its mobilization. These mechanisms were no longer operative, and everything was complicated still further by demographic factors.

The articulation of the relevant factors in a situation where labour could no longer be 'mobilized' was analysed by an expert in 1968 before a selected audience of top officials. The lecturer – E. V. Kasimovsky – was head of the Research Institute of the Russian Federation's Gosplan, and his lecture was entitled 'Problems of Labour and the Standard of Living'.[1] His richly documented presentation surveyed the problems of labour, labour productivity, and the geographical distribution of labour resources. Here we shall cite some key points.

In recent years, large urban centres had experienced labour shortages, to the tune of tens of thousands not only in Leningrad but also in Moscow, Kuibyshev, Cheliabinsk and Sverdlovsk. The situation was even worse in Siberia. 'This is a new period', said Kasimovsky, 'and we have never seen anything like it before.' No doubt demographic projections held out the hope that the next five-year plan would see a strong influx of young people into the labour market. But they also anticipated that this increase would drop off thereafter. In 1961–5, 2.6 million young people had arrived on the labour market; an additional 4.6 million were expected for the 1966–70 plan and 6.3 million for 1971–5. But the figure subsided to 4.6 million for 1976–80.

Added to this decline in the number of young people arriving on the labour market was the fact that the introduction of compulsory secondary school education would rule out employing fourteen- to fifteen-year-olds in production. In 1965 the Russian Federation had 287,000 young workers of that age, and it would still have 263,000 in 1970. But the figure would fall to 130,000 in 1980.

Obviously, demographic factors were introducing a new blockage.

---

1   GARF, f. A-10005, op. 1, d. 48, LL. 2–62, 16 September 1968.

The predicted reduction in the youth cohorts entering production was attributable to falling birth rates, which had been especially marked since the beginning of the 1960s. In 1950 the rate was still 27 births per 1,000, but in 1967 it was no more than 17 per 1,000 (14.5 per 1,000 in the Russian Federation itself). Despite the drop in mortality in these years, falling birth rates had substantially reduced natural population increase, from 17 per cent in 1950 to 10 per cent in 1967 (less than 8 per cent in Russia). Birth rates had fallen in the twelve Soviet republics – especially in Russia, the Ukraine, Belorussia, Moldavia and Kazakhstan. The phenomenon was especially troubling in the Soviet Union's two metropolises: between 1960 and 1966, Moscow's birth rates had fallen from 7 to 2.2 per 1,000 and Leningrad's from 6.4 to 3 per 1,000. According to some estimates, in 1972 Moscow's mortality rate would be 3 per cent higher than its birth rate, and in 1973 Leningrad's would be 2 per cent higher. In 2000, the figure for deaths would be 2.5 times that for births – equivalent to a population decrease of several hundreds of thousands.

Over the Union as a whole, the drop in birth rates in towns was higher than in the countryside. But an utterly novel trend had emerged: overall birth rates in the Russian Federation, where a quarter of the USSR's rural population lived, were lower than in the towns. Of the seventy-one administrative units of the Russian Federation, eighteen had birth rates below those of towns. In areas like Novgorod, Pskov and Kalinin, birth rates were lower than mortality rates.

The rate of reproduction of the population was plummeting. For the whole USSR, it had dropped from 1.4 in 1938–9 to 1.12 in 1968, which was lower than that of leading capitalist countries (1.56 in the USA, 1.13 in Canada, 1.38 in France, and 1.44 in the UK).

In the USSR (and the Russian Federation), women had an average of 2.6 children (1.9 in towns and 3.3 in the countryside). Research by the Central Statistical Office indicated that an average of 3 children was required for normal population reproduction. This meant that the urban population was no longer reproducing itself, but growing only thanks to an influx from the countryside.

The decline in birth rates in the USSR was more rapid than that experienced by the other socialist countries and the capitalist countries. What would its effects be on the supply of labour? Some demographers argued that it presented no threat to living standards. But Kasimovsky differed: if the decline in births persisted, workers' living standards would suffer.

Population density remained low in the USSR – thirty-two inhabitants per square kilometre – and was lower still in Siberia. Falling birth rates would slow down any increase in population density and thus further reduce the prospects of populating Siberia, which was now a major problem. If birth rates did not pick up, the outcome could be stagnation, or even reduction, in living standards, which were already too low.

THE CAUSES OF DECLINING BIRTH RATES

Births had fallen during the war and had not yet recovered. The structure of the population in terms of sex and age had changed. In the first instance, this involved the disparity between men and women. But there was also a gap in the 30–50 age groups. In 1959, the 20–24 age group counted 106 women for 100 men in towns and 98 women for 100 men in the countryside. In 1967, the corresponding figures were 98 women for 100 men in towns and 95 women for 100 men in the countryside. Thus, the situation had almost been normalized in the towns, but it had deteriorated in the countryside. For the 25–29 age group, in 1959 there were more women than men in the towns; and in 1967 the situation was worse. In the countryside there were 131 women for 100 men. These imbalances represented a serious handicap in terms of labour supplies and demographics. They obviously had a major impact on birth rates and the reproduction of the population.

The sharp increase in the number of women employed in production (19 million in 1950 and around 40 million in 1968) was also a factor. The proportion of women in production in the Russian Federation had doubled. But the birth rate among working women (workers or employees) was 30–40 per cent lower than that of women working at home or on the family plot. The main reason was the greater difficulty experienced by working women in caring for their children. Many of them had no relatives to help out and could not afford a nanny. In many towns there were no places in the crèches and kindergartens. The fact that women (several million of them) were often employed in very heavy, non-mechanized labour – mining, machine construction, metallurgy – was a further element. Kasimovsky reckoned that the time had come to revise the list of jobs open to women, so that they could both work and bear children. Another well-known factor was birth control: the number of abortions exceeded that of births.

In the first quarter of 1968, the research institute of the Russian

Federation's Gosplan, the Health Ministry, the Finance Ministry and the Central Statistical Office studied the causes of falling birth rates in thirteen large towns and ten rural regions in Bashkiria, Krasnodarskii krai, Kaliniskaia and Pskov. The responses of 1,600 women asked about the reasons for their abortions confirmed the results of an earlier inquiry among 26,000 women: 22 per cent of them stated that they did not want a baby because of inadequate housing, which would only deteriorate with the arrival of a baby; 18 per cent mentioned the difficulty of finding a crèche; 14 per cent believed that their income was insufficient and would fall with a baby. These three reasons accounted for half of the causes invoked.

Although house construction had been accelerated, the situation remained unsatisfactory in many towns. Places for children in crèches and kindergartens were also increasing, but only half of existing demand was met. Moreover, despite the rise in the minimum wage to 60–70 roubles a month, household incomes remained too low – especially in the case of single-parent families, which were quite common. Benefits were given to only a small number of people, and more substantial help was offered to women only with the birth of their fifth child. In 1967 a mere 3.5 million women received family allowance. Of these, 2.1 million had five or more children. Many women had abortions for health reasons, often as a result of heavy labour. Because the period of convalescence following an abortion was not paid, many women resumed work immediately, which often led to complications and even sterility.

Birth rates also suffered from increased instability in conjugal relations. In recent years, the number of divorces had risen steeply, especially in the countryside. In 1960, there were roughly nine marriages for every divorce; by 1966, only three.

In the conclusion to his report, Kasimovsky indicated that, some months prior to this inquiry, a population study laboratory had finally been created at Moscow University (an institute of the Academy of Sciences that had existed before the war had not yet been re-established). Measures to increase the birth rate and a study of the whole issue had been submitted to the government and the Central Committee.

We can assume that some of the problems were attributable to living standards in the USSR. An author like Mironov would be inclined to detect the effects of modernization, which are evident in all urban societies. But that would be to underestimate some of the socially deleterious effects of modernization, especially in Soviet conditions. We must therefore round off his unduly positive picture by pointing to dangerous side-effects overlooked by him.

WERE THERE ANY LABOUR FORCE RESERVES?

Falling birth rates were not the only reason for the problem in recruiting labour. It was becoming increasingly difficult to tap the reserves represented by those who still worked at home or on private plots. In 1960 the people engaged in such activities still represented between a quarter and a fifth of the reserve labour force (19 per cent in Russia), but by 1970 the percentage was reckoned not to exceed 8 per cent. In addition, a distinction had to be made between those employed in this sector and real reserves. In fact, only half of those so employed accepted the idea of going to work outside their homes (and half of them stipulated various conditions). Moreover, the method used to count this potential labour force was faulty and a source of disappointment. In the Russian Federation, 5,700,000 had been recruited to work in the state economy in 1960–5, but the total for the next plan was 1,000,000. Projections for the one after indicated that 500,000 might be the maximum, and the number of people working their own plots might increase sharply. Furthermore, there was a great deal of regional variation in the situation. Let us note in passing that the majority of those working in and around the house, cultivating plots, or keeping animals, were women.

Thus, labour reserves were pretty much exhausted. Some local resources still existed here and there, but were difficult to release. Many people preferred working at home, since it was more likely to improve their standard of living.

Another possible source of labour was pensioners. The population was ageing and the share of pensioners in it was rising. Many areas that lacked labour had developed social services to attract pensioners. But this was a limited source. In 1965, 1.9 million pensioners were employed in the state economy; estimates anticipated 2 million in 1970 and perhaps 2.5 million in 1980.

The authorities certainly understood that development depended less on labour reserves than on improving labour productivity. Yet labour productivity rates, measured over the long term, were in decline. Labour productivity had increased by 7.7 per cent per annum between 1951 and 1960, but only by 5.6 per cent between 1961 and 1965. In 1962 there had been a temporary recovery to 6 per cent. In 1967, however, there was a new drop as a result of a sharp decrease in growth in agriculture. The rate of growth in some leading industrial branches was still high. Yet overall, it lagged substantially behind the main capitalist countries. In the USA, labour productivity was 2.5 times higher in industry and services and 4.5 times higher in agriculture (according to the Soviet Central Statistical Office). The experts sounded the alert: if productivity did not increase, the USSR would not even catch up with the West by 2000! Improving this crucial indicator was now an overriding task: the means and measures to achieve it had to be found.

POPULATION AND LABOUR MIGRATION

Better specialization and cooperation between enterprises and industrial branches was indispensable. Decisions to this effect had been taken for Leningrad and Moscow, but they would take some years to be implemented and bear fruit. The most urgent thing was to mobilize labour reserves. However, their geographical distribution presented an additional problem. Of the 128 million inhabitants of the Russian Federation (to which we shall restrict ourselves here), only 25 million lived in eastern regions (basically meaning the Urals and especially Siberia). This imbalance was hampering the economic development of these regions, where the strongest economic growth should have occurred given the abundance of natural resources there. To achieve the targets that had been fixed, it was necessary to transfer 2.6 million people (the period being referred to is apparently 1968–80). Yet in the last fifteen years, population movements had been in the opposite direction. People were leaving Russia for other republics to the tune of 200,000 a year on average and the figures for the eastern regions were even higher. Between 1950 and 1960, Russia had lost 2.8 million inhabitants to other republics. Even more disturbing was the fact that in Russia itself people were leaving areas where labour was in short supply, and moving to areas where there was a surplus. What attracted them to Northern Caucasus or the Stavropol region was a better climate and more developed small-scale farming.

The countryside suffered from its own share of miseries. Labour productivity was between four and five times lower than that of the USA, but with regional variations. The sex and age imbalance in the rural population was getting worse. There was high, unplanned migration to the towns, which was all the more alarming in that 73 per cent of the migrants were under the age of twenty-five and 65 per cent of them were women in the same age group. The proportion of young people and of thirty- to forty-year-olds in the rural population was shrinking, whereas that of older people or those incapable of working was expanding. Those who were leaving were precisely the ones whom the countryside most needed to service the increased mechanization and electrification of agriculture. In 1968 there was only one able-bodied male for every two kolkhoz households. The average age of a working member of a kolkhoz was fifty and many worked beyond retirement age.

The overall picture was thus disturbing. The dangerously distorted age profile and the conjunction of declining labour productivity and departures for the towns were bleeding the countryside dry. Accordingly, this traditional, seemingly inexhaustible source of labour could no longer even provide for its own needs. The search for labour reserves now resembled scraping the barrel. Among those who preferred to work on their own plots (particularly women), many would only accept part-time work outside the home. But their number was also dwindling rapidly – not to mention the fact that jobs which removed them from their plots (especially in the countryside) would entail an immediate drop in food production.

Did this already amount to a crisis? At all events, one was certainly brewing. The documents we used in Part Two indicate that, according to Gosplan's experts, the auguries for the 1971–5 five-year plan were far from favourable.

As labour became a rare commodity, there was a proliferation of studies, research and conferences. A continuous flow of texts ran from Gosplan to the Central Committee and from the State Labour Committee to the Council of Ministers. One expert put it bluntly: 'For the country as a whole, I believe that our labour resources are practically exhausted.' When we recall that at the same time many, if not all, enterprises were heavily overstaffed, the absurdity of this complete dead-end on the labour question (to say nothing of other aspects of the economic system) should have served to put the leadership on constant high alert. And yet, the enormous flow of information and analysis, which offered a picture of monumental mismanagement and foresaw this supposed super-state rapidly approaching a point of no return, created no visible stir. The Politburo was content to produce endless resolutions enjoining everyone to be more efficient.

25

THE BUREAUCRATIC MAZE

It is now time for us to turn once again to those who actually ran (we have not as yet said 'owned') the economic branches and services. It is impossible to tackle any aspect of Soviet society, economy and politics without constantly running into the administrative class, whether state bureaucrats, party apparatchiks, or both in their intricate inter-relations. We are therefore going to revert to this phenomenon, starting out from the findings of the Commission for the Elimination of Waste,* whose remit extended to the bureaucracy.

The history of state and party institutions is full of constant structuring and restructuring: structures were set up, split, abolished, re-established. By contrast, the last fifteen years of the regime witnessed great stability in this respect. Khrushchev's disbanding of more than one hundred industrial ministries at the stroke of a pen was the most spectacular anti-bureaucratic initiative – the only one on such a scale. And it is worth repeating that they were all reconstituted in 1965. The institutional problem we are referring to here – a systemic feature in itself – consisted in a kind of incessant tinkering, a form of 'bureaucratic neurosis' that the system was cured of only by catching another illness. The administration possessed a lot of weight, became highly influential, and sought to curb the Politburo's despotic power. The bureaucratic neurosis was a way of evading real reform, on the basis of the idea – dear to Stalin – that all that was needed was to 'correct' the administrators.

---

*   The Commission for the Elimination of Waste was subsequently renamed the Commission for Economizing State Resources (see chapter 23). Here we shall refer to it simply as the 'Anti-Waste Commission'.

All this requires some explanation. Tracking the vagaries of the administrative system is no easy task.[1] Despite having been a prime mover in Soviet history, the bureaucracy (and its administrative networks) has been insufficiently examined. Its study takes us to the very heart of the system, revealing that the bureaucracy which ran the state virtually came to own it. Changes in its structure, self-image and status must be examined not only in the framework of administrative history, but also in a political optic, contrary to the widespread view that the chief political features of the system were embodied in the party. Under Stalin, the bureaucracy was already an indispensable co-ruler, but unstable and fragile on account of the relative youth of its structures and the novelty of its tasks. Moreover, its members were 'suspect' because Stalin understood and feared its potential for consolidating itself and its thirst for power. The situation changed profoundly in the post-Stalin period: initially still deeply marked by the country's plebeian and rural traditions, during the 1950s and '60s the bureaucracy became a fully urban phenomenon in a society that was itself now urbanized. In its upper echelons, it was now a solidly established and firmly entrenched power. This emancipation of the bureaucracy was one of the key features of the whole post-Stalinist period. The state and party bureaucracy put an end to the arbitrary practices that had made its situation so precarious under Stalin. Stalinism was thereby replaced by a fully bureaucratic model that rapidly acquired a quasi-monopoly over all strategic positions of power.

Here we must recall the speed of social change in the 1950s and '60s and the consequent drastic alteration of the socio-historical landscape. The construction of a still fragile bureaucracy under Stalin, and its consolidation as a monopolistic power structure in the years immediately after his death, occurred in a primarily agrarian society. Its monopolistic position in the state and entrenchment in power preceded the definitive transition to an urban civilization. An old characteristic of Russian history, pointed out by Miliukov and reformulated by Trotsky, was once again replicated here: the establishment of a strong state

---

1 However, helpful information can be found in the 1986 and 1995 editions of T. P. Korzhikhina, *Sovetskoe Gosudarstvo i ego Uchrezhdeniia. Noiabr' 1917 – Dekabr' 1991* (Moscow); and in the very valuable reference work on *Soviet Government Officials, 1922–1941: A Handlist*, edited by R. W. Davies and his colleagues at the Centre of Russian and East European Studies, University of Birmingham, England.

preceded the development of society and enabled the former to dominate the latter. But the Soviet era also witnessed the converse: successive waves of social development on a grand scale generated new systemic characteristics and a whole series of complex phenomena, which we are seeking to untangle in this book.

The bureaucratic phenomenon would unquestionably become more palpable if we had some idea of its size, internal structure and power. We already know that ascertaining the precise number of people employed by the state and other administrative agencies is not straightforward, since much depended on the criteria used by those who counted them – in particular, the Central Statistical Office. The best data are probably those produced by the census of administrative agencies conducted in 1970. Just reading this material and enumerating its results discloses the complex, tentacular character of the phenomenon. Here we shall simply offer a brief synthesis.

The census focused on the administrative personnel of all state institutions and supplied a breakdown between the various important administrative units, enterprises and organizations. Each republican administration was presented separately, as was local government. This abundance of statistics is mentioned only to remind readers that it does exist.

The Central Statistical Office's computing centre explained that on this occasion it had included everyone not directly engaged in productive activity. Where there was ambiguity, they had split the difference: for example, an engineer working on the shop floor was not regarded as a member of the administrative personnel; but an engineer who worked in the factory's administrative office was – unless his job was planning and design work. Auxiliary and service staff were included, albeit in a separate category. Guards were a separate category again, probably because they were better paid than auxiliary staff in the strict sense.

On 15 September 1970 – the date of the census – the total administrative apparatus consisted of some 13,874,200 employees, or 15 per cent of the working population (workers and employees). Top managers (*rukovoditeli*) and their deputies numbered 4,143,400 (this encompassed all institutions at central, republican and regional levels). The next most important category was that of 'chief specialists' and their deputies, containing all the engineers, technicians, agronomists and so on, working in administration: some 2,080,400. Then came engineer-economists, economists and planners: 543,400. The rest were distributed between accountants, statisticians, computer scientists, office employees and auxiliary staff.

One particular type of institution was singled out for separate treatment – namely, central ministries and their equivalents in the republics, as well as the other major agencies of comparable status and importance (state committees). The organizations under them employed the bulk of the country's working population – 49,708,377 workers and employees. Administering all these workers were 7,996,116 officials, of whom 2,539,797 belonged to the top managerial category. In other words, one in three of them was a 'boss'.[2]

Above this layer we find the very senior officials – some hundreds of people in charge of gigantic institutions. From another source we learn that around 1977 there were 32 USSR-level ministries (25 of them industrial) and 30 Union ministries that had equivalents at republican level (10 of them industrial).[3] To these must be added some 500 institutions that were referred to as 'ministries', but which were government agencies in the 'autonomous' republics – something important for the study of local elites, but not the topmost stratum.

Before the 1970 census, the figure of 8 million was generally given for the number of employees in state administration, 2.5 million of whom were described as *nachal'niki* ('heads'). With the census, the picture changed to a more realistic total of 13 million, with some 4 million *nachal'niki*. The statisticians had rightly separated out another category: the members of the central ministerial core, who constituted the real ruling stratum. It involved six Union-level state committees (Science and Technology, International Trade, Meteorology, etc.), twelve committees with dual competence (Union and republics), and agencies like the KGB, Gosplan, the Central Statistical Office, the Finance Ministry, and so on. The officials who headed these institutions were all members of the central government.

To this hard core, composed of the heads of some eighty major government institutions, we must add the members of the Politburo, the heads of the party apparatus (at central and republican levels), and party secretaries in the regions and the capitals – a select group of some 1,000

---

2 RGAE, f. 1562, op. 47, d. 1896, LL. 1–47. These are the results of the census (*edinovremennyi uchet*) conducted by the Central Statistical Office, carefully edited and presented. The document was produced by the Office's computing centre. See also RGAE, f. 1562, op. 47, d. 1897, LL. 1–211, vols 1–2.

3 See Korzhikhina, *Sovetskoe Gosudarstvo i ego Uchrezhdeniia*.

people (of whom slightly fewer than half were Central Committee members). All of these were top players, mindful of the interests of the 2.5 million people who underpinned them. If the 'ruling elite' is what we are interested in, then the first figure (1,000) is the relevant one; but if the 'ruling class' is the subject of our study, then the second (2,500,000) is appropriate. A number of intellectuals, scientists and artists belonged here – some in the narrower circle, most in the wider one. But this is beyond the scope of our immediate concerns.

THE 'ENVIRONMENT' IN WHICH THE RULERS WERE FORMED

When wading through the mass of files and documents relating to the Politburo, the Orgburo and the Secretariat, one is struck by the intensity of the contacts between state bureaucrats and party bureaucrats within each apparatus. A factory manager, who might also be a bureaucrat in the formal as well as the pejorative sense, was in daily contact with people from other social groups – workers and technicians. By contrast, top leaders encountered workers only during official visits; typically, they made a speech and the workers applauded. The poverty of such contacts is normal for rulers, as is the fact that their milieu mainly consists of bureaucrats and that the whole politico-administrative process unfolds within it. Inside the party apparatus itself, from the Politburo to party cells, personnel issues took up a lot of time, together with minor economic and administrative details. General issues were reserved for a very small number of figures. Such was the environment and activity in which Molotov, Malenkov and Khrushchev were immersed; and this was what shaped them. An in-depth knowledge of the nuts and bolts was a sign of their mastery, and they exhibited it to impress their audience or interlocutors.

On the other hand, the capacity to deal with major problems – normally a leader's main task – was utterly lacking in most of them. They devoted most of their time to resolving budgetary and salary issues, and signing the tens of thousands of decrees drafted by various agencies. Such activities pertain not to the remit of political leadership in the proper sense, but to that of a pernickety inspector who deludes himself that he is the master of the situation (when real mastery consists in a profound grasp of broader realities). Their subsidiary skills (shrewdness, cunning, the ability to construct a clientele) mainly served their personal power games. Behind them and this 'passion for control', which consumed their best efforts and skills, we can discern the waning of their political power and their highly coveted ability to control all the levers. We may note in passing that in 1966 a very powerful state control agency, whose running costs outstripped those of the Health and Culture ministries combined, was disbanded by Brezhnev simply to counter the influence of its highly ambitious head, Shelepin.

The leaders' formation by their milieu was closely bound up with the Soviet principle that the national economy was state property. This was the source of the bureaucracy's monopolistic power and of the only type of leadership such a state was capable of producing.

The administrative strata themselves underwent changes as a result of the country's ongoing urbanization. Their educational level, professionalism, living standards and cultural habits were so many factors that necessarily impacted on intra- and inter-bureaucratic functioning. Even if the impression persisted that the general-secretary was absolute master (full stop!), the system was no longer a genuine autocracy. The general-secretary could dominate the party apparatus (though he was also heavily dependent on it), but the actual exercise of power and policy implementation took the form, as has been said, of extended bargaining between different government agencies. The latter were adept at manipulating the formal and informal lines of authority. Their rights, official and unofficial, went on expanding, to the point where their objections, counter-proposals and demands had become a component of political and administrative procedure, acquiring a quasi-constitutional status that we know too little about. For example, we have already seen that the centre was incapable of compelling the ministries to comply with planning procedures. In numerous respects, they acted exclusively in accordance with their own interests.

Given that nothing could be done without the ministries and other such agencies, events, or, more precisely, the powerful contradictory trends that were at work, forced the system's rulers to adapt not only to changing social realities, but also to the 'sociology' of the bureaucracy itself. Various trends characteristic of the bureaucratic universe can be identified as 'system-making'. After all, the state and its leading administrative personnel had become almost indistinguishable.

The formation of the complex structures of this stratum is a crucial phenomenon. As we have seen, its numbers exceeded 2 million in 1970, to restrict ourselves to the most sensitive posts. Their power allowed them to dictate acceptance of their insatiable drive for higher living standards, more perks, ever more power, and also toleration of a degree of corruption. They were the mainstay of the system. Hence another trend can be discerned, leading to the de facto amalgamation of these upper echelons of the state and party to form a single power complex. The most important ministers were members of the Central Committee, and some (KGB, Foreign Affairs, Defence) had a seat in the Politburo. Paradoxically, what facilitated this amalgamation was the procedures of the *nomenklatura*. Restored after the war to put the administrative monster in its place, it rapidly revealed its other side, which pointed in the opposite direction. If the whole elite was composed of 'nomenk-laturists' – all of them high-ranking officials, but often also high-ranking party functionaries – the question of who actually controlled whom is not without point. *Nomenklatura* appointees and the apparatuses under them were running the state: this became the overarching reality of the Soviet polity.

In these circumstances, what exactly was the role of the party or, more precisely, of its leadership? Evidently, it was a powerful apparatus that relied on the governmental administrative machinery to rule the country. But the impression that the former controlled the latter, because the bureaucracy was its *nomenklatura*, is misleading. The Polit-buro and its apparatus were also an administration and, by this token, formed part of a much larger bureaucracy. The state administration had employees and workers; the party had employees and members. To insist that these members controlled nothing would be superfluous. Since this 'party' possessed some curious features, it is appropriate to put quotation marks around the term.

FROM A 'ONE-PARTY' TO A 'NO-PARTY' SYSTEM

However paradoxical at first sight, we are going to explore the hypothesis that the 'ruling party' did not in fact hold power. This seems surreal, but Soviet history is replete with myths and shams, misnomers and deliria. Thus, such resounding slogans as 'collectivization', 'dicta-torship of the proletariat', 'communism', 'democratic centralism', 'Marxism-Leninism' and 'vanguard' had little to do with reality, at least most of the time.

As the years passed, the regime's initial orientation towards the working and peasant classes and masses gave way to a different orien-tation – towards the state administration, its 'organs', and the various categories of 'officials'. This all-encompassing process of 'statization', whereby the state's centrality became absolute, culminated in a cult of the state, which represented the mindset of the upper echelons of the bureaucracy. In private discussions, but also in public, we find top party officials declaring that government ministries deal only with sectoral matters, whereas the party alone concerns itself with the higher interests of the state. Obviously they were responding to ministerial circles, which asserted precisely the opposite. This enables us better to appreciate what 'statism' meant. Party officials were not claiming that they alone were capable of representing society's interests: they were competing with other bureaucrats to be the better spokesmen for the state and seeking to assert their primacy in the state.

In the 1930s, the organization calling itself the 'party' had already lost its political character; it had been transformed into an administrative network, wherein a hierarchy ruled a rank and file. During the next step, even this administrative creature was deprived of any power: under Stalin, it made no sense to speak of a party in power, given that its institutions did not function, no one asked its members for their views, and the rare occasional congress was just one long clapping session.

It is true that Khrushchev restored power over the party and state to the party's summit (the Central Committee) and its apparatus. However, this made no difference to various key characteristics: rank and-file members still had no political rights and the party remained a ruling hierarchy, devoid of any real political life. Under Stalin, the party had lost power to the supreme leader; after Khrushchev, it kept losing power to the state machine, which ended up absorbing its ruling network, making it into its own spokesman and representative – and this time for good. The process of 'statization' which was so important in the Soviet phenomenon, and probably its main characteristic when it came to the political system, reached its final stage. When the system entered into a prolonged phase of 'stagnation', the party, unable to do anything, powerless to impose far-reaching measures on ministries and other agencies, foundered along with everything else.

We can already formulate some initial conclusions: the 'party' was not actually always in power; and at a certain moment, it stopped being a political party and became one agency among others – the linchpin of an administration. This is why it is appropriate to put the term 'party' in quotation marks. We can even go so far as to venture that the 'one-party' system, on which so much ink has been spilt, eventually became a 'no-party' system. It may well be that if the USSR had possessed a genuine party, engaged in political life and capable of political leadership, it might have escaped its sorry fate and the country been spared a monumental crisis. However, after so many years and waves of historical change, this political structure, based on a powerful apparatus and members deprived of rights, was moth-eaten. No wonder it collapsed so easily, without any need for a strong jolt or storm.

What were the factors and circumstances that led the party system to a quasi-phantom existence, despite the awe inspired, then and now, by the Staraia Ploshchad? It was the transformation of the party into an apparatus – an old phenomenon – that entailed its de facto absorption by and into the bureaucratic realities of the state. The process started when the party became directly immersed in economic and other minutiae that were supposed to be handled by government ministries. Ministerial staff justly sensed that the party was duplicating their work, rather than concentrating on its own. The little-known conflict between Brezhnev and Kosygin over who should represent the country abroad is a good illustration of the problem.

The party's 'identity crisis' – a formula used in Part One to describe the reformist endeavours of 1946–8 – can now be further deciphered. The apparatus had been restructured in 1946 with a view to its rediscovering its political identity by withdrawing from direct supervision of economic life. The argument was that the ministries 'were buying the apparatchiks', the 'party had lost power', and it must revert to its proper functions if it wanted to recover its power. Two years later, however, it was once again restructured for the converse reasons: so that it could interfere in economic affairs and 'control' them. The contradiction was the following: when the party concerned itself with politics, it lost control of the economy and bureaucracy; when it was fully engaged in controlling the economy, and meddled directly with what the ministries were doing and the way they were doing it, it lost its specific functions – even any sense of what they were. The second logic prevailed, and it allowed the party's de facto absorption by the bureaucratic colossus.

It is worth remembering that Lenin and Trotsky (the latter in a letter to the Politburo just before the Eleventh Congress) had raised this problem, and warned Bolshevik leaders that direct meddling in the affairs of economic agencies (as opposed to ruling through them) would encourage the bureaucratization of the party, as well as increasing irresponsibility on the part of the administration. Trotsky argued that just as they had declared that the trade unions should not engage in managing the economy, but should remain trade unions, so the party should remain a party. But things did not turn out that way, prompting Bukharin 1928 to lament a virtual *fait accompli*: 'The party and state apparatuses have merged and it's a calamity.' Following Stalin's death, this was to lead to a further deepening of this trend.

THE ANTI-WASTE COMMISSION AT WORK

Growing labour shortages elicited an almost 'classical' market response. Labour is a commodity and as the state – the principal employer – became more and more dependent on it (and with forced labour no longer an option), it had to confront these shortages in various ways. As a result of the interaction of the factors involved, a different climate and new patterns emerged in labour relations. But this was insufficient to cure the illness ravaging the state economy. The regime brought in more and more measures in response to the pressures and aspirations of different social strata. However, despite the urgent recommendations impressed on it by the Anti-Waste Commission, the State Control Commission, and many other agencies, the regime failed to secure an increase in labour productivity, to prevent enterprises accumulating reserve stocks of labour and raw materials, and to stimulate the sluggish rate of technological innovation. The country's rulers faced a dilemma. On the one hand, they were desperately in need of labour and had to court the labour force. On the other, they also had to court the administrative bodies that managed the labour force. This was not an easy game to play. A 'consensual' modus operandi was now unavoidable; and bargaining with the ministries became the rule. As is always the case with bureaucracies, however, this finally amounted to sharing power with them. There was no such power-sharing with labour, although here too we could point – as we did – to many concessions, improvements and extentions of rights (the same was true for other interests and social groups). This new way of conducting affairs of state, consisting in taking account of all sorts of social pressures and responding to them, is never registered by theorists of 'totalitarianism', for whom dependency remained total and unilateral. (In this instance, one can sympathize with their predicament: by definition, a semi-totalitarian regime is as impossible as a half-pregnant woman.)

Yet this was the major novelty of the post-Stalinist period and certainly contributed to the regime's vitality in the 1960s. But the fact that the bureaucracy which managed the state obtained (or, more precisely, extracted) more than others, and reached an *entente cordiale* with the political leadership, was difficult to reconcile with satisfying the interests of workers and other social strata. Any hopes of maintaining social peace and developing the country were frustrated by a sluggish, wasteful economy. Bureaucratic planning did succeed in modernizing the economy and the 'deal' made with the bureaucracy enhanced its power, but did not improve its performance. Informal agreements with the bureaucrats did not constitute a policy; they amounted to a drift in a direction that aggravated the system's ailments.

Readers are now well aware of the system's malfunctioning and presumably keen to know what the Anti-Waste Commission proposed by way of remedies for government ministries and other agencies. For some conservatives, the indicated road was clear: the solution consisted in greater discipline – 'law and order', as they say in other political contexts. But this was a delusion.

From the outset, the history of state administration had been dominated by the Politburo's endless battles to contain (and even reduce) its expansion and improve its efficiency. The Anti-Waste Commission, which had redefined its function from 'eliminating waste' to the rather less offensive formula of 'saving state resources', met with representatives of the central and republican ministries to prepare a draft proposal, taking account of the mass of data and information it had gathered on each and every branch. Its attempt to find ways of making savings in expenditure on state administration was seemingly rather courageous. Reducing the proliferating cohorts of the bureaucracy had hitherto seemed utterly impossible, given that each administrative machine was run by one of the most powerful figures in the regime. Persuading them to make cuts would be no easy matter. Moreover, some members of the Anti-Waste Commission (its membership is listed in footnote 4 below) themselves ran sizeable administrative departments.

N. Rogovsky, a noted expert and head of Gosplan's labour department, reported on the discussions that took place during the Commission's sessions, and they certainly involved quite a battle.[4] The

---

4 RGAE, 4372, op. 66, d. 670, LL. 175–6, 3 September 1966: the report of a session of the 'commission for saving state resources'. Vested with considerable powers, it was chaired by Gosplan's head, Baibakov, and included: Starovsky, head of the Central Statistical Office; Finance Minister Garbuzov; the head of Mattekhsnab (a powerful agency responsible for supplying enterprises with raw materials and technological resources), Martynov; the head of the State Bank, Poskonov; and Tchikin, one of the heads of the State Control Committee. The Committee of Labour and Wages was represented by Volokov. The report on the meeting, which took place on 21 September 1966, was signed by Deputy Prime Minister Poliansky.

Commission initially proposed to reduce administrative costs by 1,015 million roubles, but after some long and hard bargaining agreed to the lower figure of 905.3 million. For their part, the central and republican ministries would accept no more than 644 million. Detailed discussions on expenditure and staffing were conducted with each ministry separately and the same pattern invariably emerged: in each instance, the Anti-Waste Commission made concessions on the requisite cuts, while the other side gave little or nothing. Rogovsky informed the government that the majority of central ministries and republics opposed any change, preferring to leave things as they were.

As regards the number of state employees – another sticking point – the Anti-Waste Commission wanted to abolish 512,700 posts – a sizeable chunk of the total administrative workforce projected in the 1967 plan – which would have saved 590 million roubles on wages. Needless to say, the ministries affected would not hear of it.

In the defence of budgetary cuts that he addressed to the government, Rogovsky stressed one of the biggest obstacles faced by the Soviet economy: the problem of finding a balance between the population's income and the supply of consumer goods. Reducing administrative costs would help. It is difficult not to register a certain perplexity here: eliminating half a million jobs would certainly reduce the sum total of monetary incomes, but those who lost their jobs would swell the ranks of the poor.

What actually happened? Some job cutting did occur here and there, but most of the officials affected found administrative work elsewhere or even in the same ministry. The hope entertained by some – that officials made redundant would turn to manual jobs (where there were real shortages, especially in remote regions) – was a pipe dream.

Another valuable source on the bureaucratic universe derives from the State Control Committee, which surveyed it in 1966 and made its contribution to Baibakov's Anti-Waste Commission. It also offered a series of suggestions as to how to reduce state administrative costs. We may start with a proposal that was hidden among various other items: abolition of the benefits offered to certain categories of top officials, which would of course have produced significant savings. The State Control Committee drew up a list of the various perks that officials awarded themselves, calculated in roubles (millions of roubles, naturally) for each category of 'service'. The list is revealing. Officials and departmental heads received a so-called 'healthy diet' allowance, as well as an allowance (equivalent to a month's salary) for 'social needs', with vouchers for stays in sanatoriums and rest homes at reduced prices. They had at their disposal dachas, whose maintenance and repair were carried out at government expense. The State Control Committee proposed abolishing all these benefits and some even more outrageous ones enjoyed by senior military officers and their families. It was alarmed by the fact that administrative personnel had increased by 24 per cent in the last five years, bringing their total to more than 7 million (let us recall that this number referred to the hard core of the ministerial network) and the overall wage bill to 13 billion roubles. This rate of growth surpassed that of employment in general and curbing it would easily save a billion roubles.

An especially profligate branch when it came to staffing was the network of various supply agencies maintained by most ministries. The State Control Committee offered some examples, which should not be neglected if we wish to grasp Soviet realities.

Without counting those employed in stores and canteens, these departments and directorates for 'supplying workers' employed 36,700 people, receiving 40 million roubles a year. They could often have been closed down, and the stores and canteens directly supplied by the state's own commercial network.

The Central Committee and Council of Ministers decreed that the problem of 'workers' supply' should be addressed by a single unified system, which was already in the process of being constructed, in the hope that it would be less expensive and more efficient. But a number of ministries refused to rely on other organizations and preferred to retain their own supply channels for food, raw materials and machines, continuing to create and maintain depots and offices for supplies and marketing. Some of them bought materials and products of general industrial use from enterprises and marketed them through their own networks in other regions or republics. To take one example: the Ministry of Chemical Industry was shipping all manner of equipment and semi-finished products from its Sverdlovsk marketing office to Moscow, Kiev, Leningrad and Donetsk, even though such articles were available there in the local warehouses of the bodies responsible for supplies. This system, which employed many thousands of superfluous workers and issued in such irrationality, was an endless source of good jokes (we do not need the archives to know them).

We shall return to these issues of supply and marketing (*snaby-sbyty*),★

★ An expression referring to the phases of the process: the supply of goods (*snabzhenie*) and their sale (*sbyt*).

in connection with one of their unforeseen consequences. First, however, let us turn to further examples of the 'excesses' indulged in by the ranks of the bureaucracy, and condemned as such by the State Control Committee. Among them were the 'official trips' (*komandirovki*) to Moscow – a million a year – for seminars or conferences, or even (in 50 per cent of cases) in the absence of any reason or invitation, which cost the state some 600 million roubles a year. The State Control Committee proposed to reduce the number of such trips by 30 per cent (which once again would not be easy, given that going to Moscow and enjoying its pleasures was one of the most sought-after perks). Another practice that had assumed unacceptable proportions was sending all sorts of intermediaries (*khodatye i tolkachi*) to finalize deals and find materials. In general, the State Control Committee deplored the fact that the measures and efforts undertaken to reduce bureaucratic 'mobility' had yielded no results.[5]

As we have seen, administrative officials liked to offer themselves as many services and perks at the state's expense as they could extract. They also liked to party. Even in the postwar days of penury, high-ranking officials had had a good time. But in the 1960s the libations were more lavish and the parties rowdier! No one even tried to claim that they had anything to do with serving the common weal. The pile of empty bottles consumed by civil servants at state expense spoke for itself. The government regularly received indignant letters condemning this lifestyle and became seriously alarmed about it. A countrywide campaign was launched against illegal expenditure of state resources on banquets and receptions, and large-scale investigations undertaken, which revealed the extent of the problem. All kinds of occasions were excuses for banquets – anniversaries, jubilees, conferences, visits by dignitaries – during which vodka, cognac and wine were served in generous quantities. Finance and control agencies had plenty of material on these goings-on; they knew perfectly well that managers and their accountants were burying such expenses as 'production outlays' and that the ministries and senior officials were turning a blind eye to it. The Council of Ministers drafted a decree stipulating that in future ministries could only give banquets in exceptional circumstances, following permission from the Council (or the local authorities in the republics), and that alcohol was not to be served during them. Infringements were to be

5 RGAE, 4372, 66, 670, LL. 31–8.

severely punished and the culprits required to reimburse the cost out of their own pockets.

The draft decree was jointly proposed by the Finance Minister (Garbuzov) and the Chairman of the State Control Committee (Kovanov), after they had presented their government colleagues with a 'panorama' of such excesses. In 1968, 6,500 government enterprises and agencies had been investigated (at central, republican and district levels), revealing that more than a thousand of them had staged lavish banquets where enormous quantities of alcohol were consumed and presents offered to honoured guests. In Izhevsk, twelve enterprises belonging to different ministries had each spent thousands of roubles on receptions and parties. Between October 1967 and July 1968, one of them had drained 350 bottles of cognac, 25 bottles of vodka and 80 bottles of champagne during the merry-making, at a total cost of 3,100 roubles. Sometimes the banquets were staged in restaurants, which were cited in the document together with the bills stating the price of the drinks.[6]

As we can see, there was no shortage of information on the lifestyle of officials financed by the state, and the leadership sought to remedy the situation. But it is doubtful whether the measures they took or proposed had any effect. The decree itself offered a loophole, authorizing banquets in some circumstances (it was impossible to ban them altogether), and we can be sure that the requisite permission was given. For such was the style of the system, in which everything functioned via personal contacts, exchanges of services, deals, promotions, and so on.

This detour was necessary in order to return to the crowds of 'suppliers' (*snabzhentsy*), for whom meals in restaurants, receptions and binges were part of the routine. Working without these, not to mention bribes, was inconceivable; and this was common knowledge. The KGB and prosecuting authorities could recount some especially juicy stories. In any case, libations were only the preliminary to a whole 'culture' of wheeling and dealing, profiteering and corruption. The supply agencies were the quintessential milieu that generated this culture and diffused it throughout the administration, especially to economic agencies. As we proceed, we shall discover the existence of powerful systemic springs at

---

6 GARF, A-259, op. 45, d. 7501, LL. 4962: a file of documents from the government of the Russian Federation (October–November 1968) concerning the campaign which was being conducted throughout the USSR against 'illegal expenditure of public money on banquets and receptions'.

work, transforming the whole Soviet bureaucratic scene into a setting from a different play altogether.

THE USSR'S GOSSNAB: STAFF AND ACTIVITIES (1970)

By name at least, such Soviet institutions as the KGB or Gosplan were known throughout the world. But outside the ranks of specialists, no one abroad referred to Gossnab. For Soviet economists and the whole administrative class, Gossnab – the State Committee for Material and Technical Supplies – was the engine of the economic system. Like the KGB and Gosplan, Gossnab was a supra-ministerial body, run by a prestigious economist and administrator, V. Dymshits, who had won his spurs in Gosplan.

Gossnab was supposed to provide the economy with everything it needed in order to function. Its warehouses, stations and offices were a sort of Mecca for the innumerable *tolkachi* ('pushers') and other agents from the various ministries, agencies and production units. These emissaries arrived to assure themselves that Gossnab would indeed deliver what they had been promised in order to fulfil the plan. Not receiving what had been envisaged, or receiving nothing at all, or getting it too late was a major anxiety; and given that Gossnab was frequently short of all sorts of items, the *tolkachi* were charged with making contacts with its officials, arranging deals and obtaining results.

A centralized supplier on this scale was regarded as a contradiction in terms by leading Soviet economists. Even when competently run, Gossnab, like every other Soviet agency, experienced shortages and deficiencies. It was cursed by just about everyone, with the exception of those who enjoyed the seal of government priority in procurement (the arms sector or other pet projects of the leadership).

Despite its elevated position in the Soviet institutional hierarchy, Gossnab had to submit to the same administrative routines as other bodies when it came to its budgets, personnel and structural units. Acquaintance with these procedures will help us to understand the character of this apparatus. Budgetary negotiations with the Finance Ministry were not particularly exacting, because the latter was aware of the complexity of Gossnab's duties and its high status. On 8 August 1970, Dymshits approved the list of Gossnab's staff and sent it to the Finance Ministry for registration, as procedure dictated, in order to secure the requisite personnel and corresponding budget. The document specified the number of top officials and their salaries, the number of specialists, and each specialist department together with its field of activity, for everything had to be approved by the financial auditors. Thus we learn that Gossnab comprised 34 units with 1,302 employees. Among them we find 286 holding higher managerial posts, 10 of which were leadership positions. The monthly wage bill for these 286 posts was 284,786 roubles. A separate table indicated the salary of the 10 highest officials (between 550 and 700 roubles, plus unspecified perks), or a monthly total of 5,300 roubles (though this excludes the salary of Gossnab's head). At the other end of the wage scale, we find employees earning 70 roubles a month and enjoying no perks.

As has been said, the bargaining went smoothly. At this stage, Dymshits was still in a strong position. The Finance Ministry's inspectors went through the motions of approving a central staffing level of 1,302, while trying to nibble away at numbers and wages wherever possible. When Dymshits requested an average monthly salary of 219 roubles per administrator (it had been 215 the previous year), the Finance Ministry suggested 214. Representatives of the Finance Ministry had fixed rules as regards categories of employees (*nachal'niki*, 'specialists', 'senior specialists'), and they quibbled over everything. But they readily agreed to the requested number (ten) of top officials. Next came the examination of Gossnab's activities and departments (in addition to its supply agencies, Gossnab had factories, construction teams and research laboratories). The supply activities were distributed between the specialist departments: heavy industry, energy, metals, construction, materials, and so on, as well as an import–export department and the usual internal administrative agencies.[7]

A lengthy page would be required just to list the departments and sections of this imposing body. It employed some 130,000 people, which was not excessive given its task – namely, to organize a smooth flow to the country's productive apparatus of all the supplies required for it to function: machinery and equipment, raw materials, fuel, construction materials and tools, and so on. Everything sounds perfectly reasonable – until we realize that in the USSR a single bureaucratic agency was responsible for doing what market mechanisms did elsewhere. If Gossnab had performed satisfactorily, the USSR would indeed

7 RGAE, f. 7733, op. 58, d. 2892, LL. 1–5, 85–97: a bundle of documents (dating from July–December 1970) dealing with the negotiations between Gossnab and the Finance Ministry over the numbers and salaries of top officials.

have represented the alternative to capitalism it sometimes claimed to be. Gossnab and Gosplan would have been the two cathedrals of a new world. Here we might remind the reader that a good socialist like Trotsky had explained to the Comintern executive committee in 1921 that socialism was a long-term project and that those who wished to realize it one day had to start off by following in the footsteps of the market economy.

The reality is that in the Soviet world no other centralized agency produced such a host of 'decentralized' side-effects. Gossnab, super-supplier, was in fact one of the system's bottlenecks, for it was the cause and manager of constant shortages. Consequently, it is scarcely surprising that the whole economic apparatus responded to these shortages, and to Gosplan's patent inability to furnish vital supplies consistently, with all sorts of devices and practices and an independent supply-cum-marketing system, emulating the ministries and important enterprises. This murky world of *snaby* and *sbyty* acquired a life of its own, becoming a key fixture of economic and social life. No study of Soviet reality can ignore it, and it is important not to confuse it with Gossnab.

'Murky' is the appropriate adjective to describe this plethora of operators on the margins of the official system. Even so, had the regime really wanted to know how things stood (and even if it did not really wish to know), it could have referred to the inspection agencies, which regularly conducted inquiries into the sector, or (even better) to the Central Statistical Office, which on 1 October 1970 carried out a census of these 'commercial' organizations. Although it could not claim to be exhaustive – naturally, it did not encompass military procurement agencies – the figures are impressive. The 11,184 organizations recorded in the third quarter of 1970 employed 722,289 people, with a total payroll of 259,503,700 roubles. The Central Statistical Office also provided information on warehouses, inventories and transportation costs.[8]

The census was incomplete because it did not include the unofficial personnel of these *snaby-sbyty* bodies. The notorious *tolkachi* featured on the payrolls as employees of other administrative agencies or in more or less fictitious jobs in enterprises. They actually spent most of their time dealing with all manner of suppliers and disposed of the requisite resources to 'speed things up', or simply to secure indispensable supplies

---

8 RGAE, f. 1562, op. 47, d. 1183, LL. 4–8: data of the census conducted on 1 October 1970 by the Central Statistical Office on 'indicators of the activities of supply-and-marketing organizations'.

in means of production and consumer goods. For crucial supplies were rarely obtained without a nudge in the right direction; and that was precisely the task of the *tolkachi*. Their activities were severely condemned by the party, but flourished nevertheless, for without them the economy would have stalled completely.

There was a further dimension that the census could not take account of. Possessing plentiful resources, these operators frequently meshed with dealers on the black market, who hovered around factory warehouses whose stocks were not strictly inventoried. The huge army of people engaged in *snaby-sbyty* activities formed a natural environment for all sorts of deals, and thus for the development of a shadowy proto-market economy, which was often vital and useful. At all events, it constituted a surreal aspect of Soviet reality.

26

'TELLING THE LIGHT FROM THE SHADE'?

Gregory Grossman has pioneered the study of the phenomenon known as the 'second economy', while others – and the Russians themselves – prefer the more mysterious-sounding 'shadow economy' (the literal translation of the Russian term *tenevaia ekonomika*), which refers to a much broader, more complex reality than the readily definable 'black economy'. This is unquestionably a thorny issue, with economic, social, legal, criminal, and even profoundly political dimensions. The authors of a serious Russian work, who are well acquainted with Western publications on the subject and refer to them, have enriched the debate by bringing previously inaccessible Russian sources and studies to our attention.[1]

The shadow economy is not easy to define, but efforts to circumscribe it lead us into some of the less well-known complexities of the Soviet economy. For some scholars, its causes are to be sought in the almost permanent imbalance between supply and demand, with the deficit in consumer goods and services leading to inflationary pressures. According to the Hungarian economist Janos Kornai, bureaucratic planning creates shortages of capital and goods and the shadow economy emerges as a partial correction of the straitjacket imposed by an economy of shortages. As wages lose their purchasing power, the population

---

1 I. G. Minervin, 'Tenevaia ekonomika v SSSR - prichiny i sledstviia', pp. 103–27, in I. Iu. Zhilina and L. M. Timofeev, otvet. red., 'Tenevaia ekonomika: ekonomicheskie i sotsial'nye aspekty'. This set of essays is to be found in a periodical published under the auspices of the Russian Academy of Sciences, *Ekonomicheskie i Sotsial'nye Problemy Rossii*, vol. 4, Moscow 1999.

is forced to find other sources of income, prompting many to engage in some additional activity on top of their regular state jobs. Experts who have tried to assess the extent of the shadow economy for the years 1960–90 estimate that it multiplied eighteen-fold in this period: one-third of it in agriculture, a further third in commerce and catering, and the remaining third in industry and construction. In the case of services, the main activities in the shadow economy were home and car repairs, and private medical services and education at home.

I. G. Minervin, who contributed the chapter dealing directly with the Soviet period, made ample use of Western works and recent Russian contributions. The majority of Western authors (Grossman, Wiles, Shelley) concur that the emergence of a shadow economy is inevitable in the so-called socialist economies, and this is mostly confirmed by later Russian studies. But how exactly is it to be defined? For some, it comprises all economic activities not included in the official statistics or all forms of economic activity conducted for personal profit that flout existing laws. Others (Western scholars) regard it as a 'second economy' or a 'parallel market'. However, because the dividing-line between legal and illegal activities is often difficult to draw, some of them include all activities that were acceptable in practice, but which did not pertain to the official economy. Thus, Grossman's 'second economy' encompasses activities that were common to the Eastern bloc and Western Europe, such as the cultivation of a private plot or the sale of its produce in kolkhoz markets – activities that were legal in the USSR, but which might sometimes be connected with illegal practices. The situation was similarly ambiguous in construction: building materials from dubious sources, bribes, illicit use of state transport, helping private citizens or influential bosses to build a house or dacha. The same applies to repair work of all kinds carried out by private individuals or teams: this could be legal, semi-legal or illegal (the latter two categories belonging to the 'shadow economy').

What was peculiar about the phenomenon was that it involved the circulation of legal goods and services on illegal markets. The sources and character of the 'deals' were semi-legal or illegal. Such semi-legal markets provided services that were not declared for purposes of taxation (privately rented housing, medical care, private lessons, repairs), as well as barter deals between enterprises seeking ways to make up for their failure to achieve the targets laid down by the plan.

The unambiguously illegal sphere included the sale of all kinds of scarce goods (like spare parts and consumer goods), and illegally produced or stolen merchandise. A separate category contains such criminal activities as embezzlement, smuggling, drug-trafficking and so on, which are prohibited the world over. But the criminal economy proper accounted for only part of the shadow economy, even if it was the most dangerous, and as such deemed unacceptable by many who were themselves engaged in parallel economic activities.

The US scholar Louise Shelley has offered an illuminating alternative definition. Within the 'second economy', she distinguishes between legal and illegal activities, but excludes anything that is obviously criminal. The legal private sector essentially corresponded to markets where peasants, but others too, sold what they had grown on private plots. The illegal economy was much larger and had two components – one of them operating within the official economy, while the other functioned in parallel to it. The principal illegal activities in the official economy consisted in speculation on scarce goods, bribes to influential people, corrupt practices in the education system, the formation of work-teams for hire in construction, the manipulation of accounts and false data in response to investigations (e.g. adding 'dead souls' to pay-rolls), and, finally, the construction of illegal factories concealed within official ones and using their raw materials.

THE EXTENT OF THE SHADOW ECONOMY

In addition to the problem of defining the shadow economy, we face the difficulty of estimating its extent. Researchers are agreed that it was sizeable, supplying large quantities of goods and services. Gosplan's research institute estimated that at the beginning of the 1960s it involved less than 10 per cent of the annual average number of workers, employees and kolkhoz members, whereas by the end of the 1980s more than a fifth of the working population was engaged in it (some 30 million people). In some branches of the service sector (house building and repairs, car repairs), it was responsible for between 30 and 50 per cent of all the work undertaken – and often much more than an equivalent state service performed (Menshikov's estimate). For example, the quantity of vodka distilled at home – an important branch of the 'private sector' – was difficult to assess, because official and unofficial production of alcohol were interconnected.

Researchers point out that the parallel economy also exists in the West, where its development reflects the growth in state regulation. In the Soviet case, the shadow economy may be considered an adaptation and reaction on the part of the population to state controls and the deficiencies of the state-run economy.

At the beginning of the 1980s, Gosplan's research institute proposed the following classification, which was probably the optimal one in the Soviet case:

(1) The 'unofficial' economy, involving mostly legal activities that included the production of goods and services which, although subject to taxation, were not declared. These were tolerated.
(2) The 'fictitious' economy: false accounting, embezzlement, speculation, bribes.
(3) The underground economy, comprising actions forbidden by law.

This picture must be rounded off by what we had to say about the *snaby-sbyty*. Therewith we obtain a more realistic image of Soviet economic activity, the interaction between different economic agencies, and the innumerable varieties of private or semi-private initiative. We shall shortly address the political implications of this complex economic scene.

The whole set of shortcomings and malfunctions afflicting the bureaucratic system – phenomenal shortages of goods and services had become systemic – prompted or forced different institutions to seek solutions in private arrangements, bartering of merchandise or raw materials, and falsifying results. Even if personal gain was not necessarily the principal objective, it increasingly became a powerful motive force, especially at the beginning of the 1980s, when it was clear to everyone that the leadership was displaying little zeal when it came to the prosecution of highly placed offenders. Louise Shelley notes that in the 1970s, 90 per cent of cadres accused of breaking the law got off with a simple reprimand from the party. A double standard could be discerned in the attitude of party and state leaders to the unofficial economy, which certainly complicated the task of streamlining and improving leadership at the centre.

For its part, the population quite naturally strove to maintain or improve its standard of living by obtaining additional income, at a time when the consumer market was defective and open or hidden inflation high. The discrepancy between widespread corruption in the state administration and the official ideological rejection of any private enterprise helped to fuel the economic and psychological factors pushing people into the shadow economy, or even directly into the black market.

Some researchers believe that the shadow economy actually enabled the system to survive, by supplying a partial corrective to its malfunctioning; that it helped most citizens to make ends meet; and that it thereby preserved the regime. In my view, the positive function of informal economies should not be exaggerated. The same authors reckon that such practices inculcated new motivations among economic managers, which supplemented the official ones attaching to their duties. On the other hand, the existence of a whole range of parallel networks led some sections of the Soviet elite to separate themselves from the official system and forge closer links with 'unofficial' elites. The two elites had much in common. Leaders of the unofficial elite (who were implicated in the black market, if not directly connected with criminal mafias) themselves retained official positions, or maintained close ties with the official elite, enabling them to play a background role as pressure groups for dubious causes or undesirable elements. Such activities might be characterized as pertaining to a 'shadow polity'.

The Soviet system guaranteed all its citizens social security, public health services, education, and pension entitlements, whereas employment in the shadow economy was mostly part-time and unregulated. Thus the official sector provided social services to the unofficial one, thereby contributing to the reproduction of the labour force in the shadow economy.[2] R. Ryfkina and L. Kosals have aptly summarized the situation: it was no longer possible to distinguish between legal and illegal activities in many enterprises. A 'black-and-white' market had emerged.[3]

Others believe that although the shadow economy made it much more difficult to create a healthy contemporary economy, it was still better than the savage, mafia-style capitalism that descended on Russia after the fall of the Soviet system. At all events, the phenomenon is an additional aspect of the trends that emerged in the Soviet system, conditioning, maintaining or undermining it. The resources the population found, and which it could rely on in coping with the system's vagaries, formed one of them. The low intensity and low productivity of the working day, which were at the heart of the 'social

---

2   See A. Portes and J. Boroch, in *Ekonomicheskie i Sotsial'nye Problemy Rossii*, p. 121.
3   Ibid., p. 125.

contract' between workers and the state, facilitated 'work on the side' (cultivation of private plots, etc.). Such resources, officially unacknowledged, became increasingly sizeable with the growth of the shadow economy, which not only supplied supplementary foodstuffs, but also provided additional income through part-time employment that became available to ever more people. Criminal activities are excluded from these resources: they could lead to prison.

SOCIOLOGISTS AND LIVING STANDARDS (1972–80)

While the managers of the state-run economy were seeking ways to remedy a labour shortage and a drop in labour productivity, sociologists, and particularly experts in economic sociology, were confirming the significance of the shadow economy and arriving at some startling conclusions. Despite the bad news announced by the planning authorities and clear signs of a system in decline, living standards actually rose during the years of stagnation. The population's reaction and adaptation to changing economic conditions produced new patterns of behaviour and new values, which official statistical data were incapable of assimilating.

The data used by the sociologists derived from two sources: their own studies conducted in the Siberian city of Rubtsovsk (Altai region) in 1972 and repeated in 1980 and 1990; and those carried out among the rural population in the Novosibirsk area in 1975–6 and 1986–7.[4] The development indicators in Rubtsovsk approximated to the general Russian average for the 1970s and '80s, while those of the Novosibirsk area (one of the most important in Western Siberia) were close to the Russian inter-regional average. Thus, the data collected in these studies, conducted by the Moscow and Novosibirsk academies of science, may be regarded as faithfully reflecting the national situation.

From them we learn that the housing situation had improved; that the purchase of consumer durables had increased appreciably; that there were more recreational facilities for city dwellers; and that many families had a private plot near their residence or in the neighbouring countryside (even though demand still outstripped supply). A third of the population had access to collective vegetable gardens. During the

---

4 T. I. Zaslavskaya and Z. I. Kalugina, otvet. red., *Sotsialnaia Traektoriia Reformiruemoi Rossii – Issledovaniia Novosibirskoi Ekonomiko-sotsiologicheskoi Shkoly*, Novosibirsk 1999, pp. 577–84.

twenty years under study, in line with increased house construction, many garages, garden sheds and various types of summer houses had been built. On the whole, the least well-off sections of the population had seen their incomes rise, attesting to a general trend towards decent minimum living standards. The most marked differences, as measured by key indicators like housing, incomes and personal means of transport, had decreased significantly.

These findings provide an explanation for the paradox of nostalgia among the population of post-communist Russia for the Brezhnevite 'good old days'. The 'miracle' of improving living standards in a declining economy was based on the existence of untapped labour energy that was not mobilized by the state-run economy, of under-employed resources, and an abundance of other resources that had yet to be squandered (the country remained fabulously wealthy). However, as the authors of the study confirm, improved living standards in the 1970s and '80s came at a very high price. While economists and the leadership were seeking to raise output and labour productivity, to reduce waste and use resources more rationally, the latter were being systematically plundered.

Everyday life in the 1970s and '80s would sooner or later reflect the decline of the state economy, in the form of an increased unpaid personal workload on private plots or at home. Many people had to find a second job; many others said they would like to. A similar increase in the workload also occurred in the countryside, with men and women investing more time in their private plots or home-based work – the main source of additional income – which enabled them to support relatives in town and exchange agricultural products against manufactured products.

The same trend of greater worker workloads and lower monetary incomes could already be observed in the years 1972–80. Following the collapse of the USSR, in the 1990s the role of the private plot or garden became indispensable, taking up much of many people's working time. The garden, a place of leisure in developed urban societies, reverted to its pre-industrial function. A similar regression was evident in many spheres of existence, where survival strategies led to the devaluation of one of the most obvious successes of previous decades: the improvement in educational standards, which became less and less useful (a trend already apparent at the end of the 1970s). This was attested by the falling numbers of those taking after-work courses. The authors deplore the decline in what they call the economic and cultural function of higher education and higher professional qualifications, in favour of a pragmatic search for material benefits. The reduction in the time given over to leisure activities is explained by the need to work more in order to make ends meet, as a result of the failures of the state economy in the 1970s and '80s.

In conclusion, improved living standards in the regime's final years, though genuine, were no 'miracle'. They were more of a mirage, like cheeks that glow after they have been pinched – the prelude to a slow decline that would witness the ruin of many past achievements.

PRIVATIZING THE STATE?

In order to make do, the population of the USSR had to increase its workload. By contrast, its ruling networks, especially at the upper level of the *nomenklatura*, saw their material well-being improve – by expanding existing income streams – without being obliged to work harder or change their leisure habits. We must therefore turn our attention to them once again.

Our examination of the shadow economy deepened our understanding of the processes at work within the ranks of state officials, particularly with the *snaby-sbyty* – the procurement and sales networks that supplied production units with what the state should have provided in the first place. Despite being officially frowned on, such semi-legal activities rapidly became indispensable, because they played a vital role for the enterprises they supplied. The availability of partially or completely concealed reserves of materials, financial resources or even manpower; the increase in bargaining and lobbying; the vast scope for activity on the borderline between the shadow economy and the black market – all this indicates the emergence of a model, even a system, which was at once indispensable and parasitic (like a body that produces beneficial pathologies). In the behaviour of enterprise managers, we witness a progressive blurring of the boundary between state and private property. Another boundary was blurred concurrently: between the official incomes and privileges allocated to top officials on the one hand, and the considerable room the latter enjoyed for increasing them by exploiting their position in the state hierarchy, on the other. And this avenue led to something even more significant in the behaviour of some heads of institutions or enterprises. It is one thing to strive to extract ever more perks from the state. It is quite another no longer to be content with such perks and to seek to accumulate wealth. Networks for that very purpose now existed within the state sector – in the various forms of the shadow economy – but also outside the state sector – in the form of the 'black market', itself spawning the mafia connections that flourished as never before under Brezhnev.

A longer-term historical perspective enables us at this point to discern broader political transformations – to distinguish successive stages in the bureaucracy's position in the system and their consequences for the whole regime. Once the administrative class had been liberated from the rigours and horrors of Stalinism, it attained a higher status and became co-ruler of the state. But it did not stop there: the senior ranks of the bureaucracy actually began to appropriate the state as the collective representative of its interests and were highly conscious of the fact. The heads of ministries or other agencies referred to themselves as 'those in charge of the state'.

The autobiography of A. G. Zverev, who served as Finance Minister both under Stalin and after him, provides a good illustration of this self-image. He barely mentions the party: membership of it is taken for granted as an obvious formality. For this to have occurred, the party, as we saw in Parts One and Two, had to have undergone a transformation. Having itself become an administrative apparatus and a hierarchy, it not only found itself in a position of utter dependency, but ended up being absorbed by the class of top state officials we just mentioned. This allowed the latter to take a further step in their 'emancipation': although formally subject to all sorts of rules, they now existed as an uncontrollable bureaucracy, free of all curbs. They began to attack the sacrosanct principle of state ownership of the economy. The spontaneous processes at work emptied a series of ideological and political principles of any content. The most important of them – state ownership of assets and the means of production – was slowly eroded, initially issuing in the formation of veritable fiefdoms inside ministries, and then in the de facto privatization of enterprises by their managers. This process must be called by its real name: the crystallization of a proto-capitalism within the state-owned economy.

This point has been very aptly highlighted by Menshikov, an economist whom we have already cited in connection with the shadow economy.[5] He pays particular attention to the illegal sectors within the

---

5 Menshikov is cited by Zhilina and Timofeev, *Tenevaia Ekonomika*, pp. 116–17.

state economy that he calls the 'internal shadow economy', and which exercised strong influence on the official economy. This powerful sector became possible because of the division between the functions of ownership and those of management. What was evolving was, on the one hand, private management of the social capital of state enterprises; on the other, private appropriation of the products of that capital. It involved not only those who operated in the shadow economy, but also the official managers of enterprises in league with the highest reaches of the *nomenklatura*. All these figures, Menshikov argues, played an important role when the capitalism that emerged through the pores of central planning matured, in due course, into a decisive and potent force that shattered the system. Thus it was that the *nomenklatura* metamorphosed from covert owner of state property into its overt owner.

This interpretation foregrounds the inevitable consequences of a prior social reality: the takeover by the upper strata of the bureaucracy of the totality of state power and hence of the economy. The principle of state ownership – the system's main pillar – was progressively subverted, preparing the ground for the transition from quasi-privatization to the fully-fledged variety.

Readers will now probably appreciate why we needed to deal with the *snaby-sbyty* in some detail: they were the 'termites' that helped to accomplish this task. No wonder that with the advent of perestroika these supply offices–depots–warehouses were the very first Soviet agencies to declare themselves 'private firms' and adopt an openly commercial status. This looked like a step in the right direction. But they were privatizing something that did not belong them, whereas the first principle of the market economy is that if one wants to acquire assets, they have to be paid for. Otherwise, it is a matter for the criminal law. And the intimate connection in the course of the post-Soviet reforms between 'privatization' and criminal activity is now widely known.

But we have not yet reached the phase of perestroika. We are examining the era of so-called 'stagnation', when the system's chief pillars were crumbling. Not only had the economy lost steam, but the main thing it generated was waste. So what was Gosplan up to? Its collegium (the assembly of top officials) seemed to be in agreement with the conclusions of its research institute, which had diagnosed a fatal tendency in the economy: extensive trends were outstripping intensive trends. In 1970 it issued a statement, serene in its tone (it contained not a single alarmist word), in which it formulated a quite chilling diagnosis-cum-prognosis: the projections of the eighth five-year plan (1966–70) contained inbuilt disproportions. As a result, 'all basic indicators will decelerate, deteriorate or stagnate'.[6] The reason was that the very low efficiency indicators on which the calculations were based were leading to a dual imbalance: on the one hand, between the state's resources and the needs of the national economy; on the other, between the population's monetary income and the output of consumer goods and services (this remark implies that some previous version of the plan did contain the requisite proportions and balances). Hence the fear of a looming deterioration in the circulation of money and marketable goods in the course of the ninth five-year plan: a decline in the incentivizing role of wages in raising labour productivity and other ways of managing production was to be anticipated. It was as if the report was actually claiming that the eighth plan had programmed a deterioration of the economy in the course of the subsequent plan. In other words, Soviet economists were perfectly well aware of the downward slope the economy was set on.

'Stagnation' was marked by the impossibility of extracting anything from the bureaucracy and a lack of will and ideas at the top about how to stop the rot. All attempts to reduce the size of the bureaucracy, or force it to change its habits, were so many losing battles. Post-Stalin, the new rules of the game – the 'bargaining' between government agencies and central government (the Politburo and Council of Ministers) – allowed the bureaucracy to become a colossus that was not only the real master of the state, but also formed bureaucratic fiefdoms under the eyes of the party apparatus, which was reduced to a mere spectator and gradually yielded to the inevitable.

The diagnosis was simple: the system was sick while the bureaucracy was in fine fettle. Reforming the system entailed reforming the bureaucracy: no one was in a position to impose this and why should it undertake the task itself? This meant that the writing was on the wall – of the Kremlin this time.

It was imperative to resolve the problem of growing labour shortages and arrest economic decline by a dramatic rise in labour productivity. But this implied nothing less than a revolution. It could not be done without switching to a mixed economy, which was only conceivable on certain political conditions – and these too amounted to a revolution.

---

6 RGAE, 4372, 66, 3717, LL. 1–9.

Technological and economic reforms were inextricably bound up with political reforms. The party machine had to be divested of its last power: the power to prevent change. A mass uprising against state institutions would have accomplished this, but it did not occur. The alternative was reform from within, directed in the first instance at the party. Only a revitalized political force could compel the bureaucracy to make the transition to a mixed economy, bringing pressure to bear on it from above and from below, and threatening it with full-scale expropriation. The establishment of a transitional system would make it possible to preserve minimum living standards, avoid economic collapse, and open the way to individual and group economic initiative. The next task would be to begin to empower the population politically. Since none of this happened, what (it might be asked) is the point of mentioning it? I do so for a simple methodological reason – namely, in order to arrive at a better understanding of what actually did happen.

The political aspects of the system, which we already know a fair amount about, demand our attention once again at this point. The erosion of political systems, and of the ability of ruling groups to act, is a frequent enough phenomenon in history. Each instance is a combination of general features and particular characteristics. Observers detect such erosion when they find a system stuck in the groove of a successful past, not unlike generals who tend to stick with the winning strategies of the last war. The scenario is one that periodically re-emerges in different historical circumstances, and is regularly observed in the case of regimes in decline. Politicians and political analysts should always bear it in mind, even when dealing with seemingly thriving systems.

The Soviet system was successful, albeit in truncated fashion, when it responded to the call of history by mobilizing the country's wealth and large population. No great thinker, Boris Yeltsin once said that the Soviet system was nothing more than an experiment which had wasted everyone's time. This might have been true of his own years as party boss in Sverdlovsk and as Russian President in the Kremlin, but such remarks, endlessly repeated with no regard for historical realities, are empty chatter. I have devoted many pages to describing the decay of the system, for this is a reality that needs to be studied. But that does not license distortion of the whole historical record. The Soviet system saved Russia from disintegration in 1917–22. It rescued it again – and Europe with it – from a Nazi domination that would have stretched from Brest to Vladivostok. Let us imagine – if we dare – what that would have meant for the world. To these achievements must be added others, measured by twentieth-century criteria for defining a developed country: Soviet Russia scored quite well on demography, education, health, urbanization, the role of science – so much capital that was to be squandered by the lacklustre reformers of the 1990s.

So where did things go wrong? All the social changes that enabled the country to 'marry its century' represented a job only half-done. The other part of the job – state-building – proceeded in the wrong direction. When the historical circumstances changed (in part on account of the regime's own efforts), the USSR found itself confronting a fatal bifurcation and contradiction: the social sphere exploded, while the politico-bureaucratic universe froze. The turn of events that I have referred to as the 'second emancipation of the bureaucracy' ultimately consisted in the de facto absorption of the party apparatus by the ministerial cohorts. This process had a further dimension, to which reference has already been made. The Soviet economy and the whole of the country's wealth were formally owned by the state; and the state administration existed to serve the nation. But who was the real owner of this 'property'? The ideology and practice of nationalization derived from Communist Party notions about how to build a supposedly socialist system. It was for the party to take charge of the integrity of the system, whose core was precisely the principle of state ownership. But the huge bureaucratic machine that managed the 'common wealth' imposed its own conception of the state and made itself the latter's sole representative. It laid claim to equal status with the party apparatus, even to first place. The other side of this process was the social and political fusion of the party apparatus into a single bloc with the state bureaucracy. The party always maintained that it retained a dominant position, but in reality the bureaucratic directorates in the ministries and enterprises had become the country's true masters. No matter that the Constitution continued to proclaim otherwise. The party cells in ministries and enterprises served no purpose and its central bodies merely repeated what the Council of Ministers and ministers themselves had initiated. A political organization is only justified if it performs a political function: as soon as it is content to reiterate what has been decided elsewhere, it no longer possesses any *raison d'être*.

I subsume this process under the category of what I have called the 'de-politicization of the party'. The party's role changed once its function of political leadership had been eroded on account of its submersion in the bureaucratic milieu. It might be said that the party and its leadership had been expropriated and replaced by a bureaucratic hydra, which formed a class holding state power. Henceforth any political will was paralysed. The summit of this over-centralized state impeded any explicit reformist endeavours, deemed unacceptable by the various components of the bureaucracy. Party leaders could no longer afford to antagonize the latter. Quite the reverse, the privileges of those who now constituted the regime's mainstay were allowed to increase, in order to keep them happy. Worse still, with political volition at an all-time low, illegalities and a high degree of corruption were tolerated. The periods of stagnation and decay encouraged the privileged to engage in what were, to put it mildly, reprehensible practices – another dubious pay-off.

We are now in a position to offer a response to a question that we have raised several times: Can a bureaucracy be controlled by another bureaucracy or even by itself? Our answer is a categorical 'No'. Control can be exercised only by a country's political leaders and citizens. It is for them to define the relevant tasks and the means required to implement such control. But it was this ability that the leadership of the USSR had lost, generating a set of fatal paradoxes: the party was 'de-politicized' and the ever more bureaucratized economy was managed and controlled by an administrative class more intent on preserving its own power than increasing production; more concerned with maintaining its cosy routines than cultivating creativity and technological development. Hence another series of paradoxes: an 'ailing economy' but a 'flourishing bureaucracy', which thrived on its sloth; bureaucratic privileges on the increase, even as the system's performance deteriorated; rising investment combined with dwindling growth; a marked expansion in the number of educated and qualified people whom the regime, unable to tolerate independent talent, excluded – in short, a veritable magical formula for systemic breakdown.

The various phenomena and processes that unfolded at the summit had an impact on the population, which sensed that the factories and other national assets simultaneously belonged to everyone and no one – that there was a swarm of 'bosses' and yet no one was taking charge. This explains why Andropov's arrival in the post of general-secretary was so well received across most of the social spectrum: the country finally had a 'boss' (*khoziain*). The task awaiting him was colossal: to overcome the effects of a process set in train by Stalin, which had stripped the party of any political rights. This trend had not been reversed after the death of the supreme leader: the party remained an organization whose members possessed no rights and whose leaders

were fooling themselves when they asserted that policy was their preserve. They remained without a voice and paralysed in the face of an
administrative class that had ceased to listen to them. A party had to be
reconstituted that would respond to its leaders' call to embark on
reforms: confronted with a determined leadership that was ready to
mobilize its base, a recalcitrant bureaucracy would have little chance of
prevailing. Andropov was seemingly readying himself to reiterate
Lenin's famous question of May 1917: 'Which party will have the
courage to take power on its own?' – to which he had replied: 'There is
such a party', provoking guffaws among the assembled anti-Leninists.

I would characterize the Soviet regime as a 'state without a political
system' – an imposing skeleton without any flesh on its bones. This
should have been realized (apparently it was by some), prompting a
series of initiatives aimed at gradually creating what was lacking: more
freedom of inquiry, information and discussion, free trade unions, the
re-creation (or re-politicization) of the party. Reviving the party's
internal political life (whether in the form of fractions, a programme,
currents of opinion, statutes), as recommended by Osinsky-Obolensky
in *Pravda* in 1920 – such was the programme formulated by Andropov
some six decades later, one year before he succumbed to illness.

THE BURDEN OF HISTORY

What happened to the Soviet system from the late 1960s onwards marks
the re-emergence of a whole series of traits that had plagued Tsarist
Russia for centuries, and which Russia never managed to divest itself of.
It was as if the country was weighed down by a historical burden, which
was thought to have been shaken off, but that returned to haunt it. Old
Russia, where the development of the state and its power always preceded social advance, had ended up stumbling: the political system
became blocked, impeding any economic and social progress. And here
was the same scenario repeating itself – and in the course of the same
century.

The rise and fall of the Soviet system is perfectly encapsulated in the
fate of the Mir space station. At the outset, it represented an unprecedented technological breakthrough, with a long life ahead of it. But it
soon fell victim to endless manufacturing defects and malfunctions: it
was constantly being repaired by the incredibly resourceful operators
responsible for it (confirming my own wartime observations of truck-

drivers who managed to keep their vehicles moving by fixing or connecting missing or broken parts with shoe-laces!). The episode ended with Mir's plunge into the ocean, sufficiently well-directed as to inflict no damage on anyone . . .

On the other hand, it is worth reminding readers what did not happen. Post-Stalinist Russia did not experience the omnipresent, omniscient hyper-control predicted by some writers. Had it been faithful to, and capable of, any kind of 'decent' totalitarianism, it would have lasted for ever. The terrifying literary phantasmagorias (some of them written when the spectre was present and horror reigned) both did and did not come to pass: Zamiatin, Huxley and Orwell prophesied that a monopolistic power would bring about the total enslavement of human beings, transforming them into the numbered cogs of some huge machine. But despite its dark pages, history avoided this terrible man-trap. In reality, whatever the regime's policies and ideology, historical processes were at work that are missed when the whole focus of study is the regime or, in one of its variants, denunciation of the regime.

When I refer to a return of Russia's historical burden, what I have in mind is secular historical trends which, after having initially benefited Russia, came to plague much of its history. The Russian historian Solovev perceived the process of Russian colonization – small groups of people migrating to and populating huge territories – as a characteristic feature of its history, which he qualified as 'drawn out'.[7] In other words, this history involved quantitative expansion in space, complicating any transition to a qualitative – i.e. intensive and in-depth – modus operandi. For a while it looked as though the Soviet regime was overcoming this handicap. But in the twilight of the Soviet era, when nearly all vital signs were fading, Russia once again found itself stuck in the syndrome of quantitative expansion, portending an ineluctable exhaustion of its economic, social and political resources. The extraordinary momentum of Soviet development had modernized the country, and yet perpetuated a mode of extensive development; and of this Gosplan's experts were sadly conscious. It should be noted that this tendency in Russian history is far from exhausted.

Once again, these observations require qualification. Paradoxically, such extensive, quantity-oriented development was also embodied in

---

7 Quoted by G. Vernadsky, *Russkaia Istoriografiia*, Moscow 1998, p. 106. The Russian formula is 'zhidkii element v russkoi istorii' ('the drawn-out element in Russian history').

the vigorous Stalinist mobilization that made victory possible in 1945, saving Russia and Europe with it. In other words, the traditional impetus from above – from the state – could accomplish many things. But such prowess had its limits and was only fully effective in the transition from a profoundly rural civilization to an increasingly urban one.

Irreplaceable when it comes to reflecting on Russia's past and its burdens, the Russian historian Kliuchevsky (who died in 1911) suggested that a huge country like his own was unwieldy to govern and that it would be very difficult to alter its historical course. Kliuchevsky was no fatalist: he was registering the existence of a 'burden' that had yet to be lightened.

27

WHAT WAS THE SOVIET SYSTEM?

Reflection on the USSR has been marred – and still is – by two frequent errors, which need to be cleared up before we address the question posed by the title of this chapter. The first is to take anti-communism for a study of the Soviet Union. The second – a consequence of the first – consists in 'Stalinizing' the whole Soviet phenomenon, as if it had been one giant gulag from beginning to end.

Anti-communism (and its offshoots) is not historical scholarship: it is an ideology masquerading as such. Not only did it not correspond to the realities of the 'political animal' in question, but waving the flag of democracy, it paradoxically exploited the USSR's authoritarian (dictatorial) regime in the service of conservative causes or worse. In the United States, McCarthyism, or the subversive political role played by the FBI head Hoover, were both based on the communist bogey. The unsavoury manoeuvring by some on the German Right to whitewash Hitler by foregrounding Stalin and his atrocities entails such use and abuse of history. In its defence of human rights, the West proved highly indulgent towards some regimes and very severe with others (this is not to mention its own violations of these rights). Such behaviour did not serve to enhance its image and certainly did not aid an understanding of the Soviet experience and related important phenomena.

David Joravsky has been especially scathing in his critique of the methods used by the West to embellish its image, as if hymns to the market economy, and the defence of human rights, democracy and liberties by 'anti-communists', were conducive to understanding the USSR.[1] As for 'totalitarianism' – an historically inadequate and purely

---

1 See David Joravsky, 'Communism in Historical Perspective', *The American Historical Review*, vol. 99, no. 3, June 1994, pp. 837–57.

ideological tool – it served to mask the various dark pages in the history of the West (starting with the horrific mass slaughter initiated by the First World War), and to gloss over the contradictions and weaknesses of Western democratic regimes and the misdeeds of imperialist policies that were still current. Joravsky has also criticized the contradictions and failures of German Social-Democracy: its highly praised renunciation of class radicalism, and conversion to supposedly democratic procedures, served to emasculate the SPD and make it an auxiliary and then a victim of obscurantist regimes it was not prepared to fight.

This commonsensical appeal to stop drawing a veil over the numerous failings of Western civilization and its terrible crises (thereby magnifying the sombre realities of the other side) was also a call to restore dignity to historical scholarship and recognize an inescapable truth: however specific and shaped by its own particular historical traditions, the 'other side' was itself a product of the crisis of the civilization dominated by the West and its imperialist world system.

But where is the Soviet system to be situated in the great book of history? The answer is all the more complicated in that there were at least two, if not three, versions of it (excluding the Civil War period, when it was just a military camp).

We have already posed this question in connection with the Stalinist period and proposed an answer. Russian history is a remarkable laboratory for the study of a variety of authoritarian systems and their crises, up to and including the present day. So let us now formulate the question rather differently, focusing on the system after Stalin's death: was it socialist? Definitely not. Socialism involves ownership of the means of production by society, not by a bureaucracy. It has always been conceived of as a deepening – not a rejection – of political democracy. To persist in speaking of 'Soviet socialism' is to engage in a veritable comedy of errors. Assuming that socialism is feasible, it would involve socialization of the economy and democratization of the polity. What we witnessed in the Soviet Union was state ownership of the economy and a bureaucratization of economy and polity alike. If, confronted with a hippopotamus, someone insisted that it was a giraffe, would he or she be given a chair in zoology? Are the social sciences really that much less exact than zoology?

The confusion derives from the fact that the USSR was not capitalist: ownership of the economy and other national assets was in the hands of the state, which in practice meant the summit of its bureaucracy. This is a crucial defining characteristic, entailing that the Soviet system should be placed in the same category as traditional regimes where ownership of a huge patrimonial estate equalled state power. Such was the historical process at work in the constitution of Muscovy and its monarchic autocracy. It too had an influential bureaucracy, but it was the sovereign who possessed absolute power, not his bureaucracy. In the Soviet case, it was the bureaucracy which, in the final analysis, collectively acquired undivided and unchallenged power. 'Bureaucratic absolutism' – a relative of the older 'agrarian despotisms' – was much more modern than that of the Tsars or Stalin. But it belonged to the same species, especially when we factor in political control of the population by the state.

This line of argument also implies that the Soviet bureaucratic state, despite its revolutionary innovations in both terminology and recruitment of personnel from the lower classes, directly inherited many of the old Tsarist institutions; and thus it was inevitable that it continued Tsarist traditions of state-building. In large part, this stemmed from the fact that after the revolution the agencies reactivated under Soviet auspices could function only with the help of officials from the old regime. Lenin himself had noted with regret that entire sections of the Tsarist administration remained in operation under the new regime, leading to a much greater degree of historical continuity than had been envisaged prior to October. The new regime had to learn how to handle finances, foreign affairs, military matters, intelligence operations, and so on; and it was obliged to turn not just to the expertise of some specialists, but to whole agencies, which in many respects continued to function according to established procedures. The old officialdom could not be replaced or changed overnight. A new state had been created, but its officials derived from the old one. The problem now, as Lenin saw it, was how to get them to work better.[2] Such continuity with the practices and traditions of the past was, of course, unavoidable, especially inasmuch as the relevant personnel numbered in the tens of thousands and traditions in state institutions were so entrenched. The new authorities did not know how to reconstruct them. In fact, they had no alternative but to take over these institutions, alter some of the details, and let them conduct business as usual.

The Soviet system ended up erecting a rather 'classic' bureaucratic state, run by a pyramidal hierarchy. Accordingly, once the phase of

---

2   See T. P. Korzhikhina, *Istoriia Gosudarstvennykh Uchrezhdenii SSSR*, Moscow 1995, p. 45 and *passim*; and Lenin, *Sochineniia*, vol. 45, p. 290.

revolutionary fervour was over, there was no real need for it to distance itself from old models – except, perhaps, in the case of institutions that had no counterpart under Tsarism. Moreover, every time a new agency had to be created, a special commission was appointed to oversee its organization, and it became common practice to ask a specialist scholar or experienced bureaucrat to study how a parallel institution had operated in Tsarist Russia. Where no precedent existed, Western models were consulted.

Recourse to historical precedents is natural anywhere, but in the Soviet case it was especially pronounced. In practice, Stalin's Russia adopted the ideological principles of the Tsarist state on a well-nigh official basis. Even if the specifically Stalinist practice of displaying old nationalist symbols was abandoned after his death, the Soviet bureaucratic model retained a good many of its predecessor's features, if not its ideological accoutrements. The tradition it continued defined the very essence of the system: an absolutism representing the bureaucratic hierarchy it was based on. Even the supposedly new position of general-secretary had more than a little in common with the image of the 'Tsar, master of the land'. If the symbols and scenarios of the public manifestations of power were not the same, the imposing ceremonies staged by the Tsarist and Soviet regimes hailed from the same culture, in which icons had pride of place. They aimed to project an image of invincible might, which was sometimes nothing more than a way of concealing, exorcizing or distracting attention from internal fragility. But the Tsars' successors must have known, especially in the twilight years of their regime, that systemic crisis and collapse were also part of the historical repertoire.

Given that from the end of the 1920s the construction of a strong state was at the heart of their endeavours, the issue of how to classify it arose. In the end, the old Tsarist term *derzhava*, especially cherished in conservative statist circles and among those in the military and public security bodies, was widely and openly used. In Lenin's time, *derzhavnik* was a pejorative term for supporters of an oppressive, brutal chauvinism. As for *derzhava*, it harks back to the past in its kinship with two other terms used to define the essence of Tsarist power: *samoderzhets*, denoting the absolute ruler (the autocrat); and *samoderzhavie*, characterizing the regime as an 'autocracy'. No doubt the hammer and sickle replaced the golden sphere topped off with a cross – the symbol of imperial power – but they represented nothing more than relics of the revolutionary past, much to the amusement of the bureaucratic ranks.

Ownership of all the country's land by the state, as vested in the autocrat, had been characteristic of a number of old Eastern and Central European states. In the USSR, such ownership, laying claim to socialist credentials, extended to the whole economy and many other spheres of national life. Notwithstanding a more modern outlook (unlike their Tsarist predecessors, Soviet bureaucrats ran factories that built machines and even 'atomic cities'), the affinity with the old model of ownership of all the land (the main economic resource in earlier times) was preserved, and even reinforced, by the state power exercised over the direct producers.

Throughout our explanation of the nature of this state we have encountered 'bifurcations' in the pattern of development and a whole series of ambiguities. If the system belonged in the old category of land-owning autocracies, it was nevertheless performing a twentieth-century task − that of a 'developmental state' − and we have described in detail how it proceeded to develop the country. It is to this category of 'developmental state' that the USSR belonged in the initial stages of its existence. Such states have existed, and still do exist, in several countries − in particular in the immense territories of the East and Middle East (China, India, Iran), where ancient rural monarchies ruled. This historical rationality was at work in the construction of the post-Leninist state, even if its transformation into 'Stalinism' was something that dictatorial systems are readily prone to. But the transition to a despotic model is not an incurable pathology, as is demonstrated by the elimination of Stalinism in Russia and Maoism in China. And despite the pitfalls, the presence of a state that makes possible and directs economic development remains a historical necessity.

Towards the 1980s, the USSR had achieved a level of economic and social development superior to China's, but its system was stuck fast in a self-destructive logic. The kind of reforms envisaged by Andropov could have given the country what it needed: a reformed, active state able to continue its developmental role, but also capable of renouncing an authoritarianism that was now obsolete, inasmuch as the social landscape had been profoundly transformed.

However, the recourse to the venerable symbolism of the *derzhava*, which expressed the mindset and interests of a significant component of the ruling elite, was the sign of a loss of vigour on the part of the state apparatus, the members of which, stuck in a groove, now used its power solely to further their personal interests. It also signalled the interruption of any reformist dynamic at the very moment when the country was crying out for reform. Rather than adding the computer to the hammer and sickle, the leadership took refuge in conservatism, embarking on an inglorious path. If the population lived under a system with an ancient pedigree and characteristics, they were no longer living in the eighteenth century, but the twentieth. The state had remained behind and such 'bifurcation' (society going in one direction, the state in another) was fatal.

The term 'bureaucratic absolutism', which seems apt to us to characterize the Soviet system, is borrowed from an analysis of the Prussian bureaucratic monarchy in the eighteenth century, wherein the monarch was in fact dependent on his bureaucracy despite being its head.[3] In the Soviet case, the party's top bosses, putative masters of the state, had actually lost any power over 'their' bureaucrats.

Insignificant ex-ministers of the USSR, writing nostalgically in their memoirs about the glory of the superpower they have lost, do not realize that the fashion for the term *derzhava* precisely coincided with the period when the state had ceased to accomplish the task it had once been capable of performing – and had indeed performed. It had become a shadow of its former self, the last gasp of a power about to join the grave of a family of antiquated regimes to which it remained bound by too many ties.

THE FOREIGN FACTOR

The Soviet phenomenon was a profoundly typical chapter in Russian history – not in spite, but because, of the role of the international environment, including the use of ideologies borrowed from abroad. The autocrats who have proved most successful in Russian history also maintained such links with the external world. A country with a highly complex history, constantly engaged in friendly or hostile relations with neighbours near and far, Russia had to develop relations not only on the military, economic, commercial, diplomatic and cultural levels, but also by responding culturally and ideologically to a series of challenges. It did so either by borrowing ideas from abroad, or by counterposing indigenous notions – which explains why its rulers' antennae were pointed in two directions, inwards and outwards. Similarly, in the history of the

---

3 See H. Rosenberg, *Bureaucracy, Aristocracy and Autocracy*, Boston 1966.

USSR the outside world constantly helped to determine the form the regime took, in a variety of ways. The First World War and the concurrent crisis of capitalism had a lot to do with the Leninist phenomenon and the phases Soviet Russia went through in the 1920s. The crisis of the 1930s and the Second World War likewise had a direct impact on Stalin's Soviet Union.

The 'distorting mirrors' we referred to in the case of Stalinism influenced the images that populations and rulers formed of the opposing camp. Since both competing systems experienced crises and phases of development, the 'distorting mirrors' on both sides projected and reflected images in which reality and fiction were almost impossible to disentangle. If in the 1930s Stalinism, then at the peak of its momentum, enjoyed great prestige and benevolent attention in the West despite the misery and persecution endured by Soviet citizens, it was largely because of the negative image of capitalism projected by global economic crisis – particularly that afflicting Central and Eastern Europe. Russia reflected back the image of its industrial momentum, and the poverty of the population was relativized by the notion that this impressive progress would rapidly overcome it. A similar distorting effect can be seen in the case of Stalin and Stalinism at the moment of its triumph over Germany in 1945, when the country was once again plunged into a profound poverty for which the ravages of war were not exclusively responsible. The exchange of distorted images had significant political consequences: divining the intentions of the other side often became a guessing game.

The Cold War was an unusual contest. Seen from Moscow, it was dramatically unleashed with the dropping of atomic bombs on Japan. But if Berezhkov's memoirs are to be believed, it began earlier with the American delay in opening a second – western – front: Stalin regarded this as a deliberate ploy on the part of the USA, intent on entering the thick of battle only after the German and Soviet contestants had exhausted one another.[4] This delay, compounded by the use of atomic weapons against Japan, had been perceived as evidence of the American desire to let it be known that a new era had opened in international relations – a declaration made not to Japan, but to the USSR and the rest of the world, which the Soviet leadership had interpreted accordingly. That the USA did think in this way at the time cannot be ruled

---

4 See V. Berezhkov, *Riadom so Stalinym*, Moscow 1999.

out. What effects the opening of the second front a year earlier, or abstaining from the atomic bombardment of Hiroshima and Nagasaki, might have had on postwar relations can only be speculated about. The fact remains that the war and postwar developments propelled the USSR into the role of a superpower and pushed it into an arms race that helped to perpetuate the worst, most conservative features of the system and to reduce its ability to reform itself.

Among the consequences of the Cold War, we should note the fact that the US found itself in a position to exercise considerable influence and pressure on the Soviet leadership's way of thinking. The Old World (England, France, Germany), which had hitherto served as a model, was replaced by the New World: the US became the Soviets' yardstick for assessing their own performance when it came to the economy, science, military capability and, needless to say, espionage. The impact of this reorientation to the US was concealed from both the Soviet population and the West (this is a vast subject awaiting exploration). We may assume that on account of the US the Soviet leadership came to realize the systemic nature of their country's grave inferiority, though it could be that some of them refused to acknowledge the reality. After having been beaten in the (utterly useless) race to get to the Moon first, the country's inability to embark on the new scientific and information revolution – even though a special ministry was created to supervise the task! – must have engendered a sense of powerlessness in some ruling circles, while the conservatives stuck with their immobilism and hard line.

It was this same image of the US as superpower that led so many ex-members of the *nomenklatura* to bid for American favours after they had taken control of the Kremlin under Yeltsin's mantle. However, this episode belongs to the post-Soviet era and is of interest to us here only in so far as it casts some additional light on the historical record of the system – a system that is dead and buried, and yet remains present in the constant search for a national identity which will only be defined when the past, warts and all, has been seriously re-examined and mastered.

POSTSCRIPT: A COUNTRY IN SEARCH OF A PAST

It is perfectly natural that researchers studying the state of Russia in the 1990s should use data from the later Soviet period as their starting point. The situation becomes ironic only when sociologists who have a profound knowledge of this past, from the studies they conducted at the time (when they were very critical of the system), now treat it as some kind of Eldorado, on account of the living standards and social benefits enjoyed by the population not so long ago, but which have deteriorated inexorably since the beginning of the 1990s.[5] The picture they present is highly instructive: decreasing numbers of people go to the theatre, concerts, the circus or libraries; the reading of literary works and subscriptions to newspapers are in sharp decline in town and countryside alike. The whole structure of leisure activity has been transformed because of increased workloads. Leisure is now much more passive (essentially 'restorative'), whereas it was becoming culture-oriented in the late Soviet era with the growth in free time. The phenomenon is particularly striking in the case of specialists and managers. The need to increase household incomes compelled many Russians to rear more cattle and poultry on their mini-farms to improve their diet and earn a little more money, or simply in order to survive, with a corresponding reduction in their time for rest and cultural recreation.

The expansion of liberties and rights, as well as the emergence of expensive services, have benefited only the best off, the best qualified, and the most enterprising. A majority of people saw their access to national and international culture reduced. The sociologists we are referring to are highly critical of the quality of television programmes. Television has become the dominant leisure activity, with especially deleterious effects on children who, left to their own devices in the afternoon, sit glued to bovine broadcasts.

According to the authors, two processes are at work: an ever-deepening social stratification, and withdrawal by individuals into their own selves (fewer social and family contacts, lack of interest in culture and politics), which is less pronounced in the major urban centres of European Russia, but very marked in the provincial towns and the countryside. They do not deal with the decline in scientific research, education, and medical and social services, or the fall in demographic indicators, producing a catastrophic situation in which the country's very survival is at stake.

To conceal this woeful state of affairs, the new power-holders – most of them from the old *nomenklatura* but now rebaptized 'democrats',

---

5 T. I. Zaslavskaya and Z. I. Kalugina, otvet. red., *Sotsialnaia Traektoriia Reformiruemoi Rossii – Issledovaniia Novosibirskoi Ekonomiko-sotsiologicheskoi Shkoly*, Novosibirsk 1999, pp. 577–84.

'liberals', or 'reformers' – embarked on a massive propaganda campaign against the old Soviet system, using all the devices previously employed in the West and even outbidding them: the system was nothing but a monstrosity run by monsters, from the original sin of October 1917 right up to the failed coup d'état by conservative party stalwarts against Gorbachev in August 1991. Thereafter, a miracle supposedly occurred, with the dawning of a new era of freedom under President Yeltsin. As a result of this kind of political discourse, contemporary Russia, already woefully diminished and still in a state of shock, also suffers from a kind of self-denigration of its historical identity. Not content with looting and squandering the nation's wealth, the 'reformers' also mounted a frontal assault on its past, directed at its culture, identity and vitality. This was no critical approach to the past: it was sheer ignorance.

The mendacious and nihilistic campaign against the Soviet era was accompanied by a kind of frantic shopping around for alternative pasts to offer the nation for it to identify with. It began with a wholesale readoption of anything Tsarist and pre-revolutionary – a pathetic attempt to find a worthy predecessor in a decaying system. Then, when the rejection of anything Soviet became yet more intense, crystallizing in a hatred of Lenin, Leninism and Bolshevism as issuing from Hell, attempts were made to rehabilitate the Whites in the Civil War – the most reactionary right wing of the Tsarist political spectrum, which lost precisely because it had nothing to offer the country.

Identification with anything and everything detested by the Bolsheviks or the Soviet regime simply attested to intellectual feebleness. The first wave of 'new elites' who conquered the Kremlin and power were regarded by many Russians as something approaching a new 'Tatar invasion', attacking the country's political and cultural interests. The nation's best minds and moral authorities feared lest its only prospect was the nightmarish one of sinking to the level of a Third World country.

It takes time to recover from the ravages of obscurantism. But various cultural events offer positive signs that a slow recovery is under way. We should remember the historian Kliuchevsky's reaction to those who, at the beginning of the twentieth century, claimed that 'the past is in the past'. No, he said: with all the difficulties crowding in on us and the errors that have been committed, the past is all around us, enveloping reforms, distorting and almost swallowing them up.

As if taking up where Kliuchevsky had left off, the political philosopher Mezhuev, speaking at a conference in Moscow organized by Tatyana Zaslavskaya, forcefully argued that 'a country cannot exist without its history'.[6] His highly stimulating thoughts are worth quoting at length:

> Our reformers – whether communists, democrats, slavophiles, or people fascinated by the West – all make the crucial mistake of failing to identify a rationally and morally justified continuity between Russia's past and its future, between what it has been and what (according to them) it should be. Some negate the past and others identify it as the only possible model. The result is that for some the future is merely a mixture of past themes, while for others it is the mechanical acceptance of the opposite – something without any analogy in Russian history. But the future must be conceived in the first instance in relation to the past – in particular to the past we have just left behind.

Mezhuev proceeds to criticize the liberal economist A. Illarionov, who regards the twentieth century as a wasted one for Russia: having lived under socialism, the country deviated from its liberal trajectory and that is why yesterday's giant has become today's midget. For Illarionov, the only salvation consists in a return to liberalism. According to Mezhuev, such nihilism is historically absurd. It is easier to be wise after the event than to analyse what happened and why. To rail against Russia for not having become liberal at the beginning of the century is to demonstrate a profound ignorance of Russian history and liberalism alike. The triumph of liberalism was the product of a protracted historical process: the Middle Ages, the Reformation, the Renaissance, and the revolutions that emancipated societies from absolutist monarchies (but not everywhere!). England itself, the mother of liberalism, took time to embark on the liberal road. Russia and many other countries did not develop a liberal market economy. Should they be blamed for this? That would be pointless. The important thing is to understand the past century and the role it will play in future developments.

For Mezhuev, the key to twentieth-century Russian history is to be found in three revolutions, not exclusively in the Bolshevik revolution. The first – in 1905 – was defeated. The second – in February 1917 – witnessed the victory of moderate revolutionary forces. The third – October – which saw the triumph of more radical revolutionaries, was only the last phase in this revolutionary process. That is how such

---

6   See V. P. Mezhuev, 'Otnoshenie k proshlomu – kliuch k budushchemu', in *Kuda Idet Rossiia? Krizis Institutsional'nykh Sistem: Vek, Desiatiletie, God*, Moscow 1999, pp. 39–47.

processes always unfold. Once triggered, there is no one to blame; the process pursues its course to a conclusion. The philosopher Berdyaev had understood this well: the Bolsheviks were not the revolution's authors, but the instrument of its development. It is pointless adopting primarily moral criteria and denouncing the cruelties inflicted, for it is always thus in situations of civil war or struggles against oppression. A revolution is not a moral or legal action, but a deployment of coercive force. There are no 'good' revolutions; they are always bloody:

> If you condemn revolutions, you should condemn virtually the whole Russian intelligentsia, and the whole of Russian history for that matter, since it provided the soil for these revolutionary events. Revolutions do not appease; they do the opposite. They always disappoint expectations, but they open a genuinely new page. The important thing is to understand what this page consists in – without placing too much faith in what either the victors or the vanquished say . . . Our socialism was in fact a 'capitalism à la Russe' – capitalist in its technological content and anti-capitalist in its form.

On this point, Mezhuev reviews the opinions of such thinkers as Berdyaev, Fedotov, Bogdanov and others. He himself leans towards the following interpretation. It is difficult for a country located on the periphery to combine modernization with democracy and freedom. For a time, one of them must give way to the other. The Bolsheviks understood this, and that is why they won the Civil War and why the USSR emerged victorious from the Second World War. China too appreciates this: it has opted to combine rapid modernization via the market with an undemocratic political system. Whatever the regime in question, wisdom consists not in refusing the past as if it were a barren desert, but in regarding it as a springboard for further development and preserving its genuine (not its mythical) grandeur.

In this respect, the Russian variant of socialism must be credited with its faith in science. The prestige of the scientist and engineer was never higher in Russian history than during the Soviet period and the regime opened the doors of science to many. Here its rulers were realists and pragmatists. Taking their speeches literally, the West was wrong to perceive any hostility in this. Contemporary Russia, with its nostalgia for pre-revolutionary times, is more distant from the West than the Bolsheviks were:

> Our liberals have nothing to boast about except the destruction of these achievements. Russia's future must be constructed on the basis of preserving and developing past achievements. Continuity must be preserved even as

new tasks are defined. As of now, this link with the past has been broken. But it will be restored one day. This does not involve returning to a pre- or post-revolutionary past. Ask what in the past is dear to you, what must be continued or preserved, and that will help you to face the future ... If the past contains nothing positive, then there is no future and there is nothing left to do but 'forget it all and sink into slumber' ... Those who want to erase the twentieth century – an era of great catastrophes – must also bid farewell to a great Russia.

Mezhuev remains convinced that the Russian revolution will one day receive the same recognition as revolutions in the West – a recognition that would hopefully open the way for a genuine Russian renaissance.

The preceding paragraphs do no more than summarize a long and impassioned address. Mezhuev is not a historian, and his interpretation is not unproblematic. The terms 'socialism', 'Bolshevism' and 'communism', but also a whole set of ideas about the revolution, derive from a terminology and approach that need to be reconsidered. But we are here in the presence of a real challenge to 'nihilism' and an illustration of the battle for history as a remedy making it possible for a nation in the throes of a painful decline to rediscover its identity and discover its future.

It is well known that history is subject to constant use and abuse. Listening to a non-historian plead for an objective historical knowledge as indispensable to a nation, whether in its torment or its glory days, is unusual in a media and computer-dominated age fixated on the present instant. But the instant is just that – it passes – whereas history remains. It continues to provide some of the building-blocks for the future, whether sound or defective. It is the basis that nations rest on and which they add to. It is not absurd to believe that history, in common with the applied sciences, has a practical dimension – even if it cannot provide immediate, guaranteed remedies.

GLOSSARY OF RUSSIAN TERMS

apparat: party administration. (We sometimes use *apparaty* for administrative bodies in general, but *apparatchik* always refers to an official of the party apparatus.)

belye: the 'Whites' – the predominantly monarchist camp that fought the 'Reds' (*krasnye*) during the Civil War.

derzhava: an old Russian term for the state. It derives from the verb *derzat'*, meaning to hold or keep, and implies a holding or someone's property. It refers directly to the political essence of the Tsarist state: *samoderzhavie* (autocracy) and *samoderzhets* (autocrat). The term *derzhavnost'*, which is also found, refers to a conception of the state as a great power.

Esery: Socialist Revolutionaries (or SRs) – non-Marxist socialists who were very active in the soviets and the Provisional Government. They cooperated with the 'Whites' on and off. Their left wing briefly cooperated with the Bolsheviks, but broke with them over the Brest-Litovsk peace treaty with the Germans, which they opposed.

generalnyi sekretar' (shortened to *gensek*): General-Secretary of the CPSU, elected by the party congress. In addition, there existed Central Committee secretaries, whose status varied. Some were in charge of spheres of activity, but not members of the Politburo. Members of the latter (with the exception of the general-secretary) could not have secretarial functions. This was true of Gromyko, for example, who was in charge of the Foreign Affairs Ministry.

Gosplan: State Committee for Economic Planning.

Gossnab: State Committee for Material and Technical Supplies – a kind of super-ministry organizing supplies of the raw materials, machinery and finished products required by enterprises. The remainder of the exchanges between economic ministries and their enterprises were carried out by their own purchasing (*snaby*) and marketing (*sbyty*) agencies.

Gulag (*Glavnoe upravlenie lagerei*): the General Camp Directorate, located in the NKVD. The official name for the camps was *ITL* (*ispravitel'no-trudovye lageria*, corrective labour camps). Under Stalin, *ITK* (*ispravitel'no-trudovye kolonii*, corrective labour colonies) were reserved for lesser offenders and juveniles. There were also *spetsposeleniia* (places of deportation) for those condemned to periods of exile: they were supervised by the NKVD, but not subject to the camp regime. Camp inmates – *zakliuchennye* – were referred to in shorthand as *zeki* (singular: *zek*).

ITK: See Gulag.

ITL: See Gulag.

ITR (*inzhinerno–tekhnicheskie rabotniki*): engineers and technicians, holding positions entailing supervision, higher in rank than manual labourers or people without qualification (*rabochie*).

Kadety: Cadets – Constitutional Democrats – the broadly liberal party in Tsarist and post-Tsarist Russia, who joined the 'Whites' during the Civil War and pursued their activity abroad thereafter.

khoziain: broadly used to refer to a manager-owner (e.g. of a farm) and anyone holding the senior position in a workplace hierarchy. In popular usage, it also refers to the evil spirit haunting the house.

kolkhoz: collective farm (*kollektivnoe khoziaistvo*: 'collective enterprise'). Its members were known as *kolkhozniki*.

kollegia: here mostly a collegium composed of the top officials in any ministry.

Komsomol: Union of Communist Youth – the party's youth organization.

kulak: pejorative nickname given to better-off, entrepreneurial peasants (*kulak* means fist). The kulaks were persecuted during Stalinist collectivization. Many were deported to remote areas (mainly in Siberia).

mensheviki: members of a Marxist Social-Democratic party, which played a leading role in the soviets in 1917 and the Provisional Government. They did not collaborate with the Whites, but were excluded from political life by the Bolsheviks. They continued with their political activity from abroad.

MVD: See *NKVD*.

nachal'nik: a boss. *Nachal'stvo* refers to the whole layer of such bosses. For senior party officials, the term *rukovodiashchii rabotnik* (literally 'leading worker') was used.

nepmen: beneficiaries of the NEP (New Economic Policy) introduced in 1921; neo-bourgeois.

NKVD: People's Commissariat for Internal Affairs, which became the Interior Ministry (MVD). In 1962, it was transformed into the MOOP (*Ministerstvo Okhrany Obshchestvennogo Poriadka*, or Ministry for Public Order), but lost its status as a ministry covering the whole USSR. Union status was restored to it in 1966 and it reverted to its old name (MVD) two years later. Under Stalin, this commissariat contained a special extra-judicial body responsible for dealing expeditiously with the mass of people accused of treason or political offences. At a local level, the same task was performed by a *troika* – a body of three officials comprising the local party secretary, prosecutor, and NKVD chief.

nomenklatura: the list of posts to be filled under Central Committee supervision.

Orgburo: organizational bureau of the Central Committee.

Politburo: leading body of the CPSU. Stalin replaced it by the Presidium of the Central Committee. It was restored after Khrushchev's dismissal in 1964.

politrabotniki: party cadres.

praktik (plural: *praktiki*): people in technical or administrative posts who had no formal training for them, but learned their trade on the job.

profilaktika: prophylaxis, or the 'preventive' policy adopted by the KGB under Khrushchev and continued after him. It consisted in warning people suspected of engaging in forms of political opposition of the consequences if they persisted.

prokuratura: the Prosecutor's Office (State Prosecutor). Prosecutor General refers to the central official at Union level.

sekretariat: office serving the Central Committee.

sluzhashchie: literally, 'employees'. The term refers to officials at all levels, from blue-collar workers to the highest-level *nachal'stvo*.

snaby-sbyty: supply and marketing agencies in ministries and enterprises.

sovkhoz: state agricultural enterprise (*sovetskoe khoziaistvo*).

sovnarkhoz: council of the national economy (*Soviet narodnogo kho-ziaistva*). This was the name taken by several central or local agencies. But they are best known as the economic councils introduced by Khrushchev throughout the country to replace the economic ministries, which were temporarily disbanded.

Sovnarkom: Council of People's Commissars (*Soviet narodnykh kommis-sarov*), later the Council of Ministers. The two terms are used interchangeably here.

STO: *Soviet Truda i Oborony* (Council of Labour and Defence), a government coordinating body in Stalin's time.

tenevaia ekonomika: the shadow economy, or a variety of economic activities, from the wholly illegal and criminal to the semi-legal and legal (but performed in a private capacity).

tolkach: from the verb *tolkat'* (to push). Refers to a semi-legal figure dispatched by an organization or enterprise to 'push' supply agencies into delivering the requisite goods.

Uchreditel'noe Sobranie (abbreviated to *uchredilka*): the Constituent Assembly that convened in Petrograd in January 1918 with an SR majority, and which was dispersed by the Bolsheviks.

uklady: designates social layers or strata.

upravlentsy: literally 'those who perform leadership roles'.

zastoi: stagnation. The term is used to refer to the post-1970 period (often also characterized as *zastoinye gody*, or the years of stagnation).

zek: See Gulag.

APPENDICES

APPENDIX I

Source: B. P. Kurashvili, *Istoricheskaia Logika Stalinizma* (Moscow 1996, pp. 159–60).

Numbers of people sentenced for counter-revolutionary and particularly dangerous crimes, and type of penalty imposed, 1921–53.

Years	total sentenced (persons)	death sent.	camps, colonies prisons	Exiled to* Exiled from	other measures
1921	35829	9701	21724	1817	2587
1922	6003	1962	2656	166	1219
1923	4794	414	2336	2044	–
1924	12425	2550	4151	5724	–
1925	15995	2433	6851	6274	437
1926	17804	990	7547	8571	696
1927	26036	2363	12267	11235	171
1928	33757	869	16211	15640	1037
1929	56220	2109	25853	24517	3741
1930	208069	20201	114443	58816	14609
1931	180696	10651	105683	63269	1093
1932	141919	22728	73946	36017	29228
1933	239664	2154	138903	54262	44345
1934	78999	2056	59451	5994	11498
1935	267076	1229	185846	33601	46400

1936	274670	1118	219418	23719	30415
1937	0665	353074	429311	1366	6914
1938	554258	328618	205509	16342	3289
1939	63889	2552	54666	3783	2888
1940	71806	1649	65727	2142	2288
1941	75411	8011	65000	1200	1210
1942	124406	23278	88809	7070	5249
1943	78441	3579	68887	4787	1188
1944	75109	3029	70610	649	821
1945	123248	4252	116681	1647	668
1946	123294	2896	117943	1498	957
1947	78810	1105	76581	666	458
1948	73263	–	72552	419	298
1949	75125	–	64509	10316	300
1950	60641	475	54466	5225	475
1951	54775	1609	49142	3425	599
1952	28800	1612	25824	773	591
1953 (first half)	8403	198	7894	38	273
TOTAL	4060306	799455	2634397	423512	215942

★ The punishment of exile could take one of two forms. *Ssylka* refers to being exiled to a specific area and remaining there under police supervision, whether for a set number of years or for life. This was neither a camp nor a prison, but a 'settlement', where it was possible to live with one's family in separate accommodation and perform paid work depending on local possibilities. *Vysylka* consisted in being banned from living in some particular location (Moscow, say, or Leningrad). Those so condemned could live and work anywhere else. Files on such persons would undoubtedly follow them to their new place of residence.

APPENDIX 2

We may add some data from a source used by Kurashvili – and V. N. Zemskov, a well-known researcher from Moscow, who made a name for himself by publishing reliable figures on the camps and purges long before others. Here I give only a few examples of the widespread practice of proposing enormously inflated figures for Stalin's repression.

Zemskov engages with Roy Medvedev and Olga Shatunovskaya in his article 'Gulag – istoriko-sotsiologicheskii aspekt' (*Sotsiologicheskie Issledovaniia*, no. 6, 1991, pp.12–13). Medvedev claimed that the Gulag expanded by several million people during the 1937–8 purges and that between 5 and 7 million persons fell victim to repression. In fact, the camp population rose from 1,196,369 inmates in January 1937 to 1,881,570 in January 1938, and dropped to 1,672,438 on 1 January 1939. There was indeed an explosion in numbers in 1937–8, but in the hundreds of thousands, not millions. The declaration by Vladimir Kriuchkov (KGB head under Gorbachev) that in 1937–8 'there were no more than one million arrests' corresponds to the Gulag statistics. Zemskov stresses that, according to the official document reproduced in Appendix 1, approximately 700,000 people arrested for political reasons were executed between 1921 and 1953. Shatunovskaya (herself a victim of the repression and later active in the rehabilitation campaign under Khrushchev) asserted that, for the period 1935–41 alone, more than 19 million people were arrested, of whom 7 million were shot – a figure enthusiastically taken up in the West – while the remainder perished in the camps. According to Zemskov, Shatunovskaya has multiplied the figures tenfold – no small exaggeration! Reliable statistics exist for the period 1 January 1934–31 December 1947 indicating that, throughout the Gulag camp complex, 963,766 prisoners died. This figure comprises not just 'enemies of the people', but also common law criminals. This number, along with that for those who died during the deportation of the kulaks (*raskulachivanie*), can be added to the 'terrible price' that was paid.

1.5 MILLION SOVIET TRAITORS DURING THE SECOND WORLD WAR

In his *Novyi Sotsializm* (Moscow 1997, pp. 22–7), B. P. Kurashvili offers something of an apologia for the regime, reminding readers that it did have enemies and suggesting that the war saw approximately 1.5 people actively collaborate with the Nazis. No source is given for this estimate, which – and he is right about this – involved around 1 per cent of the active population. But the existence of such collaborators indicates that the purges launched against 'enemies of the people' struck blindly at innocent people and spared some real or potential traitors. Many of those who fought with the Germans were captured but not executed. After the war, they were not treated with excessive severity. According to Kurashvili (and certain documents in my possession), many of those who served with the Nazis (Vlassov's army, Cossack units, units composed of non-Russian nationals), when arrested, were not accused of any concrete crimes but sent for five years to 'labour battalions'. The same was true of many of the Ukrainian and Baltic state partisans who fought against the regime after the war. This involved some hard-fought battles, with many casualties. However, the majority of partisans who were captured were sent into exile and later amnestied and allowed, from 1960 onwards, to return home. It is possible that such comparative indulgence was designed to placate nationalist circles in the Ukraine and the Baltic countries.

APPENDIX 3

Source: R. G. Pikhoia, *Sovetskii Soiuz – Istoriia Vlasti, 1945–1991* (Moscow 1998, pp. 365–6).

Criminal prosecutions versus 'prophylactic' measures by the KGB, 1959–74.

A. Criminal prosecutions

	1959–62	1963 6	1967–70	1971–4
total brought to court	5413	3251	2456	2423
treason	1010	457	423	350
spying	28	8	0	9
antisov agitprop	1601	502	381	348
smuggling	47	110	183	474
illegal currency operations	587	474	382	401
illegal frontiers crossing	926	613	704	553
divulging state secrets	22	31	19	18
other crimes	1003	1011	321	258

B. 'Prophylactic' measures
(These actions were not registered in earlier years)

	1959–62	1963–66	1967–70	1971–74
'profiled' total	–	–	58298	63108
suspicious contacts with foreigners nurturing treasonable intentions	–	–	5039	6310
politically damaging manifestations	–	–	35316	34700
'profiled' with community participation	–	–	23611	27079
official warning issued	–	–	–	981
brought to court from those previously 'profiled'	–	–	100	50

APPENDIX 4

The Interior Ministry as an industrial agency and the Gulag as a supplier of manpower (1946).

Source: RGAE, f. 4372, op. 84, d. 271.
In December 1946 the Gulag's statistical department produced a report on the number of inmates and 'special contingents' that worked for various ministries, the MVD supplying the manpower. A list of forty-seven ministries and government agencies was provided, with the number of inmates employed: heavy industry, military and naval concerns, construction sites for petroleum enterprises, aircraft construction, construction of agricultural machinery, Ministry of Electrical Energy. In a document dated 13 September 1946 addressed to Beria, Kruglov, the Interior Minister, complained that forty-five of the government agencies using labour supplied by the Gulag had not paid for it. They had accumulated a debt of 50 million roubles, putting the Gulag in a difficult financial position. There was no longer enough money to buy food for the inmates (not only were they not paid; they were not even fed!).

Source: RGAE, f. 7733, op. 36, d. 2097, LL. 253, 256.
On 1 November 1946, the same Kruglov sent a report to Voznesensky, head of Gosplan, to inform him that the MVD had exceeded the Plan's targets for industrial (and other) construction sites, and asked for 222 million roubles, on the grounds that he had exceeded the plan as regards investment. A table drew up a list of some seventeen MVD agencies and their investments. It discloses a flourishing network of administrative agencies, managing an ever-growing number of branches (the

organizational structure is increasingly difficult to follow). Their administrative creativity is remarkable, and the greater their investment, the higher the salaries of the agencies and the enormous bonuses of the bosses. Especial attention is paid to work linked to defence requirements – the name of these departments and agencies is generally preceded by the prefix *spec* (abbreviation of the adjective 'special' in Russian).

Source: RGAE, f. 7733, op. 36, d. 2291, L. 315.

April 1947: the MVD now possessed twelve branch directorates, managing the production of metals, mining, forestry, sawmills, machine factories, textile enterprises, shoe factories, refineries, gas facilities, concerns processing cobalt and nickel, glass works, rubber factories – the list is long and gives the names of camps (Norilsk, Vorkuta, Uhta, Dal'stroi) celebrated for their output and their very harsh conditions. The very 'businesslike' tone ignores or conceals the misery underlying these 'businesses' and the moral degeneracy of the managers of this regime.

NOTE ON SOURCES AND REFERENCES

Most of the documentary evidence used in this book comes from Soviet archives. Some of it was discovered by the author himself in the Moscow archives, while the rest has been published in specialist journals or collections of documents. In the latter instance, the references supplied in the footnotes give the name of the compilers and other indispensable details.

The archives from which most of the material derives are as follows:

GARF: Gosudarstvennyi Arkhiv Rossiiskoi Federatsii (State Archive of the Russian Federation), which contains a separate section for the RSFSR – GARF Berezhki – with a slight difference in the coding of documents.

RGASPI: Rossiiskii Gosudarstvennyi Arkhiv Sotsial'no-Politicheskikh Issledovanii (Russian State Archive for Socio-Political Research) – previously RTsKHIDNI.

RGAE: Rossiiskii Gosudartsvennyi Arkhiv Economiki (Russian State Economic Archive).

RGVA: Rossiiskii Gosudartsvennyi Voennyi Arkhiv (Russian State Military Archive).

TsKhSD: Tsentralnoe Khranilishche Sovremennoi Dokumentatsii (Central Depository of Contemporary Documentation). The author did not personally work in this Central Committee archive and the documents cited from it have all been published.

Each reference to a document begins with the name of the relevant archive, followed by the number of the collection (f.), the number of the catalogue (op.), the number of the document (d.), and the page numbers (L.). But it is also common practice for historians to omit the first letters of the coding categories and simply supply four consecutive numbers in the appropriate order.

Autobiographies are an important and legitimate source for historians, especially in the case of the Soviet Union, because they contain eyewitness reports of events or secret meetings in more recent years that cannot as yet be studied from the documents they generated. Biographies are a further valuable source when their authors have also come upon otherwise inaccessible evidence.

INDEX